Finnegans Wake - some Eastern Aspects

James Augustine Aloysius Joyce, 2.2.1882-13.1.1941
Published Finnegans Wake in 1939

Finnegans Wake
some Eastern Aspects

Dr Zulfiqar Ali Chaudhry

We plant a tree
for every book sold

Non Fiction ISBN 978-8792632-40-1
First edition

Design and layout by Whyte Tracks
Type set in Sakkal Majalla, La Lique, Gill standard

Published by Whyte Tracks, Denmark

Forward

In May of 1894, when James Joyce was twelve years old, a Grand Oriental Fête was held in Dublin in aid of the Jervis Street Hospital. The fête was called "Araby" and, if we are to believe the narrator of Joyce's short story on the subject, this "magical name" cast an "eastern enchantment" over the future writer. In Dubliners his puerile fascination with the mysterious East is balanced by a short-lived fascination with the Wild West in the story "An Encounter." But Joyce's Oriental interests, once awakened, continued to develop. His friend Stuart Gilbert, one of the earliest interpreters of Ulysses, remarks on the frequent references to the East, to its occult sciences and to the "oriental sources of all religion" in that book. Even in Ulysses, however, Joyce's horizon does not extend very far beyond the Jews, Greeks and Phoenicians of the Mediterranean littoral and the Near East. In Finnegans Wake his last and most difficult book, it is very different. Here—as Dr Zulfiqar Ali Choudhry shows in this fascinating study—Joyce may truly be said to have become "Europasianized." His manifold allusions to the Koran and to the Thousand and One Nights are apparent to the most casual reader of a book in which the heroine appears in one of her incarnations as "Annah the Allmaziful," and the hero as "Haroun Childeric Eggeberth."

Even the long, looping opening-and-closing sentence of Finnegans Wake may be interpreted as initiating a geographical movement towards the East. The book begins in mid-sentence with "riverrun, past Eve and Adam's," a reference to the eastward-flowing River Liffey and, we are told, to Adam and Eve's Church in Dublin. The ensuing "commodius vicus of recirculation" suggests, at the most literal level, that the river waters describe a tight circle around Dublin Bay ending abruptly at the phallic promontory of Howth Castle and Environs. But Dublin, in this book, encapsulates the whole of human geography and history, so that "Eve and Adam's" is also the Biblical paradise. Passing to the east of Eden we come (according to the Book of Genesis) to the Land of Nod, which Joyce's Irish predecessor Jonathan Swift identified with the land of sleep—a land that any book offering, as Finnegans Wake claims to offer, the "keys to dreamland" must necessarily enter. During the seventeen years that he spent writing his book set in the Land of Nod, Joyce greatly extended and deepened his knowledge of Asiatic cultures, religions and languages.

Within the vast critical literature on Joyce there are, needless to say, a few introductory commentaries on Finnegans Wake as well as a much larger number of specialist studies. Practically all of them have been written by Westerners brought up in the Christian and Jewish traditions, so that Dr Ali Choudhry is thoroughly justified in claiming that his is a sorely neglected topic. Whereas the Eastern aspects of the thought of Joyce's contemporaries W. B. Yeats and T. S. Eliot are relatively well known and well understood, scholars with the relevant qualifications have fought shy of the linguistic and narrative challenges thrown up by Finnegans Wake. Dr Ali Choudhry is not so easily daunted, however. Among his few predecessors we might mention J. S. Atherton, who in his pioneering study of The Books at the Wake identified the Koran as one of the Wake's "sacred books" and listed its references to individual suras. Clive Hart in Structure and Motif in "Finnegans Wake" explored Joyce's use of cyclical structures, including the Indian cycles outlined in H. P. Blavatsky's Isis Unveiled. And there, more or less, the matter stood when Dr Ali Choudhry first came to ithe study of Joyce. (Fittingly, Clive Hart became one of his mentors). Dr Ali Choudhry differs from his predecessors in being an expert in the languages and cultures of the Subcontinent, but like any good Joycean he is an incarnation of the "ideal reader" possessed by an "ideal insomnia." His study of Finnegans Wake's roots in the Koran, in Hinduism, in the Thousand and One Nights and in Persian vocabulary and thought is at once a definitive work in itself, and a source of inspiration for future Joyce scholars and students. May they share something of the determination, the intrepidity and the endless curiosity that have gone into the making of this book.

- **Patrick Parrinder**
The University of Reading, England

Patrick Parrinder is a Professor of English at the University of Reading, England. His books include James Joyce (1984).

Acknowledgements

I particularly wish to thank my supervisor, Professor Patrick Parrinder, *for always furnishing me with advice and assistance through the long process of writing this work, and for helpful criticism whenever I was in danger of losing sight of the best way to proceed.*

I am also grateful to Professor Clive Hart *of the University of Essex, who convinced me from the outset that the work I wished to undertake was worth pursuing, and might in due course become a significant contribution to scholarship.*

As well as thanking the staff of the British Library and the Bodleian Library, Oxford, I must express my gratitude to Mr Peter Massett *and* Mr Malcolm Walker, *the Librarians of High Wycombe Public Library, who were kind enough to arrange for copies of the Wake Notebooks to be sent from collections which I was unable to visit.*

I thank Professor Akbar S. Ahmad, *Fellow Iqbal Chair, Cambridge for his propitious guidance and encouragement when I was working on this book.*

I have also benefited from consulting the Joyce Collections at the University College London Library, and thank the staff there for their help.

In June 2004 I met Professor Vincent John Cheng *in the 19th International James Joyce Symposium, Dublin. He took the Manuscript to his room during the Symposium, and I believe that he made up his mind after scanning the contents. Later on, he spoke to* Sebastian Knowles *and this is how the Manuscript got his lynx-eyed attention.*

My thanks to all who have helped make this book possible.
- Zulfiqar Ali

Abbreviations:

AP:	*A Portrait of the Artist as a Young Man.*
AWN:	*A Wake NewsLitter, ed.* Clive Hart and Fritz Senn.
FW:	*Finnegans Wake.*
JJQ	*James Joyce Quarterly.*
OPP:	*On Poetry and Poets,* (T.S. Eliot).
PBUH:	*Peace Be Upon Him*
Q:	*Quatrain.*
S:	*Surah of the Quran.*
U:	*Ulysses.*
V:	*Verse of the Quran.*
HCE:	*Here Comes Everybody*

Contents

Introduction

*J*oyce's interest in the East has not been fully explored. A glance at the catalogue of material in this area written by critics and researchers on his contemporaries, such as W.B. Yeats and T.S. Eliot, shows that the focus of attention has fallen on them: numerous papers, theses and books on the relationship of Eliot and Yeats to the East have been produced over the years from both East and West. Joyce has not been appreciated on this scale despite the works of John Bishop, Vincent Cheng and Aida Yared in recent years. All these writers focus on Joyce's Eastern motifs but none of them makes a book length study. Vincent Cheng's work is remarkable, discussing Finnegans Wake in the last two chapters. Does this mean that Joyce was not as much interested in the East as Yeats and Eliot? As the present thesis illustrates, that would be a difficult position to defend. Secondly, unlike Eliot and Yeats, whose main interest was in Eastern metaphysics and mysticism, Joyce absorbs and transposes into his art not only various Eastern cultures but also religions; he lets the diversity and variety enmesh like "Chutney graspis" (FW 405.26). There is no wavering of faith or doctrine in him similar to what one discerns in Yeats and Eliot. His detached observation is like that of a "lunger" (FW 131.04, 165.10, 331.06, 349.35). "Lunger" is a gesture reflecting the philanthropic sentiment of Indian culture; the meal is served without discrimination, religious or social, it is open for everybody to partake of and is usually distributed to all-comers at the shrines of the Indian mystics. Even the-well-to-do are proverbial for such benevolence. The people of the subcontinent adhere to cultural values of this kind, which received a new impetus with the arrival of Islam.

Observe, for example, the comprehensive vocabulary, circumscribing the entire culture, in the following quotation from the Notebook, VI.C. 6-16, p. 84: "chew of betel, brahimn, Kshattriyas, Vaisiyas, Sudras Subcaste, transmigrant, dravidian, anna, sherbet, epedermics, endemic, sporadic." Not only religion, the caste system and the heat, but also endemic diseases are encompassed here. Hindu society is divided into four castes reflecting the classical Greek pattern of life. The Brahmin is the priest-teacher while "ksatriya" is the king or military leader. Both Brahmin and Ksatriya are like the philosopher-king of Plato except that the former are divided into two ostensible classes and the latter is not only a sage but also a de facto ruler. It is ironic that in Hinduism, the power

is wielded by the Brahmins who use the military leaders more or less like the guardian class of Plato's Republic. The merchants ("vaisya") and ("sudra") are comparable to their Greek counterparts though the master-slave dialectic, say in Aristotle, is far more civilized and ultimately beneficial to the slaves.

Again, in the following instance we find the way Joyce transposes Buddhist "avidya" into a metaphor relevant to ALP and the girls who tempted Buddha: "whichever you'r avider to like it and lump it, but give it a name" (FW 455.07-08); "avider" is not identified by McHugh but, according to Burnett Hillman Streeter, it means "avidya": nescience, spiritual ignorance.[1] The word is used in virtually identical meaning when applied to Marge, one of the avatars of ALP. Marge is "avidously" looking at her "sweet" garment, but in reality she is "ovidently on the look out for him" (FW 166.10-11). Her feigning posture smacks of her spiritual ignorance or "avidya". Further, Marge is sitting on the "benches" but is in reality in search of "him" (not identified here), echoing the "apsaras" who sat on the branches of the Bo-tree (Ficus religios) below which Buddha meditated. Marge is crazy to the point of narcissism "over the shirtness of some "sweet" garment". Her shirt is synonymous with Issy's "skirt", which implies the mysterious dark realm (noumenon) beneath the ephemeral appearances (phenomenon).

With the arrival of the European colonizers, a new vocabulary was coined in the cultural melting-pot of India, as shown in these words and phrases: "Batt in, Boot! Sell him a breach contact" (FW 374.19-20) is "breach of contract" (McHugh) in business like the give-and-take reaffirmed by the phrase "Sell". The Indian term nearest to "Batt in, Boot!" is batta (1632 [EF] The English Factories in India (1618-1669) ed. William Foster; (1670-1677) ed. Charles Fawcett: 1680 Oxford English Dictionary), which means difference in exchange or extra allowance. "Bazaar" (FW 597.14) (or "Bazar" (FW 497.25)) is an Indian word (c.1599 OED) for market. "Begum" (FW 526.26) (or "Begum by gunne!" (FW 590.24)) is an Indian word (1626 ED, 1634 OED) for queen, princess or a well-to-do lady.

In the following references, there is an evident reminiscence of the Sepoy Mutiny (the first Indian war for independence), when the sepoys felt deeply insulted at being asked to bite the cattle-greased caps off shells: "hinndoo

---

I Burnett Hillman Streeter, The Buddha and the Christ: An Exploration of the Meaning and the Purpose of Human Life, (London: Macmillan, 1932), 51.

waxing ranjymad for a bombshoob" (FW 10.09); "to insoult on the hinndoo seeboy"[2] (FW 10.14). How one of the sepoys was tied over the mouth of a cannon and blown to pieces echoes in the sentence "This is the dooforhim seeboy blow the whole of the half of the hat of lipoleums off of the top of the tail on the back of his big wide harse" (FW 10.19-21). There are many more allusions to 19th- and 20th-century colonialism in India: "M.A.C.A. Sahib", "Syringa padham", "nack haul of Coalcutter" (FW 492.15, 22, 23); "dustungwashed...of the lost Gabbarnaur-Jaggarnath. Pamjab" (FW 342.13-14); "allafranka" (FW 343.23); "besant" (FW 432.31); "chutney and cloves" (FW 456.16); "Outcats in India" (FW 307.26); "Day the Dyer works, in Dims and deeps and dusks and darks" (FW 226.15-16).

Language is the sum-total of a culture's experience. At this level, experience embodies both the most intricate metaphysical interpretations and also the everyday colloquial idiom. An artist can express these extremes of reality only through his own language. Joyce uses language to create a puzzle. Somewhere, in a word or sentence, the letters or phrases communicate the main thrust providing the clue. The style of the Wake is cryptic in that it rejects meaning through language, as the latter is incapable of substantiating reality in its true spirit, but that is not the whole of the truth. The essential point about the Wake is that each reader understands it in proportion to his or her awareness of his or her own culture; the words are only the means by which sudden insight into the Wake's Aladdin's cave of encyclopaedic conglomeration is sparked. Such enlightenment is equivalent to Joyce's "epiphany." The European reader steeped willy-nilly in Christian culture, however imbued with post-modernism, would pass over a word of Sanskrit or Persian without feeling the spirit enclosed in it, whereas a reader in the Indian subcontinent would feel in it a warmth like that which Wordsworth describes in "Tintern Abbey." It is thus words, and only words, which enshrine the otherwise ungraspable metaphysical aspect of reality. This is very relevant to the Wake. True, the reader in

---

2   Vincent J. Cheng, Joyce, race, and empire (Cambridge University Press, 1995), 185. Vincent Cheng discusses the phrase "seeboy" (FW 10.14). Cheng, here, no longer attaches the cult of "subservience" to Indian soldiers of the Raj. As he puts it "mad as a hater in his anger, the "hinndoo" responds to Wellington's famed rallying cry ("Up, guards, and at "em") with a Hindu war cry of his own: "This is the seeboy, madrashattaras, up jump and pumpin, cry to the Willingdone: Ap Pukkaru! Pukka yurap!" (FW 10.15-17). As Cheng rightfully comments that "Madrashattaras" is a combination of two words: Marhatta and Madras. The latter is a city populated by Marhattas who were defeated by Wellington in the "Marhatta War." The "hinndoo's war cry, says Cheng, identifies a note of defiance. On the same page, Cheng refers to "Jam Sahib." The "seeboy" (soldiers of the Raj), used the title "Sahib" for their British Officers.

the Indian subcontinent would fail to respond to the episodic names of the *Odyssey* mentioned in the *Wake*, but sight of the Arabic word "skoule" (for "Scylla" or rock) would disclose to an eastern reader levels of meaning that he or she could develop according to his or her ability.

In addition to the allusions to colonialism, in both India and the Middle East, Joyce's Orientalism also includes a wide-ranging series of references to eastern cultures of different regions and times, religions and politics: the Mediterranean regions in their historic, strategic and cultural role; Confucius in China; the Tatars and Mongols of Central Asia; the Abbasids of Baghdad; the Fatimids of Africa; and, above all, the Turks old and modern. Joyce's encyclopaedic consciousness balks at the purely mystic, ancient wisdom of the East, in which Eliot and Yeats were mainly interested; Joyce, in this respect, does not show any of the rejection or reservation that one observes in Eliot and Yeats.

Eliot eventually returned to his own culture ("while all systems lead us back to the point from which we started"),[3] and Yeats too remained ambivalent towards the East. In *A Vision*, one can discern at least three meanings of "the East", viz. Asia; the Middle East; India and China. Asia and the Middle East illustrate the "primary", the "physical and religious" (*A Vision*, p.168), the binary opposites of the "antithetical" Europe. In the 1937 edition of *A Vision*, East stands for "Egypt and Mesopotamia" (p.257), symbolising wisdom and indifference towards life. Yeats's understanding of India and China are quite simple and pertain to meditation, non-attachment and karmic cycles of spiralling progress, up the ladder of the spiritual tower.

In his choice and selection of Eastern themes and vocabulary, Joyce is akin to other writers of the Orient like Kipling and E.M. Forster, but with a difference. In one of his incarnations, Finnegan is a dreamer like Vishnu; hence the "cultural gap" which haunts Mrs Moore in the caves of Malabar does not apply to the *Wake*. The range of Joyce's Indian material is far more limited than Kipling's and Forster's, yet it has essence and substance equal to theirs. Joyce interweaves myriad shades of reality into a fabric which defies any one conclusion. With respect to the Islamic component, Joyce regresses to the centre, the Kaba which connects to the unknown through the known. The Kaba is where Adam's fall and rise come together, while Adam and Eve connect Islam to the other revealed religions. From the Hindu perspective, the cosmic

---

3   Cleo McNelly Kearns, T.S. Eliot and Indic Traditions: A Study in Poetry and Belief, (Cambridge: Cambridge University Press, 1987), 133.

dreamer *Vishnu, one of the avatars of HCE, embodies the universal self; in the words of David A. White: "It seems true to say that an individual self apprehends other selves as other by existing in relation to those selves. The more individual egos a given self has experienced, the more the limits of that self are extended".⁴This endless chain assumes bigger and bigger proportions ("all that has been done has yet to be done" (FW 194.10)), accumulating into a cosmic memory which sheds its light "on the outermost reaches of time, with human life itself reflecting this never-ending and unlimited universality".⁵White adds that the individual human self, though fused inextricably, is but a "monad" or "flicker" in this unfathomable and endless process. Memory is karma, reward or punishment from previous incarnations, and Vishnu rules endlessly over the universe through the balancing act of karma. Vishnu's dream initiates an endless chain of cycles marked by the void of successive regression and regeneration. This void, known as "Sandhyas" enables contraries to melt into each other in a state of twilight, ready for the next cycle. Regression to the void, the unknowable, is where all systems, Eastern or Western, coalesce. In other words, Joyce attempts to discover the common roots of the different religions, the revealed religions on the one hand, and the pagan, secular, man-oriented religions such as that of (India, ancient Egypt, and ancient Greece, for example), on the other.*

Finnegans Wake is a kaleidoscope of Joyce's maturity.⁶From Dubliners onwards, the kinetic element of ephemeral reality eventually rises from,

4   David A. White, The Grand Continuum: Reflections on Joyce Metaphysics, (University of Pittsburgh, 1983), 39.

5   Ibid., 44.

6   Maturity implies the completion of the journey that Joyce began, as L.A.G. Strong puts it, "from objective scrutiny" to "the most deeply introspective" approach in the history of the novel (Sacred River: Approach to James Joyce, revised edition (Haskell House Publishers U.S.A., 1982)),1-15. His composing of the earliest verses as "pastiche" and Dubliners give the objective, realistic impression. A Portrait of the Artist as a Young Man is more a study of the young artist's growing soul though in the hostile, backward environment of Dublin. The spectrum of vision in Ulysses both expands and deepens as awareness and experience increase. The citizen Bloom stands for civilized understanding and adjustment in a place like the paralyzed Dublin. Since life is a constant yearning for new horizons, the Stephen of Ulysses would, even while he feels disgust and rebellion against his culture, carry on making new experiments on the very soil that he abjures. If Dubliners present the "paralysis" of life in Dublin, then A Portrait is a strong revulsion against it. Ulysses adds prudence and compromise. Hatred is always of one thing against another, it springs from the roots of love. Love is an association of a personal kind; we hate when we no longer find the previous attraction in a thing. This "loving wounding doubt," as Richard says in Exile, is both a bane and a boon in stirring up the currents of revulsion and attraction at a much higher and diversified level in the dreamlike condition of Finnegans Wake.

and returns to, a momentary silence or the "still point" as destination. Joyce observes the same rule in the Wake. Where he differs from his previous works in Finnegans Wake is in the level and magnitude of allusions. In A Portrait of the Artist as a Young Man, Stephen's range of mind is rooted in Joyce's aesthetics but we hardly read of any of the Eastern doctrine being assimilated. In Ulysses, Joyce shows a keen interest, especially in Hinduism, as Stuart Gilbert illustrates. Accounting for Bloom's Oriental tropes of a Promised Land in Ulysses Stuart Gilbert illustrates Joyce's keen interest in karma or "metempsychosis." We even come across a few allusions to Islamic culture. It is only in Finnegans Wake that we decipher such a rich "Aludin's Cove" (FW 108.27) of human cultures, both West and East. Joyce does not leave his reader in confusion in asserting such an interest "In that european end meets Ind" (FW 598.15). Whatever the scale of opaqueness, Joyce's vocabulary, after a little twinge of a puzzle, unravels its mystique. "Earopean" is European and "Ind" is India. "Earopean" is also the opening of the ear or the gathering of sense experience before the consummation of death. Joyce's stasis lies at the meeting-point of the two civilizations. His concept of this meeting explains his mental boundaries, which include Islam as well. Here, a new element is being added. The Islamic concepts of monotheism and the human accountability of deeds link it with Christianity and Judaism. The basic pattern of Finnegans Wake begins to take shape as Joyce brings together Eastern religions like Hinduism, Zoroastrianism and Confucianism, mixing them up with the systems of monotheism. Do these various faiths coalesce at any point? Joyce must have found the answer, among other books, in "The Terminal Essay" in Richard Burton's translation of the Arabian Nights.[7] In this way, another aspect of Joyce's orientalism is added into his system.

Out of the great range of Eastern themes in Finnegans Wake, this book will consider the following themes in four parts:

    1) The Arabian Nights in Finnegans Wake
    2) Joyce's Use of the Indic Canon
    3) Islam and Joyce
    4) Persian vocabulary and thought in Finnegans Wake

---

7   Le Mille e una notte, tr. Armando Dominic (Florence, 1915); The Arabian Nights, tr. Sir Richard Burton, (London: 17 Vols. 1886). Ellmann "Joyce's Library in 1920: Appendix" in Richard Ellmann, The Consciousness of Joyce, London: Faber, 1977). See also Thomas E. Connolly's, The Personal Library of James Joyce (Buffalo, New York: University of Buffalo Studies, 1955).

PART I *The Arabian Nights in Finnegans Wake*

A code of human empiricism is aptly applicable to the Nights, for they are an invention of the human mind alone and are based upon human beliefs drawn from various sources: cultures like those of Hinduism and Zoroastrianism; Chinese folk literature; pre-Islamic and Islamic beliefs.

The idea of Hinduism known to Blavatsky rests largely on cyclical patterns or renewal and repetition, as we have no idea of time's beginning or end, except what impinges upon our mind in the form of day or night. The revealed religions all have a beginning and an end, as the code of instructions is revealed from above the canopy of nature which we see around us. Blavatsky's concept of Hinduism, the Arabian Nights and Finnegans Wake are based upon indiscriminate multiplication of these and many more factors of human belief and reality. Moreover, the Arabian Nights lack any single source. They have grown with the developing and expanding interactions of human cultures. Finnegans Wake too is a compendium which welds together numerous cultures in the mind of the unprejudiced author.

In the first chapter, "Joyce and the Arabian Nights: the importance of Richard Burton", I further expand the sources and processes of cross-cultural assimilation in the Wake and the Nights. Like Finnegans Wake, Richard Burton's and Edward Lane's editions of the Arabian Nights are also compendia of the human past. The Arabian Nights consists of fables and stories not only of Persia and Arabia but also of China and India. Burton's "Terminal Essay" (See Volume VIII of the Arabian Nights) discusses its material and genesis in such detail that by reading it one is able to gain insight into the spiritual achievements of Hinduism, Zoroastrianism and Islam. Burton also establishes Greek links with the above eastern religions in this essay. He evolves a pattern of metaphysical understanding of reality by bringing in the Graeco-Persian, Hindu and Moslem systems. Like chapter 10 (FW 260-308) of Finnegans Wake, which goes to the heart of the major mystical, scriptural and mythical systems of the world, both East and West, this part of the "Terminal Essay" develops another such synthesis of human beliefs. Joyce must have found Burton and Lane crucial for incorporating Eastern material into his works. He owned an Italian translation of the Nights when he was in Trieste and later replaced it with the Burton Club Edition in Paris. Grace Eckley has identified a certain erotic story in the Wake as taken from the 1840 translation by Edward Lane, the first translator

of the Nights into English. Hence, both Burton's and Lane's translations are assimilated in Finnegans Wake.⁸ Most of the Arabian allusions from the Nights also appear in previous works of Joyce, particularly Dubliners and Ulysses. What is new in Finnegans Wake is its striking closeness to the manner and style of the Nights—its scheme of chiaroscuro and the recurrence of themes with variations within the stories and characters at every turn of the cycle. Finnegans Wake is the story of a single family involving transformations of the characters at every turn — giving the impression of "metempsychosis", as Bloom explains to Molly in "Calypso": "It's Greek: from the Greek. That means the transmigration of souls". Souls migrate from person to person and age to age in search of what has remained unfulfilled. This urge for satisfaction is an existential condition of life. Since everything in the universe is in motion, each living thing is in quest of its true entity or "entelechy". Sons inherit the traits of their fathers and grandfathers endlessly. In Finnegans Wake, this process keeps on haunting the protagonist"'s family as a unit configuring the fate of humanity.

The second chapter is about Harun al-Rashid and H.C.E. In Finnegans Wake, Harun al-Rashid emerges as one of the avatars of Finnegan, while in the Arabian Nights, Harun al-Rashid is the protagonist. This indicates his character as of central value for consideration in this chapter. Harun al-Rashid as an incarnation of H.C.E. is discussed next. Taking the cue of the symbol of the egg from Yeats's A Vision, I examine the letters "H.C.E." as a protean force relevant to Harun al-Rashid. Furthermore, I examine the general characteristics that Harun al-Rashid and Finnegan have in common. The chapter closes with a description of Harun's relations with the Bermic family, and of the latter's tragic fall as well as their fabulous feasts. Joyce refers to the Bermics in two places in the Wake.

If Harun al-Rashid is the male protagonist, then Shaharazad and Dunyazad are the two equally prominent females of the Nights. The role of these two women is examined in chapter three. According to the Wake, these two characters of the Nights are the "inseparable" sisters. Their strategy was that, the moment the king stopped making love to Shaharazad, Dunyazad was to request the next tale. In this way, the king was to be kept enthralled both by

---

8   Grace Eckley, Children's Lore in Finnegans Wake, (Syracuse: Syracuse University Press, 1985), 62. Eckley refers to the tale "The Rogueries of Dalilah the Crafty and her daughter Zaynab-the Coney-Catcher" (the Nights 7: 144).

the narrative web and by the web of erotic pleasure. The Wake's use of the erotic material in the Nights is discussed in this chapter and the dialogue of the Two Washerwomen in ALP's chapter "O, tell me all about Anna Livia" (FW 196) is evaluated by comparison with the women of the Nights. The telling of tales, and its relation to the darkness of night, bring in the motif of the hidden creative potential that is possessed by Shaharazad and also by ALP.

The character of Sindbad the Sailor is another aspect of Joyce's attraction to the Arabian Nights, examined in chapter four. Part of the cycle of Travel Stories, Sindbad's tale was popular in the East even in the age of Alexander the Great, as G. E. Von Grunebaum explains.[9] Sindbad the Sailor is mentioned in Book I of the Wake: "Singabob, the badfather". (FW 94.32-37). In the same passage, the stinking apparel of a sailor is stated as "comes off his body, the stench of a goat". Since Sindbad is also a teller of his own tales, there is an important parallel between Shem and Sindbad. This contrast draws attention to chapter 9 of the Wake (FW 219-259), in which the behaviour of the playing children is described. In this chapter, the children are staging a play in which the girls ask different questions of Shem. Every time that Shem returns after being exiled on account of his failure to solve the riddle, he appears as Sindbad the Sailor: the first riddle is "jeeremyhead sindbook", (229.32); the second is "sin beau.. the seagoer" (233.5-11); the third is "Singabed sulks before slumber" (256.33-4). In the next chapter of The Study Session, Sindbad is mentioned as "Sinobiled" (263.f.n) in an overlapping collection of theosophical themes. There is also an allusion to Sindbad's physical appearance as "Somhow-at-Sea (O little oily head, sloper's brow and prickled ears!)". (FW 291.26-7). This, in fact, foregrounds Sindbad's story with what Richard Ellmann terms the "final tri- ad" of Ulysses.[10] Sindbad the Sailor's relation to "Sindbad the landsman" is also considered. The section on Sindbad's tales closes with discussion of two other tales of the Nights: "The Sleeper Awakening" and "The Hunchback's Tale."

PART II *Joyce's Use of the Indic Canon*

We have seen Joyce's fascinating interest in the tales of one culture leading

---

9   G.E. Von Grunebaum, Medieval Islam, "Greece in the Arabian Nights," (Chicago: University of Chicago Press, 1945), 294-319.

10   Richard Ellmann, Ulysses on the Liffey (London and New York: Oxford University Press, 1972),151.

into another and the common characteristics of these stories whether Persian, Arabic and Celtic, in the previous section. Joyce's quest for such similarities also expands into human religions. In Reading Joyce Reading Derrida[11] (p.5), Alan Roughley uses the term "equivocation" for Joyce's method. Roughley says that whereas Husserl may be described as interested in geometrical form having "univocal ideal", Joyce was occupied in "generalized ideal forms" of "equivocation." Equivocation, as we know, is a deliberate attempt to avoid a direct, clear answer to a question. In this enterprise of manufacturing a language epitomising nearly all the languages of the world, Joyce, according to Derrida (as Roughley quotes) was minting "equivocation itself, utilising a language that could equalise the greatest possible synchrony with the greatest potential for buried, accumulated, and interwoven intentions within each linguistic atom, each vocable, each word, each simple proposition, in all worldly cultures and their most ingenious forms"[12] (Derrida 1989: 102).

Why all this amalgamation of diversity? Joyce is a 'modern', writing with the sensibility of modernism in his bones. Joyce looks at reality like the Cubists of the first and second decades of the twentieth century. According to Gleizes and Metzinger, Cubism permits an artist in "moving around an object to seize from it several appearances, which, fused into a single image, reconstitute it in time."[13] The Wake's phrase "the annihilation of the etym" (FW 353.21) is in one sense the annihilation of the atom, the work of the physicists. On another level, "etym" is Adam whose expulsion from the Garden of Eden and its consequences are hinted at. A nuclear scientist and a religious person could each bring their own understanding and logic to it. Both are right in their own approximation.

Joyce, as we know, leaves multiple possibilities of interpretation to his text by emphasising "equivocation." This may be applied to his use of the Indic thought. His knowledge of Hinduism was based upon the information obtained from the works of H.P. Blavatsky, H. Zimmer, H.S. Olcott and above all the 11th Encyclopaedia Britannica. There is hardly any evidence of his having a scholarly interest in the classic sacred Hindu texts such as Puranas and Vedas.

---

11   Alan Roughley, Reading Derrida Reading Joyce (University Press of Florida, Gainesville, FL. Publication Year: 1999), 5

12   Reading Derrida Reading Joyce, 5

13   (Jo-Anna Isaak's "James Joyce and the Cubist Esthetic" in Mosaic 14 (!981): 61-90. See also Albert Gleizes and Jean Metzinger's "Cubism" in Modern Artists on Art, ed. Robert L. Herbert (Englewood, Cliffs, N.J. :Printice Hall, 1964), 15.

Among his contemporaries, T S Eliot, for example, had more formal training in the Indic religions. In fact, Joyce's awareness of the Indian thought owes mainly to the literary scene of Dublin in particular and the nineteenth century explorations of the Eastern systems by the Orientalists.

Joyce's use of Eastern imagery can be generally described as theosophical in the sense that theosophy was an attempt at complete synthesis of all religions as one. Joyce in Finnegans Wake adapts all kinds of religions and philosophies into a system of his own without committing himself to any one in particular.

Tracing the history of Joyce's interest in Yeats's theosophical and oriental outlook, Richard Ellmann draws attention to Dublin's literary scene in 1902. The copy of H.S. Olcott's A Buddhist Catechism that Joyce bought dates as May 7, 1901. The younger generation of writers like Padraic Colum, Seumas O' Sullivan and numerous others had attracted the attention of the older figures like George Russell, Synge, Lady Gregory and above all Yeats. In the summer of 1902, Joyce met George Russell whose interests in eastern mysticism were well known. A friend of Blavatsky and organiser of her theosophical branch in Dublin, Russell discussed the themes of karmic cycles, the succession of gods and "the eternal mother-faith that underlies all transitory religions"[4]with Joyce. His meeting with Russell was fruitful because it brought Joyce nearer to Yeats. Russell's opinion of Joyce at this stage was intriguing. "The first spectre", Russell announced to Yeats "of the new generation has appeared. His name is Joyce. I have suffered from him and I would like you to suffer."[5]Ellmann eloquently sums up the differences between Joyce and Yeats: "the defected Protestant confronted the defected Catholic, the landless landlord met the shiftless tenant. Yeats, fresh from London, made one in a cluster of writers whom Joyce would never know, while Joyce knew the limbs and bowels of a city of which Yeats knew well only the head."[6]

Despite many divergences, there were some basic interests that Joyce and Yeats were pursuing in common. J. Eglinton mentions the passion of Yeats for the East: "It was from the east that Yeats snatched the clue to the interpretation of Dublin culture."[7]Stuart Gilbert mentions P.W. Joyce as saying that "From

---

14   Richard Ellmann, James Joyce, revised edition, (Oxford: Oxford University Press, 1982), 102.

15   From George Russell's article "Some Characters of the Irish Literary Movement", cited by Ellmann, James Joyce, 104.

16   Ellmann, James Joyce, 104.

17   John Eglinton, "Yeats and his Story", The Dial, (May 1926), 358.

Scythia, their original home, they [i.e. the Druids] began their long journey. Their first migration was to Egypt, where they were sojourning at the time that Pharaoh and his host were drowned in the Red Sea; and after wandering through Europe for many generations they arrived in Spain. Here they abode for a long time, and at last they came to Ireland with a fleet of thirty ships under the command of the eight sons of the hero Miled or Milesius."[18]

Finally, Richard Burton's knowledge of India may simply have helped Joyce learn about its civilization. Burton's erudite knowledge of Hinduism earned him great respect in the religious circles of Indian Brahmins. This helped him in his work of translating the Arabian Nights, as these tales are not confined to the cultures of the Near East alone. India's geographical and historical relations with this region had permitted a close interdependence among these peoples of the East. No wonder that the waves of conquerors from the Near East had always succeeded in consolidating their hold on India. Even the pre-Islamic Hindu rulers, like the dynasty of Chandargupta, had annexed parts of Persia and Central Asia. Such currents of military conquest played a part in transferring both literary and moral values.

Book IV begins with Sandhyas, the prayer word of Sanskrit. The question, however, arises as to the reason for invoking Hinduism at the very start of Book IV when Hinduism is referred to only occasionally throughout the Wake. The chief answer, however, is the way Finnegans Wake is designed and structured. The first sentence begins with the subject "river run," which is left without a grammatical article. This alerts the reader to look elsewhere, and completion is readily available, if we put in place the "the" with which the Wake ends. This artifice of joining together the beginning and the end of Finnegans Wake is further implied in the ever-flowing "river run," an epithet of ALP, the everlasting creative feminine principle. This unceasing process of creativity binds the two

---

18 P.W. Joyce, A Concise History of Ireland, quoted in Stuart Gilbert, James Joyce's Ulysses: A Study (New York: Vintage Books, 1955), 67. Also observe Lady Ann Blunt's Bedouin Tribes of the Euphrates, (Wilfrid Scawen Blunt and Lady Ann Blunt publishers and translators, London, 1879) Vol. I, vii. She argues that the condition of Celtic Ireland must have been similar to that of the Arabs prior to Islam. In her translation of the Seven Golden Odes of Pagan Arabia, (Wilfrid Scawen Blunt and Lady Ann Blunt publishers and translators, London, 1903), ix, she says, "In Europe the nearest analogy to it [Arabic poetry] is perhaps to be found in the pre-Christian verse of Celtic Ireland, which by a strange accident was its close contemporary, and lost its wild natural impulse through the very same circumstance of the conversion of its pagan bards to an overmastering new theology." (Wilfrid Scawen Blunt had been seen by Yeats at Lady Gregory's house).

extremes as the body links the head and tail of a snake. On this plan, every moment and every place is both a beginning and an end in which the past operates in the present and vice versa. Thus, the insertion of Hindu themes in Book IV is as relevant to any other part of the Wake as that part or Book to it. Moreover, Joyce's application of Vico's theory states the same idea.

Sandhyas itself verifies the truth of mergence with, and divergence from, a point of stasis, stillness or momentary silence subsuming the various ages. Sandhyas is here first defined in detail in chapter one and then applied to the Hindu myth of creation. In this chapter, an attempt is also made to identify the role of Sandhyas in establishing the Hindu doctrine of existence. Like any other system in the world or, for that matter, the Arabian Nights, what ignites Sandhyas from its depthless silences, or dark womb, is desire. Madame Blavatsky (referred to in the Wake) is relevant here and reference is also made to H. Zimmer's work on Hinduism. Chapter two is about ALP and the Mystery of the Article "the." The reason why the Wake ends with the letter "the" and how such an ending is related to the system of Blavatsky and to Hinduism in general is explored. Since the birth of desire means the impact of "maya" or illusion, parts of Book IV are analysed as an outcome of such an impact. Chapter two also examines the Indian topography in ALP's "untitled mamafesta." (FW 104.04). In this chapter, I also discuss the passages which Joyce has assimilated from Zimmer's The Myths and Symbols in Indian Art and Civilization. Some aspects of the life of Buddha are also considered. Chapter 3 is about the value and techniques of Yoga. In this final chapter of the section, I attempt to bring out the central message of the Hindu wisdom which lies in mystic contemplation and painstaking spiritual exercises. I begin the chapter by considering St. Kevin, whom the Wake remembers as "a naked yogpriest" (FW 601.01). The last part of the chapter deals with the yoga system of Buddhism since it too is incorporated in the Wake.

PART III *Islam and Joyce*

Islam, as understood by Joyce, originated in Arabia in the late sixth century AD. This means that Islam, as revealed to the Prophet Mohammed (pbuh), comes much later in human history than the ancient religions such as Hinduism. On chronological grounds, therefore, Islam is discussed in the third section of the book.

Joyce's interest in the family, faith and prophethood of Mohammed is indicated

by his inserting the name of the Prophet's mother Amina in chapter 10 of the Wake (the central chapter in which he synthesises his system by bringing in as much as he knew): "...and as for Ibdullin what of Himana" (FW 309.13-14). Mohammed's father "Ibdullin" (Abdullah) died only weeks before the Prophet's birth. His mother too died when he was an infant of five or six. As was then the custom, the infant was entrusted to a Bedouin family in the desert. After some years, the future Prophet returned home and his mother decided to take him on a visit to her maternal home in Medina, also visiting his father's tomb. During the return journey, the mother fell ill and died. The grandfather, Abdul Muttalib, took over care of the orphan, but he too died soon after.

In the Wake, Khadijah is not directly referred to, though McHugh has glossed the phrase "his cousin" (FW 20.03) as relating to Khadijah, the Prophet's cousin. HCE is examining the Arab culture by means of his "infrarational senses" (FW 20.01). The verb "ban" in Persian means "farsightedness," the capacity to foresee coming events or happenings. It is also used as a noun meaning microscope and telescope in the South Asian languages. HCE's "infrarational senses" thus embody the same idea as "ban." Joyce's use of vocabulary is such that he selects words from different languages carrying the same sense as prototypes. He also juggles with words by changing their grammatical structure although the thought remains implicit. Extrication of meaning requires a familiarity born of or belonging to a particular culture, without which the effort remains deliberate, conscious and laborious. The sentence under discussion is a clear example of this: "under the ban of our infrarational senses for the last milchcamel, the heartvein throbbing his eyebrowns, has still to moor before the tomb of his cousin charmian where his date is tethered by the palm" (FW 20.01-04). The passage describes the Arab custom of tying a camel to the grave of a dead person in the belief that the camel would ease the soul in journeying to the hereafter. The prophet's deep sorrow at the death of Khadijah is quite explicit in the phrase "moor before the tomb of his cousin."

Khadijah was Mohammed's first wife. According to Shibli, a Moslem scholar, Khadijah's family had branched off from Mohammed's some five generations back.

Twice widowed and now forty, Khadijah still received marriage proposals from the Koreish because of her unblemished character and business acumen. She had a son, Hala from her first husband Abudulah ibn Zarara and

a daughter was born of her second marriage. The deaths of her guardians compelled her to look for someone who could take care of her business. She chose Mohammed, a man in his mid-twenties, mainly because of his reputation in Mecca as "El-amin" (the trustworthy). Joyce refers to Mohammed's title "El-Amin" in his Notebook (VI.B.31). Khadijah was the first to vow allegiance to the prophethood of Mohammed (pbuh) after he received his first revelation on mount Hira. As he returned home, his face was wrapped in a cloth—"(the rapt one warns)" (FW 20.10), and a phrase from the Quran: "O thou who art wrapped, rise up and warn" (s.24). Following this first revelation, Mohammed was stricken by fever. Khadijah stood by him and persuaded her clan to soften their antagonism towards him. Mohammad and Khadijah had two sons and four daughters. The sons died as infants. Two of Mohammad's daughters married sons of Abu Lahab, who became the sworn enemy of the Prophet, and about whom the Quran says: "The power of Abu Lahab will perish, his wealth and gains will not exempt him. He will be plunged in the flaming fire, and the wood carrier will have upon her neck a halter of palm-fibre" (s.III v.32). James Atherton, in the chapter on the Quran, refers to this Quranic verdict on Abu Lahab rendered by Joyce as "and a hundered and eleven other things,...I will commission to the flames" (FW 425.31). It is interesting to note that the surah in which the Quran relates the story of Abu Lahab is numbered III. The name Lahab means being put into the flames of hell.

The year of Khadijah's death is commemorated as a year of mourning. It was Khadijah who supported the Prophet through the trials and tribulations of the early years of his preaching—the time of idolatry, ignorance and internecine war.

In Finnegans Wake there are a number of references to Aysha such as, "then, Aysha" (FW 282.25-26), Prophet's second wife.

Following the death of Khadijah, the prophetic task became even more challenging for Mohammed. The epoch-making "Hijrah" (FW 62.03) was approaching, with the Prophet's decision to migrate to Medina. While Mohammed (pbuh) and his friend Abu Bakr hid themselves in the cave of Hira, the same cave in which the Prophet had received his first divine call, Aysha and her sister supplied them with food, keeping their whereabouts secret. Aysha was Abu Bakr's daughter. R.W.J. Austen has divided Mohammed's life into two eras: the time spent in Mecca, in introspection, and his time at Medina, where the

mystic musings of the Meccan period were given practical effect.[19]

Khadijah completes the mystic Meccan period, while Aysha initiates the practical period in Medina during which the Prophet emerged as a statesman and general. Aysha played a decisive role in the future development of Islam. Whether in battles, as at Badr and Uhud, Notebook (VI.B.31, p.53) "2 A.H i.e A.D 624" or the final conquest of Mecca "Mecca evacuated 3 days" (FW 127.12-13), Aysha remained in the forefront.

Another passage in the Wake may refer to the Prophet's life:

> Yet never shet it the brood of aurowoch, not for legions of donours of Gamuels. I have performed the law in truth for the lord of the law, Taif Alif. I have held out my hand for the holder of my heart in Annapolis, my youthrib city. Be ye then my protectors unto Mussabotomia before the guards of the city. Theirs theres is a gentlemeants agreement. Womensch plodge. (FW 318.22-27).

This has the tone of an extempore speech, perhaps indicating the Prophet's farewell address on his last pilgrimage. The passage pertains to a time when the Prophet had been successful in establishing Islam, the idol worshippers of Mecca and Taif (who had attacked Mohammed during his earlier missionary visit to Taif while Khadijah was still alive), had been brought into the fold of Islam, the Meccan Koreish humbled and their three hundred and sixty idols (Notebook VI.B.31) destroyed from "the Annapolis" for the sake of Alif Allah, the Omniscient and Omnipotent.

There are two references to Fatimah, Prophet's daughter in Finnegans Wake: "with the role of ... Ahdahm this way make, Fatima...!)" (FW 205.29-31); and, "for teaching the Fatima Woman history of Fatimiliafamilias, repeating herself" (FW 389.14-15). The first reference "Ahdahm" stands for Adam, while denoting the rhythmic drawing in and out of breath in Urdu. Breathing sustains

---

19 R.W.J. Austen, "The Prophet of Islam" in The Challenges of Islam, ed. Altaf Gauhar, (London: Islamic Council of Europe, 1978), 68. Austen states: "As the final religion, Islam draws together many strands of truth expressed earlier in the Judaic and Christian traditions, creating from the synthesis the complete and final form of God's religion. The life of its Prophet Mohammad unites in one man the differing truths about man revealed in these religions. Two phases of the Prophet's mission — the Meccan and the Medinan — symbolize respectively the Judaic emphasis on law and community, and the Christian emphasis on the dual roles of man as solitary and social being, as slave and vicegerent of God, as servant and messenger, prophet and king. He is the archetype or norm of humanity par excellence in whom all aspects of being unite at the centre in perfect harmony and balance."

life; hence Adam as "Ah" (intake) and "dahm" (expiration) is understood as the bestower of life. The second reference suggests the repetitive pattern of history in which the Fatimids continually asserted and reasserted themselves in the name of Allah and the Prophet Mohammed. It is Fatimah's esoteric, mystic aspect which accounts for her vital symbolic role.

Moreover, in Finnegans Wake, Joyce begins the introductory pages with a paragraph which conveys the whole story and achievement of Islam. In chapter one, I discuss the truth about the Kaba. The Kaba, to which Joyce refers in this paragraph and elsewhere in the Notebooks, is the very navel of Moslem faith and an earthly counterpart of heavenly. existence. Joyce's references to the life story of the Prophet Mohammed (pbuh) and his family, and to the spiritual relation of the Prophet with Christ, Moses, Ibrahim, and Adam and Eve are noted. In chapter two, I set out Joyce's sources on the Quran. Hughes's Dictionary of Islam, George Sale's translation of The Koran and Richard Burton's Personal Narrative of a Pilgrimage to El-Medinah and Mecca are the major sources of information about the Quran for Joyce. He inserts the names of the surahs quite frequently, with occasionally the verses of the Quran, in Finnegans Wake. Sometimes, the Quranic allusions appear in those paragraphs which are conspicuously related to Moslem culture in general. In others, words or a passage could be applied to any of the revealed religions. At times, the general themes of, for example, "Fall" and "Apocalypse" connect the revealed religions into a single pattern, though this pattern is not confined to these religions as Joyce diversifies his meaning by adding myths old and new into a bigger whole in a constantly evolving system. After identifying the word "al-cohoran" (FW 20,09) as taken from Sale's translation of the Quran as "Al Koran" in chapter three, I explain how the same word resonates in different combinations underlining the message of Islam which is coherent and unifying. Since Allah is omnipotent and omniscient, His control over the universe and the entire creation is emphasized in this chapter. Allah is the one unifying force in the multitudinous universe. The chapter, then, cites those words and phrases that allude to the names of the "surahs" of the Quran spread diffusely in the Wake. Such a vocabulary may also be considered as the Wake's peculiar method of punning the texts.

PART IV *Persian vocabulary and thought in Finnegans Wake*

Because of Joyce's interest in Persian vocabulary, Zoroastrianism and Omar Khayyam's Rubaiyat, the chapter discusses all these aspects. The Wake as we know is also "persianly literatured". (FW 183.10). The chapter also touches upon Zoroastrians, the ancient kings of Persia, and cultural and literary exchanges between Persia and India. Since Joyce transcribes Fitzgerald's translation of Khayyam's Rubaiyat in the Wake, an attempt is made to identify these references. Khayyam's doctrine of mysticism is briefly described. The chapter also brings out those words and phrases which are commonly used in both the Persian language (Farsi) and its sister languages of South Asia. Joyce's choice of vocabulary is narrow, so that the words themselves reflect the mainstream South Asian cultures.

Additionally, in the Appendices:

In this section, an attempt is made to identify the meanings of various words of Sanskrit, Persian, Urdu, Punjabi and Arabic which occur in Finnegans Wake and in the Finnegans Wake Notebooks at Buffalo..

Joyce's eastern themes need a thorough digging in the Wake. The reader knows that unravelling the complex text of the Wake is like groping to understand the modern self. The reader is only a mediator anatomising the text and the self, objectively.

Mediation is the scintillating node of the point in time when the characters finally move from ignorance to self-recognition. Discovery takes place when the facts are sifted from fiction, the "tying" or "untying" the events as David Weir in James Joyce and the Art of Mediation,[20] quotes from Aristotle. How complicated the modern self and Joyce's text is, may be illustrated through an example. In the case of Odysseus (who represents the Greek civilization) and Sindbad the Sailor (whose story preserves many common shades of Eastern stylistics), for example, the "untying" of the knotted plot takes place in the "end" of the linear time: the cabman's shelter and the Sailor's residence. The tavern where Bloom and Stephen meet in Ulysses, occasions a chance interaction between the two. The action moves towards discovery in the case of Odysseus and Sindbad.

---

20 David Weir, James Joyce and the Art of Mediation (The University of Michigan Press).

It hardly helps resolve the psychological dilemmas Bloom and Stephen in here. This is due to the nature of the modern "self", which, as Weir quotes Walter Pater as saying that it is "a tremulous wisp constantly reforming itself upon the stream, to a single impression, with a sense in it, a relic more or less fleeting, of such moments gone by...." Contrary to a conscious, deliberate construction of a story out of myth and tradition derived from folk culture as the Odyssey and the Arabian Nights are, the modern "self" is a groping for the construction of the consciousness itself. Consciousness implies the feelings, sensations, impressions, responses, perceptions that lay the casus belli of behaviour and mediation between the "world within" (or Aristotelian possibilities) and "the world without" of the actual or the objective as Stephen meditates on Shakespeare that he "found in the world without as actual what was in his world within as possible" (U 9.1040-41). The elusive Wake can be deciphered from the bits and pieces which are like "a tremulous wisp." These "relics" are the clues to a culture. "Relics" the Wake embodies when examined in the light of that culture, identify its salient features known mainly to the Orientalists.

∾

Finnegans Wake:
some Eastern Aspects

PART I

The Arabian Nights in Finnegans Wake

1.

Joyce and the Arabian Nights: the importance of Richard Burton

Richard Ellmann in "The Consciousness of Joyce"[1] and Thomas E. Connolly in "The Personal Library of James Joyce"[2], mention the Arabian Nights as having been read by Joyce. He owned an Italian translation, "La mille e una notte", translated by Armando Dominicis (Florence, 1915). When he settled in Paris, he purchased the set of the Nights translated and transcribed by Sir Richard Burton. Within the English literary tradition, the list of authors familiar with the Nights and read by Joyce is fairly large. Peter L. Caracciolo in his introduction to The Arabian Nights in English Literature makes a lucid survey of the Nights influence on the English and European literary tradition.[3] Thus even unconsciously Joyce was to

---

1   Richard Ellmann, The consciousness of James Joyce, (London: Faber and Faber, 1977), 99. "Joyce's Library in 1920: Appendix" La Mille e una notte, translated into Italian by Armando Dominic, Florence: Adriana Salani, 1915.

2   Thomas E. Connolly, The Personal Library of James Joyce, (Buffalo NY: University of Buffalo Studies, 1955, 10. Sir Richard Burton, The Arabian Nights, Luristan edition, ca, 1919.

3   The Arabian Nights in English Literature, ed. Peter L. Caracciolo, Basingstoke, Macmillan, 1988). In the "Introduction," 1-61 titled "Such a storehouse of ingenious fiction and splendid imagery" Caracciolo says that Chaucer evidently became acquainted with the Nights during his stay in Spain and Italy, and that the "Magic Horse" of the Squire's Tale is proof of this. The Crusades had helped in mellowing the literary environment (if not political). Cervantes, Boccaccio and the French trouveurs were also familiar with the literary achievements of the Moslem East. In the The Bride of Lammermoor, Sir Walter Scott alludes to "The Sleeper Awakened" in the eastern tales as does Joyce. Swift, Pope and Addison were the first to read the French and English translation of the Nights by Antoine Galland in 1704. Caracciolo mentions the opinion of Gibbon that these tales could be compared with Homer and Virgil. The eighteenth century sensibility found the Nights most striking and exotic: ..."nothing is so striking as the degree to which...English writers are able to tame and demonstrate what comes to them originally in the form of a genuinely exotic item." Mohsin Mahdi compares Coleridge's Ancient Mariner with Sindbad the Sailor. Dorothy Wordsworth mentions the influence of the Nights in The Prelude and describes how enchanting it was "... to express the enchanted effect produced by this

register the enormous and popular appeal of these tales.

His basic interest was to grasp the common elements between various cultures, as Mary and Padraic Colum state in considerable detail:

> And because Finnegans Wake dealt with night life he wanted to know about other books that proceeded from night life. One was The Arabian Nights ... the frame work has to do with nights, and, we are told, the art of collection originated in night walkers stories. Joyce wanted the Arabian Nights read by someone who could tell him some of its features, so he sent over to my apartment a sixteen volume set of Burton's translation. The first thing I reported interested him: back of the Arabian stories were Persian stories; in fact, the names of the story teller and her sister were Persian. The fact of one culture leading into another was always fascinating to Joyce, and he wanted to know if there was a parallel between the Persian stories giving rise to the Arabian and the Celtic stories giving rise the Arthurian cycle. And what did the names of the storyteller and her sister mean? I read the sixteen volumes with great delight, naturally (I had read only Lane's four volumes previously), and talked to Joyce about various features in them. The Caliph walking about at night with his Vizier must appear on some page of Finnegans Wake, but the only lines I am sure derived from my reading are those about the night talking sisters.[4]

Here, Mary and Padraic Colum aptly summarise Joyce's interest in the Arabian Nights. First, there is the fact of the cross-cultural migration of the tales. The Nights actually originated in Persia. "The first people to collect stories were the early Persians"[5] writes Ibn Ishaq al-Nadim. According to him, the rulers of the Sassanid dynasty (third to seventh century A. D) were in the habit of listening to the "evening stories and fables." How early these tales took root in Arabia is a matter of conjecture. According to Abu al-Hassan al-Masudi, it took nearly three centuries

---

Arabian scene behind which we stood" (Letters of W and D. Wordsworth, Vol, I, p.280). In The Preface to Arthur (1-3), Hole praises the heritage of humanity preserved in these tales during the Middle Ages when Europe was living in the Dark Ages. Among the other Romantics, Byron was definitely fascinated by the Nights, as his hero Don Juan says "after a dwarf buffoon stood telling tales." In the nineteenth century Thackeray speaks of "...the charming Scheherazade." Dickens refers to the Nights "talking bird, the singing tree, and the golden water" enjoyed by Parizade and her brother in "The Story of the Sisters who Envied their Younger Sister" (Letters, ed. House et al., p.54 and n.4). In the rest of the nineteenth century, the Bronte sisters and the twentieth, Thomas Moore, Conrad, H. G. Wells, E. M. Forster, Walter De La Mare, Yeats and Joyce are mentioned by Caracciolo as having benefited from the Arabian Nights.

4   Mary and Padraic Colum, Our Friend James Joyce, (London: Gollancz, 1955), 161-2.

5   Bayard Dodge, (editor and translator), The Fihrist of al-Nadim: a Tenth century Survey of Moslem Culture (New York: Columbia University Press 1970), Vol, 2., 712-13.

for them to become assimilated into the regular Arab culture.[6] Islam, which was established in Arabia in the sixth and seventh centuries, was their staunch opponent. The Quran had this to say about them: "There is one person who purchases frivolous stories so as to lead people away from the path of God; ignorant, he makes mock of God's path. For persons such as this there will be a humiliating punishment" (s.31:v.6-7). Al-Masudi illustrates by quoting al-Zamakhshari and al-Nadir ibn al-Harith. Commentators like al-Zamakhshari (A.D.1143) explain the phrase "frivolous stories" as meaning baseless fairytales and legends meant to entertain on a merry-making-evening with drink and music. Ibn al-Harith, an Arab merchant, would purchase them from Persia and recite them to the tribe of Koriesh or the Prophet Mohammed saying: "If Mohammed has been reciting for you tales of Ad and Thamud, well then I am going to recite for you tales of Rustam and Behram, and of the Persian shahs and the monarch of Hira!."[7] The people found them more entertaining than the Quran, as al-Zamakhshari reports. Rustam and Behram are heroes of the Persian saga and Hira was the capital in the north east of Arabia whose rulers were allies of the Sassanids. The Quranic recitations to the tribes of Ad and Thamud by the Prophet were a serious warning. According to chapter seven of the Quran, these ancient inhabitants of the Arabian peninsula had been punished and destroyed by God because their refusal to listen and practise Divine injunctions. God had been sending them prophet after prophet for this purpose. McHugh mentions the names of these two tribes as having been known to Joyce through Stanley Lane Poole's book The Table Talk of Prophet Mohammed. Joyce glosses the phrase "destroyed in prehistoric days" from this book in the Notebook VI.B.31.[8]

The cross-cultural transmigration of literary exchange is not confined to geographically contiguous regions such as Arabia and Persia. McHugh, for example, identifies the name of Antar Bayard in the Notebook. (VI.B.31, p. 51). In Finnegans

---

6   Abu al-Hasan al-Masudi, Muruj al-dhahab (Paris, L'Imprimerie Imperiale, 1861-1877),Vol.4, 90-91; cited and translated by Abbott, op.cit.,150. Nabia Abbott, Journal of Near Eastern Studies 8 (1949): 129-164,"A Ninth Century Fragment of the Thousand Nights: New Light on the Early History of the Arabian Nights."

7   Mahmud ibn Umar al-Zamakhshari, Al-Kashshaf an haqaiq al-tanzil, (Beirut: Dar al-marifah, n.d), Vol.3, p.210) quoted by David Pinault, Story-Telling techniques in the Arabian Nights, (Laiden, New York and Koln; E.J. Brill, 1992), 2

8   A W N L (August, 1979), 55.

Wake Book IV, we find the exclamation "By the antar of Yasas!" (FW 596.34). "Yasas" is a Sanskrit word meaning that which is beautiful in appearance. "Antar" is also a Sanskrit word used for internal purity of the heart, whereas in Arabic culture Antar appears as a famous hero of sixth century AD folk literature. The Sanskrit abstract noun meaning a heroic character in the Arabic stories indicates quite clearly the impact of Sanskrit on Arabic language and culture. R.A. Nicholson identifies his real name as Antar b. Shaddad. He belonged to the tribe of Abs and, during the inter-tribal War of Dahis fought in the sixth century, he proved to be a man of prowess and heroism. According to Nicholson, he was respected as "the Bedouin Achilles" among the Arabs.[9] This Ode was "one of the seven Golden Poems suspended in the temple of Mecca," just before the time of the Prophet. This famous folk hero is also mentioned in the Quran: "We remember the story of Antar, the Bayard of pagan Arabia" (s.16). The legend of Antar became even more popular when, in the golden age of Harun al-Rashid, he appeared as the hero of the romance Sira Antar, written by Al-Asmaii in the ninth century. The Sira Antar, according to E.L. Ranelagh, is connected with western tradition in two ways: it looks back to the heroic age and it looks forward to the knightly hero. As Clouston perceived a hundred years ago, it is "the prototype of the European romances of chivalry."[10] Ranelagh elaborates by saying that the concept of such a literary genre as the "romance" developed in the Near and Middle East, and was then further developed by the Greeks and Romans. Antar's mythic, heroic figure shares some of the following characteristics with the European tradition. A man of versatile prowess and chivalric passion, he is an Arab avatar of the European King Arthur. Like King Arthur, he cuts his gigantic foe Usak through the middle so that he and his horse are divided into pieces. The freeing of Antar by Monzar on condition of helping the latter against Khoserwan is a deed repeated in the Arthurian stories. In Guy of Warwick, the king returns Sir Heraud because of the knight's help against the king's enemies. Another common trait is the frequent but sudden appearance of the hero in disguises, taking the enemy by surprise and rescuing his friend or lover. Antar's rescue of Nazir from the Aamir tribe is an example. In the

---

9   Reynold A. Nicholson, A Literary History of the Arabs, (Cambridge: Cambridge University Press, 1977), 114.

10   E.L. Ranelagh, The Past We Share: The Near Eastern Ancestry of Western Folk Literature, (London, Melbourne and New York: Quartet Books 1979) chapter IV, See "Antar and Abala," 85-89.

Arab tradition, female warriors are introduced in the chivalric epic of Antar and Abla. In the European tradition, Renaissance epics contain female warriors such as Bradamante in Orlando Furioso, Clorinda and Gildippe in Gerusalemme Liberata and Britomart in The Faerie Queene. In both traditions, the heroic knights-errant are fond of singing, composing, and making love to their ladies.

It is not merely the cultural symbiosis of the Arabs and the Persians that one could decipher in the Arabian Nights. Richard Burton's classic translation of the Nights and his "Terminal Essay" in volume VIII establish still deeper common literary and cultural roots among the Arabs, Persians and Hindus on the one hand, and the Greeks on the other. The name of Burton appears twice in the Wake: "Old Burton" (FW 595.18) and "an allburt unend" (FW 598.07). In the following passage, there are some strong suggestions about this translator of the Nights:

> He had fled again (open shunshema!) this country of exile...sidleshomed via the subterranean shored with bedboards, stowed away and ankered in a dutch bottom tank, the Arsa, hod S.S. Finlandia, and was even now occupying, under an islamitic newhame in his seventh generation, a physical body Cornelius Magrath's...in Asia Major, where as Turk of the Theater...he had bepiastered the buikdanseuses from the opulence of his omnibox while as arab at the streetdoor he bepestered the bumbashaws for the alms of a para's pence/ Wires hummed. Peacefully general astonishment assisted by regrettitude had put a term till his existence (FW 98.04-16).

"Sidleshomed" appears as "the Earwickers of Sidlesham" (FW 30.09) for W. Sussex; "subterranean" is something situated, living or operating underneath the earth or "those throne open doubleyous (of an early muddy terranea origin whether man chooses to damn them agglutinatively loo" (FW 120.02-04). "Subterranean" is the hidden power operating in the manifest world for being "doubleyous." It is also active in the rise and fall of humanity as "as one generation tells another. Ofter the fall" (FW 589.19-20).

"Islamitic newham" is the new name taken after conversion to Islam. The phrase "seventh generation" again suggests someone who is a new convert to Islam. "Seventh generation" may also be considered in the light of "the seventh city of Christendom" as we read of in A Portrait of the Artist as a Young Man (Chapter IV) as "like a scene on some vague arras, old as man's weariness, the

image of the seventh city of Christendom was visible to him across the timeless air, no older nor more weary nor less patient of subjection than in the days of the thing mote." HCE converts the statement in a dream sequence as "from Wildu Picturescu or some seem on some dimb Arras, dumb as Mum's mutyness, this mimage of the seventyseventh kusin of kristansen is odable to os across the wineless Ere no þdor nor mere eerie nor liss potent of suggestion than in the tales of the tingmount. (Prigged !)" (FW 53.02-06). On the same page, HCE also uses the name of Morya-one who contributed to the Mahatma Letters along with Blavatsky as "bannocks of Gort and Morya" (FW 53.30).

Generation in the Wake applies to human generations "generations, more generations and still more generations" (FW 107.35); the growth of language as "to be the contonuation through regeneration of the urutteration of the word in pregross" (FW 284.21.23); and, the Christians "disgeneration by neuhumorisation of our Christianisation" (FW 331.31-2).

"Bumbashaws" is a head of one thousand soldiers in army. One could trace such a system of ranks in the Ottoman military structure.

The reasons behind why HCE decided to flee has its own history. Initially, he is being slandered for his indecent behaviour in the Phoenix Park. Once his image has been tainted among the general public, he becomes the victim and a scapegoat. To this, he responds variously. On one occasion, he becomes the butt of the king's joke. During His Majesty the sailor king's foxhunt, the king stumbles into HCE's garden which is next to his "mobhouse" Chapelizod pub. The king takes the turnpike-keeper by surprise as he was hunting the earwigs like "cabbaging Cincinnatus." The king gives him the nickname of an "earwigger" (FW 31.28), there and then. He is hailed as "our kingable khan" (FW 32.02) by the prophets Nehemia and Malachi. To add to the Eastern colour of the Wake, it may be worthwhile to mention that the king appears in public wearing a "topee"...and "solascarf" (30.23). Returning to the ordeal of Mr Earwicker, it behoves to add that on another occasion when he was walking across the Phoenix Park clothed in a costume tailoring seven different items together, one "a cad with a pipe" (FW 35.11) .... "a luciferant" (FW 35.11), intrudes asking the old Earwicker the time. This embarrassed Earwicker in his old age as it made him feel guilty of the sin he committed in this Park when young. Earwicker now named "Humpheres Cheops

Exarchas" (FW 62.21) is attacked by someone who "had a barkiss revolver placed to his faced with the words: you're shot, major: by an unknowable assailant" (FW 62.30-31). On another occasion, when Cad and Buckley visit him as "unsolicited visitors" (FW 70.13), also insult him "blew some quaker's ...through the house king's keyhole to attract attention" (FW 70.18-19). Furthermore, during the trial when Earwicker appears as "the plaintiff" (FW 80.04), he is "struck" again. He reacts thus by escaping. Even then he is pursued like a fox by Fitz Urse. Considered in the context of Burton, to return to the main argument, the escaping of HCE or Earwicker is also a comment on the political scene: the colonial wars of India, the struggle for power and expansionism in Africa and the religious values of the Arabs.

The passage interweaves some important motifs of the Wake. The phrase "open shunshema!" (FW 94.04) has been interpreted as "Open Sesame" by McHugh. This phrase is a well-known phrase in English used as the magic formula for unearthing the treasure caves in the story of Ali Baba. Secondly, the passage alludes to the theme of exile, common to Joyce and Burton. The Encyclopaedia Britannica (15th edition), quotes Burton as saying that "England is the only country where I never feel at home" (p.668). He was expelled from Oxford University on certain disciplinary charges in 1842. He straight away joined the military service in India with the Bombay Native Infantry under the command of Sir Charles Napier. After the departure of Napier (the commander of the English forces operating in Sindh), Burton was forced to resign again on disciplinary grounds. His long career as a Moslem Pathan (an inhabitant of Afghanistan) in disguise in the cities of Cairo, Suez, Mecca and Medina was an attempt to gain information about the cultural behaviour of these peoples, yet he was again to suffer expulsion in disgrace from Damascus because the local Moslems intrigued against him, and because of his wife's proselytizing indiscretions as a Catholic. According to Grace Eckley the following remark in the Wake is directly applicable to Burton's expulsion from Damascus: "Wires hummed. Peacefully general astonishment assisted by regrettitude had put a term till his existence:...resigned" (FW 98.14-16).[11] He

---

11 Grace Eckley, Children's Lore in Finnegans Wake, (Syracuse, N.Y.: Syracuse University Press, 1985), 58-65. Eckley enlarges the perspective by saying that W.T. Stead had been exposed to similar defamation after insulting the Dutch in Cape Town. In the passage under discussion, the phrase "bedstead" is, she suggests, the nickname of W.T. Stead. Eckley applies the phrase "stowed away and ankered in a dutch bottom Tank" to the ship on which he was

"put off his remainders" (FW 98.17) may be interpreted as the various identities in which he had cloaked himself in the Arab world. He "was recalled and scrapheaped by the Maker" (FW 98.17) indicates the public imprecations heaped against him because of his flagrant disregard of the established Victorian decencies in his works. His wife defended him against the charge that he died of "infamous private ailment" (FW 98.18-20) though at Trieste Burton virtually thought of himself as being in an "ignominious exile" (Encyclopaedia Britannica).

As we know the dreamlike metamorphosis of HCE's mind, Burton is only one such segment of the dream though what happened to him, also happens to others in these pages. Burton had to hide like Parnell. So was James Joyce forced to flee. Scandals pursued them in their exiles. Along side Burton, the stigma of having "an infamous private ailment" may also apply to James Joyce, Parnell and Burton. It shows the public's reaction which thrives in spreading gossips "envenom loped in piggotry" (FW 99.19) - a truth that circumscribes humanity like Vico's cycles, generation after generation "A human pest cycling (pist!) and recycling (past)...here he was (past) again" (FW 99.04-06). In the case of Burton, exile, sexual excesses and disease may simply be partially due to his adventures in the East, provoking jealousy at home in England.

Burton's dealings with Arab civilization in the Arabian Nights are foregrounded by the mention of the Arab goddess "Arsa." The phrase "under an Islamitic Newham" (FW 98.08) indicates the veiled identity and the assumed name with which he was able to penetrate the holy precincts of Medina and Mecca during the annual pilgrimage. How he must have kept himself safe from being caught is described as "he had bepiastered the buikdanseuses from the opulence," (FW 98.11-12), summarised by Campbell and Robinson as "even while as street arab he was pestering the public for alms."[12] He describes his experiences and the Moslem way of life in his book Pilgrimage to El-Medinah and Mecca.

---

forced to leave Cape Town. She establishes the nexus between Burton and Stead by showing that the latter worked as Assistant Editor to the Pall Mall Gazette and had been a commentator of the Nights. Furthermore, Eckley says that the erotic behaviour for which his office in London was pelted with stones smacks of the latitude accorded by Burton and Joyce to the theme of eroticism in the Nights and the Wake. These three contemporaries had in common a flagrant disregard of the public moral values of their societies.

12 Joseph Campbell and Henry Morton Robinson, A Skeleton Key to Finnegans Wake, (London: Faber and Faber, 1947), 82.

Besides Islam, Burton's erudition with respect to Hindu thought had earned him the title of the "second born."[13] Moreover, Burton had found eastern wisdom implicit in the sacred ritual of sex. In order to make his views known to the public in this respect, he translated books like The Kama Sutra of Vatsyayana (1883), Aranga Ranga (1885) and The Perfumed Garden of the Cheikh Nefzaoui (1886). Despite Burton's translation of The Kama Sutra and the tremendous interest shown by Joyce in the erotic, mystic implications of sex, we have no proof that Joyce was influenced by Burton in this respect.

Burton's third field of interest was the exploration of the origins of the Nile. In Finnegans Wake, both Burton's failed adventure and his relations with John Hanning Speke are referred to. In the first journey, they were attacked by native Africans near Berbera as they planned to enter Somaliland. Speke was badly injured and hence the excursion had to be dropped. After the Crimean war was over, both planned to venture inland from the side of Zanzibar in 1857-58. After suffering a great deal of hardship from the hot, humid African climate, Burton decided to retire from the expedition. Speke continued, travelling to the north-east till he had discovered Lake Victoria. Back home, he received lavish funds and praise while Burton was ignored — which prompted the latter to challenge the former's discovery. In Book IV of the Wake, there is a reference to the squabbling between these adventurers: "Wisely for us Old Bruton has withdrawn his theory" (FW 595.18-19).

Instead, Burton decided to devote his life to understanding and translating the literary heritage of the Arabs. Quite appropriately, he attempted to discover the East through the Arabian Nights in which Shaharazad and her sister emerge as the protagonists. It is to these two sisters that Joyce refers as prototypes of Issy. Issy is

---

13 The title the "second born" alludes to one who is originally born into the Hindu class system which accepts the three castes "Brahmin," "ksatriya" and "vaisya" as pious,and rejects the "sudras" as outcasts. The phrase "seventh generation" (FW .98.08-09) can also be interpreted as the most sublime pedestal of the soul. In the words of Blavatsky, the seventh generation or race would be the purest race of all, enjoying "rest" like that of Brahma insulated and cordoned off from the mirage and delusion of "maya" or the cravings of human greed. Blavatsky also alludes to the supreme status of the sun above and beyond and yet ruling the seven planets which are always gravitating towards it. The Secret Doctrine, (Vol.II, 747). The "seventh generation" is directly opposite to that of the present generation of "kali yoga." Our present birth, according to Hinduism, is sullied with the sin of incarnations. Our second birth would mean the complete sundering of the cycles of incarnation.

the daughter of ALP and one of the sisters of ALP is the river Nile. ALP is concerned about the explorer, as indicated by the talking washerwomen: "will find where the Doubt arises like Nieman...found the Nihil" (FW 202.18-19).

The washerwomen are directly referring to the dispute between Burton and Speke. John Hanning Speke is again questioned as "You take Joe Hanny's tip for it!" (FW 455.11). Where Burton failed, Speke had succeeded by saying "I saw that old father Nile without any doubt rise in the Victoria Nyanza, and as I had foretold, that lake is the great source of the holy river which cradled the first expounder of our religious belief."[14] In Finnegans Wake, Joyce refers to this comment of Speke, "Nuctumbulumbumus wanderwards the Nil. Victorias neanzas. Alberths neantas. It was a long,...an allburt unend, scarce endurable, and we could add mostly quite various and somewhat stumbletumbling night." (FW 598.05-09). "Nuctumbulumbumus," according to McHugh, is the Latin for "we were wandering in the night." "Victorias neanzas. Alberths neantas" are the two Western reservoirs of the Nile. Moreover, the frame story of the Nights establishes how dangerous it was for the two sisters to cope with the murderous king. Their nighttime agony is suggested by "It was a long,...an allburt unend, scarce endurable, and we could add mostly quite various and somewhat stumbletumbling night." This remark is also applicable to the explorers of the Nile and the readers of Finnegans Wake.

Most of HCE's knowledge about the Nile valley civilization comes from sources like The Book of the Dead by E.W. Budge. Accounting for the cultural impact of the Nile lands, Burton says that with the "only advanced culture," the Egyptian Hirseshtha of Pharoah's court was able to impart knowledge to such learned and monumental figures as "Pythagoras, Solon, Plato, Aristotle, and possibly Homer,"[15] Thoth, the god of letters who appears quite often in Finnegans Wake, was able to transfer his divine gift to many parts of the East. His invention of the cuneiform alphabet spread from the Nile valley to Phoenicia, Judaea, Phrygia and Asia Minor.

14 John Hanning Speke, Journal of the Discovery of the Source of the Nile...(With maps and portraits, and numerous illustrations chiefly from drawings by Captain Grand) (Edinburgh [printed] and London, 1863)).
15. Richard Burton, "Terminal Essay," The Arabian Nights, Vol. VIII, (Luristan edition, ca. 1919), 105-07.
15 Richard Burton, "Terminal Essay," The Arabian Nights, Vol. VIII (Published in London: The Burton Club for the private subscribers only) 17 Vols., 1886), 107.

One of the basic ideas which Burton elaborates in his "Terminal Essay" [section A-The Matter] is that of the apologue or "Beast-fable." Appraising it as the most antique symbol of human consciousness, Burton reminds us that the "Beast-fable" was in fact the invention of an advanced human culture. It originated in the days of the oligarchy and was used as a tool to suppress the rising danger of those who, by speaking "plain truth," could have contributed to the overthrow of the established system. In addition to the "Beast-fable," Burton says that the number of fables and historical anecdotes in the Nights exceeds four hundred. He believes that both the "Beast-fable" and those referred to in the Nights had originated in Egypt, and it was from there that their cult spread to civilizations like those of Mesopotamia, Babylon, the Indus and China.

Burton divides the fables of the Arabian Nights into two kinds: first, the fables whose author is generally known as Aesop; second, those fables which embody the Hindu doctrine of karma or (as he uses the phrase) "metempsychosis." In the first kind, the animals act according to their own species in a normal, natural way. In the second, the animals appear as interlocked in the conflict of good and evil. To the second, Burton attributes the quality of human beings as the animals demonstrate human behaviour acutely. Among the second kind, the role played by the "hunter" is the reflection of the brute in human nature, whereas the "herdsman" represents the benevolent aspect. The instinctive "Ego" of the hunter is tempered by morality in this process of bringing about the desired balance of mind.

The fact that animals behave according to their species points to doctrinal determinism. We are goaded to make the best of the opportunity available to us. This shows the idea of the revealed religions like Judaism, Christianity and Islam in which the destiny of mankind is to be found in the hereafter, but with no second birth in mortal shape. The principle of "metempsychosis" removes the distinction between the created and the Creator. Until the human soul is purified in the fires of divine light, man's cyclical births and deaths continue with the exception of a momentary cessation — a pause like that of the distending heartbeat. The former notion of reality is reflected in Aesop's fables, and the latter describes the impact of Hinduism. Exactly like the Nights fables, Finnegans Wake merges the divine religion and Hinduism together. Burton insists that from their homeland in Egypt, the Nights fables made their literary pathway to Phoenicia, Judaea, Phrygia,

Asia Minor, Greece until "In after centuries, when the conquests of Macedonian Alexander completed what Sesostris and Semiramis had begun, and mingled the manifold families of mankind by joining the eastern to the western world, the Orient became formally Hellenised."[16]

One basic feature of Burton's findings is that symbols like the "Yoni" and the "Lingam" stood for similar meanings in vastly distant cultures like those of Egypt and India. Deciphering the meanings of the stamp seals which belong to the Harappa culture of the Indus Valley (now in Pakistan), Campbell says that the stones sculptured like a cone mean the lingam of phallus whereas those stones which are round with a hollow in the centre denote the female yoni.[17] Burton indicates the various customs among the different peoples who worship these engraved deities. According to him, the images encrusted on metal, stone or wood could be found in every city of Egypt to bewitch the masses with awe and wonder. He believes that the goddesses Diana of the Greeks and Pasht or Osiris of Egypt could be identified with the Mambogh or Michabo of the indigenous Americans, underpinning the same theme which the revealed religions invoke from holy cities like Jerusalem or Mecca. According to Monier William, quoted by Burton, these symbols (the lingam and yoni) "are the mystical representations, and perhaps the best possible impersonal representatives, of the abstract expressions of paternity and maternity."[18] Although Joyce may not have taken these concepts from Burton, as he had resource to the works of Jung and Frazer's The Golden Bough among others, yet the Nights must have added to his aim of finding out the common meanings behind these symbols. The Lingam is the phallus HCE, the father figure whose logos does not suffer change. In his quest for understanding such an unfathomable mystery as that of ALP's "Yoni," Joyce, in Finnegans Wake alludes to Nora's "redtangles"[19] (FW 298.25), and to the maternal source of fertility as "doubleviewed seeds" (FW 296.01) lying "bluishing refluction below" (FW 299.17-18)

---

16 Richard Burton, "Terminal Essay," The Arabian Nights, Vol. VIII (Published in London: The Burton Club for the private subscribers only) 17 Vols., 1886), 107.

17 Joseph Campbell, The Masks of Gods: Primitive Mythology (London: Secker and Warburg, 1960), 437. These forms of worship can be found everywhere in India. Campbell, however, suggests that this cult came to India from the Mesopotamian mythogenetic zone by way of Iran in about the third millennium.

18 Burton, "Terminal Essay," 106 note referring to Prof. Monier Williams, (Folk Lore Record), Vol. III, Part I, (118).

19 Richard Ellmann, James Joyce, revised edition, (Oxford: Oxford University Press, 1982), 398.

where her double circles interject "twain of doubling bicirculars," (FW 295.31).

Like Burton's use of heterogeneous material in identifying certain truth, whether through fable or by means of the symbols like the "Lingam" and the "Yoni," HCE touches the nerve centre of a pattern operating in many cultures at the same time. In Finnegans Wake, the bull cult summarizes the paradox of the active and passive aspects of metaphysical reality. Its universality as a symbol can be seen from its appearance in three civilizations, in the cults of Osiris, Shiva and Dionysus. The bull's roar is like the wind, or a certain spirit which causes the stones to crack at the door of the tavern and hence is termed "unpleasant bullocky." (FW 72.26) The wind which is felt by Jarl van Hoother as "van Hoother was to git the wind up" (FW 23.14) is openly attendant upon Kate in delivering the message from the deity: "And the Bullingdong caught the wind up." (FW 333.18). The spirit which causes the wind to blow resides in the Himalayas or "immortality," (FW 580.13) the abode of the Hindu gods Shiva and Shakti. Its roaring nature is essential for creation: "Somular with a bull on a clompturf. Rooks roarum rex roome!" (FW 17.09).

But before the creation takes place, a fall is inevitable in which too the image of the bull participates: "Here one might a fin fell. Boomster rombombonant!" (FW 52.36-53.01). "Rombos" is the roaring of the bull in Greek. The bull's roar is related both to the sun and the moon. With the former, it functions as the fertilizing agent. Its curved horns look like the crescent moon. The tides which are raised by the moon are thus associated with the bull described in the Wake as "bullseabob" (FW 580.14). "Boob" in Urdu as well as in English means the tender breasts of a young damsel, whereas in association with "sea," "boob" is synonymous to "bab" and "aab" meaning lesson and water in Persian. In raising ripples in the sea, the bull suggests the cult of Dionysus. It reflects the amorous gesture of ALP: "her bulls they were ruhring, surfed with spree" (FW 198.04-05). "Spree" according to McHugh is a river and its roaring of surf shows the inherent, divine energies of ALP. According to Edward William Lane, the bull is holding the seven earths on its body. When God created the seven earths, there arose the necessity of holding them intact. An angel of immense size was asked to go underneath the lowest earth: but, on what was the angel to stand? God then created a rock and in order to support this rock of ruby, the bull was sent, while below the bull there resides

the fish swimming on the water of infinity.[20] R.C. Zaehner says that the bull was used in Zoroastrian religion as the sacrificial object: "the cruelty was inseparable from sacrifice"[21] in the creative process.

If we examine the footnote on page 106 of "The Terminal Essay", it is evident that Burton is reporting his ideas in a purely modern style. He is interfusing various contradictory doctrines in order to articulate a new way of looking at reality. He calls this style that of "scientific investigation". After mentioning the idol worship prevailing among the Egyptians and the pre-Christian Romans, he directs his attention to the mystical signification of the masculine and feminine symbols. At the same time, he quotes the surah of the Quran (Chapter 39) in which fetishism is declared sacrilegious. The irony is that Burton, after explaining the spiritual value of these images, alludes to their counterparts like "the Catholic host" and the Moslem "Kiblah" in Mecca. Burton, thus, interfuses themes like those of erotic infatuation and the universal conflict of male and female principles with the spiritual omphalos (Jerusalem and Kaba) of the revealed religions. Such a methodology must have given Joyce readily available material to play with.

Continuing to sustain and preserve the original spirit of the Nights, Burton, like Joyce has nothing to preach except the nature of human behaviour. Though he lived in the Moslem world and is acclaimed for his transliteration of the Nights, he does not show any special regard for Islam. In this respect, he is akin to Joyce. Despite Joyce's Catholic upbringing, his personal life and literary characters often display more than one set of values. Similarly, Burton's way of looking at the Eastern cultures gives an impression of secularism which he attains first by neutralizing the overbearing impact of Islam on these regions. Burton believes that the Persian civilization on the one hand and the "Law of Moses" on the other, were the readily available materials on the basis of which Islam established its metaphysical entity. The pull of Platonism and Christian Gnosticism was so strong that within a few centuries of the establishment of Islam, creeds like Sufism and mysticism replaced the hard and fast injunctions of the Quran in most of the East. How people performed their worship and with what sincerity, Burton exemplifies

20 Edward William Lane, The Arabian Nights, (New York: Tudor PublishingCompany, 1927), "Notes To The Introductory Story," 972.

21 R.C. Zaehner, The Dawn and Twilight of Zoroastrianism (London: Weidenfeld and Nicolson 1961), 84-5.

through a story. In the story The Queen of the Serpents ("that strange exotic serpentine ... a rightheaded ladywhite ... seems to uncoil spirally" FW 121.20-21:22:24), the queen saves the life of a hapless lad abandoned to die in the wilderness by the vanishing caravan. As a gesture of consolation, the queen narrates Adventures of Bulukiya to the boy. In these stories, the protagonist is "an Israelite converted by editor and scribe to Mohammedanism; but we can detect under his assumed faith the old creed."[22] The queen then explains her own version of the history of religions by pointing out that Solomon is buried at Jerusalem. The mystic idea that his mausoleum is "beyond the Seven (mystic) Seas," is incorrect as he had died a natural death.

Describing Solomon's ring, the queen says that it "suggests the Jami-i-Jami," "the crystal cup of the great King Jamshid." About the Archangel Gabriel, she says that he helped and guided the Prophet Zoroaster to walk over the forbidden zones of divine mystery. Like Zoroaster, Bulukiya enjoys these splendid scenes by flying across the Seven Oceans. The queen says that they were shown the co-eternal battle between Good and Evil principles, Ohrmuzd and Ahriman. This story explains a number of things relevant to Finnegans Wake. Like the incidents of the Wake which generate a chain of links between East and West, religion and secularism, this story, as Burton states, was originally an Egyptian myth. In its Persian version, it was first a romance before being shortened into a tale for the Nights. Second, the human head and reptile bodies of the snakes ("That a head in thighs under a bush at the sunface would bait a serpent" FW 89.31-32)) are a reminiscence of similar Indian myths. Third, the most important role in the story is played by the queen of these serpents in saving the life of a young lad. Her task is similar to that of ALP who saves and collects the precious material as the litter heap of history. Fourth, the story teaches us that differences between religions are a mere figment of imagination, for the Archangel Gabriel known to a Moslem or Christian, is the first Intelligence of Pluto known as Bahman among the Zoroastrians. Finally, though the story was compiled in the Moslem culture, the teller and listener have taken its secular spirit for granted.

ༀ

---

22   Richard Burton, "Terminal Essay", The Arabian Nights Vol. VIII, 117.

2.

Harun al-Rashid as "pseudo-caliph" of the Nights

Another figure recognized throughout the cross-cultural consciousness is that of the famous Abbaside[1], Caliph Harun al-Rashid appearing both in the Arabian Nights and the Wake. In the words of Robert G. Hampson, Harun al-Rashid is "one of HCE's avatars".[2] As such, he is "Haroun Childeric Eggeberth" (FW 04.32). The paragraph from which this reference is taken is packed with overlapping themes both from East and West:

> Oftwhile balbulous, mithre ahead, with goodly trowel in grasp and ivoroiled overalls which he habitacularly fondseed, like Haroun Childeric Eggeberth he would caligulate by multiplicables the alltitude and malltitude until he seesaw by neatlight of the

---

1   In Notebook, VIB 27-8 (p.226), Joyce enters the name of the Abbasides as "Abacides". Known in Arabic as "Abbasiyah", English Abbasides is the name of the dynasty of Caliphs descending from al-Abbas, the son of Abdul-Muttalib, and a patriarchal uncle of the Prophet. The Abbasides were indeed highly respected members of society but couldn't assert their rightful claim to Caliphate until 749 A.D. when Abu al-Abbas was recognised as the right caliph after defeating Marwan II, the Umayyad. Thirty-seven Caliphs who ruled the Islamic world from 749-1258 A.D. The Abbaside reign came to a sad end in 1258 after the destruction of Baghdad by Jingiz Khan, the grandson of Hulaku. Caliph Mamoon (One of the illustrious Abbasides) is remembered as "…remembore long ago in the olden times momonian" (FW 397.17) who according to Burton's tale "The Caliph Al-.Maamun and the Pyramids of Egypt" (The Arabian Nights, Vol. V, P.105-6), cherished to get to the ancient treasures by burrowing deep into the Pyramids. Burton analogizes "pyramids as "haram" for well-esteemed in Arabic to which the Wake refers as "haram's way round … bestpreserved whole Wife" (FW 532.32). According to Encyclopaedia Britannica (11th edition which Joyce consulted), the Pyramids are named separately and one among these is coined as "The Glorious" by Burton who draws the name from the Encyclopaedia (see vol.22, p.684). As Scheherazade puts it, the curious caliph enters the Great pyramid or "the Glorious" to dig out the "mysteries preserved until the day of resurrection" because "there is none of the face of the earth aught like them for … mysteries; … for they are built of the rocks" "mysterbolder" (FW 309.13). Joyce transposes these images variously as "glorisol which plays touraloup with us in this Aludin's Cove of" (FW 108.22). "… the glory of a wake …allatheses" (FW 309. 6-8). The Caliph could only dig in a small tunnel given the formidable nature of these ancient mysteries Scheherazade puts it as "he expended his mint of money, but succeeded in opening only a small tunnel in one of them" transcribed by Joyce as "we all would fain make glories. It was minely well mint" (FW 313.27).

2   Robert G. Hampson, "The Genie out of the Bottle" in The Arabian Nights in English Literature ed. Peter L. Caracciolo, (Basingstoke: Macmillan. 1988), 229-237. One relevant aspect of Harun al-Rashid is that he is one thing for his court during the day and another for the public during the night. His majesty is awe-inspiring when he is seated on the throne during the day, but at night his appearances in disguise are even more astounding on disclosure of his true identity.

liquor where twin twas born, his roundhead staple of other days to rise in undress maisonry upstanded (joygrantit!), a waalworth of a skyerscape of most eyeful hoyth entowerly, erigenating from next to nothing and celescalating the himals and all" (FW 4.30-36:5.01).

It is true that "balbulous" is the Tower of Babel, but HCE has balanced it by referring to "Toper's Thorp" (FW 4.27). "Toper's" or "tope" means the round dome over the places of religious worship in India, China and the rest of East Asia. This word belongs to the family of Sanskrit "stupa" and is attributed among others to Buddhism and Jainism. Joyce's "Toper's Thorp" is the "middenhide hoard of objects!" (FW 19.08) and appears elsewhere as "tope" (FW 615.01), "Tope" (FW 20.13), "toped" (FW 83.29), "topee" (FW30.23), "topers" (FW 322.27:386.04, 549.05), "toper's" (FW 381.11) and "topes" (FW 136.18). Similarly, "mithre ahead" is not only "mitre on head" as McHugh says, but the mythic figure Mithra. This Hindu god is interwoven with HCE and Ibsen's Master Builder ("Bygmester" in Dano-Norwegian) according to Anthony Burgess.[3] He is shown in contemplation ensconced in the Himalays, "celescalating the himals and all". Furthermore, "himals" also suggests being impregnated. Here, impregnation and spiritual enlightenment identify the generative impulse of nature. Mithra is the Persian god of light known as the sun. Mithra's influence on Christianity is noted by Barbara Walker.[4] Walker says that the god had such an enormous impact on the Christians of Rome that in ad 307 the Roman emperor designated Mithra as "Protector of the Empire". St. Augustine considered the priests who worshipped Mithra as actually paying homage to Christ. There are some interesting parallels between Christianity and Mithra. His ascension to the heavens, which is shown in the phrase "celescalating the himals" is a tradition attributed to Prophet Mohammed (pbuh) in the Quran as well as to Christ. Like Christ, Mithra celebrated his last Supper with twelve disciples representing the twelve zodiac signs. This Supper is known as "mizd" in Persian, "missa" in Latin and "mass" in English.

In addition, the passage strongly suggests the journey of the sun and its birth "fondseed" at night "neat light" just as Harun would measure the length and

---

3   Anthony Burgess, Here Comes Everybody, (London: Faber and Faber, 1965), 196.

4   See Barbara Walker's article "Mithar" in The Women''s Encyclopaedia of Myths and Secrets (New York; San Francisco; London: Harper and Row, 1983, 663-65).

breadth of the streets of Baghdad at night in his "ivoroiled overalls", as Campbell and Robinson mention of HCE: "In the morn you're vine, in the eve you're vine-gar".[5] The "neatlight of the liquor" means two things: first, the phrase "liquor" as liquid stands for the river Liffey which means ALP and her appearance in the den of HCE's unconscious, the first glimmer of life. In the case of Harun al-Rashid, it should be interpreted as the light of the lamp which fell on the water of the river Tigris during his boating at night. The caliph's name Harun or Harown reverber-ates in phrases like "around" (FW 33.36) and "haroween" (FW537.28). "Childeric" according to McHugh is the name of two of the Frankish kings. Harun is the only Moslem caliph during the Middle Ages whose relations with Europe are known to have been cordial and friendly. Harun and Charlemagne were contemporar-ies. A great patron of learning, Harun encouraged European scholars to come to Baghdad for scholarly pursuits. Because of his enlightened, tolerant and humane character, he enjoys the status of the protagonist of the Arabian Nights.

The Wake vocabulary projects the protean nature of reality in such a manner that everything seems to be in a state of flux because there is "a being again in becomings again" (FW 491.23). In such a flux, HCE attempts to create "the book of Doublends Jined" (FW 20.15) so that East is as much a part of the whole as West. The idea seems to be that things exist only in a state of relativity and that everything flows into something else. Language participates as a polysemic fea-ture in the objective determination of internal and eternal circulation. The inner message remains the same, only words differ.

The phrase "Eggeberth" means the one born of an egg – an important symbol in Finnegans Wake. As an egg transforms itself, so the three letters H.C.E. reflect the diversified forms and shapes of man's identity in time. If at one moment HCE is related to Harun al-Rashid as his avatar, at another the letter "H" symbolises the king "Harold"

(FW 30.21) or "Duke Humphrey" (FW 405.18): the letter "C" stands for "Childers" (FW 535.34), "Childeric" (FW 04.32) and "E" for "Everybody" (FW 32.19), "E" Erawan" (FW 46.01), "Eavybrolly!" (FW 315.20), "Ebblybally!" (FW 612.15) and so on. One can count some fifty-seven situations in the Wake where

---

5   Joseph Campbell and Henry Morton Robinson, A Skeleton Key to Finnegans Wake, (London: Faber and Faber, 1947).

it is referred to. Such a variegated use of this symbol suggests its protean nature. Some of the basic allusions to eggs are worth looking at more closely, for example "very like a whale's egg farced with Pemmican", (FW 120.11). The image of the whale is also used in relation to Sindbad's voyages in the Wake (discussed in a chapter). Thought does not exist outside (its) matter since an egg fuses into its shell (compare Bruno's dialectic): "just becups they won the egg and spoon" (FW 144.09). The spoon symbolises the phallus, whose identity is dependent upon the egg as the source of fertility. Closely related to the "whale" is the bird "rukh" to which the Wake refers as "So olff for his topheetuck the ruck made raid, aslick aslegs would run" (FW 225.09). The "raid" was due to the egg appropriated by the sailors. As we know that in the second voyage there is a reference to the bird Rukh which lands Sindbad into the valley of diamonds and precious metals. The roc's auk's egg experience of Sindbad occurs when, after cruising in various different waters, they land on a deserted sandy shore. Far off they notice a white dome and anticipating it to be the sign of a town, approach it, only to learn that it is "a huge Rukk's egg" with no habitation around. Without hesitation out of ignorance and in immolation of Nature's secrets, they start pelting it till they crack it open. The water leaks out of it and finding a young "Rukh" bird inside, they drag it out and cut it into pieces for food. When this was happening, Sindbad was away on board ship, and when he heard about the injury being done to the innocent bird, he cries "Stop! Stop! donot meddle with the egg, or the bird Rukh will come out and break our ship and destroy us." His fellow sailors paid no heed till "behold, the day grew dark and the sun was hidden from us, as if some great cloud had passed over the firmament." As they raised their heads, they were astonished to discover that what they had thought to be a cloud was the Rukh bird poised between them and the sun, its enormous wings darkening the day. As they hastened towards the ship, they shortly found the two parent Rukh birds flying over them and clutching two heavy boulders in their claws to destroy it.

Dismayed and stranded in a desolate place, Sindbad on finding a huge white object gets near it out of curiosity and as soon as he had began exploring it, the darkness shrouded the environment. The huge "roc" settles over the egg. In order to get away from this place, Sindbad girdles his turban after twisting it into a rope around his waist and the legs of the bird. Next morning Sinbad finds himself flown into the valley of the diamonds. "Topheetuck" suggests the "topee"(FW.136.38) or

"turban". It is also on record that the tales of Sindbad the Sailor were written in the age of Caliph Harun al-Rashid. Moreover, Mary Bell in Yeats's A Vision talks about the egg and says that she bought it from a turbaned old man of the city of Tehran. She says that the egg had been placed in the treasury of Harun al-Rashid for some time. Before this, it had been in Byzantium, from where it was to be passed on to Harun as ransom for a certain prince.[6]

Joyce had also read the theosophical works of Madame Blavatsky. She explains the mystical nature of such symbols as eggs and circles, by referring to Brahma's myth of creation: "At the beginning of each Mahamanvantara Brahma lays a "Golden Egg." The egg symbolises the cyclic nature of creation as :

> Brahma merges back into Dayus, the Unrevealed God, and, his task being accomplished, he falls asleep. Another day is passed, night sets in, and continues until the future dawn. And now again he re-enters the golden egg of His Thought, the germs of all that exist ...this Soul of all beings sleeps in complete repose till the day when it resumes its form, and awakes again from its primitive darkness."

The phrase "a niester egg with a twicedated shell" (FW 210.35) denotes the controversial issue of the date of Easter. The phrase "due to egg everlasting" (FW 220.29) occurs in the background of The Mime of Mick, Nick and the Maggies. Despite the element of "impeachment" (FW 220.29) from or on the stage of life, the play continues ceaselessly because of our birth from the "egg everlasting". "And egg she active or spoon she passive," (FW 269.28), takes further this egg-spoon (active and passive) dialectic of reality. The active aspect permits the circulatory orbit of reality: "As round as the calf of a egg!" (FW 294.11). "Calf", among other things, is an Arabic letter which is round in shape. The phrase "Rosairette's egg" (FW 376.07) indicates the spiritual value of the rose. The egg's comic role in pantomime appears in the reference to the goose that laid a golden egg "a gooth a gev a gotheny egg" (FW 394.27).

The fall of the wall of Troy is presented as "Leg-before-Wicked lags-behind-Wall where here Mr Whicker whacked a great fall" (FW 434.10), because "Bessy Sudlow" was "trying to boil the big gun's dinner" (FW 434.08-10) made of "egg" in

---

6 W.B. Yeats, A Vision, (second edition, 1937), 268. It is the same egg from which Leda and Pollux were hatched. Expounding the central idea of his system, that "all things are from antithesis", Yeats alludes to the "Spartan temple" whose roof was strung up with two eggs of Leda, one of war and the other of love. (continued note 15)

order to keep him in good spirits, "healtheous as is egg" (FW 483.23). These lines are, in fact, a pun on the ballad of Humpty Dumpty: "Humpty Dumpty had a great fall". In another instance, the image of the egg repeats the theme of Yeats's poem "Leda and the Swan": "This is the Hausman all paven and stoned, that cribbed the Cabin that never was owned that cocked his leg and hennad his Egg" (FW 205.34-36). The cock as the vocation of the phallus priest Shaun is projected by him while advising his sister Issy "Egg Laid by Former Cock and With Flageolettes in Send Fanciesland" (FW 440.20). Before the explosion or release, both Shaun and Shem "were in one class of age like to two clots of egg" (FW 489.19). Once they had come into existence, they remained "the sign of the cause" deriving "the greatest benefit" (FW 527.14-15).

The egg is the catalytic energy for the four judges — the "Mamma Lujah" (FW 614.28) and the Trinity: "...for the farmer, his son and their homely codes, known as eggburst, eggblend, eggburial and hatch-as-hatch can" (FW 614.31-32). HCE connects the egg symbol in this instance both with Christianity and with some of its Eastern aspects, though it is a machine moving "autokinatonetically" (FW 614.31-32) whose wheels keep on circling the square in terms of the Kabbala. The egg is also connected with the Yggdrasil tree for it is while looking at this "eggdrazzle" tree that Yawn discovers the male and female human couple sheltered under it. Moreover, enemies of humanity, like the snake, are there too. It shelters all, irrespective of grudge or malice.

In Book IV, the Wake alludes to the question as to which came first, the chicken or the egg: "About that coerogenal hun and his knowing the size of an eggcup" (FW 616.20), and mocks at the riddle by saying that the created being appeared first as a salesman "sulksman" before being fertilized: "Cloon's fired him through guff" (FW 616.23). The level of his original sin "coerogenal hun" corresponds to the egg of his entity or i.e. primal matter and the capacity "the size of an eggcup". The egg is also used as an idiom by HCE — "Egged on" (FW 87.27). This phrase emphasizes the role of the litigants against Shem, aided and abetted by the women in the park. The egg figures in the all-inclusive list of those who have contributed to ALP's "untitled mamafesta" (FW 104.04): "The last of the Fingallians, It Was Me Egged Him on to ..." (FW 106.18). The egg was the food — "old hospitable corn and eggfactor," (FW 380.11) — of the last king of Ireland who was unable to

repel the Norman invaders although he had the means of doing so. In the section on St Kevin, the egg is used as the aroma of sweetness "like a grace of beckoning over his egglips" (FW 603.01-02), in magnifying the morning dawn over the nearby Chapelizod Church (with which his legend is associated) along with the countryside in the neighbourhood. The egg connects the Chinese language with the Wake: "Hung Chung Egglyfella" (FW 374.34), in which "chung" according to McHugh, means "crowd". Eggs are the product of the river Liffey — "moyliffey eggs" (FW 54.24). The river Liffey's love for eggs is told as "she was kind of born to lay and love eggs" (FW 112.14). "Professor Levi-Brullo" experimented on the "Nuremberg eggs" (FW 151.13), by which HCE implies the relation between the accidents of where and when of reality as manifestations of the protean egg. HCE applies the same potential in an egg to Shakespeare: "shakespill and eggs!" (FW 161.31). In this chain of egg imagery, it should be reiterated that "whiles eggs will fall cheapened all over the walled the Bure will be dear on the Brie" (FW 163.26-28). In this statement, Shem is saying that before the splitting of the egg, the twins Burrus and Caseous were single and identical, but after the split, they have now disintegrated even though they share some of each other"s character traits.

From the eastern cultures, the egg as the source of energy both physical and spiritual, as for example in Hinduism, is well assimilated by HCE (see the chapter "Sandhyas as Hindu Concept of Genesis" in Part II). Like the diverse properties attached to the egg, Harun al-Rashid in Moslem culture has a many-sided character. As a caliph, he is the vice-regent of Allah. His nightly escapades and perambulations are proverbial. HCE reports on this feature of Harun's character: "Rambling. Nightclothesed, arooned" (FW 355.18-19). In the Arabian Nights, he appears in various disguises and mixes on equal terms with people of almost all the social groups right up to the end of the story, when he suddenly discloses himself as the representative of justice and magnanimity. Since the vocabulary of the Wake attaches various meanings to a single word, Harun's habitual wanderings of the streets of Baghdad at night echo in verbs like "rumble" in the following passage "for after a goodnight's rave and rumble and a shinkhams topmorning with his coexes he was not the same man)" (FW 41.14-15). Quite clearly, "rave and rumble" refer to his night time roving with his close friends and servants. In another situation, Shem is shown to have disguised himself by rubbing mud on his face in order to evade the "rumbler's rent" (FW 86.30).

Once Harun al-Rashid has been identified as an incarnation of HCE, phrases like "And for a night of thoughtsendyures and a day" (FW 295.02-03) or "So, bagdad, after those initials falls and that primary tancture, as I know and you know yourself, begath, and the arab in the ghetto knows better" (FW 286.04-07) suggest the mysterious and notorious scandal in Baghdad involving the Bermic Jaffer and the sister of Harun al-Rashid. Once again, the emphasis is on Joyce's interest in conflating the modern sensibility with that of the Middle Ages, both European and Asian.

Many legends surround the character of Harun al-Rashid, amplifying his myriad roles, both literary and political. In one of these legends, the Caliph, according to Burton, desired to pass through the streets of Baghdad. "Tortured by restlessness" as Burton states, the Caliph and his vizier, Jafar the Bermicide, stepped out of the palace. Both were disguised as merchants. After watching the activities of the street people, they came to the banks of the River Tigris. They asked for a boat, but received a curt rebuff from an old boatman: "who can think of pleasure-boating when every night the Caliph Harun al-Rashid sails down the Tigris accompanied by a crier who proclaims...."whosoever goes out in a boat now and cruises the Tigris, I will cut off his head or hang him on the mast of his own vessel?" Somehow the old man was ingratiated by bribery. They started their journey and then, when they were in the middle of the river there came the barge, floating down the river in midstream, ablaze with candles and lights:

> ...a man held a torch made of red gold robed in red atlas, shoulders embroidered with silver, turban of finest muslin. In the barge, they saw another man, similarly dressed and also holding a torch. In the middle of the barge were two hundred mamluks, standing in rows left and right, around a throne of red gold on which sat a young man. As he saw all this the Caliph murmured, By Allah, he who sits there is the living image of the Caliph, and the man standing before him looks like you, Jafar, and the eunuch behind him looks like Mansur![7]

Everything in this story seems mysterious. Even the bright colours and the flaming brilliant torches are blurred, as if melted into the darkness of masonry. The factual Caliph becomes a fiction, and vice versa. The Caliph is wonderstruck

---

7   Blavatsky, The Secret Doctrine, Vol. I), 376-7.

at this extravagantly indistinguishable medley of colours and phantoms. He hides in the rowing boat watching as his "other" enjoys the dream of being enthroned in the blazing light.

Harun al-Rashid as an incarnation of HCE suggests some of the latter's characteristics in a general way. The dreamer HCE, according to Padraic Colum, is "an old Finn, lying in death beside the river Liffey and watching the history of Ireland as well as that of the whole past, present and future flow through his mind like flotsam on the river of life".[8] If he is the "flotsam on the river" "Liffey" then Harun, though comparable only in general terms, is an extricable part of the river Tigris, especially in folk tales. If Harun al-Rashid is "tortured by sleeplessness",[9] then HCE in the words of Kimberly J. Devlin is "suspended between life and death, trying to look both backward and forward..." like the doomed man in Measure for Measure: "Though hast nor youth nor age, / but as it were an after dinner sleep, / Dreaming of both...".[10] According to Devlin, HCE's fissured and traumatized psychic state is eventually healed through suffering and penance, confession and grace. In the Nights, Shaharazad's time-gaining chain of tales serves the cause of truth and humane understanding. If Harun al-Rashid, in his cycle of fifty stories, plays different roles ranging from the "listener" to the disguised wanderer at night, then HCE too, is the moving spirit of universe and an avatar of many different religions.

HCE changes his costume and behaviour like Bloom in "Circe". Bloom's roles mutate as does his costume, as Devlin states that "the most salient feature of these fantasies of acclaim is the excess of cultural signifiers of significance itself: resplendent clothing, symbolic jewellery, phalanxes of titled men, a superabundance of fanfare".[11] Costume in the Wake is even more fantastical and heterogeneous in its mutations: buildings, mountains, statues, eggs, machines, barrels, clouds, rainbows, all serve as HCE's "apparels" in the dream. When they assume

---

8   Mary and Padraic Colum, Our Friend James Joyce, (London:Victor Gollancz, 1959), 161-2.The same has been quoted by Adaline Glasheen whom Dr O' Brien (one of Joyce's friends) had told that the Wake was about "Finn lying dead by the river Liffey with the history of Ireland and the world cycling through his mind".Adaline Glasheen, "Out of my Census", The Analyst, No.XVII, (1953), 23.

9   Mia Gerhardt, The Art of Story Telling: A Literary Study of the Thousand and One Nights, (Leiden: E.J. Brill, 1963), 428.

10 Kimberly J. Devlin, Wandering and Return in Finnegans Wake: (Princeton: Princeton University Press, 1991), 93.

11 Devlin, Wandering and Return in Finnegans Wake: 124.

more recognizably human colours, costumes are often explicitly marked as disguises, "dangieling his old Conan over his top gallant shouldier so was... He's like more look a novicer on the nevay" (FW 322.03-04). These costumes veil the self of HCE.

HCE as ..."folks forefather" (FW 33.04) appears "in a wardrobe panelled tuxedo comletely thrown back from a shirt well entitled a swallowall" (FW 33.07-08). His robes create a state of fantasy — "Fantasy! funtasy on fantasy, amnaes fintasies! And there is nihil nuder under the clothing moon" (FW 493.18-19) — for everything is in vain, a figment of imagination.

The dilemma of Harun al-Rashid according to Gerhardt is "fundamentally tragic; everything is his except peace of mind, the restlessness and depression that plagued him".[12] If Harun al-Rashid is restless and depressed, then HCE is suffering from the enigma of uncertainty ..."Thousand to One Guinea-Gooseberry's Lipperful Slipver cup" (FW 342.15-16), an echo of an adage which goes back to the Greek times: "There is many a slip 'twixt the cup and the lip". The reference alludes to the fatal lapsus of HCE in the park that sparked into a thousand and one forms of suspicions and rumours. The incident is woven into a complex web whose reality is beyond discernment.

The first reference to this occurs as "Barmecidal" (FW 79.06) in Book I (Chapter IV). On account of its heavily concentrated circular movement of allusions and themes, this chapter is considered by Tindall as the Wake's micro-plot. By introducing the major characters of the Wake, it emphasizes the phenomena of death and burial, the story of the cad, the trial before four judges, refuge from reality through exile and finally "a hymn to A.L.P. and the river".[13] The "Barmecidal" reference occurs in the opening sentences of the chapter, just as the first allusion to Islam occurs on the third page of the Wake. In fact, the fall of the Bermics resulted from their continuous rise in power alongside the caliphate, though as his loyal votaries. This ambiguity posed an equally frustrating challenge to their rivals. The jealous courtiers poisoned the Caliph's ears until he was left with no choice but to destroy the Bermics, glorious though their services had been. Jealousy is a powerful force once the rumours of immoral behaviour have been started in this world

---

12 Gerhardt, The Art of Story Telling: A Literary Study of the Thousand and One Nights, 425.

13 W.Y. Tindall, A Reader's Guide to Finnegans Wake, (New York: Thames and Hudson, 1959), 101-2.

of HCE and the Arabian Nights. "Barmicidal" is also relevant here. It relates to the incident of the Nights (Harun Cycle) in which certain Bermic set a number of empty plates before a beggar pretending that they contained sumptuous dishes.

The second reference is in "The Tristan and Isolde" fable, in which the four old men are sighing regretfully over the vanished feast of the prosperous days, "the barmaisigheds" (FW 387.21) of King Mark. The allusion is to rich and splendid feasts for which the Bermics were proverbial.[14] The Tristan and Isolde fable repeats the theme of downfall and calamity that befell the Bermics. King Mark fell in love with a girl with golden hair. The four old Men had warned the king strictly to avoid such a girl. The king's son Tristan was assigned the task of executing the king's desire. In the Wake, it is the law that whenever fathers are pitted against their sons, the former lose the battle. The theme of the Fall binds together the references to Harun al-Rashid and the Bermics into the universal figure of HCE.

∾

(continuing note 6:[15])

---

14 See W. M. Thackeray, Works, (London: Smith Elder, 1891) Vol. XXV, 74-5.

15   Its imminent hatching of the next generation of world history is a serious concern in A Vision
      — a grim apprehension as related in Yeats's poem "The Second Coming" W.B. Yeats, A Vision,
      (London and Basingstoke: Macmillan, 1981), p.51.Yeats's apprehension of the catastrophic end of
      the world as the precondition of another beginning is consonant with the system of Vico. Where
      they differ, however, is in the timing of this catastrophe.
            Furthermore, Harun al-Rashid, credited by Richard Burton as an icon of liberalism who pa-
      tronized artists and scholars without prejudice, (Richard Burton, The Arabian Nights, Vol.VIII,
      "The Terminal Essay", p.121), emerges in A Vision as one who desires to be instructed in human
      nature so that he will "never be astonished again". Yeats quotes the tale The Dance of the Four
      Royal Persons from the Arabian Nights, and says that one Kusta bin Luka attempts to try his luck
      by explaining human nature to Harun through geometrical figures. To the caliph, this abstract
      divination based on the calculation of figures and dots makes little sense. His displeasure is so
      grave that he sentences the "uninetlligible visitors" to be "put to death" (A Vision, [A], 1925, p.9).
      Some days later there come to Harun's palace a group of four attired in splendid robes, vowed
      to solve the riddle posed by the caliph or face the consequences. On appearing before him, they
      start dancing and, a few minutes later, the caliph issues the verdict: "This dance is dull and they
      dance without accompaniment, and I consider that nobody has ever been more unintelligible".
      Exposed to this dire predicament, each for fear of execution pleads "In the name of Allah,
      smooth out the marks of my footfall on the sand". The caliph is informed of their strange wish,
      hurries to the scene and is astonished to see the footprints scrubbed out in the sand. Kusta
      was called forth, says Yeats, "...and from the sunrise to the sunset of the day after, and for many
      days, he explained the markings of the sand. At last the caliph said, "I now understand human
      nature; I can never be astonished again; I will put the amount of the award into a tomb for the
      dancers". Kusta reiterates his right to the award by claiming: "No, Sir, for the award belongs to
      me!" "How can that be?" inquired the caliph, "for you have explained the marks upon the sand
      and these marks were not made by your feet". "They were made by the feet of my pupils", said
      Luka, "When you banished me from the palace, they gathered in my house to console me, and
      the wisest among them said, "He that dies is the chief person in the story", and he and three
      others offered to dance what I chose". "The reward is yours", said the caliph, "and henceforth
      let the figure marked by their feet be called the Dance of the Four Royal Persons, for it is right
      that you people be rewarded for dying!"
            Commenting on this story, Yeats says that Intellect alone is not enough to explain the mystery
      of Reality. The four represent the "Four Faculties", displaying the truth only cumulatively. Even
      these faculties cannot encompass reality without accommodating the supernatural. Yeats at-
      taches these concepts to Plato's Timaeus, which refers to them as the circuits of the "Other",
      the individual planets ceaselessly ascending and descending towards and away from the Equator.
      Opposite to these circuits is the abode of the fixed stars or the heavenly fixture of "the Same"
      containing the knowledge of the ultimate universals. The idea of the "spictre or my omination"
      (spectre and emanation) (FW.299.05) is stated by Yeats as "I had never read Hegel, but my
      mind had been full of Blake from boyhood up and I saw the world as a conflict — Spectre and
      Emanation" (A Vision, p.72). The sudden disappearance of Robartes in A Vision may also signify
      the value of the force outside the ordinary operations of cause and effect. This power "thwarts
      the intellect" by permeating "all visible and tangible things". In fact, the image of sand, which also
      appears in the poem "Ego Dominus Tuus" as "On the grey sand beside the shallow stream"...
      and "And trace these characters upon the sands?" always symbolises the intimate secrecy of
      "Magical shapes" which can enthrall the imagination, that other self or anti-self existing outside
      the brain's kaleidoscopic refracting and reflecting images.
            Yeats alludes to the spontaneous reaction that inspires Harun al-Rashid with love as soon as
      he "looked at the singer Heart's Miracle and on the instant loved her...[and] covered her head
      with a little silk veil to show that her beauty had already retreated into the mystery of our
      faith". "Heart's Miracle" symbolises Yeats's belief in beauty, "which is its own sanctity" (A Vision

[A], p.197). The Bishop on the other hand defines beauty as a mere sanctified abstract thing: "I looked long upon her beauty, knowing that I would be told it upon the day of judgement, and I wept to remember that I had taken less care of my soul than she of her body".

The function of Yeats's "Four Faculties" is to transmute abstract philosophical concepts into the living presence of passionate intensity by activating and accentuating conflict between part and part, part and whole. Graham Hough comments: "The Wheel with its twenty-eight phases represents twenty-eight incarnations which fulfil the whole range of human experience..."(Graham Hough, The Mystery Religion of W.B. Yeats, (Sussex: The Harvester Press, 1984), pp.113-120.). The "Wheel" consists of two cones, each representing the conflict of concord and discord "within it". The forward and backward movements of these cones are operated upon by its expansion and contraction. Each of the cones contains two antithetical forces, "Will" or ego and "Mask", or the "antiself" of "Will" or what we wish to be. Both the cones supplement one another. Joyce mentions these composite parts of the Sphere [or spheres] (based upon the antinomies) as "husk, passionate / body / spirit / celestial / body" (Notebook 47478, 70 / / 90). In A Vision, Yeats explains that no human being, nation or era is either totally subjective or totally objective. Everybody has to pass through twenty-eight phases from infancy to maturity and death. After death, or the fall to oblivion in "Hades", a human being regenerates into the next gyre. Generation after generation and stage after stage, he moves onward on the winding meandering spiritual stair, rising towards the perfection of ultimate Reality or the "phaseless sphere" defined as an agent of freedom: "it turns into a phaseless sphere when the time has come for our deliverance... Within it live all souls that have been set free" (A Vision, A B, pp.187-210). Warwick Gould describes the "thirteenth Cone" as "the End of the Cycle... the drama that men write and in which they are written is not wholly knowable. It's Yeats's way of saying "But Allah knows all" (Warwick Gould, "A Lesson for the Circumspect": W.B. Yeats's Two Versions of A Vision and the Arabian Nights" in The Arabian Nights in English Literature, ed. Peter L. Caracciolo. p..273). The "thirteenth Cone" is akin to the Islamic sphere of archetypes that exist as Aristotelian "potentia" functioning as the transformers of mysteries between the creatures He created and the Absolute in His Absoluteness. It is the sphere wherein the coincidence of contraries occurs in Joyce's work. Sheldon Brivic defines the range of such as the tenth sephiroth or Ain-Soph: "The Ain-Soph is drawn to emanate the sephiroth by an attraction to the female ones, especially the third, Binah, who completes the first triad at the top of the Tree, and the tenth" Sheldon Brivic, Joyce The Creator, (Madison: The University of Wisconsin Press, 1985), p.115. See also Brivic's article "The Mind Factory: Kabbalah in Finnegans Wake" JJQ, XXI / I (Fall 1983), pp.07-30). The tenth sephir corre ponds to the Islamic tenth Intellect. The tenth sephir, according to European theosophical traditions is the point of contact between the material world and the Divine Mother, "the place of the manifestation of the Deity". Joyce refers to it as "Ainsoph, this upright one, with that noughty besighed him zeroine" (FW.261.23-24).

Like the Moslem mystics, Yeats remained optimistic that perfection was attainable by means of the endless gyres encompassing both life before and after death as a chainless process of karmas. Joyce, basing his argument on Vico's constant cycles or the Hindu incarnations, could not look beyond the repetitive occurrences of phenomena terminating in the state of stasis before relapsing into another cycle endlessly. Stuart Gilbert, however, emphasizes the element of growth in explaining Vico's sense of history as it was perceived by Joyce:

The discoveries of the preceding civilized epoch are almost obliterated and man reverts to a brutish state, till once again he hears the voice of God...The goal of human effort is a resolution of the conflict between good and evil; after each epoch of dissolution and reconstruction, a fragment of the advance gained by the spent wave is conserved, for there is a slowly rising tide in human history and the struggle is not naught availing. (Stuart Gilbert, James Joyce's Ulysses: A Study (New York: Vintage Books, 1955) p.47).   Gilbert cites Bloom as such an example of "improvement all round", an anticipation of the perfection of "the ideareal History". Still, when

we look at the final apology sought by HCE after facing and passing through his trial in front of the twelve and four judges, we find enough ground to absolve him thanks to the Christian grace endorsed and salvaged by ALP. Yet the question remains as to why ALP, while gasping her last breaths, looks upon HCE as the possible tempter of her daughter. Joyce could not resolve the dilemma of evil and hence his belief in the ceaseless cycles of existences.

Harun al-Rashid, whether as an avatar of HCE or as an embodiment of wisdom in A Vision, is a literary character reconciling East and West. Kusta bin Luka is a Christian but Harun al-Rashid has employed him as his physician — "Christian like the Caliph's own physician" in "The Gift of Harun al-Rashid":

"but I Who have accepted the Byzantine faith, That seems unnatural to Arabian minds, Think when I choose a bride I choose for ever..."

Kusta symbolises Byzantine civilization. Harun al-Rashid represents the Moslem caliphate. As Harun in his own reign had to face hostilities from the Byzantine borders like the rest of the Abbasides, their coming together signifies the reconciliation of the two otherwise divergent cultures and political entities.

In addition, Yeats's poems such as "Solomon to Sheba" and "Solomon and the Witch" find various echoes in the Wake. The story of Solomon and Sheba is another nexus which binds Yeats, Joyce and the Arabian Nights. Queen Sheba or Saba comes from the Saba race, described in the eleventh edition of the Encyclopaedia Britannica, Vol. 23 as follows: "There are also numerous small tribes and sections of tribes about Baghdad, but none of them deserve notice except the Sabaens (Sabians), now found only in the neighbourhood of Souk Arab Hillah, and numbering in all 3000 souls" (p.964). The Sabaen traditions, as recounted in this article, say that before the Deluge, the world believed in one God and spoke the same language because all were Sabaens. Drawing their pedigree from Adam's son Shem, they believe that their first settlement was in Egypt where Pharaoh treated them with the same cruelty as he had administered to the children of Israel. Exposed thus to the fear of extinction, they migrated to Damascus and lived there until two hundred years after their prophet, John the Baptist's death. Their next destination was Baghdad where they flourished until after the decline of the Caliphate. They believe that after sacking Baghdad, Tamerlane had carried their intellectual and spiritual books to Ispahan, the city which attracts the Sabaens up until now.

Counting Sheba as a Sabaen implies an interesting and far-reaching result. The impact of the Sabaens is very deep in the history and culture of Mesopotamia. Kusta bin Luka belongs to the race of the Sabaens. Shem, who plays such an important role in the Wake, stems from the same roots.

End of Note 15

3.

Shaharazad and Dunyazad: Issy and ALP

Just as Harun al-Rashid in the Arabian Nights corresponds to HCE in Finnegans Wake, his female counterparts Shaharazad and her younger sister Dunyazad correspod to Issy and ALP respectively. If Harun al-Rashid appears on page 4 of the Wake, then the women of the Nights could be traced right in the first statement on ALP "the delldale dalppling night" (FW 07.02). The phrase signifies the sound and rhythm of the water like the Irish river dance. Moreover, "the delldale dalppling night" (FW 07.02) is the telltale Anna Livia Plurabelle's night. ALP, Stella, Vanessa, Swift, Peter, Jack and Martin are sitting around HCE who is lying flat on the land between Howth "Bailywick" and Chapelizod "Shopalist." The attendants are making a meal of him as he symbolises Christ, Adam and an old ailing father. What they actually do in literal and symbolic terms is first brought out in phrases like "a cooin her hand" and "a ravin her hair" (FW 08.31-34) through the two jinnies. In this passage, the erotic provocation "git the band up" of Wellingdone is like the eroticism of the king of the Nights contrasted with the coldly calculated self-exposure of the women in both books. As antithetical representatives of the "Lingam" and "Yoni" or Bruno's "Coincidentia Oppositorum," both male and female are inextricably textured in the structures of the Nights and the Wake.

We can read the following passage in the first book of Finnegans Wake as directly concerned with the female protagonists of the Nights:

> Heave we aside the fallacy, as punical as finikin, that it was not the king kingself but his inseparable sisters, uncontrollable nighttalkers, Skertsiraizde with Donyahzade, who afterwards, when the robberers shot up the socialights, came down into the world as amusers and were staged by Madame Sudlow as Rosa and Lily Miskinguette in the pantalime that two pitts paythronosed, Miliodorous and Galathee (FW 32.06-12).

"Punical" is Latin puinicus -a variant of Poenicus Carthaginian or a later form of Phoenician. "Finikin" is Finnegan. Joyce has used the word "robberers" signifying a number of themes. In the following excerpt, the robbery has amorous, greedy resonances which caused havoc in an extremely peaceful, ideal bliss of

that of Paradise "when Adam was delvin and his madameen spinning watersilts, when mulk mountynotty man was everybully and the first leal ribberrobber that ever had her ainway everybuddy to his lovesaking eyes and everybilly lived alove with everybiddy else, and Jarl van Hoother had his burnt head high up in his lamphouse," (FW 21.06-10). "Mulk" is king in Arabic. Robbery also applies to Finnegans stark hatred for the religious institutions "when Robber and Mumsell, the pulpic dictators," (FW 185.01-02); secular "like hale King Willow, the robber-er" (FW 583.28). Willow, as we know is wood used in making cricket bats. Wood, in Finnegans universe stands for pen and the bat for playing. Perhaps Finnegan is playing his cryptic game of borrowing from others. The phrase "the robberers shot up the socialists" may simply be taken as the revenge of the exploiting class's upon the Socialists. "Pitts paythronosed," (FW 32. 10) is patronised.

The Nights women are mainly entertainers or "amusers." They provide recreation by telling stories which they invent under the threat of death. These sisters also stage a show and entertain through jokes or "scherzi" (jokes in Italian). The "uncontrollable nighttalkers" is an epithet which links them explicitly with ALP. After a catalogue of the "muse room," ALP is introduced among other things as "She is livving in our midst of debt and laffing through all pores for us (her birth is uncontrollable), with a naperon for her mask" (FW 11.31-33). Like the "nighttalk-ers," ALP's birth is "uncontrollable." Her "mask" (FW 11.33) is essentially relevant to the scheme of Joyce's "The seim anew" (FW 315.23), or as Clive Hart notes "The primary energy which maintains the highly charged polarities of Finnegans Wake is generated by cycles of constantly varied repetition."[1] In fact, her "naperon" is the traditional clothe with which women cover their faces in the East. She is the "same" but at the same time "new." In the second to the last page of Book 1, Chapter 1, in which the name of Shaharazad can only be determined after a careful culling of the subject matter, the twelve gentlemen are consoling the dying Finnegan. He is being told to remain at ease as his household affairs are going smoothly. His wife is fine. About his wife, we are reminded "Arrah, it's herself that's fine, too, don't be talking! Shirksends?" (FW 28.01-02). The word "Shirksends" is further modified to "Shakeshand" in the next sentence. If we observe the whole of the paragraph and rearrange these various words into a probable pattern, we find the following structure. "Shirksends" and "Shakeshands" sound like Shaharazad

[1] .Clive Hart, Structure and Motif in Finnegans Wake, (London: Faber and Faber, 1962), 31.

whose vocation of story telling "storyan" (FW 28.02) is appreciated as "herself that's fine, too, don't be talking!" Sitting on "tabouretcushion," she is being watched as "sewing a dream together, the tailor's daughter, stitch to her last" (FW 28.06-08). Her cunning is revealed as "She was flirtsome then and she's fluttersome yet" (FW 28.15-16). She can devise her escape as "She's seeking her way, a chickle a chuckle, in and out of their serial story" (FW 28.25-26) to "ZeeEnd" (FW 28.29). "Shirksend?" also means the secret plan of the sisters: the tale teller is meant not to end or shirk from telling. The question mark suggests that there can be no such thing as "ZeeEnd." The king whom the two sisters entertain is Scheherazade - a prototype HCE. His name in the Wake, so basic, appears for the first time on this page as "Here Comes Everybody" (FW 32.18-19). He signifies someone who epitomizes all the Stephens, Leopold Blooms and many more, in fact the whole of the race of his gender on this world's stage "world stage" (FW 33.03) where the sisters of the Nights, Lily, Rosa and others play their parts, endlessly.

The next explicit reference to Shaharazad in Finnegans Wake can be found in Book 11, Chapter 3. In the words of Clive Hart, the chapter is "the central expressionistic development of themes, on to which Joyce made his material converge and toward which he himself worked during the process of composition."[2] From the precariousness of Earwicker as sinner and the stupidity of war as the common heritage of mankind, to the apology sought by the tavern keeper for the "Russian General" by saying that "the guilt of the High Personage is shared by mankind at large"[3] as Campbell and Robinson put it, the chapter spans almost all the important themes of the Wake. It also includes Earwicker's desire to be absolved from the "felix culpa." Mysteries of the earlier chapters are evoked by references to the Prankquean riddle, and to religious rituals like Holy Communion and the Last Supper. The chapter also includes scientific themes like the invention of television and the exploitation of atom. The last pages of the chapter refer to the last Irish king, King Roderick O' Connor. In the midst of all these themes of the Wake, an allusion to the Nights magnifies the importance of the oriental aspect of Earwicker's concentric mind: "What ravening shadow! What dovely line! Not the king of this age could richlier eyefeast in oreillental longuardness with alternate nightjoys of a thousand kinds but one kind. Shahrryar cobbler on me when I am

2   Hart, Structure and Motif in Finnegans Wake, 131.
3   Campbell and Robinson, A Skeleton Key to Finnegans Wake, 191.

lying" (FW 357.17-19). "Cobbler" is the protagonist of the Nights tale Maruf the Cobbler. Maruf the Cobbler's dilemma is woven into the structure of the Nights. Cursed by a shrewish wife, he had to comply with her ever growing exaction and demands. Once he failed to live up to her expectations, she revenged herself by filing a false case against him. Compelled to pay the costs of the bailiffs, he had to sell everything he possessed at a low price to the governor's agent. After his wife's second complaint against him, he fled in terror from the approaching police, but this time his suffering led him into a new course of life which proved amazingly fruitful for him. The central idea seems to be that of female deceit and perfidy which is a theme common to the Nights and the Wake.

In the same passage, "ravening shadow" could be interpreted as the terror of death which engenders the poetic utterance or "dovely line!" Here the conflict between the sword and the creative act is held suspended, just as in Keats' Ode the pursuer and the pursued are poised in between the lover trying to achieve his goal and the beloved in foiling the mad pursuit of her lover.

"What ravening shadow! What dovely line!" (FW 357.17) may be explored further. Here, Finnegan is drawing a stark contrast between the opposing forces of aggression "ravening" and peace "dovely" by punning on John Keats lines "Ode on a Grecian Urn"

> "What men or gods are these? What maidens loth?
> What mad pursuit? What struggle to escape?
> What pipes and timbrels?
> What wild ecstasy?"

Oriental languidness "oreillental longuardness" (357.18) owes to an ingrained attitude about East among the Occidental intellectuals. It could be because of the weather which sapped the new-comers from Europe into the Middle East or the rest of Asia. Joyce's imagery here is full of sensuous saturation. The arousal of desire and its fulfilment is common both to this passage and the Arabian Nights. If we compare this passage with Bloom's fantasy in "Lotus Eaters," we find that despite Bloom's Eastern characteristics, his karma or kismet denies him the true

love that he is in need of.

Critics have proposed the following explanations of the Wake passage. Earwicker in the words of Grace Eckley "waxes enthusiastic about his sexual pleasures."[4] The voyeurism of HCE is the source of his sensuous pleasure as Campbell and Robinson observe — "Not the king of this age could feast his eyes more richly"[5] — though the reference eventually boils down to the basic sense of conflict represented by the symbols of raven and dove. The "raven" in the context of the Nights is a cruel king, and the "dove" is the peaceful Shaharazad. This conflict between "raven" and "dove" or "Dovesandraves" (FW 363.07) is found in various combinations in the Wake such as "coocoo him didulceydovely to his old cawcaws huggin and munin" (FW 327.35-36). "Coocoo him" is the sweet, amorous song of the peace loving, passive dove to her master's call of "cawcaws." McHugh glosses "huggin and munin" as mind and memory, Odin's messengers, ravens. "Didulcey" is the dove who has been married to the keeper of the tavern. Though a "mighty man of valour" (FW 325.13), his characteristic haughtiness which provokes the past memories "huggin and munin" is being broadcast by the radio. Furthermore, the voice of the radio which utters "I wish auspicable thievesdayte for the stork dyrby" (FW 325.06) wishing an auspicious day for her king is what we read at the end of each night in the Arabian Nights: "It will be a thousand's a won paddies. And soon to bet. On drums of bliss" (FW 325.07). "Paddies" are pities — the feelings of tenderness aroused by suffering.

The theme of erotic corruption is another feature common to the Nights women and the Wake. In order to establish the erotic perversity of the Nights, Grace Eckley quotes the tale The Rogueries of Dalilah the Crafty and her Daughter Zaynab the Coney-Catcher. It is full of "unrelieved fraud, roguery, and swindling that ends with the female perpetrator receiving not only a pardon but also a position."[6] This tale had been omitted by Lane "on account of its vulgarity" (Arabian Nights, 7:144). Eckley scrutinizes the traces of this tale in the Wake by starting from the excessive rumours about Ear wicker's "camelback excesses" motivated by "those rushy hollow heroines in their skirtsleeves" (FW 67.31), one of which is

---

4   Grace Eckley, Children's Lore in Finnegans Wake, (Syracuse: Syracuse University Press, 1985), 62.

5   Campbell and Robinson, A Skeleton Key to Finnegans Wake, 191.

6   Grace Eckley, Children's Lore in Finnegans Wake, 63.

a "dilalah, Lupita Lorette" (FW 67.33) who "paled off" (FW 67.35) and the other her "sister-in-love, Luperca Latouche" (FW 67.36) whose promiscuity wells up as "that same hot coney a La Zingara which our own little Graunya of the chilired cheeks dished up to the greatsire of Oscar, that son of a Coole. Houri of the coast of emerald, arrah of the lacessive poghue, Aslim-all-Muslim" (FW 68.09-12).

The names of women mentioned here belong from diverse backgrounds: Lupita is St. Patrick's sister. Loretta is a whore who attended the church at Notre Dame while Luperca is the she-wolf suckling Romulus. Dilalah may be from John Milton's Samson Agonistes. On the same page the name of James Joyce himself appears as "jimpjoyced" (FW 68.02). He is flirting with an Indian nauch girl "the nautchy girly" (FW 68.02-03) "selling her spare favours" (FW 68.05). It has to be said that the passage cited does not contain a direct reference to either Shaharazad or Dunyazad. However, the theme of eroticism, temptation and desire reinforces the general motif of the Nights. The beauty of the women in the Nights and Islamic culture is usually compared with the "houris" of Paradise. A "houri" who belongs to the "coast of emerald" is hard to locate in Islamic literature. The "coast of emerald" may be viewed as a metaphor expressing scenic beauty and appeal. An "Emerald" is a precious green gem in French (old French) "esmeraude," "smaragdus" in Latin and "smaragdos" in Greek. In Sanskrit, it is termed as "marakata" emerald.

One word used differently in various languages and sometimes in the same way, is one thing that Joyce was particularly zealous in deploying. However, when we look at the nature of the business transactions of the middle ages involving the Middle East and Europe via the Mediterranean and the Red Sea, we find that the Arabs in the south (along the Persian Gulf and the Arabian Sea), were famous for selling precious gems, perfumes and spices. Joyce may have borrowed these words from Burton's works on the Arab Civilization or from the translations of the Quran, which he knew in French and English. "Coast of emerald" could be the Emerald Coast of Florida. "Houri" appears in different associations such as "Unsightbared embouscher, relentless foe to social and business succes! (Hourihaleine)" (FW 156.35-6). If "embouscher" is an ambusher who has bad breath, then "Houri" is "haleine" who breathes nice. "Sheols of houris in chems upon divans," (FW 177.10) strongly suggests the chair, seat of power of an oriental lord studded with gems. In another context, "houris" appear as a reward: "when they were

all in the old walled of Kinkincaraborg (and that they did overlive the hot air of Montybunkum upon the coal blasts of Mitropolitos let there meeds be the houri-horn)," (FW 316.13-15). The rest of the images are straight forward to explain: "La Zingara" is Italian for a gipsy girl; "Oscar" is Finn's grandson; "lacessive" is to get incited; "arrah of the lacessive pogue" is Boucicault's play Arrah-na-Pogue.

The theme of sex is a dynamic catalyst in the Nights. Even the prologue to the Nights revolves around perfidy and promiscuity. According to Burton, Shaharyar and Shahzaman were two brothers. After the death of their father, the king of kings, they divided between themselves the immeasurable territories which sprawled across India, China and Central Asia. Once it so happened that Shaharyar sent his brother Shahzaman a message, inviting his brother to visit his kingdom. Shahzaman accepted the invitation. Right at the moment of departure, the king had to walk back into his palace in search of something that he had for-gotten, "and the world waxed before his eyes to see the queen asleep on his own carpet-bed embracing a black cook of loathsome aspect and foul with kitchen grease and grime."[7] When Shahzaman met his brother Shaharyar, the latter was astonished to find the former stricken with grief. Deeply alarmed at his brother"s discomfiture, Shaharyar was anxious to know the reason of it, but Shahzaman evaded his questions. He preferred to keep the secret to himself by spending his time hunting. On one of these excursions, the king Shaharyar accompanied his brother. At the appointed hour, according to Edward William Lane, when Shaharyar had not as yet left the precincts of the palace, he returned for some reason and found some twenty female and twenty black male slaves stepping out of the palace into his royal garden:

"and the king's wife who was distinguished for her extraordinary beauty and ele-gance, accompanied them to a fountain, where they all disrobed themselves, and sat down together. The king's wife then called out, O Masod! and immediately a black slave came to her and embraced her."[8]

Shaharyar disclosed this breach of royal honour to his brother and since both had suffered at the hands of their faithless wives, they decided to abandon the

7 .King of Susan in Iraq, the last ruler of the dynasty overthrown by Moslem invaders.
8 Edward William Lane, The Arabian Nights, Vol. 1, 10

worldly life. Both took to wandering until one day they approached the seashore. Out of the water there appeared an "afrit" with a chest of glass encasing a handsome damsel. No sooner did they see this, than the giant "afrit" fell asleep and the fairy invited them to make love to her.

The sexual intrigue that befell HCE in the Phoenix Park is twice repeated in the very first story of the Nights. The fairy coerces them under duress, as Lane narrates. She induces them to hand her over their gold rings, adding to her store of a hundred and seventy such rings gained by similar methods. Sexuality, therefore, remains a universal temptation both in the Wake and in the Nights.

Elucidating the theme of incest in the Arabian Nights and the Wake, Grace Eckley traces the background of the term "coynt"[9] in both works. Shem for example hints "he winged away on a wildgoup's chase across the kathartic ocean and made synthetic ink and sensitive paper for his own end out of his wit"s waste" (FW 185.05-08). Furthermore:

> "...when the call comes, he shall produce nichthemerically from his unheavenly body a no uncertain quantity of obscene matter not protected by copriright in the United Stars of Ourania or bedeed and bedood and bedang and bedung to him, with this double dye, brought to blood heat, gallic acid on iron ore, through the bowels of his misery...this Esuan Menschavik and the first till last alshemist wrote over every square inch of the only foolscap available, his own body (FW 185.28-36)."

"Nichthemerically" (FW 185.28) is from nichthemeron for a period of twenty four hours. "Nicht" in German means not or night, cited as "(in the Nichtian glossery which purveys aprioric roots for aposteriorious tongues" (FW 83.10-11). Darkness or night is the unconscious retaining the potential roots, among other things, of human languages. In the following excerpt, night is a harbinger of the morning and thus, readiness for prayer "As Lord the Laohun is sheutseuyes. The time of lying together will come and the wildering of the nicht till cockeedoodle aubens Aurore." (FW 244.31-33). "Esuan Menschavik" is Russian for a Socialist of a moderate nature. "Foolscap" a printing, publishing term may also be viewed as space which was being used up fully on his body. "Scape" may also be considered as landscape as "gives relief to the langscape as he strauches his lamusong

---

9 Grace Eckley, Children's Lore in Finnegans Wake, 62-66.

untoupon gazelle channel and the bride of the Bryne," (FW 595.03-05).

What Shem narrates is the tale in which a husband, while on his return from travel's abroad, finds his wife sleeping with another person. The wife, as a defence, lures her husband by telling the Nights' tale, The Tale of the two coyntes. In the Wake, we find the name of the tale being used as a pun: "Quoint a quincidence!" (299.0), a coincidence of contraries, among other things. Not only Shem but also HCE can be heard as saying in his defence "Not for one testey tickey culprik's coynds ore for all ecus in cunziehowffse!" (FW 538.15). "Testey" is sixpence and "tickey" is three (pence) in Slavonic; "culprik" is culprit; "ecus" is a coin; and, "cunziehowffse!" is Cunzie House: mint in old Edinburgh. Furthermore, the phrase occurs when HCE alludes to "Ali Baba and The Forty Thieves," "Hold the raabers for the kunning his plethoron. Let leash the dooves to cooin her coynth" (FW 579.14-16). "Rabbers" are the criers; "plethoron" is plethron for ancient Greek linear measure, c.101 ft; and, "the dooves to cooin her coynth" signifies the passive, yielding of the doves. Shem's involvement with the Nights can be probed further. His filth-ridden body on which he writes with his own excrement and urine seems to have been drawn literally from the Nights' sentence, "the tale should be written with a filthy fluid for ink upon a filthy solid for paper, more expressive than elegant" (The Supplementary Nights, 5:215). Applied to Shaharazad and Dunyazad of the Nights, it may be asserted that the waste material they were using for an indelible "ink" was the fear and anxiety. Shaharazad was using her own wits in desperation.

The Nights use of phrases like "dirty brine" and "dung cakes" suggest Shem's apparel, signifying also, the taint of sin which is being rinsed by the two Washerwomen: "the old cheb went futt and did what you know" (FW 196.06-07). Now both these phrases are used to illustrate the character of Issy, "The infant Isabella from her coign to do obeisance toward the duffgerent, as first futherer with drawn brand" (FW 566.23-24). Even here, the feminine gender expresses the "obeisance" to the Wake's father "futherer with drawn brand." It is interesting to note that Issy thus combines both the transcendental and the excretory aspects while fecundating like ALP. Her transcendental aspect can be seen from the fact that in the house of HCE, she is placed (John Gordon explains) in the third storey interconnected through the chimney pipe to the lower storey[10] of the pub, while

---

10 John Gordon, Finnegans Wake: A Plot Summary, (Dublin: Gill and Macmillan, 1986), 10.

HCE is placed in the middle storey between these two extremes.

We can say that like Issy, Shaharazad combines both sexual and narrative characteristics. Issy is the major symbol of such a creative fecundity. It is the desire for life which drives Shaharazad to such an exploration of her hidden potential. Desire thus is the motivating force which, under the guise of sex, stimulates the huge chain of tales within tales, cycles and repetitions of these cycles. "Any reflection on novelistic beginnings" Peter Brooks says while discussing Freud's Beyond the Pleasure Principle, "shows the beginning as an awakening, an arousal, the birth of ambition, desire's intention."[11] Desire is "the very motor of narrative, its dynamic principle." "Sister, listen well to what I am telling you," says Shaharazad, "When I go to the king, I will send for you, and when you come and see that the king has finished with me, say, sister, if you are not asleep, tell us a story." "Then I will begin to tell a story, and it will cause the king to stop his practice, save myself and deliver the people" (Thousand Nights and one Night, Burton, 9:272).

The ALP episode begins with the same desire, as one washerwoman asks the other, "O, tell me all about Anna Livia! I want to hear all about Anna Livia. Well, you know Anna Livia? Tell me all. Tell me now. You'll die when you hear" (FW 196.01-06).

Joyce had written to Harriet Shaw Weaver in March 1924 saying that the "Anna Livia Plurabelle" episode in Finnegans Wake was a "chattering dialogue across the river by two washerwomen who as night falls become a tree and a stone. The river is named Anna Liffey." The "Anna Livia" chapter was to be read aloud as Joyce's own reading of it testifies. Reading of this nature is the strongest cue of the tale teller's gift. Moreover, the letter "O" serves as ALP's mouth or orifice emitting her voice "babbling, bubbling, chattering to herself...gossipaceous Anna Livia" (FW 195.01-04). The letter "O" also relates to her private parts — the origination for her "daughter sons," as well as a symbol implying the cycle of infinity and perfection. This symbol is linked with the nature of ALP as the water of fertility, the river which encircles the phallus HCE and joins the two ends of the novel with the last word "the" left making sense only if correlated with the Wake's first word "river run."

---

11   Peter Brooks, Reading For the Plot: Design and Intention in Narrative, (New York: Vintage Books, 1985), 291.

One washerwoman wishes to know "all about Anna Livia". The emphasis on "telling" echoes throughout the chapter: "O, tell me all I want to hear" (FW 198.14). "Tell me moher. Tell me moatst" (FW 198.28). "Listen now. Are you listening? Yes, yes! Idneed I am!" (FW 201.03). "Onon! Onon! tell me more. Tell me every tiny teign. I want to know every single ingul..." (FW 201.21-22). Telling the tale is a "never" stopping process of "continuarration!" (FW 205.14) as "every telling has a taling" (FW 213.12) terminating at the close of the episode only. "Tell me of John or Shaun? Who were Shem and Shaun the living sons or daughters of? Night now! ...Telmetale of stem or stone. Beside the rivering waters of, hitherandthithering waters of. Night!" (FW 216.01-05). The tangible identities of day-like reality are obscured by the dark night. One becomes a stone and the other a tree. Night thus is regression in which, as in the Nights, Shaharazad and Dunyazad can execute a circumspect plan in winning over the king. In the confusion of the darkness, identities are caught between the real and the figurative. The real is the "sword of certainty" (FW 51.03-06), the figurative is the potential treasure of her telling. The desire to escape death intensifies as the vocal dialogue between the two washer-women indicates. Intensification of desire means the continuous realization of "A being again in becomings again" (FW 491.23). One incident in the Nights may be a reminiscence of an earlier one just as the central action of a certain sequence or episode or cycle recurs throughout the narrative as the same event can happen to different characters who are essentially replicas of one another. Joyce in the Notebook (VI.B.I) explains this feature of the tale telling sisters and says that they begin with the story A, add its elements to B and then keep on supplementing and supplanting the former by the latter by reflecting, refracting and flashing back and forth across the entire cycle: "Begin story A+B, then B+C, C+D."

Shaharazad interrupts the narrative only at the end of each night "But morning overtook Shaharazad, and she lapsed into silence." She interferes during the narrative though only occasionally as she says at the beginning of each night "I heard, O happy king". The rest of the narrative time is occupied with the tale tellers of the individual tales within the cycles. The voices of these tale tellers are further diversified ranging from the voices of the human beings to that of the animals and the supernatural beings. The general pattern of this huge web can roughly be summed up as follows. At the end of the first tale ("The Tale of Three Ladies and the Porter" - The Wake refers to the "porter" severally "FW.069.26; 327.34; 368.11;

372.04; 531.25; 548.12; 570.15; 570.19; 570.19; 570.20; 571.20; 622.27) the first dervish is heard as saying finally "But God drove us to your house, and you were kind and generous to let us in and help me forget the loss of an eye and the shaving off of my beard." The narrative is further dramatised by one of the Ladies of the house "Stroke your head and go! To which he replies "By God I will not go until I hear the tale of the others..." "It is related O happy king,that those who were present marvelled at the tale of the first dervish." This is the voice of Shaharazad speaking to her king Shaharyar.

Unlike the other speakers whose voices are clearly mentioned or identified, the voice of Shaharazad is heard but her identity remains illusive although all along it is she who is the only speaker of all this huge chain of voices and tales. Immediately after the above sentence of Shaharazad, we hear the voice of the caliph which further diminishes her presence as she always addresses her king and the caliph Harun al-Rahid. The caliph Harun al-Rashid said to Jaffer "In all my life I never heard a stranger tale." The caliph's speech complicates the pattern further. Harun here is a disguised tale teller or dervish. In reality he is a caliph. In other words, Shaharazad like Harun al-Rashid is wearing the mask of every tale and character which undergoes transformations assimilating different tales and characters into a pattern addressed by her. The phrase "In my life I have never heard a stranger tale" is also attributed to Shaharayar as he is heard as saying quite often. In other words, everything comes out of the mouth of Shaharazad, yet her own voice is split up into the metonymy of the melange of voices. This essentially is her depersonalisation- so important in keeping the horrendous flow of voices in operation through tremendous regression. This regression of hers is eventually an anchorage into the unconscious from where the cultural archetypes articulate under the stoking fire of desire, utterance, tale of life and its riddles, of cultures and their myriad values by interacting constant feed up of shuttle-like to and fro, a movement between the conscious and unconscious — a metonymy of night flanked by the dichotomy between dusk and dawn.

Henriette Lazards Powers attributes to Shaharazad's capacity of such a regression into various discourses as "...which attempt to certify and specify the meaning of a given prior text, yet which become themselves discourses to be specified - or

questioned by another witness"[12] This unspecified flow of uncontrollable libido is

12 Henrietta Lazaridis Power, "Shahrazade, Turko the Terrible, and Shem: the reader as Voyeur in Finnegans Wake"- in Coping with Joyce: Essays from the Copenhagen Symposium, "We may consider this dialectic of masculine and feminine phenomenology by recapping the characters again. The basic polarity is worth noting: like Shaharyar, HCE is a "male fist" just Shaharazad is "women formed mobile" (FW.309.21-22) like ALP. Both HCE and Shaharyar are in a state of moral dilemma: the consciousness of guilt of his sin in the Phoenix Park in the case of HCE and an eye-witness experience of the infidelity of the ladies of the Harem, in the case of the latter. Whereas HCE represents the Western tradition of guilt of incest and violence as attributed say to Charles Parnell, Romulus and Remus, Zeus and Leda, Isis and Osiris, Finn MacCool, the myth of Oedipus and the stories of Old Testament; Shaharyar manifests the kind of terror as inflicted by the monarchs and their nobles on the ladies of the Harem. Etymologically, "Shaharyar" means the one who befriends the city - the cities built and established along the fertile soil of the river banks: "Allalivial allalluvial" (FW.213.31). Unlike these, Shaharazad and ALP in their nature are like a river which gushes forth, back and forth endlessly without sticking to anyone and only form.
 Female infidelity causes intolerable grief and despondency to their sense of patriarchal self. Shaharyar and his brother Shahzaman are further traumatized when they experience incest with the faery whose abductor, the afrit releases her out of the chest by emerging from the river. The brother kings are stunned at the coercing invitation: "we seek the aid of God against the malice of women, for indeed their craft is great." Shaharyar's anger becomes an obsession and rather than rationalise the nature of womanhood, he resorts to ruthless violence.
 Shaharazad's role, on the contrary is that of a redeemer. By pandering to his appetite, she schools him gradually. Soon Shaharyar is reduced to the status of an eager listener spell bound to the narrator who now enjoys the role of a dictator as an active master to her passive agent. The way she gains her objective shows the paradox of the displacement of power: the limits of physical, political power and the limitless potential of the feminine libido made possible to find its release in special circumstances by the circumspect Shaharazad. Her nightly activities draw an interesting parallel to that of the Wake. In the Arabian Nights, Shahzaman returns to his palace to collect the forgotten item at night. His nerves fray as soon as he discovers that his own wife is lying in bed with a slave as black as the pitch darkness. On seeing this "the world became black before his eyes" so that incited, he commits the deadly act of killing the two. Both night and darkness function as concealment and revelation. What Shahzaman initiates, becomes the horrible custom with Shaharyar unless the intervention of Shaharazad: "and henceforth he made his regular custom, every time he took a virgin to his bed, to kill her at the expiration of the night. This he continued to do during a period of three years" to expiate "an internal sore". Her discourse opens this "sore" from the womb of his unconscious by putting him in a state of trance just like HCE's "substance" (FW.597.07. Once the cave of his mind opens, a torrential stream of the strife and struggle among individuals, nations their cultures and languages flows out at random.
 Shaharazad has another valuable parallel. She is not only charming but amazingly scholarly. As Lane reports: "Shaharazad had read various books of histories, and the lives of preceding kings, and stories of past generations: it is asserted that she had read a thousand books of histories, relating to preceding generations and kings, and works of poets" (The Thousand and One Nights, 1:10).
 Her abilities of intellect suggest those of "diva deborah" in the Wake. Deborah, as Sheldon Brivic argues (p.28 Joyce's Waking Women, The University of Wisconsin Press, 1995) by referring to Harold Bloom's The Book of J that "fundamental parts of Genesis were written by a woman but they were later covered over by layers of male writing." Deborah had also led the Israelites to victory against the Cananites.

what Colin McCabe considers as an "infinite regress of meta-languages"- a state of mobility through invisibility, to which Powers alludes in the song "the boy / that can enjoy / Invisibility"

(U 10). Shaharazad engages the reader, states Powers "in a kind of shell game". The moment the reader attempts to determine her visibility in a specific guise, she eludes by disguising herself into another form. She challenges the fixed patterns of language like Kristava's "chora" Powers mentions. If masculine economy is "centralised, short, cutting, an alteration of attraction and repulsion then the feminine economy is "continuous, overabundant, overflowing".[13] Her profusion of desire enables her to exceed the determinable or the nameable and thus by transcending, she enables the contraries (like that of Bruno's active and passive, Hegel's master and slave, Aristotle's soul and body), fuse together.

Shaharazad defers the King's habit of killing young damsels by telling him endless tales which serve as the Arabic "kinayah" - an indirect way of expressing meaning. Shaharazad is heard as saying "Thus he spent the rest of the night with her in embracing and clipping, playing the particle of copulation in concert and joining the conjunctive with the conjoined, while her husband was a cast out ... construction" (The Thousand and One Nights, 9:272). We can use this passage as an illustration of the textual code of creativity. The Arabian Nights in short is a long "kinayah" a fruit of metonymy... the consequence of a sexual act made word through fables, parables, dialogues and narrative. One of the finest example of "kinayah" can be studied in "The Porter and the Three Ladies" from Sandra Naddaff's in Arabesque.[14] The porter is asked to take off his clothes by the Ladies and jump into the pool. A little later, he is ordered to rush out and plant himself "in the lap of the fairest girl, put his arms on the lap of the doorkeeper" while the Ladies were now rollicking with laughter by referring to erotic organs.

During this period, the porter was hugging, kissing, pinching biting and nibbling them to the satisfaction of the entire company. Some such use of "kinayah" can be identified in the Wake as meanings remain constantly deferred: "Ay Exhibit his relics! Bu! Use the tongue mor! Give lip less! But it oozed out in Deadman's Dark

---

13 Julia Kristeva, Desire in Language: A Semiotic Approach to Literature and Art, ed. Leon Roudiez, tr. Thomas Gora, Alice Jardine & Leon Roudiez, Blackwell 1982

14 Sandra Naddaff, Arabesque (Northwestern University Press, Evanston, Illionis, 1991). P.55

Scenery Court through crossexamination of the casehardened testis that when and where that knife of knives the treepartied ambush was laid (roughy spouting around half hours "twixt dusk in dawn.."(FW 87.30-35). The Nights women lay an "ambush" around the king and keep him in darkness but the king also is the one who poses the phallus riddle-another kind of "ambush". Nevertheless, these women execute their plan and keep him in darkness till the emergence of dawn of their lives and their release: "Fine feelplay we had of it mid the kissabets frisking in the kool kurkle dusk of the lushiness" (FW 95.20-23)... "and she and myself, the redheaded girl, firstnighting down Sycomore Lane." Furthermore, "Whence it is a slopperish matter, given the wet and low visibility (since in this scherzarade of one's thousand one nightinesses that sword of certainty which would indentifide the body never falls) to idendifine the individuone" (FW 51.03-06). The "wet" and "low visibility" of the Wake means the dream like "fatal slip" of the "foetal sleep" which is so propitious to Shaharazad in evading the sword of certainty. The king is so impressed by the tale teller's capacity to captivate his mind that his indecision, like the linguistic flux of the Wake, is easily exploited by the sisters. Just as the king is hamstrung both by eroticism and the charm of the tales, so is the language of the Wake which affects each reader differently every time because of the indeterminacy of its code. To reiterate, it may be said that the "slop perish method" is the characteristic of the Wake narrative strategy, just as Shaharazad and Dunyazad hide their true intention of saving themselves by telling the tales. "Wet and low visibility" applies to the darkness and weather at night though we could stretch the meaning to wetness of the beds in which the two won over the heart of the cruel king through erotic temptation and story telling. The identity of the individuals becomes as obscure as the intention both in the Wake and the Nights.

The story of Shaharazad interfuses the erotic desire and language under the tremendous cataclysm of desire itself. Both of these nocturnal activities are interconnected. In the Notebook (VI.B.I) under the heading "Sisters" (p.53) Joyce notes "The arabian nights, serial stories, tales within tales, desperate story telling, one apes another to reproduce a rambler mockberdic tale (cg). Once upon a time So they put on the kettle and made tea." Here making of tea is associated with telling of the tales and these tales are based upon mutual imitation as "one apes

another." As Margaret C. Solomon explains, tea is associated with sex and "micturition."[15] Micturition is implicit in the spelling out of "pee ess" (FW 111.18-22). In the Notebook (VI.B.I) we read of the use of the letter "t" as "queen of teatable and W.C." In the same notebook, Joyce relates the phenomena of "pees" as "strophes of Omar a bowl of merest pisse." The bowl is Omar Khayyam's "jug of wine." Tea fuses together the male and female: "Homo Capite [cup of tea] Erectus, what price Peabody's money" (FW 101.12-1), or "the souffsouff blows her peaties up and a claypot wet for thee" (FW 117.17-18). She blows the "peaties" the dried peat for fuel softly and then warms the water in the clay pot for him. It could also be a metaphor for two things: first, the excitement of sexual nature, and second, the enticement of the mind of the king to listen to the tales with ever-growing interest. The Latin "homo Capite [cup of tea] Erectus," (FW 101.12) is man erect as to the head while "what price Peabody's money" (FW 101.12-13) is the philanthropist George Peabody. The Prankquean's micturition at the "dour" establishes not only

15 Margaret C. Solomon, Eternal Geomater (Carbondale and Edwardsville: Southern Illinois University Press, 1969), 77. Like ALP washing off HCE's stain-ridden shirt "I know by heart the places he likes to saale, duddurty devil" (FW.196.14-15) by urging him to sail in the soil of her river-identity, Shaharazad finally, enables Shaharyar to regain sanity as Burton puts it "and comes to himself, and awakens from his drunkenness" [Burton 12.269], by acting like ALP as "proximate" (FW 198.17) a proxy, an object of the King's desire which brims over "feefee fiefie" (FW 204.15)in its creative, productive process. Though the most ingenious plan of harnessing the virile instincts of the king keeps the sisters vulnerable, uncertain as Doddpebble pleads to Quick enough "Forgivemequick" (215.07) as the latter replies "Forgetmenot" (FW 215.08) because both are aware of the challenge "...love!...We'll meet again, we'll part once more" (FW 215.4-5).The two sisters are fully aware of their role - "a kitchernott darkness" (FW 107.20-25), yet they must roll on "we must grope on till Zerogh hour" in countless roles like the rolling sun "the eternal chimerahunter Oriolopos" "with guns like drums" (FW 107.14:17) in achieving the goal of "..So is My Washing Done by Night" (FW 107.01). In their vocation of washing, they are "the twinfreer type" of "the Coucousien oafsprung of this sun of kuk" (FW 162.) whom "Fonnumagula" or Finn MacCool had picked up from "the Persic-Uraliens hostery" and had fixed their destiny "as the knew kneck and knife knockouts" (FW 162.10) in removing the "sandhurst out of his eyes" (FW.162.07).Even though Sandhurst symbolises the military academy, "sandhurst" in the "Persic-Uraliens hostery" points to the Oriental dust and sand storms. But then, Finnegans reveries are endless. In the discussion in this chapter,"Sesthers" may be interpreted as sisters or"Esther" for star (Persian), even the queen Esther from Persia in Old testament. The phrase "twone nathandjoe" may be seen as the title of the Arabian Nights. The noun" English" becomes "inglis" (FW 8. 23) and "anglease" (FW 16. 6) when pronounced by an Asian, not used to the learning of the English language. In "dam night garrulous, slipt by his side" (FW 139. 18-19), the "garrulous" is the king of the Nights, whom Shaharazad entertains by her meandering tales: "what a meanderthalltale to unfurl and with what an end" (FW 19. 25-6) like the endless rivers that appear in the Wake. Max Eastman, quotes Richard Ellmann in James Joyce, about the river reverie of the author that he "liked to think how some day, way off in Tibet or Somaliland, [or even in Persia] some boy or girl in reading that little book would be pleased to come upon the name of his or her home river."

the fact of female fecundity but also the truth of "baptismal waters" with the wine of communion, as Hart explains.[16] In a note in the Scribbledehobble Notebook (p.178) Joyce's "bedtime, teatime" applies to the Nights protagonists. Teapot as "kettle" stands for the woman that wets the "weapon" symbolised by the tea-spoon: "And where was hunty, poppa the gun? Pointing up to skyless heaven like the spoon out of sergeant major's tay" (FW 330.36; 331.01-02). "Poppa the gun" is the hunter's Popgun while "skyless" is the cloudiness and "heaven like the spoon" is the tasting of the tea which is so strong that spoon stands upright in it.

The Arabian Nights end on a happy note. The king, as Burton states, is convinced of Scheherazade's "chaste, self-sacrificing and learned; bold and re-sourceful" demeanour, yet the three sons that are born to her ultimately become the source of rescue. As the Nights draw to a close, we find her requesting the king "May I then make bold to crave a boon of thy Highness?" The king replies "Ask O Shaharazad and it will be granted to thee." She asks for the sparing of her life for the sake of their children. The king replies "By Allah O Shaharazad, I pardoned thee before the coming of these children, for I found thee chaste, pure, ingenu-ous and pious." The king was pleased to make her his queen, and in celebrating this unprecedented marriage all the ceremonies were lavishly accomplished. Similarly, king Shahzaman was married to her other sister Dunyazad. The nobles, courtiers and mamluks could find their daughters freed by Shaharazad, "the freer of the city."[17] In Finnegans Wake, the Nights" happy ending come after the "old Gallstonebelly" has established his "honours from home, colonies and empire" (FW 393.14); these sisters, the "assisting grace" whose profession was that of "counting and contradicting every night" like Bruno's inseparable co-existence of contraries were "now happily married" (FW 393.18-20). These "beautiful sister misters" were married to "their four hosenbands" (FW 393.17-22) — the four judges reaffirming Bruno's idea of indissoluble relation between spirit and flesh. In Arabic, "hosen" means "beautiful" - a sign of Allah. Women according to Islam, stand for such a "hosen."

∾

---

16 Clive Hart, Structure and Motif in Finnegans Wake, 207.

17 Richard Burton, The Arabian Nights: "Conclusion," Vol.VIII, 56-7.

4.

Sindbad and the Sailor and Two Other Tall Tales

Sindbad's voyages come under the category of Travel Stories. In making some references to the Sindbad of the Nights, Joyce is reaffirming the tradition and value of the literary and cultural interpenetrating of the West into the East and vice versa. Narration of the unseen wilds of land and sea provide an excellent allegorical framework for moral instruction and aesthetic edification. Where such tales originated is a matter of speculation only. As G.E. Von Grunebaum states: "Geographical lore seems to lend itself particularly well to being borrowed and re-borrowed, and this fact reduces considerably the number of cases where we are able to assign a definite origin to a motive."[1] Von Grunebaum thinks that four of Sindbad's voyages are indebted to a Greek source. Similarly, Richard Burton believes that: "Egypt-Greece-Indian stories over-ran the civilized globe between Rome and China. Tales have wings and fly farther than the jade hatchets of proto-historic days."[2] Joyce's approach is exactly similar to that of Burton. Like Aladdin's lamp, Joyce's imagination travels thousands of miles for an appropriate theme echoing in a different vocabulary at the spur of the moment.

According to Von Grunebaum, the first translation of Homer's two books into Arabic occurred in the age of Caliph al-Mahdi (p.775-85). Joyce mentions the name of this caliph in his Notebook (volumes. C. 6,8,9,10,16,15 - p.211 "Mahdi"). "Theophilus of Edessa" (d.785), explains Von Grunebaum, "a favourite of the caliph al-Mahdi and a celebrated astrologer, translated the two books of Homer into Syriac."[3] The name of the voyager "Sindbad", however, commemorates a native of "Western India," comprising today's Pakistan.[4] In the languages of the

1   G.E.Von Grunebaum, Medieval Islam: A Study in Cultural Orientation 2nd ed. (Chicago: University of Chicago Press, 1953), 303.

2   Richard Burton, The Arabian Nights, Vol.VIII "The Terminal Essay", 109.

3   G.E. Von Grunebaum in Medieval Islam (298-299) referring to A. Baumstark, Geschichte der Syrischen Literatur (Bonn, 1922), 341, n.4.

4   Edward William Lane, The Arabian Nights (New York: Tudor Publishing Co., 1927), 1186. He explains the etymology of "Es Sindibad" as comprising two names, viz. "El-Hind" and "Es-Sind". By "El-Hind" he means "the main portion of India," whereas "Es-Sind" stands for the whole of "Western India."

subcontinent, Sindbad implies two meanings: first, one who roves in the river Indus. Second, Sindbad taken from the Sanskrit term "siddhapat" means "the lord of the sages." The river Indus is considered as one of the sources of ancient traditions, as Joyce states in the Notebook (Book II, Chapter 2, p. 48):

> "and it is veritably belied, we belove, that not all the soupeans that"s in the queens pottage-pots and not all the green gold that the Indus contains would ever hinduce them (o.p.) to steeplechange back to their ancient habits which, cumma, having listed carefully to his continental's curses..."

According to Von Grunebaum,[5] Callisthenes, while accompanying Alexander, had written to Aristotle about such tales that he had heard in India. Grunebaum believes that Sindbad's landing on the fish (an episode to which there is a reference in the Wake discussed below) has its source in the Vita Alexandri Magni of Callisthenes which states:

> ....Some barbarians at the coast of the Indian Ocean showed us an island which we all could see in the middle of the sea. They said it was the tomb of an ancient king in which much gold had been dedicated. [When we wished to sail to the island] the barbarians had disappeared leaving us twelve of their little boats. Pheidon, my closest friend, Hephaistion, Krateros and the other friends of mine did not suffer me to cross over [to the tomb in person]. Pheidon said: Let me go first so that if anything should go wrong, I would face the danger rather than you. If everything is all right I shall send the boat back for you. For if I, Pheidon, should perish, you will find other friends, but should you, Alexander, perish, the whole world would be steeped in grief. Convinced by this plea, I gave them leave to cross over. But when they had gone ashore on what they thought was an island, after no more than an hour the animal suddenly dived down into the deep. We cried out loud while the animal disappeared, and the men, including my dearest friend, came to a horrible end. Embittered I made a search for the barbarians but could not find them.

Similarly, Von Grunebaum thinks that the Odyssey has its source in a certain Syriac text.[6] The episode of "food which puts them out of their right minds" in both the Odyssey and Sindbad the Sailor have common roots. Furthermore, Gerhardt (another critic of the Arabian Nights) mentions the monster that clings to the body of Sindbad. It looks like a human being but has a tale and is absolutely harmless. It

---

5   W. Kroll, ed., Historia Alexandri Magni, (Berlin: 1926),Vol.17, 03-07.The editor dates this recension to about ad 300.

6   G.E. Von Grunebaum in Medieval Islam chapter "Greece in the Arabian Nights" (Chicago: University of Chicago Press, 1945, 294-319) refers to A. Baumstark's Geschichte der syrischen Literatur (Bonn, 1922), 341.

"has a fish's body, a bald head, with a beard and long horns and malignant coun-
tenance. It does not hold on to the man with its legs, having none, but seems to
clutch him with its fin-like forelimbs." Gerhardt terms the monster the Old Man of
the Sea,[7] and he may be identified with the "Proteus" of the "Proteus" episode of
Ulysses and the Odyssey, as Joyce's Notebook (VI.B.I) specifies "Old Man of Sea:
Proteus: good king" (p.208). There are several references to Sindbad the Sailor
in Finnegans Wake. In Book 1, chapter 4, we come across the following passage:

> The four of them and thank court now there were no more of them. So pass the push
> for port sake. Be it soon. Ah ho! And do you remember, Singabob, the badfather, the
> same, the great Howdoyoucallem, and his old nickname, Dirty Daddy Pantaloons, in
> his monopoleums, behind the war of the two roses... (FW 94.31-36).

"The four of them and thank court now there were no more of them" (FW
94.31) is a song as McHugh quotes "Glory be to God that there are no more of us
For the four of us will drink it all alone." "So pass the push for port sake" FW 94.31-
2) is to pass the port. The four judges drop their charges against HCE, yet, they
taunt him by blaming that he stinks in his dirty "pantaloons." "Monopoleums" is
the monopoly of the Patriarchal system and its "bad fathers" or worse "howdoy-
oucallem." This shows the dreamer's conscience and disgust towards the fathers
of all kinds of monopolizing power whether in the "war of the two roses" or
elsewhere. Rose and O' Hanlon, like McHugh, identify "Singabob" as Sindbad the
Sailor.[8] "Singabob" is presented as the singer of songs ("singa"), in water ("abob"
means water in Persian). In another instance of a navel journey, Jaun sets out on a
"glorious mission" (FW 452.18) "to meet a king" (FW 452.26) in his "dutyful cask"
(FW 452.24), and there is a reference to singing: "Look in the slag scuttle and you'll
see me sailspread over the singing" (FW 453.23-24). "Slag" is to attack or strike.
The fact that Jaun is on the way to the East is stated as "eastern humming sphere"
(FW 453.22). These images reinforce the singing aspect of "Singabob." Culturally,
the sailor skimming the waves in a boat in the East is generally thought to be a
singer also. The theme of Sindbad in the above passage, is further enhanced by
the phrase "so pass the push for port sake." His oily head and prickled ears are

---

7   Mia Gerhardt, The Art of Story Telling: A Literary Study of the Thousand and One Nights, 240.

8   Danis Rose and John O'Hanlon, Understanding Finnegans Wake, (New York & London: Garland
     Publishing, 1982), 69.

recorded as "Somehow-at-Sea (O little oily head, sloper's brow and prickled ears!)" (FW 291.26-27). In another situation, the reference to the Nights women "Anna Lynchya Pourable! One and eleven. United We Stand...Don't forget" is followed by a reference to Sindbad the Sailor: "gentlemens tealer, generalman seelord, gosse and bosse, hunguest and horasa, jonejemsums both, in sailsmanship, szed the head marines talebearer, then sayd the ships housefather" (FW 325.04-06).

The word "bosse" also appears as "Bosse and string bag from Heteroditheroe's and all ladies presents" (FW 221.29-30). Here "bosse" is Harriet Bosse Strindberg's 3rd wife. Moreover, the use of this word as: "by the seven bosses" (FW 325.29, a reference is being made to the seven bosses who rose on the shield in Macpherson's Temora VII.309.

The word "gosse" in Persian means one who can hear, and "bosse" in Indian languages is used for language that one can speak. The passage alludes to the seven voyages of Sindbad, a story "the ships housefather" is telling in his house ("horasa") to the guest ("hunguest") Sindbad the Landsman. The latter is more clearly present in another passage: "lift-ye-landman. Allamin. Which in the ambit of its orbit heaved a sink her sailer alongside of a drink her drainer from the basses brothers, those two theygottheres" (FW 311.01-04). The teller (Sindbad the Sailor) and the listener (Sindbad the Landsman) may be identified with "those two theygottheres."

We learn from the Nights that the rich merchant Sindbad the Sailor is finally back at home and relaxing in ease and comfort, narrating his trials and triumphs like a romantic hero. His guests listen to him with wonder and awe, while a large retinue of servants is at his beck and call. In fact, Sindbad in his own house is no less than a king — a reminiscence of how the tales repeat the protagonist roles of the king and his entertaining women of Baghdad. In the second chapter of Book 1 there are indications of similarly majestic behaviour on the part of our hero HCE. He is "Our sailor king" (FW 31.11) and is described as "draining a gugglet" (FW 31.11) of drink. Like Sindbad, he has moustaches: "smiled most heartily beneath his walrus moustaches." Both of these heroes enjoy a "genial humour" (FW 31.12-16).

In chapter 9 (FW 309-82), we can discover two of the traits of HCE. First, he is a

tailor whose weaving is as complex as that of a web or "wordspiderweb" (Letters, III, p.422). Secondly, he is a sailor who roves in the thick jungle of confusion during sleep. Like him in this second capacity, even the customers in the pub are sunk in confusions of identity though they lack the ambition of the protagonist. The owner of the pub, our "Vakingfar sleeper" (FW 310.10), and the customers are not only the listeners but also the transmitters of the story of HCE to the equally dumfounded audience, "an auricular for fickle" (FW 310.10). Even the content of the broadcast is deafening: "the balk of the deaf" (FW 309.03). In this situation, the teller and the listener are not easily identifiable. What can be conjectured is that there are two sides to the story (the tale of Kersse the tailor and the Norwegian Captain). As tailor, Earwicker is the father of ALP — "my cold mad feary father" (FW 628.01-02) — and as a sailor he is also Persse O'Reilly [the Scandinavian invader], both the characteristics merging in him: "How kirssy the tiler made a sweet unclose to the Narwhealian captol" (FW 23.10-11). It is here that there is a reference to Sindbad the Sailor's seven voyages: "And aweigh he yankered on the Norgean run so that seven sailend sonnenrounders was he beastbare to the brinabath, where bottoms out has fatthoms full" (FW 312.05-07). "Aweigh he yankered" is to weigh anchor; "sailend" is sailing; "sonnen" pertains to the sun though "sonnenrounders" in the dreamlike strutting echoes "seven sailend." In Arabic, Persian and Urdu, Sindbad is pronounced as "Sindhbad" with emphasis on "d" and "dh." "N" as in "sailend" remains silent. "Sonnen" read from right to left evolves the name of "Nansen" the one who led the ship for polar expedition. The chaotic motion of the waves is put as "and the tides made, veer and haul, and the times marred, rear and fall..." (FW 312.11).

In fact, Sindbad's character is an aspect of HCE's oceanic life and adventures. "Where bottoms out has fatthoms full" implies two things. First, it shows Earwicker's character as a tailor, and secondly, his roaming across the sea in search of the "bottom" of reality as throughout the Wake, there is a contrast of clothes or "skirt" and the mystery inside or below the appearances. Unable to discover the truth, HCE prefers to forego much introspection in favour of Omar Khayyam's philosophy of life, "Enjoy yourself, O maremen!" (FW 312.10). This is exactly what the customers are doing in the pub — "Hump! Hump! bassed the broaders-in-laugh" (FW 312.10) — as is Earwicker, deaf to the broadcasting "(Hear! Calls! Everywhair!)" (FW 108.23) except the calls for more drinks in this

tavern of drunkards.

How the wanderings of Sindbad the sailor have been knitted into the Wake is best presented on page 182 of the book. This house which belongs to O'Shea or O'Shame, is "Asia in Ireland," metaphorically the whole of the globe comprising both East and West. It is a place of "Haunted Inkbottle" (FW 182.31) with no definite identity "no number brimstone Walk" (FW 182.31) except the "doorplate" which bears the sign "SHUT" and the "blind of black sailcloth." The "soulcontracted son" has to grope through this dark alley dejected by life from "jesuit bark and bitter bite" (FW 182.34-36). His starting point is the "midnight middy" (FW 480.09) or the Mediterranean which joins East and West, "ponenter" (FW 480.10) in this "crusade on with the parent ship" (FW 480.07). The room or the cell is like the "Infernal machinery" (FW 320.33), and the blaspheming Norwegian Captain — "blastfumed the nowraging scamp tail" (FW 320.25) — has to keep on sailing — "baffling yarn sailed in circles" (FW 320.35) — for the realization of his dream or "dhruimadhreamdhrue" (FW 320.21) (though this phrase also echoes the Hindu "dharma" or faith in becoming one with the universe after journeying through the cycles of incarnations). Like his circular voyaging from East to West, he has to pass through the challenges and trials in this baffling journey — a constant hermeneutic of hide and seek, the protean phenomena of reality in the ocean "sailalloyed ... they were all trying to and baffling with the walters of,.... High! Sink! High! Sink! Highohigh! Sinkasink! Waves" (FW 373.04-08). No less terrible are the ordeals on land for once the sun goes down and "with one touch of nature set a veiled world agrin" (FW 138.36, 139.01) they could be seen being pursued by "blick a saumon taken with a lance," the "hunters pursuing a doe" and the sailors with their "swallowship in full sail" (FW 139.03-04).

Sometimes, a reference is so vague that it can be deduced only by meticulous piecing together of these bits and pieces. For example, we come across the following phrases and clauses in the long question posed by Shem to Shaun in Book 1, chapter 6: "...changes blowicks into bullocks and a well of Artesia into a bird of Arabia;" "...walked many hundreds and many score miles of streets and lit thousands in one nightlights in hectare of windows....; O sorrow the sail and woe the rudder that were set for Mairie Quai!...;" "...a part of the whole as a port for a whale...the night express sings his story" (FW 135.14-35); "...his porter has

a mighty grasp and his baxters the boon of broadwhite; as far as wind dries and rain eats and sun turns and water bounds he is exalted and depressed, assembled and asundered; ..." (FW 136.04-07). "Blowicks" is Bullock, a place near Dalkey. "Baxters" is a baker. Page 135 of the Wake seems to be preoccupied with two themes. On the one hand, there are political terms like "yldist kiosk" (Yildiz kiosk, the seat of Turkish government under Abdul Hamid the youngest); the Irish "wide cloak" (huge cloaked Daniel O' Connell killed D'Estere in a duel on the "fifteen acres" (FW 135.21 / U 09); and the English "White horse" (symbol of William III). These political allusions have received comment from all the critics of the Wake. The cultural allusions, especially to the Orient, seem to have remained unexplored.

The reference to the Nights in the above quotation is clear: "and lit thousands in one nightlights". The oriental perspective is further embellished by the phrase "a bird of Arabia" (FW 135.14) which according to McHugh, is the "phoenix." Moreover, the phrase "well of Artesia" (FW 135.15) is about the Phoenix Park, named after a corrupted Gaelic word for well or spring. The phrase "a part of the whole as a port for a whale" (FW 135.29-30) seems to be a pun on Sindbad's first voyage, in which he landed. More accurately — the island was a part of a whole "a port for a whale."

Commenting on the protean character of HCE, Rose and O' Hanlon say that he is "almost everything: he is at once man, mountain, myth, monster, tree, city, egg..."[9] From the "phoenix" to the "whale" and the larger-than-life image of HCE, the sense of wonder is constantly evoked. On the same page there is another reference to his pathetic condition during the journey, for he "crawls with lice, he swarms with saggarts; is as quiet as a mursque but can be noisy as a sonogog" (FW 135.36, 136.01). "Sonogog" and "mursque" are places of worship. Sindbad, when in full tune is expected to be a singer of "the song of sparrownotes on his stave of wires" (FW 135.35). Even "mursque" seems a pun on "mashriq", meaning East, which occurs frequently in the pages of the Quran. "Mursque" is also mosque.

Such a singer is, however, rejected curtly by the playing children before bedtime in the "playhouse" of chapter 9. The children put on various pantomimes such as "Aladdin", "Ali Baba" and "Sindbad." The story of Sindbad is inextricably woven into the structure of the chapter. Every time that Shem is asked to solve the

9   Danis Rose and John O' Hanlon, *Understanding Finnegans Wake*, 89.

riddle posed by Isabel, the former is faced with the dilemma of failure. Forced as punishment to quit their company, Shem goes into exile. For him, however, exile is not unproductive. On his return, we find him accompanied with a "jeeremy-head, sindbook (FW 229.32). It is a book of travels like the tales of Sindbad that he returns with. The phrase "jeeremyhead" of "sindbook" suggests the convulsion during which Shem's features flush, his eyes role and his tongue squirms. There are many references to sea voyages in these pages. For example, in "(osco de basco de pesco de bisco!)", (FW 230.06) "Osco" is "bravo!" and "pesco" is "fish", though it is also a pun on Vasco da Gama, the Portuguese navigator.

The next cluster of sea imagery is preceded by Glugg's repentance, in response to which Issy takes pity on him: "Isle wail for yews" (FW 232.13). A "butterfly" (FW 232.11) "escaping" from her "zipclasped handbag" zooms across to "cumbeck to errind". The phrase "cumbeck to errind" means come back to Ireland after being in exile, though Issy is signalling her readiness to wait till he can solve the riddle. This time also Glugg appears as a disguised sailor: "doubledasguesched" (FW 232.33) "in a simplasailormade" by "shaking the storm out of his" teacup or "hiccup" (FW 232.34-35). "A bran new, speedhount, outstripperous on the wind. Like a waft to wingweary one or sos to a coastguard." (FW 232.28-30) "Waft" and "wing weary" apply to voyagers and travellers, people who undertake the challenging tasks of discovery and adding to human knowledge. His peaceful return is described as "sin beau" (FW 233.05). Sindbad "may bring to light!" (FW 233.06) something which the "Angelinas," the dancing twenty-nine girls, may not know, as Sindbad (the epitome of Shem) warns Issy: "Though down to your dowerstrip he's bent to knee he maun't know ledgings here" (FW 233.06-07). In this paragraph, the conflict between Shem and Issy is brought into sharp focus. Shem, bottled up in an inkwell house, uses his own faeces, urine and skin as ink and parchment for writing the mystery of himself and the universe.

The reference to Sindbad in chapter 10 (FW 260-308) of the Wake further embellishes his role: "And he was a gay Lutharius anyway, Sinobiled. You can tell by their extraordinary clothes."[10] Besides being "Cronwall" (261.20), HCE is "Whiteman" (263.09), religious Eucharist — "Groupname for grape juice" (261.F.3) — but also "more mob than man" (FW 261.21-22) and, above all, one

---

10 Finnegans Wake, chapter 10, footnote: 263.

whose apparel is the "orb terrestrial" (263.28). It is under this "orb terrestrial" footnote that HCE is mentioned as "Sinobiled." HCE's mate, a "noughty..zeroine" (261.24), after combining with ten "zephiroth" (FW 29.13) as his number, sets in the dynamics of the multitudinous processes of potential nature. HCE is the phallus god who inseminates his "faithful Fluvia, following the wiening corses of this world" (FW 546.30-31) and, as Sindbad, "my sumbad" (FW 548.14), is content to provide his terrestrial apparel, the "wispywaspy frocks of redferns and lauralworths, trancepearances" (FW 548.24-5), at "little crither of my hearth" (FW 549.29) in Dublin "in trinity huts they met my dame" (FW 548.12-13) (at Trinity Church I Met My Doom) after sailing in faraway places and coasts ("coataways") of "constantonoble's" (FW 548.16) (the "Impress of Asias") (FW 548.02). "Frocks" is a connector to "skert" of "Skertsiraizde" (FW 32.07) or Shaharazad. In response, ALP mentions HCE as Sindbad: "Or somebalt thet sailder, the man megallant, with the bangled ears" (FW 620.07-08). On this page, her attitude is censorious, as she wants him to be divested of impurities ("lave it") and be as pure as an infant or a peeled twig. Finding him to fall short of this, satire becomes her weapon for she knows very well his ambition to "scale the summit," a project ending in smoke: "All your groundplotting and the little it brought!" (FW 624.12), which perhaps echoes Molly's reproachful attitude toward Bloom — "he ought to get a leather medal with a putty rim for all the plans he invents" (U 765 / 630). Finally, she acknowledges the real gap between her hopes and the reality itself: "I thought you were all glittering with the noblest of carriage. You're only a bumpkin. I thought you the great in all things, in guilt and in glory. You're but a puny" (FW 627.21-24). Like Bloom, HCE does not stick to any one profession: "first he was a skulksman at one time and then cloon's fire him through guff". ALP is utterly disillusioned about her husband: "He might knight you an Armor elsor doub you the first cheap magyerstrape...And I'll be your aural eyness. Be we vain. Plain fancies. It's in the castles air" (FW 623.14-19).

There is a reference in Book II, Chapter 1, of the Wake to Sindbad's South-East Asian voyage: "...and where fishngaman fetched the mongafesh from and whatfor paddybird notplease rancoon and why was Sindat sitthing on him sitbom like a saildior, with what the doc did in the doil,...That little cloud, a nibulissa, still hangs isky. Singabed sulks before slumber. Light at night has an alps on his druckhouse" (FW 256.26; 33-34). "Nga-man" is a sea monster and "nga" is a fish in Burmese.

"Doil" is Irish Legislative Assembly. However, "doc" may be interpreted as dock, say of the Rangoon river. "Crores" (in the same passage) is Anglo-Indian figure for 10,000,000 rupees. "Pice" (FW256.35) is an Indian copper coin.

The term "fishngaman" is fishermen; "mongafesh" is an Indian edible fish; "paddybird" is a bird that eats the unripe grain of the rice crop, "rancoon" is Rangoon, the capital of Burma; "Sindat" and "Singabed," according to McHugh are the names of Sindbad the "Saildior." In his South-East Asian itinerary, Sindbad is said to have come across regions where elephants ("sin" in Burmese) abound, rice is the staple food, and "mongafesh" is available in all the rivers that flow from the Himalayas. It should be added that Sindbad refers to the elephants in the seventh voyage in which he was to represent Caliph Harun al-Rashid as Consular at the courts of this region. This shows how the tales in the Nights are mutually interconnected around the person of Harun al-Rashid.

The next passage is about the gigantic overshadowing bird the size of a cloud, "a nibulissa, still hangs isky." On finding himself in utter darkness under the colossal wings of the bird "Singabad sulks before slumber." These allusions are preceded by the following sentences: "Home all go. Halome. Blare no more sams-blares! And cease your fumings, kindalled bushes!" In the context of Sindbad, the phrase "Home all go" marks an important occasion. In the first place, it indicates the end of his adventures abroad, as "he is weatherbitten from the dusts of ages?" (FW 255.06). Back at home, Sindbad is now capable of telling the tales based upon his awesome and terrifying experiences. For this, there is a readily devised listener whose name is also "Sindbad," a beggar sitting outside the palace of Sindbad. There are two references to the second Sindbad. The first has already been dis-cussed, while the second reference can be identified as "sack on back, alack!" (FW 428.19-22) in the following passage: "...as that goodship the Jonnyjoys takes the wind from waterloogged Erin's king, you will shiff across the Moylendsea and round up in your own escapology some canonisator's day or other, sack on back, alack!" (FW 428.19-22). "Jonnyjoys," according to McHugh, was a pleasure steam-er sailing from Dun Laoghaire. "Moylendsea" is the sea that separates Ireland from Scotland. "Erin's king" was the name of a pleasure steamer. The phrase "sack on back, alack!" has not been identified by critics; but it occurs in the context of sea imagery, and there is another reference to Sindbad "Tina-bat-Talur" (meaning a

tiny Sindbad, bat) marrying the Catholic tailor's daughter (as did the Norwegian captain discussed earlier), hence the phrase evidently corresponds to the Nights' Sindbad the Landsman. Sindbad the sailor and Sindbad the landsman are thus two aspects of the same identity, a theme constantly recurring in the Wake: "tumulous under his chthonic exterior but plain Mr Tumulty in multilife" (FW 261.18-19). Thus Kimberly J. Devlin describes the different personae of Earwicker, "one of which assumes the implanted proportion of a god (chthonian: dwelling under-ground), the other appearing in a more realistic apparel the dimension of a plain man in mufti."[11] As ALP says of her husband: "Hence we've lived in two worlds. He is another he what stays under the himp of holth" (FW 619.11-12). Like HCE, Sindbad is many things; a merger of sailor and tailor, both further multiplied by "Tinker, tailor, soldier, sailor." In the Notebook (VI.B.I), Joyce mentions two Sindbads: "there are two Sindbads (U-Ps agg. L B. BMW): Wandering of Jews, he returns after each voyage, always recovers the 7th lost in 6th (s 157), So Murphy's other favourite book, the Arabian Nights Entertainment...Sindbad sailor before he sails: touching a drink: peerless Punchestown: huge joy: correspondences (fish isle: Eolus: fucking sea stallion: Oxen of sun: black ogre: cyclops: cannibals: Laestrygonians: chang: Lotuseaters: vivisepulture Hades: slaughter of roc: Oxen of sun:" (p.208).

In the Wake, Joyce inserts almost all of these references derived from the Odyssey: "Ukalepe" is the one "who is well-hidden," nymph with whom Odysseus had spent several years and who had born him a son. "Kalpe" in Greek is "pitch-er," like the topography of Gibraltar or the home of "Kalypso." "Loathers Leave" (FW 229.13) are the "Lotus-eaters," the African tribe famous for their hospitality whom Odysseus had visited (a similar version is linked with Sindbad though not as unambiguously). "Had days" is the "Unseen" Lord of the underworld. "Nemo" is Latin for "No one," the name by which Odysseus introduces himself as Aiolos (god of the winds). "The Luncher Out" is the savage Laestrygonians encountered by Odysseus. "Skilly and Carubdish" are Scylla, the rocks personified as a sea monster, and Charybdis, the dangerous whirlpool. According to Michael Seidel, "Scylla" is from the Semitic "skeula" meaning "rock."[12] The identity of Sindbad the

---

11 Kimberly J. Devlin, Wandering and Return in Finnegans Wake, 65.

12 Michael Seidel, Epic Geography of James Joyce's Ulysses (Princeton: Princeton University Press, 1976), 114. Seidel explains "Scylla" as meaning "rock" in Arabic, ranging from Molly's Gibraltar to

sailor is thus assimilated into numerous forms as he is not only Sindbad the sea-man but also Sindbad the landsman, Murphy and the Norwegian Captain, and above all Odysseus.

Two Other Tall Tales:

At least two additional tales from the Nights are notable: both not only being mentioned in the Wake but also bearing specific similarities with Joyce's work. The first is the Tale of the "sleeper awakened" or Abul Hassan. This title occurs in the ricorso, Book IV of the Wake. As the darkness of HCE's night begins to wear out and the signs of another dawn appear, we find the cosmic dreamer stirring up out of the fevered delusive "maya" ("... resty fever, risy fever,...") (FW 597.27) in his bed to begin another eon.

Both Clive Hart and Robert G. Hampson cite the phrase "sleeper awakening" as having been taken by Joyce from the Arabian Nights.[13] They believe the phrase to allude to two different tales, "Abul Hassan, The Sleeper Awakening" and "The Two Lives of Sultan Mahmud," both of which hinge on oscillation between one world and another, between dream and wakefulness: "...all-a-dreams perhapsing under lucksloop at last are through...It is a sot of a swigswag, systomy dystomy..." (FW 597.20). Like the to- and fro- motion of a swing, the difference between the state of being asleep and being awake according to the Hindu "Shavarsanjivana" (FW 597.19) is but the contraction and expansion of breathing.

The tale "The Two Lives of Sultan Mahmud" does not appear in the Arabian Nights as translated by Richard Burton. It is, however, Hampson states, part of the Nights as translated by Mardrus (vol.13. ref.1). It was first translated into English under the title "The History of Chec Chehabeddin" in the Turkish Tales published in 1708. The tale was further embellished and modified by Addison (The Spectator, no.94, 18 June 1711). It subsequently appears in C.R. Maturin's Melmoth the Wanderer, (vol.11 ch.8); Dickens's Hard Times, (Book II, ch.1); Elizabeth Gaskell's North and South (1, ch.3); and Zimmer's Maya: Der indische Mythos (Berlin, 1936). Joyce might have read it in Zimmer's book, which was in

---

Sindbad's 'roc's auc's egg' (U.737).

13 Clive Hart, Structure and Motif in Finnegans Wake, 104-8 and Robert G. Hampson, "The Genie out of the bottle" in The Arabian Nights in English Literature, ed. Peter L. Caracciolo, 234.

his library, especially as the date of composition of Book IV, in which this reference occurs, is given by Walton Litz[14] as 1938. Zimmer describes the tale in the chapter "Vischnus Maya," in which he elaborates the theme of the cosmic nature of creation in terms of the expansions and contractions of Vishnu's state of sleep or being awake.

According to Peter L. Caracciolo, the other title, "Abul Hassan, The Sleeper Awakening," is first referred to by Sir Walter Scott in The Antiquary. Moreover, Caracciolo cites Wilkie Collins as an admirer of this tale's "double consciousness" poised between illusion and frustration.[15] On the psychological level, Joyce found in these tales an imagination enriched by subsuming the states of being asleep and that of dreaming. In the Wake, the dreams are developed into a potential chain of tales within tales, broken at random into pieces which require an ingenious subtlety in order to knit together the seams of the fabric; as Stuart Gilbert quotes Joyce as saying:

> I was looking at a Turk seated in a bazaar. He had a framework on his knees and on one side he had a jumble of all shades of red and yellow skeins and on the other a jumble of greens and blues of all shades. He was picking from right and left very calmly and weaving away.[16]

In the Arabian Nights, numerous anecdotes present kings, queens, princes and princesses, viziers, afrits and people from all walks of life sleeping and dreaming. In these stories, the unconscious pours and swamps the conscious self. The humble

14 A. Walton Litz, The Art of James Joyce: Method and Design in Ulysses and Finnegans Wake, (Oxford: Oxford University Press, 1964), 149. (See also Clive Hart, Structure and Motif in Finnegans Wake, 104-8).

15 Peter L. Caracciolo, ed., The Arabian Nights in English Literature, 45, 163. Robert G. Hampson shows that the following passage of Ulysses was taken from either "The Two Lives of Sultan Mahmud" (Mardrus: The Arabian Nights) or "The History of Chec Chahabeddin" from The Turkish Tales (1708) or from Heinrich Zimmer's Maya. Der Indische Mythos (Berlin 1936):"The Lord Herry put his head into a cow's drinking trough in the presence of all his courtiers and pulling it out again told them all his new name" (U 328). Hampson also endorses Hart's opinion that Abu al-Hassan is an avatar of his father, like Shaun of HCE. Abu al-Hassan's spendthrift, careless ways contrast with the industriousness of his merchant father in the tale. Abu's mock death and his speech from under his shroud prefigure Finnegan's revival and his outburst from his bier, while Abu's "oscillation from one world to another" parallels the spatial oscillation of Finnegans Wake.

16 The Letters of James Joyce, ed. Stuart Gilbert, (New York: Viking Press, 1957), 251.

"Sleeper Awakening," Abul Hassan, having squandered his father's property, is standing listless and frustrated on the banks of the Tigris when Caliph Harun al-Rashid passes by. The Caliph discovers the cause of his grief and is astounded to learn about Abul Hassan's dream of becoming caliph of Baghdad, at least for one day. Abul Hassan is taken to the palace, is drugged to sleep and, on his awakening, is amazed to find twenty-eight girls at his beck and call, ready to satisfy his lust and other desires: "several successivecoloured serebanmaods on the same being white drawingroams horthrug" (FW 126.19). Shaun, in "The Mime of Mick, Nick and Maggies" (FW 219-59), is encircled by the heliotropic girls in the same manner. The royal palace in which Abul Hassan is kept as pseudo-caliph consists of a pavilion decked out in "gold" and "ultramarine," with roof of red gold, curtains of embroidered silk, vessels of gold, chinaware, crystal, furniture and carpets of finest quality — a palace more elegant and impressive than that of the Caliph himself. "By Allah," proclaims Abul Hassan on awakening in this wonderland, "either I am dreaming or this is paradise." Soon he realizes, however, that he is in a real world, with grandees, courtiers, mamluks, attendants and other retinue to reassure him with thousand fold homage and allegiance. As the busy day ends, he is escorted to the four halls to rest and amuse himself, accompanied by seven rainbow girls for each of the luxurious, splendid mansions. This heavenly delight vanishes, when he is once more drugged and taken back to his true home. He returns to consciousness in the dark of his true home, but still he craves the slave girls of his dreams. His loud complaining fills his mother with perplexity and alarm, and eventually he is taken off to a madhouse.

The next time that Abul Hassan meets the Caliph on the bridge, after his release from the asylum, the Caliph plays the same trick on him as before. Once again he is drugged with Hashish and finds himself surrounded by twenty-eight girls and issuing royal decrees. Then suddenly he starts on his mad behaviour once more, throwing the bed coverings one way and the cushions another, casting his nightcap into the air, leaping from the bed, tearing off his clothes and throwing himself amongst the girls; jumping, twisting, contorting and shaking his belly, all in a storm of laughter which grows as the scales begin to fall from his eyes. But finally the generous Caliph showers him with bounties, giving him a palace and a slave-girl.

The second part of the story is an ironic reversal of fortunes, for now it is the turn of Abul Hassan and his wife Nuzhatul Fuad to hoax the Caliph. Abul Hassan devises a plan, more imaginative than that of the Caliph, whereby Nuzatul Fuad makes it known to the Queen that her husband is dead, while Abul Hassan tells the Caliph that his wife is dead. When the Queen and the Caliph meet in the evening, they fall out squabbling. Just as Abul Hassan scandalised his mother, so the Caliph calls his Queen an imbecile. Finally, they resolve the issue by sending one Masrur, who reports back that indeed Abul Hassan has died.

The Queen refuses to accept this and she in turn sends a maidservant, who reports back that it is Abul Hassan's wife who has died. The Caliph and the rest of the court decide to go and see the truth for themselves. They find that both are dead, lying corpse-like side by side on the bed. Even this does not solve the mystery. Harun al-Rashid, refusing to be in the wrong, starts arguing as to which of the two died first and swears to pay a thousand dinars to the one who first tells him the truth. Abul Hassan, who has waited impatiently for so long to hear something like this, springs up, declaring, "I died first, O Commander of the faithful! Now give me the thousand dinars in fulfilment of your solemn oath!" (Burton's translation, Vol.III, p.487). According to Hampson, Abul Hassan's sudden and agile springing up is like HCE's coming alive from his death-bed in Book 1 of the Wake: "He's duddandgunne now" (FW 25.23).[17]

In this story, the Caliph remains disguised from the start until Abul Hassan"s fantasies have worn off in the palace. Abul Hassan in return entertains the strangers only in his house. When they meet for the first time, the Caliph asks him: "O youth, how art thou?" Abul Hassan makes the Caliph understand his circumstances by relating an anecdote.

In a second tale, "The Tale of the Hunchback," there are strong suggestions of at least one aspect of HCE's character. Like "The Sleeper Awakening," "The Tale of the Hunchback" tells of people not actually dead, but feigning to be dead, in the way that Earwicker is found to be asleep most of the time. A tailor who loved "pleasuring and merry-making" in the words of Burton's translation was returning, accompanied by his wife, when they met a hunchback "whose semblance

---

17 Robert G. Hampson "The Genie out of the Bottle: Conrad, Wells and Joyce" in The Arabian Nights in English Literature ed., Peter L. Caracciolo (234).

would draw a laugh from care and dispel the horrors of despair." They invited him to accompany them and enjoy their hospitality. During the meal, the tailor's wife put a great piece of fish in the hunchback's mouth and, closing his mouth with her hand, said, "By Allah, thou must down it in a single gulp; and I wouldn't give the time to chew it." For the sake of his honour, the hunchback swallowed it, but a fish-bone stuck in his gullet and he died on the spot.

Filled with grief and fear, they mourned the dead man and at the same time devised an ingenious plan to dispose of the corpse. Pretending the corpse was that of a child, they wrapped it and took it to a Jewish doctor late at night, paying the servant a bribe. The doctor came out of his house in order to examine the corpse and, as he was coming down the steps, his feet struck blindly against it. As he looked at the corpse, he was not only filled with grief but also convinced himself that he had been the cause of its death. "O Ezra!," he exclaimed in dismay, "O Heaven and the ten commandments! O Auroun and Joshua son of Nun! It seemeth that I have stumbled against this sick person, and he hath fallen down the stairs and died." His wife learnt about it and, after bewailing the death a little, they devised a stratagem by which the corpse was to be thrown into the garden of a Moslem steward of the Caliph, their neighbour. When the steward saw the corpse he mistook it for a thief and started beating it. Finding the supposed thief to be dead, he believed himself to be the killer. He hastily dragged the corpse away, and left it in the street.

Next a Christian broker, drunk as a lord, fell to fighting with it. When he was caught red-handed by the night watchman at a street corner, he was assumed to be the culprit and was sentenced to death. At the time of execution, to the astonishment of all, each of the supposed culprits, conscience-torn, appeared from among those assembled, one after another. The Caliph asked them to tell a tale surpassing any told by the king's dead entertainer, the hunchback. To each his judgement was: "This story is not more amusing than the story of the Hunchback. And so you shall have to hang, all of you" (vol.1, p.318, 330, 343).

The character of the Hunchback corresponds in many respects with that of HCE. Rose and O'Hanlon, for example, allude to the ballad of Tim Finnegan, which describes the death and resurrection of HCE:

One morning Tim was rather full,
His head felt heavy, which made him shake;
He fell from his ladder and broke his skull,
So they carried him home his corpse to awake.[18]

A laughable incident presented in a humorous style, the tale initiates a chain of stories following the accidental death of the hunchback like that of Tim Finnegan: "one thousand and one stories, all told" (FW 5.28-29). Joyce refers to the motivation of these inserted tales in the "Sisters" section of his Scribbledehobble Notebook: "desperate storytelling, one caps on another...1001 Nights, Decameron, Interpreters = at point of death" (p.25). Furthermore, the section entitled "An Encounter" in the Workbook begins with "Barber's story (1001 N) self and onanism: on booby trap" (p37). The "booby trap" is a chain of tricks used against the barber's eldest brother, the hunchback. The barber's brother is thus victimized all night; for this Joyce uses the phrase "millwheeling vicociclometer" (FW 614.27) or, as he writes in his Notebook "An Encouner whose mind was slowly circling round and round in the orbit" (p.29), like Patrick Morkan's horse walking round and round "king Billy's statue" in "The Dead" (p.258). There are additional parallels between the Wake and "The Tale of the Hunchback." Characters from different walks of life are collected under the theme of death and resurrection in the tale. A single tale covers almost the entire framework of society from the common people to the Caliph. Furthermore, the story incorporates characters from different religions living in a cosmopolitan city.

The tale's ambiguous geographical location is another interesting aspect. Burton, for example, states that it originated "in a certain city of China," and, alluding to other versions, he conjectures that it might have been written in "Bassorah" or even "at Bassorah and Kajar," which is "somewhat like in Dover and Sebastopol" (Nights, vol.1, p.234).

"The Tale of the Hunchback" is also about the transmission of guilt. One person's death involves the entire community in its vicious circle of sinfulness.

---

18 Danis Rose and John O'Hanlon, Understanding Finnegans Wake, 05-06. See also Jane S. Meehan in "Tim Finnegan's Wake" AWN, Vol.XIII, No.4, August 1976, (69-73) for the history of the ballad.

Similarly, HCE is the focal point of primordial guilt; as Margot Norris explains, the Wake attempts "to plumb the conflict of the individual, confronted by primordial guilt, who is tempted to deny and confess, to evade and embrace responsibility for an involuntary, non-volitional sin."[19] His is an insoluble guilt precisely because the question of guilt is "circulatory," she maintains. There are more entries in the Scribbledhobble Notebook suggestive of Joyce's knowledge of "The Hunchback's Tale." Joyce notes "cabbaging...(tailor steals cloth) pejorative" (p.175). Another note on "The Barber's Tale of his First Brother" reads: "The tailor in the East, as in southern Europe, is made to cut out the cloth in the presence of its owner to prevent cabbaging" (Nights, Vol.1, .296).

Finally, the deathbed scene in "The Tale of the Hunchback" is a regression like Shaun's travelling backwards, as Joyce pointed out in a letter: "Shaun (sic)...is a description of a postman travelling backwards in the night through the events already narrated. It is written in the form of a via crucis of fourteen sections but in reality it is only a barrel rolling down the river Liffey" (Letters, Voll.1, p.214). Such a travelling backwards applies to the pseudo-murderers of "The Tale of the Hunchback." Once the final culprit, the drunk Christian, is to be hanged, there occurs a strange and comical reversal whereby the supposedly guilty ones come forward, annoying and even astonishing the hangman. The moral note remains paramount, though. Each tale ends with "evil" punished, good reasserted and the characters enobled through self-confession.

꩜

---

19 Margot Norris, The Decentred Universe of Finnegans Wake, (Baltimore: John Hopkins University Press, 1976), 39.

PART II

Joyce's Use of the Indic Canon

5.

Sandhyas and its Implications

Book IV of the Wake opens with the proclamation of "Sandhyas! Sandhyas! Sandhyas!" (FW 593.01). The dreamer is letting the world know of the birth of another day. "Sandhyas" provides the medium for his utterance. HCE's first signal is also his last, and as a clue to "Sandhyas" Joyce discloses scores of Indian words in Book IV. Clive Hart terms this phenomenon of the Wake as the "leitmotiv,"[1] and David Hayman explains that by concentrating on a certain word as the "prime node," HCE elicits a "certain act, activity, personal trait, allusion, theme, etc."[2] The "prime node" serves as the generating centre from which spring the Wake's paraphernalia of description, expansion and exhaustive elaboration. Thus, the Indic canon appears as an essential part of the structure of Finnegans Wake.

Most probably we can say that the dreamer HCE is poised between the two worlds, dreaming of the world to come from the recesses of the fast receding night but unable to escape unscathed as his previous incarnations are already sullied with the taint of sin. This momentary unity between "contemplation and desire," the point of intercession between "the sign Aries" and "the solar east of the Great Year"[3] where all contraries interpenetrate in the substratum—is known to the Hindus as Sandhyas with which Book IV begins.

---

1   Clive Hart, Structure and Motif in Finnegans Wake, 165. "Real leitmotiv" Hart explains "entails a use of statement and restatement in such a way as to impel the reader to relate part to part; each recurrence of such a motif derives in some necessary way from all its previous appearances and leads on to future resurgence, pointing to correspondences and relationships far beyond those that hold between the individual motif and its immediate context."

2   David Hayman, "Nodality and the Infra-Structure of Finnegans Wake," JJQ 16 (Fall 1978 / Winter 1979), 136.

3   Kathleen Raine, Yeats the Initiate: Essays on certain themes in the works of W.B. Yeats, (the Dolmen Press, Mountrath, Ireland; London: George Allen and Unwin Limited, 1986, p.165).

Defining "Sandhyas," a Sanskrit term, McHugh quotes Madame Blavatsky [a probable source for Joyce in this respect] as saying "a sandhi or the time when day and night border on each other, morning and evening twilight." Clive Hart adds to the Blavatskyan concept of "sandhyas" as the realm of space "filled with strange beings" by pointing out these "beings" in Book IV of the Wake: "horned...Cur... beast..Dane the Great snout ... bylegs ... chuckal ... ... cur..noxe..Gallus... ducksrun.. gazelle..."[4] There will be room for more on Blavatsky's implications of Joyce's use of Indic canon shortly. B.P. Misra looks at this term as a "Junction": "When the opposites come together. Europe and India, empirical knowledge and intuitive wisdom, are now one."[5] The point of interfusion between India and Europe is indicated in the Wake as "In that european end meets Ind" (FW 598.15). Endorsing Misra's opinion, W.Y. Tindall attributes traditional mysticism to India and rationalism to Europe. His Indian representative is St Patrick and Bishop Berkeley stands for Europe.[6] By lighting the paschal fire on the hill at Slane in contravention to King Ardri's prohibition, St Patrick was igniting the Christian light of a revealed religion in the darkness of paganism and bringing about spiritual awakening in Ireland. Darkness, here, implies the subjective and light, the objective manifestation of reality. This act, according to Berkeley, is movement from abnormal to normal acquisition of vision by the blind man.[7] A blind man, on acquiring the faculty of sight suddenly and for the first time, would have difficulty in establishing a normal relation between his previous sensation of touch and the experience of vision. Conversely, a normal man would consider the objects perceived by his eyes and the impressions gathered by his sense of touch as natural manifestations of the same object. For a blind man, a period of learning is inevitable before regaining or associating the visual impressions with particular perceptions of touch.

Berkeley believes in the subjectivity of visual impressions, as they exist within the mind itself with no latent connection with the external, objective aspect of

---

4   Clive Hart, Structure and Motif in Finnegans Wake, 53. Referring to Frank Budgen, Hart says that the latter had assured him of Book IV's emphasis on "forgetfulness." About Anna's emotional indifference, Hart opines that "Anna, as she passes to her cold, mad father, is losing all remembrance of her past joys and sorrows" in this Book.

5   B.P. Misra, "Sanskrit Translations," AWN, vol. 1.6, August., 1964, 9.

6   W.Y. Tindall, A Reader's Guide to Finnegans Wake (New York: Thames and Hudson, 1959), 317, 319, 320.

7   George Berkeley, An Essay towards a New Theory of Vision, (Jeremy Pepyat: Dublin), 1709, para. 49.

reality. The organ of touch is a tangible objective factor.[8] Apparently, the objective and subjective, the visual and tangible do not coalesce, yet once the blind man develops the capacity of reasoning that a certain set of visual sensations always accompany particular sensations of touch, he begins to predict the future with the help of his vision. By vision is meant the simultaneous operation of the visual and the tangible. For Stephen on the Sandymount shore in "Proteus," visual objects look like the "coloured signs" which are his subjective impressions, "thought through my eyes, at least that if no more" (U 3, 12).

Like Berkeley's blind man, Stephen closes his eyes and fears to stumble over a cliff: "If I fell over a cliff that beetles o'er his base" (U 3, 14-15). Yet, he hears the voice of the rhythmic crushing of his boots producing sounds: "Sounds ...Rhythm begins, you see. I hear" (U 3, 16-24). Despite his closing of the eyes, the objective reality cannot be escaped. Rather, it arouses his vision of diaphane and omphalos. This coexistence of the subjective and the objective can be observed in the "Patrick and the Druid" section of Book IV of the Wake. St. Patrick sees light as a language of solid exterior sense, a foreboding like Stephen's composing of his poem — "signs on a white field": "Who watches me here? Who ever anywhere will read these written words? Signs on a white field. Somewhere to someone in your flutiest voice" (U 40). He foretells of the rising sun "the sound sense sympol in a weedwayedwold of the firethere the sun in his halo cast" (FW 612.29-30).

In terms of Berkeley, the statement shows the splitting of vision into two component parts, the visual and the tangible — both coalescing into the language or signs of nature. These signs evolve out of darkness, the lighting of a fire in the case of St. Patrick and the emergence of the sun according to Hinduism. "Ind" is the mystic India as an end toward which the rationalistic European "ear" must "opean" or open for light (FW 71.07, 143.24, 156.03, 313.20).

The term "ind" also has other connotations. The "ind" (FW 71.07) here applies to the end of the rejoicing of the Fian ladies "foinne loidies" probably the two girls tempting HCE. The next use of "ind" (FW 143.24) is about the end of the night and the emergence of a new dawn with rainbow spread on the sky. Here HCE is the "earsighted" Shaun enjoying the "panaroma" of "collideoorscaps." He is in a state of trance staring in the mirror and hence at himself like Narcissus. It may be

8   Ibid., para.50.

added that the use of "ind" (FW 71.07) and (FW 143.02) in both contexts, relates to the warfare: Waterloo, Balakalava and Clontarf in the former and the Saxon invasion of England "Heng's got a bit of Horsa's nose" (FW 143.22) in the latter. The son of Noah Shem, Ham and Japhet are also referred to. Moreover, the "penci walls and the ind" (FW156.03) is Papal Mookse's "Niklaus Alopsius" (FW 155.31) pleading the case of St. Malachy on the conflict between the Monophysites and the Orthodox. The "ind" also is the end of the Punic Wars. The "ind" (FW 313.20) is Danish for "in." Kersse-Earwicker is asked to come in to prepare a drink for the twelve judges while they as they get ready for a hearing against him "pushed their whisper in his hairing" (FW 313.07) on his "misshapes." "Ind" also is a pun on Indra, who, appears as one of the colours of the rainbow "and the beau that spun beautiful pales out the ind of it! Violet's dyed! then what would that far gazer seem to seemself to seem seeming of, dimm it all?" (FW 143.22-24).

In addition to the mystic and the rationalistic, the eastern and western systems of the definition of "Sandhyas" as reconciliation of the visual and the tangible, Anthony Burgess (like Campbell and Robinson) looks at this term as denoting the different times of prayer in Hinduism during the day: "at dawn, at noon, at sunset, at midnight."[9] These critics must have taken this quotation from the 11th edition of Encyclopaedia Britannica (in Joyce's library at Trieste) which, under the heading "Hinduism" states "Sandhyas" to be "a commemorative rite" for the deceased souls:

> Moreover, a simple libation of water should be offered to the Fathers twice daily at the morning and evening devotion called sandhya ("twilight"). It is doubtless a sense of filial obligation coupled with sentiments of piety and reverence that gave rise to this practice of offering gifts of food and drink to the deceased ancestors...one also meets with frank avowals of superstitious fear lest any irregularity in the performance of the obsequial rites should cause the Fathers to haunt their old home and trouble the peace of their undutiful descendant, or even prematurely draw him after them to the Pitri-Loka or world of the Fathers, supposed to be located in the southern region.[10]

---

9   Anthony Burgess, Here Comes Everybody: An Introduction to Joyce for the Ordinary Reader, (London: Faber and Faber, 1965), 258. Comparing Sandhyas with Eliot's "threefold use of the prayer word Shantih" in The Waste Land, Burgess insists that the former symbolises the impregnation of time "with change." The latter is a "word of peace" denoting the aftermath of the trials of "karma". See also Joseph Campbell and Henry Morton Robinson, A Skeleton Key to Finnegans Wake, 278.

10 Encyclopaedia Britannica, (11th edition), (Vol.24, 178).

This statement conjures up the superstitions attached to the deceased in the West. Sandhyas as a prayer in the morning and in the evening for the dead, reflects respect and commitment to the acceptance of death and to the prospect of joining one's ancestors in the same graveyard. Since morning and evening commemorate the manifest signs of changes in the diurnal systems of nature, the prayers at these times reaffirm the acceptance of God's authority: "(its architecht, Mgr Peurelachasse, having been obcaecated lest he should petrifake suchanevver while the contractors Messrs T.A. Birkett and L.O. Tuohalls were made invulnerably venerable)" (FW 76.36, 77.01-03). HCE is quite satisfied for the moment that his sons are "venerable" in their "obsequial rites" as E.P. Walkiewicz comments.[11] The above quotation could also be interpreted as a satirical remark soaked in irony. The "Messrs T.A. Birkett" (Thomas Becket) "and L..O. Tuohalls" (Laurence O'Toole) are presented as contractors whose profession is bargaining. Such an occupation weighs morality as a commodity irrespective of true reverence. The deceased HCE is obfuscated and petrified forever, the sons are self-complaisant. On the contrary, HCE is meant to emerge endlessly as a protean force. Now, if we consider "Sandhyas" as the "commemorative rite" and apply it to Book IV, even then the result is the same. The emergence of light from darkness as "Sandhyas," according to Hinduism, does not imply the beginning of an era of peace and prosperity, rather every dawn is steeped further in the chaos of "kali yoga" (Notebook VI.11, 12, 13, 14, 17, 18, p.226) which is our age.

Under the entry "Sanskrit", the Encyclopaedia Britannica (11th edition), glosses one of the four grammatical aspects of the Sanskrit language as "rules of euphony (sandhi)." "Sandhyas" has also been defined by Arthur A. MacDonell who is referred to in the list of its sources for the Britannica as Walkiewicz quotes. According to MacDonell, the term "Sandhyas" signifies "the phonetic combinations...between the finals and initials of words in the Sanskrit sentence." The modest stress on the repetitive proclamations of "Sandhyas! Sandhyas! Sandhyas!" consists of two syllables, of which the syllable "Dhyas" sounds like Eliot's "Da!" in The Waste Land; Joyce uses this strange Hindu thunder epithet in the Notebook (VI. C. 1, 2, 3, 4, 5, 6, 7, p.282). If "Da!" in The Waste Land represents the voice of

11 E.P.Walkiewicz,"Sandhyas," AWN,Vol. XVII, No.6 (Dec. 1980), 101. See also Arthur A. MacDonell's *A History of Sanskrit Literature*, (London: William Heinmann, 1905), 21. (See also Narendra Nath Bhattacharyya, The Mother Goddess, Columbia, Missouri: South Asia Books, 1977.,107.)

the Hindu god as thunder and the rain of fertility, peace and prosperity, then by the same token "dhyas" should be read as a divine proclamation at the break of day in the Wake.

Finally, "Sandhyas" parodied as "shan't we, shan't we, shan't we" (Letters, vol.1, p.231), is also a mystic mantra of "Shantih," a hymn murmured by devout Hindus at the end of prayers or, as Eliot states the "formal ending to Upanishad":[12] "Upanishadem!" (FW 303.13). "Shanti, Shanti, Shanti amused Joyce"[13] says Tindall, referring to Joyce's Letters (vol.1, p.231) Tindall, and Campbell and Robinson also identify the repeated use of "Sandhyas" as a pun upon the "Sanctus, Sanctus, Sanctus" of the Catholic mass. Moreover, the term resonates the name of "Shaun." "Sandhyas" political manifestations are phrases like "Svadesia salve!" (FW 594.04) and "Sonne feine" (FW 593.08) which identify its colonial implications in India and in Europe. Its political dimension[14] has been rather overlooked in comparison with its mystic and metaphysical implications.

"Sandhyas" then is a word of manifold meanings. If, on the one hand it indicates the mysterious force poised between darkness and light then it also alludes to the political movements working simultaneously (in Ireland and India for example) against the Pax Britannica. At another level "Sandhyas" is the recurrent anastomosis of penetrative shades of light and darkness through the sun's diurnal journey. Above all, "Sandhyas" is the intertwined dichotomous reality of what Sheldon Brivic describes as the left and right lobes of the brain subdivided into the mystic versus rationalistic categories.[15] Poised between them is the state of mediating differentiation, allowing the reasoning mind to draw meaning out of the infinite treasures of infinity. Since Clive Hart (in addition to Boldereff) suggests that Joyce

---

12 T.S. Eliot, On Poetry and Poets, (London: Faber and Faber), 25.

13 W.Y. Tindall, A Reader's Guide to Finnegans Wake, 329. According to Tindall, the epithet "shanti" is naturally preceded by thunder. Joyce inserts this as "Dah!" (FW 594.02) or he means the same when he reverses the order of the letters as "Had".

14 The political dimension of Sandhyas derives from the "Swadeshi Movement" (Joyce's "Svadesia salve!" (FW 594.4). This movement was launched by the Hindu leadership against the division of Bengal planned by the British rulers of India. Since the British government refused to back down, the Hindus took to the streets. Soon Hindus all over India were demanding unified action against the British and the Moslems, and a movement for self-determination was launched by which everything foreign was to be boycotted in favour of home-spun cloth and home-made ammunition. Besides the Indic resonance, the phrase also points to the Irish struggle for independence as "Self-rule Save!" or "Salvation in Self Rule."

15 Sheldon Brivic, Joyce The Creator, (Madison: University of Wisconian Press, 1985), 3-24.

obtained his ideas of the cyclic motion of reality from Yeats's A Vision and Blake's The Mental Traveller, it should be added that even these literary figures (Blake and Yeats) were attempting to apply a universal concept enshrined in the idea of "Sandhyas." The East-West mutual interposition can also be understood if we take the Wake's "Sankya" (FW 60.19) as echoing "Sandhyas."

As Walkiewicz states,[16] "Sandhyas" then is a version of the Hindu metaphysical system of Sankhya which Joyce must have read about in the Britannica under the heading "Sanskrit." According to this system, the creation of the universe (as stated in the Britannica) is based on the First Material Cause which in itself is beyond the cognition of the human mind. However, it has developed with the passage of time into the actual "forms of the phenomenal universe, excepting the souls...To account for the spontaneous development of matter, the system assumes the latter to consist of three constituents (gunas) which are possessed of different qualities, viz "sattva", of pleasing qualities, such as "goodness," lightness, luminosity; "rajas," of pain-giving qualities, such as "darkness," rigidity, dullness, and which, if not in a state of equipoise, cause unrest and development" (vol.24, p.178). "Gunas," "sattvas" and "rajas" are three states of matter developing into a spiral like Yeats's gyres. Matter allows what Eliot calls a "spontaneous apprehension of thought or a recreation of thought into feeling."[17] Between the seeker and the sought there develops a pari-passu so that both are now constituents of the same process.

Joyce's utilization of the Hindu "Sandhyas" is directly relevant to the myth of human creation. The Hindu story of Creation in the works of Joyce has been variously interpreted. Clive Hart, for example, correlates the cyclic patterns of metaphysical reality according to Vico and Hinduism in the Wake.[18] Joseph Campbell

---

16 E.P.Walkiewicz, "Sandhyas" AWN, vol.XVII, No.6, (Dec.1980), 101 102.
    Commenting on the Wake's structure, Frances Motz Boldereff says that it "has no beginning nor end, is not a story, nor a novel, but an elaborate symbol, based on A Vision of William Butler Yeats." (continued: Note 32)

17 T.S. Eliot, Selected Essays, (London: Faber and Faber, 1917-32), 246.

18 In the Wake, Joyce observes the structure of life from birth to death: Birth in Book I, Marriage in Book II, Death in Book III, and the ricorso in Book IV, a system for which he is indebted to Vico. This three-plus-one pattern observed by Clive Hart is supplemented by the "Lesser Cycles," as each Book contains its own cycles based upon individual chapters. This structure is evident also within the individual chapters, which are subdivided into sections, and the sections

examines the Hindu story of Creation in relation to the hypothesis propounded by Heinrich Zimmer. Hart and Fritz Senn discover a close affinity between the structure of Finnegans Wake and the concept of the cosmic, historical cycles in Hinduism and in Vico. Hart follows Stuart Gilbert in this respect. Campbell, on the other hand, lays bare the mythic background of the Hindu genesis in the Wake. Campbell relies mainly upon the religious books of Hinduism and the psychic implications of Hindu mythology. Both Hart and Campbell have drawn heavily from the theosophical works of H. P. Blavatsky, though the former finds fault with her synthesis of the Eastern and Western, and ancient and modern systems of religious faith.

Joyce's interest in the theosophical doctrine of Blavatsky is well documented. In the Notebook, (VI.C, p.255), Joyce, after defining "Theosophy" as "to sense the universal love" mentions "our beloved H.P.B." For Joyce's knowledge of Indian archaic ontology, therefore, Madame Blavatsky is undoubtedly one of the major sources.

---

into paragraphs. Sometimes even a single sentence contains the cyclic structure, and sometimes even occasional single words. In this way, the three-plus-one structure is widened into the "four-plus-one quasi-Indian" pattern. Each of these lesser cycles symbolises one element out of four: fire, air, water or earth. The interesting thing about Book IV, as Clive Hart points out, is that it is the "hub" around which the three other Books revolve. In other words, Book IV contains the gist and, as mandala, it draws the circular order around the dark chaos of "Prakrati" (Notebook VI.C.7 p.255). It begins with the dawn of life and ends with the mergence of ALP in the ocean of infinity like the epigraph of The Secret Doctrine (volume III), "The end is omniscience." Furthermore, Hart attaches great importance to the relation of Sandhyas to the mystical Dark Hawks of the Heaven-Tree. The "Heaven Tree" (FW 215.36) is the tenth Celestial Sphere, in which the spirit is fused with matter.

In The Myth of the Eternal Return: (translated from the French by Willard R. Trask, London: Routledge and Kegan Paul, 1955, 88-89) Mercia Eliade traces the historical background of the cyclical view of history back to the Chaldean doctrine of the "Great Year," which influenced the Hellenic world, the Romans and the Byzantines. This doctrine holds that the universe remains eternal but suffers periodic destruction and renewals, whose duration varies from culture to culture. According to the Chaldeans, the congregation of seven planets in Cancer would spell disaster, while a similar phenomenon in Capricorn would mean the consumption of the entire universe by fire. These ideas, found in the earliest philosophers from Heraclitus to Zeno, are also traceable in Judaism and in the religions of Persia and India. The pattern of periodic destruction and renewal applies both to individuals and to humanity as a whole. Eliade indicates the probable root of these beliefs in the lunar system: the phases of the moon pass from "chaos" (on the cosmic plane) to "orgy" (on the social plane), to "darkness" (for seed), to "water" (baptism on the human plane, Atlantis on the plane of history p.88). Opposed to this is the basic tenet of the Hebrew religion that events are caused by a Universal Spirit as manifestations of its own Will (cf. Hegel); this is what Mr Deasy in "Nestor" believes in. As in the revealed religions, Hegel believes the terror of history will ultimately disappear.

Following Clive Hart's lead in this respect, one comes across the following definition of "Sandhyas" in The Secret Doctrine of Blavatsky. She defines it as "The interval that precedes each yoga...composed of as many hundreds of years as there are thousands in the yoga", with "sandhyamsa" as the bigger unit of "Sandhyas."[19] Such an interval of time is further illustrated by the phrase "madamanvantora" (FW 598.33). This term alludes to the original Hindu "mahamanvantara" which consists of one kalpa while fourteen such kalpas known as "Mahanvantara" are equivalent to the seven days and seven nights of Brahma's sleep. A hundred of these kalpas, that is about 311 thousand billion years, constitute the life of the supreme deity Brahma. In this enormous maze of time, each kalpa consists of a thousand mahayogas while 12 000 such mahayogas culminate in a single cosmic cycle of 4 320 000 years followed and preceded by the "pralay" (U 296.14) (Joyce uses this term in the "Cyclops" episode) or dissolution.[20] The idea of infinity is also repeated in this excerpt from the Wake "way went they. I'th' view o' th'avig-nue dancing goes entrancing roundly. Miss Oodles of Anems before the Luvium doeslike. So. And then again doeslike. So. And miss Endles of eons efter Die" (FW 226.34-6). "Way went they. I' th' view o' th'avignue dancing goes entrancing roundly" (FW 226.34) is a song "Sur le pont d'Avignon" meaning "when I was a young girl. This way I went." . "Miss Oodles of Anems" (FW 226.36) is "orders of names" as an anagram. "Before the Luvium doeslike" is antediluvian. "Luvium" is also Luvius or Ptolemy's name for river Lee. "And miss Endles of eons efter Die" (FW 226.36) is the round after endless rounds of births and deaths of human generations on the cosmic scale in terms of Indic "eons." Joyce borrows the term "eon" from Zimmer (Personal Library, p.46). The term "madamanvantora", to re-consider, is composed of madam and man, implying ALP and HCE. Dawn heralds a change and hope. The troublesome time of the night being over, the husband, wife and children should live happily together in "Ysat Loka" or Chapelizod. In this way the term suggests a peaceful and happy reunion of the family for a new be-ginning of a civil society. Dawn is also an opportunity to reflect upon the previous

---

19 H.P.Blavatsky, The Secret Doctrine, London: The Theosophical Publishing Company, Limited, 7, Duke Street, Adelphi, W.C., 1888 (vol.I, p.431; vol.II, 58, 239, 587).

20 According to Don Gifford and Robert J. Seidman, the term "pralaya in theosophy is the period of the individual soul's re-absorption or rest after death and before rebirth. In this period the soul is supposed to divest itself of earthly concerns and concentrate on spiritual growth so that it will evolve toward rebirth in an improved state." Don Gifford and Robert J. Seidman, Notes For Joyce: (E.P. Dutton &Co. INC. New York, 1974), 272.

night's dreams and nightmares and examine them in the light of our immediate reality in society for the fulfilment of desire. "Lotus spray" may also be interpreted as a prayer of thanksgiving.

Behind the stoking fire of "Sandhyas" is the desire, as Blavatsky states: "Desire first arose in It, which was the primal germ of mind; and which sages, searching with their intellect, have discovered to be the bond which connects Entity with Non-Entity." [21] Quoting from the Atharva Veda, Blavatsky says that the first

---

21 H.P. Blavatsky, The Secret Doctrine, vol.II, p.176.

In the Notebook 6-16, p.289, Atma or self means the boundaries of consciousness imposed by time and place. Self or "Atma" is relative and aware of the subject and object, a duality due to ego. Self-realization comes only when this shell of duality is broken, and a new awareness permits an initiate to see the illusion which is this world, its pains and suffering (dukha) conditioned by the sinful nature. Some of these sins are as a consequence of our predecessors in the form of prejudices which could be racial, religious, or tinctured by caste and colour. (See The Teachings of Sri Ramana Maharashi, edited by David Gorman).

Here, we may also look at the role of Agni in detail. Agni is also the messenger of the gods. "Rathgar" suggests a typical Hindu town whereas "Rathanga" may be interpreted as the godly chariot from "rath." According to the 11th Edition of Encyclopaedia Britannica (pub. 1911), the sacred text of Rig Veda begins with the name of Agni as "Agni, I entreat, divine appointed priest of sacrifice." As an immortal, Agni plays the role of a messenger to the gods. In another hymn, Agni appears as living among ordinary people "No god indeed, no mortal is beyond the might of thee, the mighty one...". As such, Agni is reborn daily "by the fire-drill, by the friction of the two sticks which are regarded as his parents" (See "Agni" main heading "Hinduism"). Besides Agni, Joyce also refers to the goddess Kali in Notebook VIB 27-8, P.208 as "Siva m Kali Olmuzd Satan Zarvas Mammon." Kali is feminine to the Sanskrit "kala," which means "time" as well as "black." Kali is a goddess who may be translated as "she who is time": "she who devours time": "she who is the mother of time": "she who is black" and "she who is black time." In contrast to her consort Shiva, who symbolises "white," Kali is "smasana" or black like cremation ashes. As Shakti, Kali is also prana or energy, which enters the body giving it life. Kali is mentioned in Rigveda as Agni's (the god of fire) black tongue.

Even the clauses "--Arra irrara hirrara man, weren't they arriving in clansdestinies for the Imbadiment of Ad Regias Agni Dapes" ....."like the messicals of great god,".... "from Rathgar, Rathanga" ....."Asia Place and the Affrian Way" (FW 497.05-13) are suggestive. "Arra irrara hirr-ara man" echoes "Array! Surrection!" that harbinger the new day. In Note book VIC 11-14, 17-8 P.132, Joyce also uses the Hindu incantation "ram hurry." "Huray Krishna, huray Ram" is a bhagan (hymn) to gods, such as "Jai Jai Ram Krishna Hari ! Jai Jai Ram Krishna Hari ! Jai Jai Ram Krishna Hari ! Jai Jai Ram Krishna Hari !" Hari. The adjective "har" means something great and intense. The term "puja" means the worship of deities, which has three different forms: temple worship, domestic worship and communal worship. In the Temple worship, the priests serve the deities. In the domestic worship, the prayers are said in a corner of the house kept clean for the ritual. In the communal worship, prayers take the form of singing of hymns such as Hare Ram Hare Krishna. Recitation from religious text is also part of the prayer. "Hari" is also one of the names of Vishnu. Vishnu as "hari" according to Vishnu sahasranama, is one who annihilates the "samsara" cycles of incarnations due to ignorance (See Commentary by Adi Sankara). In Sanscrit, "hari" means yellow or fawn-coloured/khaki (which is also the colour of the Sun and "Soma"). "Hari" is "zari" according to Avesta identified with "Zara" for Zarathustra. "Hari" means "daylight" in Indonesian, "day" in Malay and "king" in Tagalog. Such a wide spread use of the word "hari,"

movement in stirring and igniting the One was "Agni" (FW 497.05), FW 80.20). The concept of "One" here is similar to that of Judaism, Christianity and Islam. The "One" is "Him neither gods nor fathers (pitara) nor men have equalled." Pitara is the Persian "padar" for father and is equivalent to "Atama" (FW 602.12), defined by Blavatsky as the "Self-Existent" Atma Bhu. The one is also "O Jarama!" (FW 602.13), that is "the unborn" or Aja.

The Atharva Veda of Hindu scripture, mentioned as "uddahveddahs" (FW 85.03), is one of the most ancient religious books, prepared after the settlement of the Aryan migrants in India from Central Asia about ten to fifteen centuries BC. The Aryans in the Wake are mentioned as "He shall come, sidesmen accostant, by Aryan" (FW 567.22) and also appear as a pun "jubilarian" (FW 567.22). "He shall come, sidesmen accostant, by Aryan" (FW 567.22) "Accostant" (FW 567.22) may be considered as a variant of "accosting." To accost is to approach someone and confront him or solicit sexually. In Latin, however, accostare is to place side by side or "sidesmen" (FW 567.22). While "Aryan" (FW 567.22) suggests Ireland or the Irish as in this excerpt "boasts him to the thick-inthews the oldest creater in Aryania and looks down on the Suiss family Collesons" (FW 129.33-35); yet, "Aryan" connotes something exotic, exuberant, a trait of Orientalism. We may note of such an exotic tendency as "(*F4*) keep my linefree face like readymaid maryangs for jollycomes smashing (*F5*)Holmes" (FW 276). In another place, the Aryans appear as "the oldest creater in Aryania" (FW 129.34). In both instances, the Aryans are referred to as immigrants into an alien land. In Notebook, VI.C. (11, 12, 13, 14, 17, 18) the Aryans and Mongols are noted as "(Mongols of Judaism) Orang (of Asia) Mongol Orang (asia ape) Aryan" [p.37].

Blavatsky describes the above phenomenon through an allegory. "Kandu," the "yogi," like St Kevin the "yogpriest" (FW 601.01) of Book IV, is "devoid of mind." Because of his hermetic piety and austerity, the other gods become jealous. In

---

indicates the influence of Sanscrit.

One of the names of God, according to Sikhism, is "Hari". The most prestigious Sikh Temple - the Golden Temple is also called "Harimander" or "Temple of God." From "Hari" we get another clue that is "Hari Hara" which Zimmer (Myths and Symbols in Indian Art and Civilization, p.125) identifies in a footnote as the "masks" that combine "the concept and iconography of Hari Hara, ie., mixta persona of Vishnu-Shiva." Zimmer says that Vishnu and Shiva are the gods enjoying equality of status and hence are able to change roles in the dialectical process of creation and periodic destruction of the universe. For this instrumental role, Zimmer believes, Shiva and Vishnu are only wearing the masks which they exchange with each other.

order to degrade him, they seduce a nymph and send her to tempt "Kandu." The desire that is aroused in him finally destroys his godlike wisdom. Blavatsky compares Kandu with the story of Adam in Genesis, "of Adam, born as an image of clay, into which the lord-god breathes the breath of life but not intellect and discrimination, which are developed only after he had tasted of the fruit of the Tree of knowledge."[22] The birth of desire in both instances is the dividing line of consciousness between human and divine.

Campbell traces the Hindu myth of Creation by referring to the "Cosmic Being" as HCE, sleeping and dreaming about the "history of the world".[23] The Supreme Being is couched on the "Cosmic Serpent" in the waters of eternity. Grace Eckley, in the introductory paragraphs of her analysis of Book IV of the Wake, elucidates her argument by quoting from Heinrich Zimmer: "In the same image by which the Matsya Puranas presented the universe as the body of a giant sleeping god, resembling a mountain breaking out of the water," the "Hill of Hafid" (FW 595.03) gives relief to the Irish landscape "as he strauches his lamusong" (FW 595.04) to comprise its geography expressed in dioceses."[24] As Zimmer explains, a titanic giant sprawling on the Himalayas "like the limbless shape of a cloud serpent" had captured the waters of heaven in his belly.[25] The gracious god "flung his thunderbolt into the midst of its ungainly coils; the monster shattered like a stack of withered rushes. The waters burst forth and streamed through the body of the world." This flood became the source of life's flood in a thousand and one forms. As a sequel, it forced the titans to hide underneath the world and the giants to flee toward the Himalayas.

The importance of thunder words in Finnegans Wake, points to the works of Vico, Blavatsky and Zimmer[26] as major sources besides the scriptures. Blavatsky,

22 Ibid. 175.

23 Joseph Campbell,"Finnegan the Wake" in james joyce:Two Decades of Criticism, ed. Seon Givens, (The Vanguard Press, New York), 1963, 370, 373.

24 Grace Eckley,"Book IV: Looking Forward to a Brightening Day" in Michael Begnal and Fritz Senn, eds.,A Conceptual Guide to Finnegans Wake, (University Park:The Pennsylvania State University Press, 1974), 210.

25 Heinrich Zimmer, Myths and Symbols in Indian Art and Civilization, ed. Joseph Campbell, (Bollingen series VI, New York: Bollingen Foundation, 1946), 3-11.

26 Joyce's interest in the research made by Zimmer was fruitful because of its Indo-European background. For European purposes, Joyce studied Zimmer's findings of the Scandinavian hero, Finn MacCool. On 8 September 1938, Joyce wrote to Louis Gillet: "Here I find my theory on

for example, traces the origin of "thunder" by dividing the human races into seven Manus —"mundamanu" (FW 364.33) beginning and terminating through recurring cataclysms of fire or water. "Mundamanu" [Manu the clean handed, untainted or innocent] according to McHugh is the Adam of Hindu myth. At the time when "nearly the whole population of one hemisphere perished by water, while the other hemisphere was awakening from its temporary obscuration," it was this allegorical man who rescued the human race, argues Blavatsky.[27] This "awakening from temporary obscuration," can also be observed in Vico's New Science:

> the impious races of the three children of Noah, having lapsed into a state of bestiality, went wandering like wild beasts until they were scattered and dispersed through the great forest of the earth, and that with them, these bestial giants had sprang up and existed among them at the time when the Heavens thundered for the first time after the flood.[28]

Vico, Hinduism and Joyce concur with the idea of the roaming of the giants after the flood of Noah. Zimmer's discussion is relevant here as, in both Hinduism and Joyce, there is an expression of the desire for rebuilding on the ruins swamped by the floods. The Wake begins with the unfulfilled desire of building a tower as majestic as the tower of Babel. In Hinduism, as Zimmer states, we find the god Indra summoning the best craftsmen among the gods for the rebuilding of the denuded palace as soon as the titans and the giants flee to the Himalayas. Indra is twice mentioned in the Wake. In the first reference, Isabel is seen as posing her riddle: "Not Rose, Sevilla nor Citronelle; not Esmeralde, Pervinca nor Indra" (FW 233.06-07).

Indra is associated with the colour indigo, along with other colours such as

the Scandinavianism of my hero, Finn MacCool, confirmed (the Fingla of Macpherson, father of Ossian and grandfather of Oscar) by the research of a German scholar, Zimmer. It is curious to see in the resume that Professor Zimmer is engaged in on the work of his father, the boldness which I have dared in putting the gross Norwegian HCE in the skin of a mythical hero purely Celtic, justified by Teutonic doctrine with chapter and verse."

27 H.P. Blavatsky, The Secret Doctrine, vol.I, 309.

28 Thomas Goddard Bergin and Max Harold Fisch eds. The New Science of Giambattista Vico: abridged translation of the third edition, 1774, (Ithaca & London: Cornell University Press, 1970), 195.

rose, orange, citron-lemon, white, emerald and periwinkle or blue. These seven colours are the rainbow and the heliotropic girls revolving regularly around the sun Shaun against the "feinder" fiendish Shem. Indra appears as one of the seven rainbow girls "with Poppea, Arancita, Clara, Marinuzza, Indra and Iodina" (FW 572.36, 573.01). Furthermore, one of these girls tempts him again by sending a message through a butterfly. The message is in the form of a letter. In this passage, at least three names echo the Hindu characters of the Mahabharata: Cita as Arancita, Indra and Iodina. Before commenting on Indra, let us take a look at the gloss "Iodina" which resonates Ajodhya: Ajodhya as Encyclpaedia Britannica (11th Edition) describes, is one of the oldest towns of India. The town is mentioned in the Ramayana glorifying its monarch, its prosperity and devotion of its people to religion and to the royal household. It was the capital of the kingdom of Kosala during the age of the great king, Dasraratha. King Dasraratha is the father of Rama Chandra, the hero of the epic Ramayana. According to Hsuan Tsang, a famous Chinese traveller who visited India in the 7th Century, there were "20 Buddhist temples with 3000 monks" in the city.

With the establishment of Islam, numerous mosques were built in Ajodhya. Elaborating on Hsuan Tsang, it must be added that he had also collected Buddhist scripts. In the notebook VIC 6-16 P.25, Joyce jots the Sanscrit, Pali word "Abhidharma." "Abhidharma" is composed of two words: "abhi" is higher or special. "Abhi" also means "about" . "Dharma" is "teaching" or "philosophy". Abhidharma, therefore, denotes "higher teachings" or "about the teaching." Abhidharma was script based on the interpretations of the sayings of Buddha. These were in the form of manuscripts, which emerged from several monastic orders. Hsuan Tsang, the 7th century Chinese pilgrim had collected seven such texts. Two of the Abidharmas are still available in their original form: the Theravada Abhidharma written in Pali and the Sarvastivadin Abhidharma, in Chinese. It is believed that soon after his awakening or enlightenment, Buddha again slipped back into meditation. Abidharma is the fruit of this period of meditation. Buddha taught this text to the heavenly beings on his visit, which happened after the revelation of Abhidharma. This text was entrusted to Sariputra, a monk. He handed it over to the next generation. Abhidharma, therefore, is a pure, undiluted religious text of Buddhist sutras.

We find the god Indra visiting the palace for inspection. The builder Vishvakaram, a Hindu counterpart of Joyce's Hellenistic Daedalus, is required by the god to construct some "additional terraces and pavilions, more ponds, groves and pleasant grounds." [29] Indra's desire was so insatiable that whenever he came to see the place, he "developed vision beyond vision of marvels remaining to be contrived". This angered the builder god. He asked for help from Brahma, and the latter passed his message on to Vishnu, the highest in the hierarchy.

The ceaseless quest of Finn MacCool at the beginning of the Wake to build a tower is equivalent to Indra's ambition. Their eventual fall in this enterprise suggests the inevitable consequence of their excessive ambition and pride. Referring to Rumi's verse "Sleep of ignorance, in which most people pass their conscious lives," Campbell draws attention to the essence of the commonly held Islamic and Hindu Platonic truth expressed by Chwang Tzu: "The mind of the sage at rest becomes the mirror of the universe". It is in the deepest possible substratum that the human spirit exists. The seer approaches this mysterious dark womb and is amazed to discover the common root of us all. In this state of consciousness "Visions are presented to his inner eye that match, in both quantity and detail, the symbolic operations. In that which is night to all beings, the man of self-control is awake" (Bhagavad-Gita)[30] "Bhagafat gaiters" (FW 35.10), "Bhagavat" (FW

---

29 Heinrich Zimmer, Myths and Symbols in Indian Art and Civilization, 3-11. Joyce also inserts the name of Indra in his notebook (VIB 27-8) p.207 as "Ahi Indra Agni Vishnu Celestial spouse." In other words, when Indra (P.54), Zimmer says "I am the annual cycle which creates everything and again devours everything" being "the immortal lord of the waters"; we may interpret it as "the river of lives, the regenerations of the incarnations of the emanations of the apparentations" (FW 600.02). Indra also may be detected in this compound word "indradiction" as she appears wielding weapons for the battle "his shadowers torrified by the potent bolts of indradiction" (FW 61. 22) or as "Pervinca nor Indra" (FW 223.07) Rigveda sanctifies Indra as "He under whose supreme control are horses, all chariots, and the villages, and cattle; He who gave being to the Sun and Morning, who leads the waters, He, O men, is Indra." Rigveda, (2.12.7, trans. Griffith) Besides Agni, Indra who enjoys soma is one of the leading deities according to Rigveda. He defeated Vritra and smashed the stone that led to the liberation of the cows and rivers – the productive forces of life. He is engaged in a timeless battle against evil: cares for and looks after the elements – Agni (fire), Varuna (water) and Surya (the Sun) and the Devas (the gods of Heaven). As a warrior, he uses his famous weapon "thunderbolt" (Vajra), a bow and a net riding a four-tusked elephant "airavata" and lives in the clouds (svarga) around Mt. Meru. He hosts the deceased warriors and entertains them through the dance of the "apsaras" and games.

30 See Sankaracarya's commentary on Bhagavadgita, (Gita Press, Gorakhpur), 1931. In Notebook, (VI.B.21). P.69, Joyce inserts this religious script as "Bhagavat Upanishatem!" Originally, a part of the Mahabharata (Book 6), Bhagavat Gita is based on the dialogue between Lord Krishna and Arjuna at a very quiet moment – the stasis followed by the titanic warfare between good and

302.01), "names in his gitter!" (FW 320.14). "Bhagafat gaiters" may also be seen in the context of the word "ironsides" which suggests Cromwell in his military uniform "great belt" .."hideinsacks"..."fustian" and "jackboots".

Cromwell appears as one of the incarnations of HCE, who, having replaced Finnegan (a demigod or a Vico's giant), symbolises a new world of that of HCE or Here Comes Everybody in chapter II of Book 1. He represents the Patriarchal Age of human history. Costumed in seven different items and holding the "Bhagafat Gaiters" as a book of guidance, HCE bellows across the Phoenix Park that sullied his reputation. The sacred book is a talisman that shields him against jealousy and slander. Bhagavad-Gita is cited again as "quoths the Bhagavat" which again appears as a book of good omen "Ann opes" or hope, carried by Wellington "sahib" sitting on a white horse "This is Willingdone on his same white harse, the cokenhape...his big wide harse" (FW 8.17, 21). With regard to India, General Wellington is famed for his war against Marathas in the south. He played a crucial role in expanding the British rule in India as well as in defeating Napoleon in the Peninsular War. In the same passage, there is another reference to India "tipoo" (FW 302.02). Sultan Tippoo was the last major Moslem ruler to fight against the British in the south.

---

evil. Arjuna, the hero hesitates to fight against the forces of evil. Lord Krishna convinces him to stand up and face the evil even if it he were to take up arms against his own kith and kin. Arjuna is told that good will prevail. Krishna, then, surprises Arjuna when the former reveals his identity that he was Lord Krishna. Bhagavat Gita is about the problem of living clean in an imperfect world. The nature of this world becomes clear when we read the next part of the sacred text, which is about cannibals, vampires and oceans of blood and so on. Upanishad is a detailed catalogue of Hindu faith, discussing themes such as "karma" (action), "panorama" (reincarnation), "moksha" (nirvana), the "atman" (soul), and the "Brahman" (Absolute), and above all self-realization, yoga and meditation. "Upanishad" as a noun implies "sitting down near" the guru (a spiritual teacher) gifted with the knowledge of the fundamental truths of the universe. The message in Upanishad relates to a time when teaching was imparted in the pin-drop silence of the forests "ashrams" or hermitage. Upanishad also symbolizes the annihilation of ignorance by "Brahma-knowledge." For other religious books and commentaries see:

a) Jacob, A Concordance to the Principal Upanishads and Bhagavadgita (Bombay S.S. 1891).
b) Paul. Deussen, The Philosophy of the Upanishads (Edinburgh: T and T. Clark, 1906).
c) Romesh Dutt, trans. The Epic of ancient India (with an introduction by the Right Hon. F. Max Muller, J.M. Dent and Co. London 1899).
d) Sayana's commentary on Rig Veda, ed. Max Muller, (of the 14th century), (6 Vols, London, 1849-1874).
e) Sayanacharya's commentary on Rig-Veda Sanhita, the sacred hymns of the Brahmans, ed. Max Muller 1849-74, (London: W.H. Allen and Co.).

Campbell compares humanity with the old yogi Markandaya who survived the eon of dissolution and stayed on alive in the belly of the Cosmic Giant. This indifferent dreamer causes the universe and galaxies to generate and be annihilated in the wink of an eye without remorse as an atom "ex-polodotonates" (FW 353.23-24) "in that multimirror megaron of returningnties, whirled without end to end" (FW 582.20-21). Identifying him as "Brahman or Tirthankaras," Clive Hart and Fritz Senn say:

> ...if this man, in a state of suspended animation at the present moment of time — which contains all time — were accorded a close-up picture of all the people and events that have emanated from him and have influenced his life... if this man, during the watches of the night could solve the riddle of being, could see in a single vision the growth and decay of life, the battle of brothers, the acts of birth, copulation and death, what would he seem to himself to be dreaming of and to be? A kaleidoscopic synthesis of all Being. [31]

"Megaron" is the bedchamber. Returning to it means falling asleep and letting the day"s experiences to mirror through the unconscious, endlessly. In sum, as beacon of super sensual memory, HCE subsumes all times into one like anastomosis - a phenomenon interaction between the known and the unknown as complex as the interbranching flow of blood vessels and arteries. The scintillating fire remains the "sandhyas."
([32])

---

31 31. Clive Hart and Fritz Senn, AWN, (old series, 1 March 1962)

32 (continuing Note: 16) As an elaborated symbol of Yeats's A Vision, Finnegans Wake consists of seventeen chapters. Chapter seventeen consists of the whole of Book IV and is comparable, according to Boldereff, with phase seventeen of A Vision. Moreover, A Vision is based upon the gyres of the Primary and the Antithetical dialectics ascending and descending reciprocally, thus connecting the highest with the lowest recesses in their joint revolutions around the wheel of time. If the former denotes the beginning then the latter symbolises the end. This dialectical process is applicable to the Wake which, like Blake's The Marriage of Heaven and Hell (one of the favourite books of Joyce and Yeats) is based upon coincidentia oppositorum: "Without contraries is no progress. Attraction and repulsion, Reason and Energy, Love and Hate, are necessary to human existence. From these contraries spring what the religions call Good and Evil" (Letters, Vol.I, p.224). Moreover, the Wake has neither beginning nor end because it is a "whorled without aimed" (FW 272. 4-5) as Joyce told Harriet Weaver "The case is quite different with the Work in Progress, which has neither beginning nor end" (Selected Letters, ed. Ellmann, Vol.II, p.314). As the last chapter of the Wake, Book IV is structurally intertwined with the opening page of the Wake itself. What binds the beginning with the ending of the Wake also interfuses the same dialectic within Books, chapters and most of the sentence patterns throughout the Wake. The

last sentence of Book I is about the night in which one washerwoman is asking the other to tell her a tale:"Telmetale of stem or stone. Beside the rivering waters of, hitherandthithering waters of. Night!" (FW 216.03-05). "Stem" pertains to a tree which symbolises the act of creativity as in letters or words. "Stone" is cold, quiet and hence like the "Night" when the images shoot up and down swirling as if the ceaseless, torrential ripples of water. Pen only translates those images into words. The last sentence of Book II is the hour before dawn:"And still a light moves long the river" (FW 399.31). Similarly, Book III ends with the emergence of dawn:"Rumbling" (FW 590.29). Book IV ends with the beginning of another day:"So soft this morning, ours. Yes" (FW 628.08). Book IV joins both the ends together, beginning and ending with dawn. (Frances Motz Boldereff, Reading Finnegans Wake (Woodward, Pennsylvania: New York Public Library, 1959), 63-65.

6.

ALP and the Indic Theosophical Creed

B oth HCE and ALP use the article "the" in conveying the divine message of "Sandhyas". On page 598, which contains many words of Sanskrit derivation, HCE is proclaiming to the world while dreaming: "Diu! The has goning at gone, the is coming to come. Greets to ghastern, hie to morgning. Dormidy, destady. Doom is the faste" (FW 598.09-11). "Diu!" is day in Italian; "ghastern" is yesterday (Italian); "hie" is hi; "dormidy" is sleep ye (Latin); and, "destady" is destiny. The article "the" links the beginning and end here.

There is harmony in this utterance of poetic prose. The verbs swing like a pendulum around the definite article. The article "the" personifies the god, "Diu" whose original name is "dieu" in French and "theo" in Greek. If we add the letter "e" to HCE's deity, we beget the French god whereas if we add the letter "o" to the article "the," we discern the Greek deity. Hence, HCE is playing upon these words which embody the concept of divinity. "Diu" in the Indian languages echoes "Ginni" or the giants whose role in the process of creation was noted in the previous chapter. Even more to the point is the Hindu "Sandhyas" which, according to one of its versions as Walkiewicz states, is the name of a goddess. In two of the hymns of the Mahabharata, the Mother Goddess, according to Narendra Nath Bhattacharyya is addressed as Sandhyas.[1]

To HCE, the value of the article "the" is immense as it wields its powers over day and night, the entire scheme of time. It sends its "greets" (greetings) to the time which has become a thing of the past or "ghastern" meaning "yesterday." It hails the coming of the morning from the depths of night which is "a long, very long, a dark, very dark" (FW 598.06-07) part of reality. HCE acknowledges its sway over both, the state of being asleep "Dor-midy" (FW 598.10-11) and the state of being awake "destady" (FW 598.11).

Despite its pervasiveness, the article "the" has its own limitations as it too would finally be consumed because it only signals or becomes aware of

---

1   Nanendra Nath Bhattacharyya, The Indian Mother Goddess (Columbia, Missouri: South Asia Books, 1977),107.

temporality in the shape of morning or evening. There must be some other deity darker even than the night which controls the entire scheme of time, illustrated in the same paragraph as "Padma" (FW 598.12), that is "lotus flower" or the Absolute. As Zimmer puts it "from the middle of the god grows a lotus, which is a duplicate manifestation of the goddess at his feet. The flower bears on its corolla Brahma, the four-faced demiurge-creator."[2] Brahma may be considered to be the darker, mystifying aspect of "Sandhyas," though deep in its dark womb is the quiver of a new urge which is as intuitively active for self-expression as the waning, darkening side.

The use of the article "the" by ALP on page 628 as the last word of Book IV, implying the end without regard to the grammatical rules of full stop or colon or semi-colon, is more complicated. Lacking a full stop or other punctuation mark, it arouses the curiosity of neither beginning nor end, a state which induces the reader to apply to it the meaning of "Sandhyas" or the Wake's mystery of "The Suspended Sentence" (FW 106.13-14) in which contraries merge: "In that european end meets Ind" (FW 598.16).

Commenting on the sentence that tolls the bell of ALP, "A way a lone a last a loved a long the", Joyce had told Louis Gillet:

> In Ulysses, to depict the babbling of a woman going to sleep, I had sought to end with the least forceful word I could possibly find. I had found the word "Yes" which is barely pronounced, which denotes acquiescence, self-abandon, relaxation, end of all resistance. In Work in Progress I have tried to do better if I could. This time I found "the," which is the most slippery, the least accented, the weakest word in English, a word which is not even a word, which is scarcely sounded between the teeth, a breath, a nothing, the article the.

Gillet then offers his interpretation of what Joyce had in mind: "We might add that the large blank space on the last page (which, perhaps, symbolises moisture-laden air and reflects the large black dot of "Ithaca" — another sleep symbol and roc's egg) between "the" and "Paris" also forms the part of the book."[3]

---

2   Zimmer, Myths and Symbols in Indian Art and Civilization, 61

3   Danis Rose and John O' Hanlon, Understanding Finnegans Wake, 319, 320 and appendix. Rose and O'Hanlon quote Louis Gillet from his book Claybook for James Joyce, translated by Geo. Markow-Totevy (London and New York: Abelard-Schuman, 1958), 111. Rose and O'Hanlon also

Interpretation of the article "the" especially when followed by the blank space in the rest of the page, poses an enigma. If the blank space on the last page of the Wake recalls the large black spot with which the episode "Ithaca" comes to an end, as Gillet suggests, then it is an interesting coincidence that Blavatsky's The Secret Doctrine begins with a discussion of the Hindu concepts of "disk" and "black spot."

The question at the end of "Ithaca" remains unanswered:

"When?"

"Going to a dark bed, there was a square round Sindbad the Sailor roc's auk's egg in the night of the bed of all the auks of the rocs of Darkinbad the Brightdayler."

"Where?" (U.607).

We can interpret "When" as the end of Bloom's journey and "Where" as his resolve to sleep in the bed with Molly, though lying in the opposite direction to her. Walton Litz, for example, argues that the full stop at the end of "Ithaca" symbolises the novel's action, Bloom's diurnal journey through Dublin:

> As full stop it marks the conclusion of Bloom's day, the terminus of the novel's action, but as a spatial object it represents Bloom's total retreat into the womb of time, from which he shall reemerge next day with all the potentialities of Everyman. Like the Viconian ricorso, the final moment of Ithaca is both an end and a beginning.[4]

Similarly, a dot plays the central role in manifesting Hindu metaphysics in The Secret Doctrine. Referring to an archaic manuscript, Blavatsky states that "On the first [page] is an immaculate white disk within a dull background." On the following page there is the same disk but with a central spot. The first disk is "the cosmos of Eternity" — a state of existence prior to the manifestation of the "Word" or the scintillation of energy. The central spot of the next page, according to Blavatsky, stands for the "dawn of differentiation," latent and active, in periods and by turns,

---

refer to the last correction made by Joyce on Finnegans Wake: "Page 628: Please print the Place and Date much lower approximately where I indicated or lower" (BL Add. MS.47488 240). The gap between the last word of the Wake and its completion is thus intentional, further deepening the mystery of the letter "the."

4   A. Walton Litz, "Ithaca" in Clive Hart and David Hayman, eds., James Joyce's Ulysses, (Berkeley, and London: University of California Press Berkeley: 1974), 404.

as in the "Days" and "Nights" of Brahma. "Days" are the exhalation and "Nights" the inhalation in this endless process of creation and destruction. "This process has been going on," says Blavatsky, "from all eternity, and our present universe is but one of an infinite series, which had no beginning and will have no end."[5]

The point within the disk is "Aditi in that" (the Sanskrit word "Rig Veda" meaning the potential that lies unexhausted in the abstract space, differentiation and the periodical manifestation in an infinity which is beyond the categories of gender). From non-differentiation to differentiation, we arrive at the diameter as the third sage, which symbolises the "immaculate Mother Nature." In the fourth stage, a vertical line has been drawn across the diameter, suggesting the third root race of innocence and bliss. If we remove the disk around the cross, the cross, according to Blavatsky, would symbolise the "fourth race," in other words the fall of man into matter. If the cross is within the circle, then it would stand for "pantheism," while a cross outside the circle would mean the masculine phallus.

By the third symbol, that is the division of the circle in two by the horizontal line, Blavatsky means the first manifestation of Nature. Nature was passive and feminine: "The first shadowy perception of man connected with procreation is feminine because man knows his mother more than his father, hence female deities were more sacred than the male."[6] When desire was first manifested, it was feminine in nature. In this way, Blavatsky differentiates between the manifest features of reality and the esoteric, hidden part of it. It is probable that her elaboration of these symbols influenced Joyce and that the black dot that ends the day-long journey of Bloom, and the article "the" at the end of ALP's monologue, are Joyce's way of suggesting the indefatigable role of the "other," the unknowable mystery of the universe.

If we apply the above discussion to Book IV, we find that the relationship between HCE and ALP corresponds to the state of nature both in its dormant condition and in action. To the slumbering potential of HCE, ALP appears as the dynamical "Agni" which ignites him from his sleeping, latent state. This process is reciprocal in that when ALP is active, as in her last monologue, her partner is dull, dumb and completely unheard. Similarly, when in Book IV he is announcing to

---

5   H.P. Blavatsky, The Secret Doctrine, vol.I, 1-4.

6   Ibid., 4.

the world the beginning of a new dawn, we don't hear anything of ALP. The fact remains, however, that HCE encompasses both states, those of falling asleep and being awake. His wakefulness is related to the dreamlike state of mind in all the four books of the Wake. The difference, as Clive Hart states, lies in the intensity and depth of his sleep: "Thus, after the "Tiers, tiers and tiers" of dreams in these three books, we return ("Rounds"), as always in Book IV, to the first level (FW 590.30). The Dreamer, is of course, still asleep, but Earwicker's fantastic dream-night is over: "Guld modning."[7] The point at which the borders of a "fantastic dream-night" give way to a lighter level of sleep could be marked by HCE's proclamation of "Sandhyas", but this announcement is questionable because of the magnitude and complexity of HCE's character. Encompassing not only the sun and its votary planets, HCE is "solarsystemised, seriolcosmically, in a more and more almightily expanding universe" (FW 263.25-26). "Solarsystemised" is the sun and its satellites of which our earth is a part. Emphasis is being given to the influence of science and the scientific method on us. "Seriolcosmically" is seriocomically. "In a more and more almightily expanding universe" is Eddington's The Expanding Universe. "Seriolcosmically" can also be interpreted as a series of cycles in an Indic "eon." His cosmic identity reflects his multi-layered mental states which reveal multiple dreamers intertwined, intermingling so that "the traits featuring the chiaroscuro coalesce, their contrarieties eliminated, in one stable somebody" (FW 107.29-30).

According to McHugh, HCE in Book IV is asleep like Brahma dreaming about the "chaosmos" (FW 118.21). This "chaosmos" is the quadrate of the circle. The square of this quadrate is like Blavatsky's cross which represents "chaos," whereas the encirclement of the square completes the mystic, kabalistic unity — a symbol universally recognised. The reason why "the all god in human shape" wishes to remain asleep, says Zimmer[8] lies in this endless agony and chaos of the world "For eternities I have been going astray in the circle of this samsara, I am overcome by the fire of all sufferings, and nowhere could I find cessation's rest." The chaos is consummated as soon as ALP lapses into floodwater in the end. However, in the

---

7   Clive Hart, Structure and Motif in Finnegans Wake, 94.
8   Thomas E. Connolly, The Personal Library of James Joyce: A descriptive bibliography (Norwood Editions, State University of New York at Buffalo, 1977, 91.

last pages of the Wake, she is seen as warning her daughter against male tempt-ers.[9] According to John Gordon, the daughter in such instances is the medium of hope, "bringing promise of refuge from this flood, and the dove annunciation."[10] ALP is cognizant of this fact, as she says "If I seen him bearing down on me now under whitespread wings like he'd come from Arkangels, I sink I w'd die down over his feet, humbly dumbly, only to washup." If she is tottering under the weight of mortality, the sun is ripping apart the seams of a new horizon; Shem and Shaun are replacing HCE as her daughter is substituting for her and thus we hear the same cry from ALP, in her moment of extinction as at her birth, "mememormee!" (FW 628.14). The phrase "whitespread wings like he'd come from Arkangels," (FW 628.10) has three identifiable suggestions: first, the birds that Noah released from his ark to find land; second, angel of the Lord (Annunciation) according to Matt 1:2. "Archangel" is the Russian title for St. Michael.

HCE as an avatar of Brahma, the symbol of potential nature, is lying asleep subsuming the entire landscape from the "Hill of Hafid" (Howth) and Lambay is-land to Knock Gate, near Chapelizod in the Park. In his domain of "the no placelike no timelike absolvent," placeless and timeless, opposites like the Welsh people "petty Vaughan" (FW 609.02), light-haired "mersscenary blookers," and the dark-skinned "potentials" (FW 609.04) (three soldiers and three Danish girls) melt into each other: "unprobables in their poor suit of the improssable" (FW 609.05-06). The stars, the Milky Way and other galaxies shroud the terrestrial plain in darkness as the milk wagon passes by. Blavatsky uses the phrase the "milky way" for the state of primordial matter — an age preceded by the "Deluge" when the deity churned the "Ocean of Milk" for creation.[11] Buried like a pauper in Potter's Field, HCE is lying drowsily in the four corners of his bed when the morning breeze swishes through, tickling his body after an eon of sleep. As HCE wanders through the non-existent Waters of the Nile in sleep, ALP fades away "near to faint away, Into the deep" as "the book of the depth closes" under "the weight of old fletch" into "A way a lone a last a loved a long the" at the sensing of her death while her

---

9   Roland McHugh, The Sigla of Finnegans Wake, (London: Edward Arnold Ltd, 1976), 112. In one of his forms, Brahma issues from a golden egg as Prajapati. The egg hatched in water gives birth to a female with whom Brahma forms an incestuous bond. See Alain Danielou, Hindu Polytheism, (London: Routledge and Kegan Paul 1964), 235-6.

10 John Gordon, Finnegans Wake: A Plot Summary (Dublin: Gill and Macmillan, 1986), 277.

11 H.P. Blavatsky, The Secret Doctrine vol.I, 67.

little river flows into the cosmic sea of Non-entity. Here we may look at the following excerpt from Zimmer.[12] The "Allgod"

> ..."in human shape"..."as a giant", [a] "slumbering man," [is] "lying on the windings of an endless snake, which is the animal form of his being...And he saw a slumbering man who was like a mount range; half submerged, he swam in the water as a cloud floats over the sea, as if flaming with light energy...."

On page 110, Zimmer states " Male below, female above: the view of a more recent age in us [the Western world] and in India, this is an "inverted (upside-down) world."

But the ancient Egyptian cosmology still presents the same picture [as the "inverted" ancient Indian view]: the heavenly female --bracing [against] the horizon with fingers and toes--forms with the arch of her body the vault of the firmament. Beneath her lies [supine] on his back the earthling and looks up to her body whose breasts, groin, and thighs sparkle with stars."

In comparison to HCE, it is ALP who is the "Maya," Joyce's proteus, appearing and disappearing, affecting and being affected, the very source of energy and quickening, "All in All." Anna in Sanskrit means food and human body according to Vedanta is the sheath of grain. Her nature may also be viewed by referring to the compound "mayarannies." Apparentlly, it means the "wife of rajah "rawjaws" (FW.493.6-9) seen in the background of Indian "royal patron of arts" ("sun of power") "Vikramadityationists" (FW 493.15) and an allusion to colonialism "Foraignghistan" (FW 493.02). The compound word "Mayarannies" observed in the context of "morning in the end of time" (FW.493.13-14) may easily be a connector to ALP's "Maya" like sway over time and space "Mayasdaysed" (FW 597.28) for its capacity of "changing" (FW.627.15), "turning" (FW627.17) and "Imlamaya...Swimming in my hindmoist" (FW627.18). Furthermore, like Leda, she is passive: "One time you'd stand fornenst me, fairly laughing...And one time you'd rush upon me, darkly roaring," (FW 626.22-24). Her passivity is what arouses passion in HCE. She is cognizant of lust in men, "I pitty your oldself I was used to. Now a younger's there" (FW 627.06). She warns her daughter about the

---

12 Thomas E. Connolly, The Personal Library of James Joyce: A descriptive bibliography (Norwood Editions, State University of New York at Buffalo, 1977, 52.

incestuous designs of men, though the daughter, to her misfortune, dismisses these warnings as "gramma's grammar" (FW 268.17) a withered old lady's fretfulness in acting "generous" towards male "reflexes". ALP is knee-deep into her life's pond, consuming her sapping energies and body. If HCE remains asleep as the book ends, we find her shattered like a mirror into countless sensibilities each reflecting a shade of her experience ranging from amorous love stories to the riddles of life and her different acts of generosity toward men. All her acts are based on the expression of her superabundant love, as Sheldon Brivic observes:

Joyce presents her love for HCE so as to indicate something destructive in the way love has to be expressed in language. For example, she is overflowing with love when she urges him to stand up tall (620.01)...And her enthusiasm leads her to see a series of men in him."[13]

Brivic applies Lacan's concept of desire as "the metonymic reminder that runs under" the signifier HCE. Desire in this sense "always exceeds what can be gotten."

In this respect, ALP desires him to be divested of impurities. Once these are removed he is the embodiment of virtue and youthful nature:

"You make me think of a wonderdecker I once. Or somebalt thet sailder, the man megallant, with the bangled ears. Or an earl was he, at Lucan? Or, no, its the Iren duke's I mean. O somebrey erse from the Dark Countries" (FW 620.06-10). ALP fancies herself to be a new wonderful girl in her new gown "wonderdecker" as she did in the past, for her sailor lover "Soldier Rollo" (FW 202.33). She also intends to be a blond girl to tempt him. Like her own narcissus wish, she conjures up an image about him. She thinks of the Flying Dutchman, Sindbad the Sailor, an explorer like Magellan, the Earl of Lucan and Wellington.

In the words of Suzette A. Henke, ALP wants to cast off the "weight of old fletch" by "laving" (loving, leaving, washing) "her husband's flaccid" organ.[14] She wants to see him as pure as an infant, a peeled twig. Finding him to fall short of this, satire becomes her weapon. "All your groundplotting and the little it brought!" (FW 624.12-13), she says scathingly, echoing Molly's reproachful attitude toward

---

13 Sheldon Brivic, JJQ. "The Terror and Pity of Love: ALP's Soliloquy", Vol.29, 1, (Fall 1991), 150-151.

14 Suzette A. Henke, James Joyce and the Politics of Desire, (New York and London: Routledge) 1990, p.198. In the words of Suzette, ALP is "casting off" "the weight of old fletch" and "laving" (loving, leaving, washing) her husband's flaccid organs of body.

Bloom, "he ought to get a leather medal with a putty rim for all the plans he invents" (U 765 / 630) before finally discovering the real gap between what HCE and ALP thought of and what reality indeed was- "I thought you were all glittering with the noblest of carriage. You're only a bumpkin. I thought you the great in all things, in guilt and in glorry. You're but a puny"(FW 627.21-24).

The vital role of ALP as the feminine principle in fertilizing life has a topographical character in the Indian context. This is demonstrated by the number of Indian rivers in ALP's chapter and their mythical implications. Almost all the important rivers of the Indian subcontinent are mentioned in this chapter. Although the names of these rivers are well known, the river imagery at places in the chapter deserves reappraisal. In the following passage, the "nullah" requires interpretation: "Tisn't only tonight you're anacheronistic! It was ages behind that when nullahs were" (FW 202.35-36). McHugh identifies "nullah" as "none". However, in Punjabi "nullah" is the natural water channel made by the rains eroding the landscape, the mark made by the rains on the soil before their descent in rivers to the sea. There is a natural network, in Pakistan at least, of such famous water courses that spring up from the foothills of the Himalayas and flow down through the plains of Punjab where Alexander was forced to meet with the Punjabi Rajahs in an important contest near Jhelum on the river Indus. In fact, the name India is from the Persian name of the river Indus. In the Notebook (VI.C.11-18, p.194) there is an entry on the river "Indus," On page 320 of the same Notebook are added the rivers "Sutlej Helmand," "Sutlej," "Ravi," "Chenab" and "Jhelum." It seems as if these rivers have not been included in the chapter on ALP.

The true appreciation of the region demands a survey of its topography. As "river run" or reverend goddess, ALP issues forth from the head of HCE. This suggests not only the Christian belief in the origin of Eve from the left rib of Adam but also the Hindu goddesses who depend upon the Himalayas as the abode of the gods for their sustenance. This, in turn, shows the spiritual significance of the Himalayas in Hinduism, to which Joyce refers as "oura vatars that arred Himmals" (FW 599.05). "Himmals" contain the sublime spirituality of Hindu incarnations as "oura vatars," Like the raised head of HCE, the Himalayas play a vital role both in the spiritual glory of Hinduism and also in the offshoots that take root from its foothills. As the cultural womb of the East, all the rivers that

flow from it are mentioned in Finnegans Wake. The great rivers of Asia descend on every side of the Himalayas — the Oxus, the Yaxartes, the Yangtze-kiang, the Brahmaputra, along with the Indus and the Ganges. According to a Chinese saying, the Himalayas are "the nursling mother of the world's rivers," like ALP's "plenty of woom" (FW 465.08).

The chapter of ALP's "mamafesta" includes the following additional rivers from this region. The "Aimih" of Iran is mentioned as "I"ve lost it! Aimihi!...I could listen to maure and moravar again" (FW 213.06-09). "Aimihi!" is Latin for woe is me; Aimihi is also a river like "moravar" or Morava, while "maure" is more over. The river Maur is in Malacca. "Hydeaspects" (FW 208.11) is the Indian river, though the phrase "Hydaspes" could also be read as a pun on the hidden aspects of reality lying below consciousness. Thanks to his acute hearing HCE can discern the "least sound!" in his state of sleep despite some "wadding stack in (his) ear." But he sometimes becomes unconscious of this sound of the bloodstream flowing through his arteries as something "sankh neath" (FW 202.32) his consciousness. "Sankh" is an Indian river. Lying asleep, HCE can hear only vague echoes of languages like Hebrew ("ebro"), Russian ("reussischer") or "Honddu" (FW 198.18) — both Hindu and Japanese because of the rapidity of the protean waters moving ceaselessly like the "affluvial flow and flow."

In another cluster of river names, we learn about HCE's state of lying dead in "Funglus grave" (FW 198.33) in Dublin's Prospect Cemetery: "old Humber... sittang sambre on his sett" is dreaming "drammen and drommen and drumming" (F.198.28-34). In this phrase, "drammen" is river Drammen; and "drommen" is river Drome while "and drumming" (F.198.28-34) suggests dreaming. "Sittang" is a river in Burma. As the waters surge strongly on the shore of his global topography, he hears, though obscurely, the "all thim liffeying waters of" his offspring, "all livia's daughter sons." These are the living sons or daughters of his own "blood veins" or family tree. These rivers of his blood veins include the "Ganges" and "Ma" in Burma: "And the dneepers of wet and the gangres of sin in it!" (FW 196.18) and "Think of your Ma!" (FW 206.03) carry the filth accumulated during their flow in "the body politic" (FW 165.27) toward the "backtowards mother waters" (FW 84.30).

At the heart of Hindu river mythology lies another river which flows through

Burma: "Its that Irrawddyng" (FW 214.0). This phrase refers to the River Irrawaddy whose alternative name is Ravi, which is also the name of a famous river of Punjab that flows through Lahore. Ira means "flow." As fluid, it replenishes health and gushes forth from "the cosmic Milky Ocean". The feminine name "Iravati," according to Zimmer, symbolises "she who is possessed of fluid." She was born when her mother "Daksha" (originally a bisexual), consorted with a god "kashyapa." Along with her fecund nature, she is both the beginning or initiator of movement and its termination.

Iravati, according to Zimmer, was the first divine elephant to originate from Daksha's left side, and was followed by a group of eight female elephants from her right side. Elsewhere, the elephants are mentioned as "Like four wise elephants inundating under a twelvepodestalled table?" (FW 513.35). Though the phrase "under a twelvepodestalled table?" means the Twelve Tables of the Law. Furthermore, they are the ancestors of all elephants whether earthly or heavenly and are the fourfold supporters of the sky. In this dialectic, the river Irrawaddy is the opposite pole of Iravati as space. As the elephant space, she resides, according to Zimmer, in the towering "snowcapped summits"[15] where the lord perspires and space melts into time flowing into many rivers, crossing and re-crossing each other as they transverse the Indo-Burmese landscape. In her liquid state she is "Maya," but as a solid substance she is spread over the Himalayas in dream-like, milky clouds, the "Maya" queen of infinite treasures. The queen in Sanskrit is "maha" as well as the temporal "Maya" and hence "mahamaya," as in "mahamayability" (FW 597.28). The phrase "mahamayability" has been linked by Misra with the mother of Buddha, the Queen Maya or "Mahamaya," an allusion to the book The Light of Asia by Sir Edwin Arnold. Misra says that the sentence "son soptimost of sire six sixtusks, of Mayaqueenies sign oscure, hevnly buddhy time" (FW 234.12), is from The Light of Asia describing the legendary birth of Buddha.[16] In one of the incarnations, Buddha was born as a six-tusked elephant "son soptimost of sire sixtusks." Buddha's birth marks a great awakening or spiritual enlightenment "hevnly buddhy time" (FW 234.12). Fritz Senn, however, contends that Joyce's

---

15 H. Zimmer, Myths and Symbols in Indian Art and Civilization, 104. Zimmer attaches deep respect to the elephants, specially white, and writes that their ancestors belong to the "Universal Milk" or white clouds. One of the branches among their ancestors had alighted on the Himalayas too.

16 Fritz Senn, "One White Elephant", AWN, vol.I, No.4, (Aug.1964), 1

source must have been Henry Clarke Warren's Buddhism in Transition. Senn states of Queen Maya that

> In her dream she was bathed and clothed and anointed by the form of guardian angels and placed on a divine coach. Now the future Buddha became a superb white elephant, and was wandering about at no great distance, on Gold Hill. Descending thence, he ascended the Silver Hill, and approaching from the north, he plucked a white lotus with his silvery trunk, and trumpeting loudly went into the golden mansion. And three times he walked around his mother's coach, with his right side towards it, and striking on the right side, he seemed to enter the womb...On the next day the queen awoke, and told the dream to the king...Now the instant the future Buddha was conceived in the womb of his mother, all the ten thousand worlds suddenly quaked, quivered, and shook...[17]

The wandering white elephant on "Gold Hill" is the cloud of the potential space that would quake, quiver and shake once the ice melted after Vishnu's symbolic perspiration: "sleeper awakening...a flash from a future of maybe mahamayability through the windr of a wondr in a wildr is a weltr as a wirbl of a warbl is a world" (FW 597.26-29). These words "the windr of a wondr in a wildr is a weltr as a wirbl of a warbl is a world" (FW 597.26-29) express the amazement of religious enlightenment or "a flash" which enables the sleeper to awaken "sleeper awakening" (FW 597.26). Though Joyce conjures up the message of hope with sorrow and conflict which is inevitable in life. The Wake, like the reality of society and human politics is a welter "weltr" of human languages (expressing action) "wirbl" and warfare "warbl" (FW 597.29. "Warbl" usually accompanies feminine gender such as "woman wordth warbling" (FW 56.27). The phrase "Coil me curly, warbler dear!" (FW 316.14) is from Tennyson's The May Queen "Call me early, mother dear." On another occasion "warbl" is used for marble as "where I'll dreamt that I'll dwealth mid warblers" walls when throstles and choughs to my sigh hiehied," (FW 449, rephrased from the song "I dreamt that I dwelt in marble halls. With vassals & serfs at my side" (McHugh). This "flash" is the lightning which provides energy to the world created, under creation and to be created, in an infinite process of Maya.

It is, therefore, less important to discover the specific legends linked with the birth of Buddha than to learn of the supernatural powers that operate behind the

---

17 Ibid., 2.

physical phenomena of creation. Joyce would allude to any religion if it suited his purpose. Before he forsook his palace and glory, Buddha was like any prince. It was only when he abandoned hearth and home for Nirvana that the power of the waters both liquid and frozen, or the temporal and spatial dimensions, began to be harnessed by him through yoga and he became their celestial avatar, which could be symbolised in a variety of ways in the vast corpus of Indian mythology.

In conclusion, we may say that water implies "unconscious" depths of darkness in the case of ALP, HCE and the Indic divines. To make the case more specific, we may consider a few passages and words that Joyce underlines from Zimmer's Maya der Indische Mythos (refgive number). According to Zimmer[18] if "day" stands for "conscious" like "earth" then "wasser" (water) symbolises the "unconscious." We may consider the following excerpt from the Wake for comparison "Look at here. In this wet of his prow. Don't you know he was a kaldt a bairn of the brine, wasserbound the water baby. Havemmarea. So he wast! HCE has a codfisck..." (FW 198.6-9). The Wake's "water baby" is the "child" (Zimmer, p. 52) "fast asleep" after having played in "the world-bereft of all beings" - "a single lonesome sea." The holy one (Markandeya) then ponders over the child whom he had seen "once before" and comes to the conclusion that the world was "a game of the Maya of the Gods."

The holy one then "entered the body of the sublime one" listening to the swan's immortal voice "I assume many shapes and I glide slowly along in the great world sea when moon and sun have seized to be. I am the Lord and I am the Swan. I brought forth the world out of myself. And I linger in the circling passage of time." HCE in comparison, in the darkest hour of the night, is asleep like a foetus "O, foetal sleep!" His memory has slipped away from the "tropped head" and he lapses into "an unknown body", "backtowards mother waters" (FW 80.30-31). In his case, the image of "the water baby" evokes the sweetness of the sonorous sounds of the bloodstream arising from the heart and returning to it, rhythmically, in perfect measure after coursing through by journeying across the body-politic of human existence on earth. This music has also the babbling sounds of "all the livvylong night, the dell dale dappling night...flittaflute in tricky trochees..." (FW

---

18   Thomas E. Connolly, The Personal Library of James Joyce: A descriptive bibliography (Norwood Editions, State University of New York at Buffalo, 1977, p.46.

6.35, 7.01). The phrase "flittaflute in tricky trochees..." (FW 7.01) is the musical sounds produced by the movement of the water.

According to Zimmer, the "worldfullness which the male god shelters in his belly arches out as its first offspring a womb- the lotus on the umbilicus of the stem- in order to bear the world out of this womb into the light" (p.110). HCE, on the other hand, mesmerized by the "majik wavus" recollects the primordial time [Zimmer uses the noun "primordial"] when not yet "ripe before reason" (FW 212.16-17) or "the night", "unconscious" [Zimmer] the way he had been "engendered" from "heavengendered, chaosfoeted, earthborn", "belows hero" (FW 137.14) "hystry" (FW 535.18), the "whome of your eternal geomater" (FW 297.01).

Joyce conjures up the themes of water, womb and infinity "Now day, slow day, from delicate to divine, divases, Padma, brighter and sweetster, this flower that bells, it is our hour or risings. Tickle, tickle, Lotus spray. Till here next. Adya" (FW 598.11.14). According to Zimmer, the world in which "Allgod" rests "has become one single sea" or the "primal waters" ..."a single lonesome sea." From this state of Absolute darkness, the divine form has its "hour or risings" as Zimmer puts it "he swam in the water as a cloud floats over the sea, as if flaming with light energy, like the sun and its rays, even as if awake in the night..." (p.52), proclaiming "I am Naryana: the primal being from whom everything emerges..." (p.54). From the absolute darkness emerges the quiver of life. It is the water of infinity. It is like the emergence of "vegetation", as Zimmer explains

> Much as water brings forth vegetation, as a pond sends up the lotus from the bottom to the light of the surface, so Vischnu, human shape of the life flood, great with self-begotten young, brings forth from his navel a lotus, whose blossom is the world. Vischnu's navel is itself called as lotus, and the lotus flower is a symbol of the womb; the lotus opens its calyx above the moist surface much as an opened womb in the body of the waters. The worldfullness which the male god shelters in his belly arches out as its first offspring a womb-- the lotus on the umbilicus of the stem--in order to bear the world out of this womb into the light. This lotus carries the primordial earth in the midst of its thalamus. [The earth] is called the "goddess lotus."

There are several references to lotus in the Wake such as "lotus" (FW 492.2);

"Lotus" (FW 598.14); "lotust" (FW 620.3); "lote us" (FW 267.1) and "luting" (FW 448.35). Heinrich Zimmer's Maya der indische Mythos dealing with the lotus, which Joyce marked in his copy of the book (p. 111) remains the most authenticated source. The prime god Vishnu and his earthly avatar in human form, Markandeya, are known to HCE as "Humbermouth. Our Human Conger Eel! -- Hep ! I can see him in the fishnoo ! Up wi'yer whippy ! Hold that lad! Play him, Markandeyn! Bullhead! -- Pull you, sir! Olive quill does it. Longeal of Malin, he'll" (FW 525. 26-7) ..."Humbermouth. Our Human Conger Eel!" "Humbermouth" is river Humber while "Our Human Conger Eel!" is HCE, making his appearance as Vishnu "-- Hep ! I can see him in the fishnoo ! Up wi'yer whippy !" One of Earwicker's name is "Mr Eelwhipper" (FW 496.12). "Whippy!", is HCE . "Fishnoo" is also a fishnet. According to Blavatsky (McHugh), Vishnu is the 2nd god of triad: reincarnated on earth as half-man, half-fish for some time during and after flood. "Bullhead!" may be glossed as "with a bull on a clomp turf" (FW 17.09) for Clontarf the bull meadow. "Longeal of Malin"...or Malin, Co. Donegal is the most northerly point in Ireland. Zimmer (p.45) states that Markandeya is a privileged saint plunging into "the water, the substantial aspect of Vishnu's Maya." Moreover, Zimmer's "radiant as a swan" (p.52 Personal Library) is Joyce's "while gleam with gloom swan" (FW 600.31)."...shrillgleescreaming. That song sang seaswans" (FW 383.15).

℘

7.

St. Kevin and the Yoga Way

This elaboration of the water-related topography of Hinduism and Finnegans Wake strongly suggests that underlying Joyce's thought there is a conception of the power of yoga. It seems as if the entire universe is a hymn, an outpouring of love through self-extinction by immersion into the rivers. Total annihilation of the self is exemplified by St Kevin, whose character suggests the sublime aspect of "Sandhyas," because "Sandhyas" is the union between the "human level of padapatha [and] the divine level of the samhitapathas" according to J.F. Stall's definition.[1]

Chronologically, the St Kevin section comes after the mentioning of "Sandhyas" and "Maya" in Book IV of Finnegans Wake. This also establishes the structural feasibility of the mystic "buddhi" or spiritual purgation after the mist of the delusive "Maya" has evaporated. Broadly speaking, such a character suggests a Hindu Brahmin who, in old age, has chosen the traditional life of isolation in a place in the forest as his nirvana. In this way, a Brahmin earns for himself a special blessing "anander" (FW 581.33). Joyce uses the phrases "Ancient Brahman" .... "Brahman's prayer" in Notebook (VIC 6-16 P.139). Joyce must have borrowed it from Blavatsky. She refers to Jacolliot as describing the supernatural powers of a Hindu "sannyasi" - demonstrating that he was both, present and absent at the same time. The "spectre" is that of an "old Brahman." "He bore on his forehead the signs sacred to Vishnu and around his body the triple cord, sign of the initiates of the priestly caste. He joined his hands above his head, as during the sacrifices, and his lips moved as if they were reciting prayers. At a given moment, he took a pinch of perfumed powder, and threw it upon the coals; it must have been a strong compound, for a thick smoke arose on the instant, and filled the two chambers." Brahman's prayer is described as "his lips moved as if they were reciting prayer." Blavatsky, Isis Unveiled, Vol.II, PP.104-5 "The Living Spectre of a Brahman")

Can St Kevin be identified with such a Brahmin? There are several reasons to

---

1   J.F. Stall "The Origin and Development of Linguistics in India" in Studies in the History of Linguistics: Traditions and Paradigms, ed. Dell Hymes (Bloomington: Indiana University Press, 1974), 65.

confirm such a hypothesis.

In the first draft study of St. Kevin, the saint is an Irish figure who has nothing to do with the world outside Dublin and its waters.[2] His connection with the esoteric East begins with his description as "A naked yogpriest" (FW 601.01). It is the terms such as "naked" and "yog" which open up a Hindu perspective in the interpretation of purely Christian phrases like "the sacrament of baptism" linked with St Kevin. Nakedness is the first removal of the mortal grafting imposed by social conventions, in the journey toward unification with the god Vishnu. "Yog" amplifies this urge, as Heinrich Zimmer defines it as "To yoke, join together, harness; to bestow anything upon anyone; to grant, to confer."[3] P.D. Ouspensky says that The word yoga can be translated by the word "unity" or "union" or "subjugation;" in the first meaning it corresponds to the word "harnessing", from the Sanskrit word "yog", to which correspond the English "yoke" and the Russian "uto" [ego]."[4]

Quoting Aubery's study of St. Kevin, Tindall[5] says that the saint, holding the

2 A. Walton Litz, The Art of James Joyce, (London: Oxford University Press, 1961), 145. According to the chart prepared by Walton Litz, Joyce worked on the St Kevin section, Tristram and Isolde (F.W.384-386) and "pidginfella Bilkilliy-Belkelly" (F.W.611.26) in July-August 1923. In March of that year, Joyce had, according to Ellmann, drafted the first written content for Finnegans Wake, dealing with King Roderick O' Connor (F.W. 380-82). The chronology of the Wake indicates that, though the story of St Kevin occurs in the last Book just before the final monologue of ALP, its drafting had been completed in the very first year of its 17-year gestation.

3 Heinrich Zimmer, Myths and Symbols in Indian Art and Civilization, 48-49.

4 P.D. Ouspensky. A New Model of the Universe, Arkana edition, (London: Routledge & Kegan Paul, 1984). See chapter "What is Yoga?" Ouspensky is cited at several places in the Wake, e.g. the word "cubehouse," whose six dimensions, three of space and three of time, are a "Euclidean continuum" according to Ouspensky. Out of these, three-dimensional reality draws the boundaries of normal human life based on the experiences perceived by the human senses. Where we touch the fourth dimension is the point of intersection; Joyce reiterates this in St Kevin's section of Book IV: "touring the no placelike no timelike absolent...When the messenger of the risen sun...shall give to...each spectacle his spot and to each happening her houram." (FW 609.01). The fourth dimension, as Ouspensky explains, is the aggregate of all time, permitting the actualization of possibilities which remain latent and unrealised. St Kevin's renunciation and his mergence with water are a clear signal of such a realisation. His bathtub is circular and his altar is square. St Kevin symbolises the circle which circumscribes the square of "prakrati," "rajas" and "Maya." By rising higher than this melange of confusion and chaos, St Kevin symbolises the tenth Heaven, which links the Islamic hierarchies of Intellect with those of Dante's paradise; such a mandala is the essence of esoteric systems (whether East or West), mythical doctrines (such as that of Hinduism) and the revealed religions including the thought of St Augustine, Dante, Berkeley and Avicenna.

5 W.Y. Tindall, A Reader's Guide to Finnegans Wake, 314. Tindall writes that Kevin's spiritual journey to Glendalough and the setting up of the bathtub altar are an example deriving from Yeats's building of a house at Lough Gill. The meeting of the waters of "Yssia and Essia" is like that of

cross, was escorted to Glendalough by angels. At Glendalough, where the two waters "Yssia" and "Essia" meet, he intoned "Sanctus, Sanctus, Sanctus," before building a "honeybeehivehut" (FW 605.17-24). We have already looked at the parody of the Catholic mass "Sanctus, Sanctus, Sanctus" as "Sandhyas! Sandhyas! Sandhyas!." St Kevin's litany reflects Joyce's use of puns to bring together different spiritual meanings.

St Kevin's asceticism ascertains the need for meditation. Henry S. Olcott in "A Buddhist Catechism" (a book that was in Joyce's personal library, as is noted by Ellmann) explains how Buddha one night left the privileges of a wealthy up-bringing for the forests in order to discover "duhkha" or sorrow. He spent about six years in deep meditation, and during this period of penance, he mortified his increasingly emaciated body. According to Olcott, "He took less and less food and water, until, it is said, he scarcely ate more than one grain of rice or of sesame seed each day."[6]

The second point that deserves attention is St Kevin's "honeybeehivehut" — an allusion to Yeats's Lake Isle of Innisfree and possibly also to the shape of an ancient Celtic building. Critics of the Wake have not touched upon the spiritual value of "honey" and "bees" from the Hindu perspective of the Upanishads. According to R.C. Zaehner, Brahma or the World Soul can only be expressed through parables. He refers to one of these in the Upanishads: "Bees for instance are seen to collect the pollen of different trees and the whole is reduced to honey, the different pollens remaining unaware of what has happened to them. Individuality, then, is transcended in a higher reality to which it has nonetheless made its individual contribution. Or it is like the sea into which individual rivers flow, losing themselves and merging in the great whole."[7]

Mergence "in the great whole" whether of the rivers into the sea or that of bees with the beehive, is described as "padapodopudupedding" (FW 599.07-08). According to The Rig Veda, the word "pada" means the place of mutual dwelling

---

the watering of the two girls in the Park.

6 W.Y. Tindall, A Reader's Guide to Finnegans Wake, 314. Tindall writes that Kevin's spiritual journey to Glendalough and the setting up of the bathtub altar are an example deriving from Yeats's building of a house at Lough Gill. The meeting of the waters of "Yssia and Essia" is like that of the watering of the two girls in the Park.

7 R.C. Zaehner, Hinduism (Exeter: Exeter University Press, 1962), 61.

of men and gods.[8] There they are served with honey which springs from the honey-fountain, lying under the feet of a cow which unearths the "ocean" by scratching its feet and thus allows honey to serve as the "elixir of immortality." "Pada" is combined with "pedding," a pun on pudding. In the same passage of the Wake, the word "hoof" (FW 599.07-08), has been used more than once suggesting the cow in The Rig Veda from beneath whose hoofs the immortal nectar springs forth. The word honey is often used in both The Rig Veda and the Wake: "And honey is the holiest thing ever was, hive, comb and earwax, the food for glory," (FW 25.05); "silent as the bee in honey" (FW 133.01); "I am your honey honeysugger" (FW 141.33); "bracelets of honey" (FW 235.34-5); "will wend a way of honey" (FW 267.27). The phrase "Millickmaam's honey" (F.277.27) reveals the association between milk and honey applicable figuratively to the cow mother of The Rig Veda.

References like "Noah's ark," "Moses cradle," "lake born," "sources of Nile," "floating grass," "floating isles," and "isle-form-raft" (Notebook, 29:18-19) in relation to St Kevin indicate another dimension of his character. All of these allusions confirm the immense sanctity attached to water though they also reflect the impact of Yeats's Lake Isle of Innisfree. Applied to St Kevin, they show his purification of soul.

In Hinduism, such a tradition of meditation goes back to antiquity. "Shiva" (FW 80.24), the third in the triad after Brahma and Vishnu, is a god of destruction followed by regeneration. Among other things, he is the archetypal Divine Yogi. Zimmer refers to the Himalayas and it is there that Shiva meditates in isolation. The initiate Bhagiratha goes to the Himalayas and during penitence becomes severely emaciated, living on "dry leaves, finally on one leg to win over benevolence", comments Campbell.[9] In the Hindu traditions, the ascetic yogis have been found to stand on one leg in water or forests and caves. The tradition of forty days' standing in water is like a proverb in the subcontinent. An interesting parallel has been mentioned by Katherine Scherman. Tracing the legend of St Kevin from Irish mythology, Scherman writes of St Kevin's standing so still for forty days at Lent

---

8   The Rig Veda, (Penguin Classics, 1983), 226.
9   H. Zimmer, Myths and Symbols in Indian Art and Civilization, edited by Joseph Campbell, Bollingen Foundation, 1946, 115.

that two birds built nests in his hands, laid and hatched their eggs.[10] In the Wake, there is a clear reference to this:

"... changed endocrine history by loeven his loaf with forty bannucks; she drove him dafe till he driv her blind up; the pigeons doves be perchin all over him one day on Baslesbridge and the ravens duv be pitchin their dark nets after him the next night behind Koenigstein's Arbour; tronf of the rep, comf of the priv, prosp of the" (FW 136.28-32).

"Changed endocrine history" is also CEH for HCE. "Endocrine history" is endocrine or ductless glands. "Bannucks' is loaves though "forty bannocks" is "Forty Bonnets" - a nickname of Mrs Tommy Healy of Galway. "Dafe" is deaf. "Baslesbridge" is a district of Dublin. "Koenigstein's" means a king in German. "Tronf" is tronfio in Italian meaning puffed up. "Tronf of the rep" in Latin is triumphus republican meaning triumph of the state. "Koenigstein's Arbour" is also Kingston Harbour and "prosp" is prosperitas or prosperity. It is quite clear that apart from the phrase "the pigeons doves be perchin all over him" the rest of the passage is about HCE.

The quest for self-realisation is further consolidated by a number of images. "Lotus spray" (FW 606.10-12) taken from Isis Unveiled has been commented on by Blavatsky as, "The spring of water-lilies of creation and generation, worked into the earliest dogma of the baptismal sacrament."[11] "Lotus spray" also expresses an urge for prayer, and moreover, we find Bloom sitting in water in "Lotus Eaters."

Commenting on the sentence "I yam as I yam" ... "mitrogenerand in the free state on the air" (FW 604.22-23) "Mitrogenerand" (FW 604.22-23) is free nitrogen (atmospheric) and "in the free state on the air" (FW 604.22-23) is the Irish Free State. To go back to the Indic interpretation, Misra states that the phrase "I am as I am" in Hinduism is equivalent to "I am as He" or "Hamsa."[12] According to Misra, "Hamsa is an imaginary bird which has the capacity to separate water (matter) from milk (spirit)." Zimmer defines "Hamsa" as "the highest gander" ("paramahamsa"). It swims on the surface of the water, "but is not bound to it." It alternates

---

10 Katharine Scherman, The Flowering of Ireland, (Boston, Little, Brown, 1981), 117-119.

11 H.P. Blavatsky, Isis Unveiled: second edition, vol.I, (J.W. Bouton: New York, 1872), 92-93.

12 B.P. Misra, "Sanskrit Translations", AWN, vol.II, No.1, (Feb.1965), 10.

freely between the water and the air according to the season. "Thus it is the home-less free wanderer, between the upper celestial and the lower earthly spheres, at ease in both, not bound to either."[13] The essential feature of this symbolic bird is that its free movements ranging from the celestial to terrestrial spheres are spread over the East and West, as the soul of the universe or the paramount force behind Joyce's "In that earopean end meets Ind" (FW 598.15-16). Though, "I yam as I yam" (FW 604.22) is from Exodus 3:14 "I am that I am."

According to Zimmer, the relevance of Hamsa to the yoga exercises is that yoga develops the rhythms of breathing: "The inhalation is said to make the sound, ham, the exhalation, the sa."[14] This continuous humming of Hamsa, hum-sa enriches the very breath and living presence of this hamsa and hence deepens spiritual awareness. Blavatsky tells many such anecdotes of mesmeric flights in Isis Unveiled. The rhythm reaches its climax and the conscious exercise of Hamsa, ham-sa is unconsciously transposed into saham, sa-ham. "Sa" is "This" and "ham" means "I." Translated into English, the whole exercise means "This is I am." Here "I" is the limited horizon of human consciousness and "This" is the "Highest Being," the unlimited. Hamsa thus means "I am He who is free and divine."

Such an exalted freedom can also be found in the character of Buddha. Some fundamental episodes of Buddha's life can be found in Book 1, chapter 3 and Book II chapter 1 of the Wake. Buddha was popularly known as Siddhartha or "Sid Arthar" (FW 59.08). This interpretation is further supported by the mention of Buddha's stepmother: "Maha's pranjapansies" (FW 59.14). Buddha's mother had a dream in which a star was seen shooting through the void. Buddha's birth, according to the "Deva" (FW 287.04, 614.25) was to usher in an auspicious era of innocence: "from the feeatre of the Innocident" (FW 59.09). On the same page, the name of the hermit who sheltered Buddha after his exile from his father's pal-ace appears as "Aratar Calaman" (FW 59.25). The first hermit who recognised the divinity in the new born Buddha is named as "saint Asitas" (FW 60.16). Buddha's sister, who asked him to wear bracelets, is alluded to in the phrase "where he is being taught to wear bracelets" (FW 60.17). HCE, however, turns the whole situ-ation into parody by saying that so long as Buddha or "Sankya Moondy" spends

---

13 H. Zimmer, Myths and Symbols in Indian Art and Civilization, 48.
14 Ibid., 48-52.

his time in meditating vigils — "played his mango tricks under the mysttetry, with shady apsaras" (the entertaining maidens of Buddha) — "there would be fights all over Cuxhaven" (FW 60.19-22).

In Book II, chapter 1, Buddha's practical steps for reforming society can be found. First, Buddha was not in favour of preaching his laws but he was urged by Divinity to do so — "You don't want to peach but bejimboed if ye do!" (FW 238.18). He decided to preach in the Gazelle Park: "We feel unspeechably thoughtless over it all here Gizzygazzelle" (FW 238.36). His departure into a wood of bamboos after becoming the spiritual Guru, is given as: "bimboowood so pleasekindly communicake with the original sinse" (FW 239.01). Buddha's habit of playing upon the flute while preaching appears as "And whenever you're tingling in your trout" (FW 239.07-08).

In Buddhism, according to Blavatsky and Olcott, ignorance is the root of human suffering. Olcott mentions the following causes of ignorance: "Twelve Niddanas are specified, viz: Avija, ignorance of the truth of natural religion; Samkhara, causal action; Virannana, consciousness of personality, the I am I; Nama rupa — a name and form; Salayantana — the six senses; phasa, contact; vedana, feeling; Tanah, desire for enjoyment; Upadanas, clinging; Bhavaa, individualising existence; Jati, birth, caste; Jara, narana, sokaparidesa, dukha, domanassa, upayasa, decay, death, grief, lamentation and despair."[15] The following passage is a literal transcription of Olcott's A Buddhist Catechism, which was in Joyce's library:

In the ignorance that implies impression that knits knowledge that finds the name-form that whets the wits that convey contacts that sweeten sensation that drives desire that adheres to attachment that dogs death that bitches birth that entails the ensuance of existentiality. But with a rush out of his navel reaching the reredos of Ramasbatham (FW 16.24)

This sentence from Finnegans Wake, according to James Atherton, transcribes one of the passages of Vishna Rama avatar as well.[16] The rooting out of ignorance means the cessation of incarnations. This sets in a chain of emancipation ranging

---

15 Henry S. Olcott, A Buddhist Catechism, 59.
16 James Atherton, The Books at the Wake, (The Viking Press New York, 1960), 225-227.

from the emptying of consciousness, name and form, and the sense organs which establish contact with the world. The removal of contact terminates desire and the quenching of desire eliminates existence which eventually means liberation from the constrictions of the mundane for the everlasting nirvana. In addition to the spiritual message of this passage, it is typical of Joyce in that he conflates as many meanings as possible from as many religions and philosophies into a single phrase or sentence. In the words of Atherton, Joyce "liked to fit as many religions as he could into his allusions."[17] One advantage of such a technique is that it provides a safeguard against anyone taking offence at the use of any one, separately identifiable religion.

The Hindu system of the world Maya operates as an allegory in the Wake. The three soldiers, two girls and the Phoenix Park contrive the misfortune of HCE and hence as agents of the world process, they in turn are themselves the images of disillusionment like their scapegoat. The basic unit of Finnegans Wake is a family of five members: parents, two sons and a daughter. The family as a unit is common throughout human society, whether East or West. In the Wake, this family unit or "holon" expands to such a magnitude that the characters encompass the entire story of humanity, irrespective of culture, creed and colour. The expansion takes place through transformations or Hindu incarnations of Maya. There are two such clear references on incarnation in the Wake besides others: ".. and Memmy and the old folkers below and beyant, wishing them all very merry incarnations in this land of the livvey and plenty of prosperousness through their coming new yonks" (FW 308.25-27).

"Incarnations" in this excerpt implies all those ancestors "the old folkers below" and "beyond." The passage is about the greetings of their children to "Pep" and "Memmy." The children have grown up and we are told that their mother had been feeding them with eggs. The symbol of an egg, as usual in the Wake signifies fertility and procreation. The new generation of Box and Cox are having a great time "in this land of livvey and plenty," that is America. The message is being communicated to the living and the prosperous. The idea of "incarnations," however, is overlapped by the Christian use of mystical terms in this page. There is overwhelming evidence of the impregnation of the divine Logos into human form

17 Ibid., 89

through Christ, for which the passive feminine libido remains a latent, potential receptacle.

On another occasion we read of:

> ".. whereinn once we lave tis alve and vale, minnyhahing here from hiarwather, a poddlebridges in a passabed, the river of lives, the regenerations of the incarnations of the emanations of the apparentations of Funn and Nin in Cleethabala, the kongdomain of the Alieni, an accorsaired race, infester of Libnud Ocean, (FW 600.09-15).

"Incarnations" pertains to the apparitions and emanations of and from the progeny of Finn and Ann living in Baile Atha Claith, Dublin, Ireland. Here the incarnation is rooted in the "river of lives" and HCE names one of these as the river Nile.

HCE impersonates various such roles in response to the multifarious situations. At one time he is "Father Times" (600.02), at another he is King Mark of Cornwall; at others variously the Russian General, Napoleon, Ibsen's "Mysterbolder" 309.13), Oscar Wilde, Parnell, Noah and Adam. His wife is not only "Mother Spaces" (FW 600.02) but also Eve, Sarah, Ann Hathaway and Anna Karenina. Shem is Abel "shembleable" (FW 489.28); Noah's son, Shemuel Tulliver or Gulliver, Nick if Shaun is Mick. Shaun is Cain; Ham, Noah's son, Shaunathaun or Jonathan Swift. Both Shem and Shaun also appear as the Burrus and Caseous, and the Mutt and Taff dichotomies. Issy is successively incarnations of the Isolde of Isolde and Tristam, Swift's Stella, Alice in Wonderland, etc. By subjecting the family to the theme of Fall, or temptation and fratricide, the dreamer accelerates a stupendous wheel of tales: "totalled is toldteld and teldtold in tittletell tattle" (FW 597.08-09). The story remains the same, though cast from the furnace of a new culture every time, with variations of tone, inflexion, lexicon, pun and portmanteau.

By the disruption of the linear concept of events, the Wake becomes a porous matter in which events enter from so many unpredictable directions, feeding and breeding upon one another, covert and overt, of action and reaction that other than the overall diffuse hazy whole, nothing concrete of classical temper is discernible. What remains as residual substratum is the basic pattern of concepts in the characterization, over which ephemeral existence floats like the illusory "motion" of the moon in white clouds. It is precisely the characters that embody various "archaeological" layers of different versions. By interweaving various

phases of history and culture into a pattern, these basic characters become symbols configuring the flux of reality. They, nonetheless, preserve the pressures of time in their capacity as symbols. Yet there is something in them which escapes the erosion of time and so escapes permanent extinction. This maintains their identity, and in this uninterrupted existence these characters make possible a multiplicity of interpretations of human systems, whether divinely established or the products of human ingenuity.

How the Wake transcribes the nature of "Maya" is worth noting. HCE uses the phrase "Sarga, or the path of outgoing" (FW 294.09-10) and then alludes to the different states of "Maya": "Maya-Thaya. Tamas-Rajas-Sattvas" (FW 294.18-20). In Sanskrit, such a path of pouring out from within means "the process of world creation or emanation."[18]

Just as millions of sparks twinkle on the sea's surface and owe their light to the moon, so is mankind capable of existence only when breathed upon by Brahma. The reason for our evanescent existence lies in the fact that we live an illusive life enveloped by Maya, like the dance of light on the sea's surface. Maya means dependence and lack of understanding, screened by the veil of temporality. What the Lord creates is pure and brilliant — that to which HCE refers as "Sattva." In the esoteric system described by Blavatsky, "sattva" is the "rootless root of all."[19] The term "sattva" is also used in Hindi, Punjabi and Urdu to mean the rare gift of being able to look beyond the veil of appearances and understand truth by ascetic enrichment of the soul through incessant meditation and perfect silence. It is the energy which fecundates the Divine Egg, from which arises the primeval matter that fills the cosmos. The "Rajas" are the "Intelligences," which consist of the five senses, mind and understanding. The "Rajas" are of two kinds, the sensuous and the spiritual. The sensuous Rajas are controlled by the mind, without which, Blavatsky observes, they are like sleeping fires. On the spiritual plane, the mind owes its existence to the Supreme Self or Spirit which is also the breath of Brahma.[20] This purity is soon sullied with "Thaya" or the darkness of corporeality. Blavatsky discusses this term as "theo," underlying the state of chaos. It represents

---

18 Joseph Campbell and Henry Morton Robinson, A Skeleton Key to Finnegans Wake, 185.

19 H.P. Blavatsky, The Secret Doctrine, vol.I. 68.

20 Ibid., 96.

the existence of the four elements in an undifferentiated form which, when organised and filled with Brahma's breath, took the shape of the "Soul of the World." [21]

Maya's state of "Thaya" is exemplified by ALP in Book III. It has obsessed and enveloped her mind. She does not confess that her husband (to whom she refers as "my dodear devere revered mainhirr" FW 492.16-17) was imprisoned because of her eating of "forbidden fruit" (FW 492.31). Instead, she petitions — "mepetition to Kavanagh Djanaral" (FW 492.29) that her husband was imprisoned where he was infected with "maladies...below the belch" owing to the "sexular clergy" (FW 492.34-36). This disease had been injected into her, for which reason she had to approach her "family drugger" (FW 492.21) so that he could explain to her whether "was my water good," by which she means the water of India "I hindustand." Her being infected thus is due to Maya, which Campbell and Robinson consider to be the mother of the world.[22]

In Book IV, which contains most of the Hindu thought content, the scope of Maya as a veil of illusions is worth noting. As soon as Book IV opens we hear the speaker murmuring:

> The eversower of the seeds of light to the cowld owld sowls that are in the domnatory of Defmut after the night of the carrying of the word of Nuahs and the night of making Mehs to cuddle up in a cuddlepot, Pu Nuseht, lord of risings in the yonderworld of Ntamplin, tohp triumphant, speaketh" (FW 593.20-24).

The word "tohp" means a town or city like "Ntamplin" or Dublin. The ruler of the world proclaims to the world that by dint of his supernatural powers, he will make the dead souls arise again after the dreadful night of Noah's Age. Moreover, he will cuddle Finnegan (Meh) gently to sleep as soon as his sons replace him in the wake of a new dawn. This new dawn is the "Pu Nuseht." "Pu" according to McHugh is the solar deity of the ancient Hindu Vedas. "Nu" in many Eastern and Western languages means the "new" or "fresh" while "seht" is "health" that allows one to participate actively during the sun"s diurnal journey. The "seeds" depend upon a healthy environment for nourishment. In Hinduism, "seeds" are the "bejas"

---

21 Ibid., 342-343.

22 Joseph Campbell and Henry Morton Robinson, A Skeleton Key to Finnegans Wake, 185.

or sowing of human actions in this world whose fruits, good or bad, are latent in the next cycle of incarnation. The budding of these "seeds" in the month of May is an interesting coincidence as HCE is telling his story in this month. The phrase "making Mehs to cuddle up in a coddle pot" can be related to Fitzgerald's Rubaiyat of Omar Khayyam. "Mehs" is the moon in Persian and "pot" is the sky whose elliptical shape is similar to the "tohp" or stupa of Buddhist religious buildings. He who makes the moon cuddle in the sky is the old Potter of the universe. Pot is synonymous with "Bowl," as in "the Bowl of Night" in Fitzgerald's first quatrain.

The word that engages our immediate attention here is "Pu." It existed in ancient Sanskrit before its transmission first into Hindi, then into Punjabi and finally into Urdu. Urdu, Punjabi and Hindi are successive linguistic offshoots of the metamorphosed form of the original Sanskrit, in this context. "Pu" is the bursting of light from the womb of sheer darkness. After the initial blast, the process is one of gradual but inevitable movement toward the light which unfolds the seams of darkness. As the night retreats imperceptibly, its edges are eroded by the rising fingers of sunlight until it disappears, only to reappear in the evening as "Maya." It is "Maya" because it cannot sustain its grip constantly, though like the timeless recurring cycles of life, eras, eons, it is permanent. It is illusive only in contrast to the "essence of darkness."[23] "Pu" in fact is the differentiation of light and darkness in the human mind. As Blavatsky says, "Light and Darkness are identical in themselves, being only visible in the human mind."[24] "Light" is matter and "Darkness" pure spirit. She believes darkness to be the subjective and absolute form of light whereas light, though glorious in appearance, in reality "is merely a mass of shadows,"[25] as the Gospel of St John says: "And the light shineth in darkness; and the darkness comprehendeth it not." This permanent Darkness is invisible to mankind, who live and breathe in the illusive light of the phenomenal world.[26]

---

23 H.P. Blavatsky, The Secret Doctrine, vol.I, 69.

24 Ibid., vol.I, 70.

25 Ibid., vol.I, 70.

26 According to Hinduism, the universe in which life is possible is itself encased in a darkness from which "Pu" bursts forth. Smaller or finite darkness is circumscribed by greater and greater darkness like the chain of "holons" or Leibnitzian "monads". See Images and Symbols by Mercia Eliade, trans. Philip Mairet (London: Harvill Press, 1961), 71. See also David A. White's Heidegger and the Language of Poetry, (University of Nebraska Press Lincoln and London, 1978), 46- 7. The mystery of this infinite darkness according to Heidegger is like the "peel of silence" ("The Peel of Stillness" U.215). In the words of Heidegger stillness means "the pre-linguistic mode

What we term as light and darkness is in fact the "Maya" which enshrouds us in its folds, as HCE declares. On examination, the entire page with which Book IV begins appears as a strange mixture of far-fetched images illustrating the modern perceptions of the lack of a nexus, centre or omphalos. It begins with "Array! Surrection! Eireweeker to the wohld bludyn world" (FW 593.02-03) (the whole bloody world). Here we should observe the Indian word "Array," and compare it with "Hello!," its nearest equivalent in English. Both "Array" and "Hello" are used to attract the attention of the other which "Eireweeker" is doing by addressing to the rest of the world. Even if this paragraph is interpreted as a call to prayer, we do not find the traditional symbols of humility invoking the guidance of the Almighty. "To what lifelike thyne of the bird can be. Seek you somany matters" (FW 593.04-05). McHugh discovers in the phrase "Seek you somany matters" an echo of Thomas Moore's "What Life Like That of the Bard Can Be!" from Phlanty O'Reilly.

The next sentence takes another turn: "Haze sea east to Osseania Here!" (FW 593.05). According to McHugh, this alludes to the sun worship of the Japanese and other Pacific peoples. "Here! Tass, Patt, Staff, Woff, Havv, Bluvv and Rutter. The smog is lofting" (FW 593.06-07). The smoky fog could be lifting from the Pacific Ocean at the break of day. The image of smoke could also refer to the press agencies whose reports are full of prejudices and mystification, a fact that has also been observed through the eyes of Bloom in Ulysses. The spokesman, an advertiser by profession, portrays a materialistic life permeated by lies and fraud and literary cliches. "Guld modning, have yous viewsed Piers aube? Thane yaars agon we have used yoors up since when we have fused now orther" (FW 593.09-11). The image of soap recalls the tramp portrayed in a "Punch" cartoon. "The old breeding bradsted culminwillth of natures to Foyn MacHooligan" (FW 593.12-13). This "Foyn MacHooligan" is an agent of bloodshed from time immemorial. "We have highest gratifications in announcing to pewtewr publikumst of pratician pratyusers, genghis is ghoon for you" (FW 593.16-18). Here, the ruthless conqueror of the Middle Ages is juxtaposed with the empire of Earwicker, lord only over his pub which provides for the poor, humble Dubliners with drink and gossip. The introduction to Book IV of Finnegans Wake indicates a strange conglomeration of

---

of existence of all the entities in so far as they are linked together within the limits of saying." "Stillness" or "silence" is a potential for "the collection of all entities" says Heidegger, that are transposed into each other by the fourfold earth, heaven, Divine and mortal concurring.

physical phenomena, brought together despite the difference of time and place.

The call for prayer "O rally, O rally, O rally!" at the break of day, signifies the desire to seek refuge from the age of "kali yoga." In Book I of Finnegans Wake, we come across a precise statement which introduces a few Indian deities of fire and light pinpointing the chaos of kali yoga:

> For hear Allhighest sprack for krischnians as for propagana fidies and his nuptial eagles sharped their beaks of prey: and every morphyl man of us, pome by pome, falls back into this terrine: as it was let it be, says he! And it is as though where Agni araflammed and Mithra monished and Shiva slew as Mayamutras the obluvial waters of our noarchic memory withdrew, windingly goharksome, to some hastywasty timberman torchpriest, flamenfan, the ward of the wind that lightened the fire that lay in the wood that Jove bolt, at his rude word (FW 80.20-28).

We may look at the literal aspect first. "Sprack for krischnians" is also to speak for the Christians a propaganda "propagana fidies" carried out by the missionary work, led probably, form the Papal Headquarter. "Every morphy man" is the mortal nature of humanity. The phrase "and his nuptial eagles sharped their beaks of prey" carries the undertones of Shelley's Promethus Unbound; "windingly goharksome," is being obedient; "timberman" is a carpenter and, "torchpriest, flame fan," is a play on words for a "flame fan" priest who lit the ritual fire on 31 October, on Hill of Ward, County Meath in ancient Ireland "the ward of the wind that lightened the fire that lay in the wood that Jove bolt, at his rude word." "Propagana" is a clear play on "propaganda" and "gana" which is Hindustani for "song."

"Allhighest" is the omniscient and omnipotent. He is above "krischnians." Does "krischnians" mean Christians? The Wake commentators don't give any clue. Keeping this phrase in the context of the passage, one could interpret its letters as denoting the Hindu deity Krishna, as indicated by the earlier reference to the "Allhighest." Joyce (Notebook VIC6-16 P.8) lists "Krishna." An avatar of Vishnu, Krishna is brave and heroic like Hercules. Krishna and Vishnu complement each other in their divine attributes. In The Bhagavad Gita, Krishna helps Arjuna drive his chariot. Krishna's sense of humour as a child is well known despite being a God. Krishna is "Sat Cit Ananda" - one who blesses and is knowledgeable. Radha and Krishna are the fountainhead of spiritual energy of the universe. In the

Notebook VIB 27-8, P.208 , Joyce also mentions Shiva, who is the Supreme God according to Vedas. Shiva means God who purifies because He cannot be affected by "Maya" or matter/nature and its three forms which are satva, rajas and tamas. As part of the Trinity, if Brahma is the creator, Vishnu the preserver, then Shiva is the destroyer. Shiva is the Lord of ascetics. He is represented by three horizontal stripes and is thought to have immersed Himself in profound state of meditation on Mount Kailash.

As Zimmer explains, the birth of Krishna took place amid the chaos which had swamped the earth with evil.[27] In the Wake, this evil is projected by alluding to the snakes which had begun to swallow the idyllic valley where Krishna lived happily. One day while wandering alone, Krishna saw the foam of vapours whirling in the stream. The region belonged to the serpent Kaliya whose fiery breath ("flame fan") had burnt the trees of the valley grown by Krishna "to some hastywasty timberman torch priest." Krishna himself fell prey to the serpent but was rescued by the intercession of the "Allhighest" Brahma. This transcendent and immanent Demiurge killed the serpent and hence let the course of creation resume itself. "Agni," "Shiva" and "Krishna" are meant to succumb the "Matamoras" or the sons and daughters of this phenomenal "Maya" as God did to the evil people of Noah's time ("noarchic"). All of us are meant to endorse the dialectical role of Maya and be content with "as it was let it be, says he!" whether Hindus, Moslems "Andoo musnoo" (FW 144.12) or Christians as "krischnians" sounds like.

Like Mithra the Persian god of fire, Agni, Krishna and Shiva are engaged in a cosmic struggle against evil which, in these pages connotes as a garbage heap of "droppings of biddies, stinkend pusshies, moggies' doggies, rotten witchawub-bles, festering rubbages" (FW 79.23). HCE also mentions "Jove bolt" and limbo (Paradise Lost) - a region between Paradise and Hell. Once the heap or the tomb is dug up, a promising new era comes into existence, instantaneously.

The operation of Maya in Book IV suggests the same dialectical process of conflict between (to use the Sanskrit, Hindi, Punjabi terms in the Wake) "vah", "Duhkha", "Parasama". "Vah" means to flow or carry. McHugh's short definition does not do justice to its profundity. It refers to the protean forces of nature that

---

27 Heinrich Zimmer, Myths and Symbols in Indian Art and Civilization, edited by Joseph Campbell, (Bollingen Series VI, New York: Bollingen Foundation, 1946), 82-4.

are ignited by the constantly changing sun: "Vah! Survan Sur! Scatter brand to the reneweller of the sky, thou who agnitest" (FW 594.01-02). "Vah" is the opposite of "Aah" and means what Joyce notes as "Sukha" Notebook (VI.B. 5, p.342) in Urdu poetry. "Vah" is a release say from the humid depression of weather after rain. Even this relief is followed and preceded by the choking suffocation caused by low pressure during the monsoons. "Survan" is the god of good shape and of precious gold. As such, it alludes to the rising of the sun out of the obscuring darkness of the night. This "iteritinerant" (FW 594.07) journey unfortunately is the course of "kal" the destroyer (FW 594.07) bounded by the dreamer "Somnionia" (FW 594.08), the sleeping giant at whose call there sets in the multiform flow carrying within it the streams of life so intertwined as to elude a definite identity, "Kilt by kelt shell kithagain with kinagain" (FW 594.03-04). In its form as "apad" (though it has its Latin overtones) which B.P. Misra interprets as "a calamity"[28] in Sanskrit, Maya is "Arans Duhkha" (FW 595.22). "Arans" echoes "Heran" —— a Persian word used when one is taken by surprise. "Duhkha" is deception, as when one is duped out of ignorance. The phrase "Arans Duhkha" reflects the difference in consciousness between what we think we are individually, and what our objective observation is, in socio-political terms. It causes a violent reaction in consciousness which provokes counter-violence and thus the unleashing of an endless vicious circle of conflict. It is that state of uncertainty, fear, and hallucination, which exists in the fate of HCE after his fall and the charges that undermine his public image and future prospects. However, the glory of "Duhkha" lies in the eventual realisation of Nirvana. It becomes a source of hope after purgation from ignorance. In the Notebook (VIC 1-7 P.389), Joyce uses the word "a sukha." "Sukha" in Buddhism is a state of profound peace achievable by meditation. In Sanskrit and Pali, "sukha" means "happiness." It is also termed as "dhyana" in Sanskrit. If "piti" or "priti" in Sanscrit means a joy, which raises a smile or laughter, then "sukha" is a joy of different nature. Sukha is joy which comes from contemplation. It does not need to be demonstrated through smiles or other outward gestures.

Maya encompasses the whole of human existence and its history. The next paragraphs in Book IV reflect its movement back and forth in many directions. Many births, marriages, deaths and burials have occurred in its cyclic patterns. From the earliest nomadic tribes the dreamer can hear the indiscriminate sounds

---

28 B.P. Misra, "Sanskrit Translations" AWN, vol.I, No.6, (Dec.1964), 9.

"hoof, hoof, hoof, hoof, padapodopudupedding on fattafottafutt" (FW 599.07-08), the footfalls of men and beasts trampling and pounding in the pursuit of power. The aggression of the stronger against the weaker does not go unnoticed by the deities living and watching from the Himalayas: "oura vatars" (father) "that erred in Himmal" (FW 599.05). Closely related to these Himalayan deities is the reference, "but nevertheless the emplacement of solid and fluid having to a great extent persisted" (FW 599.10-11), implying the "solid" HCE as the masculine Himalayas and the "fluid" ALP as the rivers that flow down from the mountains. The time changes but not the pattern. The nomads of the past have been replaced by today's "haves and have-nots" (FW 599.14), capitalist ("monetary") and "military" "systems."

Maya is something of which Blavatsky says "we touch and do not feel it; we look at it without seeing it; we breathe it and do not perceive it; we hear and smell it without the smallest cognition that it is there, for it is in every molecule of that which is our illusion."[29] Despite our perception of it with all our senses, "Maya" still eludes us. Maya is the composition and decomposition of "Vah" and "Duhkha." It is the cell with its protoplasm and its unchanging nucleus, both of which are interdependent. The cells form an organic unity and congregate around the nucleus.

The "Egg" in this section is the protein of "Maya" which has been extensively symbolised. As Brahma's cosmic egg, it is the lotus which is evolving out of the infinite dark waters. The egg is also engaged incessantly (in this section) in preparing new tissues. It enters the stomach which churns a "wholemole, millwheeling vicociclometer" (FW 614.27), setting in motion wheels within wheels of Vico's cycles, as chaos (compare Blavatsky's disc discussed above). Maya as an automatic machine can "autokinatonetically" create mixtures of all kinds by absorbing anything "preprovided with a clappercoupling smeltingworks exprogressive process," (FW 614.29-30), in this process of the composition and decomposition of the very "heroticisms, catastrophes and eccentricities transmitted by the ancient legacy of the past" (FW 614.34-35: 615.01). On a psychological level, it works out through the eruption of what has been repressed in the unconscious. "Clappercoupling" is the creative process after the mating of two opposite genders while "smelting"

---

29 H.P. Blavatsky, The Secret Doctrine, vol.I, 330.

is a kind of fish. Fish breed fish in natural fashion in water. "Clipperclappers" (FW 614.13) is gossip. As usual with the Wake, the fecund processes of nature may turn out to be a mere gossip as in this case.

If "Sandhyas" is an incessant struggle between the waxing and waning shades of light and darkness, of human responses to the environment, then Maya as the protean force substantiates the obvious dialectic of light and darkness through "parasama":

> ...with gygantogyres, with freeflawforms; parasama to himself; atman as evars..... whitelock not lacked nor temperasoleon; though he appears a funny colour; stoatters some; but a quite a big bug....also the hullow chyst excavement; astronomically fabulafigured; as Jumbudvispa Vipra foresaw of him (FW 596.23-30).

"Gygantogyres" may be considered as the gigantic cycles of time or "eons". "Gyres" is Yeats's word for the dialectical system in which history and time flow in cycles. To this may be added the "freeflawforms" as the spirit of the universe coursing through the cycles of life and history or time and space. This spirit could be that of Brahma or Christ "astronomically fabulafigured." In human form, this enormous figure bears white complexion with a stutter, obviously HCE "hullow chyst excavement."

"Jumbu" is the eternal Tree of life and knowledge. Once it came into contact with matter through the Judeo-Christian, Islamic "serpent," the tree of eternity became mortal and hence assumed the form of our earthly tree whose shadows are termed as "parasama."[30]

B.P. Misra has confined "parasama" to its literal Sanskrit translation as "equal to himself."[31] "Parasama" is another icon of the Punjab. Its roots should be assimilated to those of "Maya" and "Duhkha." As the shade of a tree, it expands and contracts like the heliotrope in the wake of the ascending and descending sun. The nearest allusion to it in Ulysses occurs when both Stephen and Bloom in the early hours before noon experience simultaneously at different places the overshadowing of the sun by a cloud.

---

30 Ibid., 40.
31 B.P. Misra, "Sanskrit Translations" AWN, vol.I, No.6, (Dec.1964), 9.

"Parasama" could be interpreted with reference to the esoteric system of Cabala. The Jumbu Tree would have remained a potent slumbering force in heaven had it not been dynamised by the gnawing serpent, Nidhogg.

> The worms of materiality covered the once healthy and mighty roots, and are now ascending higher and higher along the trunk; while the Midgard snake coiled at the bottom of the seas encircles the earth, and through its venomous breath makes her powerless to defend herself.[32]

According to Blavatsky's quotation from Bhagavata Gita, the roots of this tree are the first cause, logos, its boughs are Brahma and its leaves are the Veda. The Tree remained green so long as it didn't touch "the terrestrial mud of the Garden of Eden, of our Adamic race." The despoiler was the serpent known to the revealed religions. This reptile which soiled the Tree's boughs with earthly mud and mortal life, had to assume various forms since it originated as a beam of light from "the abyss of dark Mystery."[33] Blavatsky's "These forms were cosmic and astronomical" on this page can be detected in the Wake's "astronomically fabulafigured" (FW 596.29).

Sheldon Brivic says of Blavatsky and Joyce that both had a strong faith in projecting woman as the tenth sephir, "Ainsoph, this upright one, with that naughty besighed him zeroine" (FW 261.21). As "besighed," "ainsoph" sounds like the serpent tightening its knot as described in The Secret Doctrine.

The common ground between Hinduism, Joyce and Cabala is that in each of them woman symbolises the tenth sephir.[34] The female, according to Cabala, emanates after being attracted by the "ainsoph" as Binah. From the highest, she has been placed in the tenth Intelligence where she immerses herself as spirit with matter to complete the metaphysical marriage between hell and heaven. Hence ALP as alma mater is the "ondrawer of our unconscionable, flickerflapper fore our unterdrugged," (FW 266.30, 267.01). Brivic comments that "drugged by

---

32 H.P. Blavatsky, The Secret Doctrine, vol.I, 407.

33 Ibid.

34 Sheldon Brivic, Joyce The Creator, 127.

his underside (ISSY), HCE is dragged forward to make the narrative."[35] "ISSY" is also Blavatsky's "Isis" or Isis Unveiled. The narrative potential of languages and ideas lies in the unconscious, the "unterdrugged" of HCE from where it is being pulled out into the present by the female, as Hart quotes Blavatsky: "Imagine a given point in space as the primordial one, then with a compass draw a circle round this point where the beginning and the end unite together, emanation and re-absorption meet."[36] Seen from this angle the black spot, as Brivic comments, is evidently the private part of the woman. In short, the Cabala system in which Ain-Soph plays the role of intercession between the known and the unknown, or the serpent that injects its venom in impregnating the immaterial, is part of the essence of "parasama."

Finnegans Wake is a huge mishmash of the world's heritage of literature and history, epics and religions, fused with the contemporaneous paraphernalia and phantasmagoria of the time of its own composition; hence the section on St Kevin could be considered as the prelude in the creator's mind and the prologue to the actual scribbling of the letters on the blank sheet of paper. Since the first sentence of the book develops a natural conjunction with the last and since river-run, according to Rose and O'Hanlon (Understanding Finnegans Wake, See note 13, p.326) stands also for spiritual reverence, it makes sense to see a symbolism in the St Kevin section as the first in draft yet the last in the book; St Kevin is the holy figure who is the voice of resurrection and reverence through asceticism, like the river. The river as ALP is contrary to asceticism since she is the feminine passive potency, while the Saint is its moral and spiritual dimension since he lives in water in self-mortifying maceration.

---

35 Ibid., 115.

36 Clive Hart, Structure and Motif in Finnegans Wake, 45. Emanation and re-absorption in the creative process of convergence and divergence, of beginning and ending, are succinctly stated in the Wake :"And to find a locus for an alp get a howlth on her baryings as a prisme O and for a second O unbox your compasses...With Olaf as centrum and Olaf's lambtail for his spokesman circumscript a cyclone" (FW 287-94). The circle both ends with and begins from the "howlth" of ALP, whose shape is like the letter "O." This mysterious reality can be interpreted by applying various systems. Whether it is the unconscious, the past being pulled into the present or the serpent whose venom impregnates the spirit, the conjunction of two opposites is unavoidable. The site of the interaction, and the mediation of it, is the "alma mater," the substratum which can assume any shape. Its protean capacity of assuming any form is best illustrated in Book II, chapter 11 (FW 309-82), which contains literary, anthropological, religious, scientific, philosophical, psychological and social ideas from all over the world, the past operating in the present in the endless chain of wheels within-wheels of "mahamayability" (FW 597.26).

If ALP creates through desire by igniting the physical dimension of matter, St Kevin rinses the stain from the soul's glasses by curbing and taming the beast in his journey toward the inner spaces. ALP is nature's blind and uncertain flow, while St Kevin is nature's homogeneous stasis—a station to be attained after ascending very many spiralling spiritual stairs. On the phenomenal level, both are from Dublin, as the text indicates. The one encircles Dublin like the eternal snake that enfolds the Himalayas in Hindu mythology, the other escapes from Dublin's "the Dirt Dump Dublin," into the nearby forests. In the draft study of 1923, Joyce had mentioned:

> Kevin born on the island of Ireland in the Irish Ocean goes to Lough Glendalough, where pious Kevin lives alone on an isle in the lake on which isle is a pond in which is an islet whereon holy Kevin builds a beehive hut the floor of which most holy Kevin excavates to a depth of one foot after which done venerable Kevin goes to the lakeside and fills time after time a tub with water which time after time venerable Kevin empties into the cavity in his hut thereof creating a pool having done which Kevin half fills the tub with water which tub then most blessed Kevin then sets in the centre of the pool after which Saint Kevin fixes up his frock in his loins and seats himself blessed St Kevin in his hiptrubbeth where Doctor Solidarius....he meditates with ardour the sacrament of the baptism of the regeneration of Man by water.

Both St Kevin (in the First Draft Version of St Kevin) and ALP in the novel signify eternity by virtue of the endlessness of the saint"s spiritual destination and ALP's father Ocean"s infinite profundity. The saint signifies spiritual space, as he is in the water, the water is in the tub and the tub is in the water. On the other hand, ALP masks the boundaries of physical space, over which she scratches her bedrock in carrying out the time"s dirt and dump. The saint is purely spiritual, ALP is both spirit and matter in unison, as water is spirit as well. There is also matter in the form of the dirt and history"s dump which pollute her river. ALP is "parasama" and St Kevin is "hamsa."

PART III

Islam in Finnegans Wake

8.

The Truth about the "cubehouse"

According to Islamic traditions, Islam is a religion whose origins cannot be dated and which enfolds the scroll of time from Adam to the Apocalypse and beyond. Islam was revived and reintroduced as a universal religion in Mecca by the Prophet Mohammed (pbuh).

In Finnegans Wake, Islam can be traced from both the above perspectives. Since there are numerous references to Adam and Eve, in this respect the relevance of Islam to the Wake is similar to that of Judaism and Christianity. Islam has numerous points of similarity to the latter religions, particularly in its monotheism. In addition, the Wake contains almost all the important events of the life of the Prophet Mohammed (pbuh).

Joyce obtained material on Islam from several sources. With regard to the Notebook, VI.B.31 Danis Rose writes: "The most important cluster of notes in the workbook (Book VI.B.31) relates to aspects of Islam."[1] Roland McHugh identifies as a prime source of these notes Stanley Lane Poole's The Speeches and Table Talk of Prophet Mohammad.[2] McHugh points out that some of the items that Joyce uses were also cited by James Atherton in the "Koran" chapter of The Books At The Wake.[3] The fact that the majority of the Notebook items were inserted in the Wake reflects Joyce's universalistic approach, which refuses to align itself with any one ideology, code of behaviour or doctrine. Atherton himself takes Hughes's

---

1   Roland McHugh, "Mohammad in Notebook VI.B.31," AWN, Vol. XVI, (No. 4, August 1979), 51.

2   Ibid., 51, McHugh quotes The Speeches and Table Talk of Prophet Mohammad, ed. and trans. by Stanley Lane Poole (London: Macmillan, 1882)

3   Ibid., 51.

Dictionary of Islam to have been Joyce's major source.[4] Grace Eckley adds Burton's translation of the Arabian Nights to the list.[5] Burton's account of the holy shrines in Mecca and Medina during his pilgrimage might also have been in Joyce's mind. There is evidence that Joyce drew on the 11th Edition of the Encyclopaedia Britannica quite extensively for the Islamic themes in the Wake (as he did for nearly everything else in the book - articles on "Mahommedan Religion," "Mahomet," "Mecca" all play a featured role in Joyce's Islamic word-hoard.

The translators of the Quran into English are mentioned in the Wake. The first, "Robert of Retina" (so cited in Hughes's Dictionary of Islam; his real name was Robert of Chester), was also the first to translate the Quran into Latin; he is mentioned by Shaun: "I have his quoram of images all on my retinue, Mohomadhawn" (FW 443.01-02). In Hughes's Dictionary, the Koran is spelled "Qur-an," punned here as "quoram." According to Thomas E. Connolly, Joyce was also familiar with J.C. Mardrus's translation of the Quran.[6] Mardrus also translated the Arabian Nights. He turns up in the Wake as "the Murdrus dueluct!" (FW 374.12), or Mardrus's dialect, and "The author in fact was mardred" (FW 517.11). George Sale's English translation of the Quran was completed in 1734; his name possibly appears as "saale" (FW 196.15); "for sale!" (FW 444.22); "expositoed for sale after referee's inspection," (FW 498.35); "for the sale of"(FW 574.06); and "As soon as we sale him geen" (FW 606.36). J.M. Rodwell and E.H. Palmer occur respectively as "dodwell disgustered" (FW 212.33) and "Like as my palmer's past policy" (FW 539.08).

Cast in the form of a dream, Joyce's "nightbook" blurs identities and hence no particular book or idea can be exclusively cited as antecedent. During his reading of these books, Joyce's absorptive vision must have grasped the essence of Islam, which was then ready to be used as occasion arose in telling the tale of human history and the human mind. This is illustrated by the example of the "cubehouse" (FW 5.14). When the dreamer turns his attention to the "cubehouse" and digs deeper into the historic layers of this sacred place, the images which subsume

---

4   James S. Atherton, The Books at the Wake, (London: Faber and Faber, 1959), 201-218.

5   Grace Eckley, Children's Lore in Finnegans Wake, (Syracuse: Syracuse University Press, 1985), 57-68.

6   Thomas E. Connolly, The Personnel Library of James Joyce, (Buffalo, New York: University of Buffalo, 1955), 23.

the Islamic and the pre-Islamic cult of the "Kaba" epitomize the theme in a single sentence; Joyce has extracted this quintessence from the many sources of his reading. Even a shade of dim memory glows suddenly to magnify the dreaming mind of Earwicker. Such a sudden trace on the cosmic mind of the "Here Comes Everybody" hero is deeply rooted in the slowly accumulating, empirical and practical experience of history.

As soon as the four densely convoluted, introductory paragraphs of the Wake crisscross Earwicker's mental landscape, we read:

> Our cubehouse still rocks as earwitness to the thunder of his arafatas but we hear also through successive ages that shebby choruysh of unkalified muzzlenimiissilehims that would blackguardise the whitestone ever hurtleturtled out of heaven. Stay us wherefore in our search for tighteousness, O Sustainer, what time we rise and when we take up to toothmick and before we lump down upown our leatherbed and in the night and at the fading of the stars! For a nod to the nabir is better than wink to the wabsanti. Otherways wesways like that provost scoffing bedoueen the jebel and the jpysian sea. Cropherb the crunchbracken shall decide. Then we'll know if the feast is a flyday. She has a gift of seek on site and she can allcasually ansars helpers, the dreamydeary. Heed! Heed! It may half been a missfired brick, as some say, or it mought have been due to a collupsus of his back promises, as others looked at it. (There extand by now one thousand and one stories, all told, of the same.) (F.W.5.14-29).

This passage is Joyce's vision of the essence of Moslem culture. Examine the passage without knowledge of its Islamic background, and the meaning fragments; but observe it in the light of Islam, and all is clear. From the "cubehouse" as Kaba to "there extand by now one thousand and one stories" (the Arabian Nights), the passage is a condensation of the Moslem belief in Kaba as omphalos (navel). Kaba is the knot which binds the unknown with the known, and is emblematic of the impact of Islam on the Arabian Nights as its cultural heritage, circumscribing the Islamic approach to the force behind, for example, Bloom's "Elijah is coming"[7] by linking the supernatural to natural tangible reality. Though most of the Arabian Nights carries the indelible stamp of pre-Islamic modes of life in the East, Islam remains one of the salient features of the tales. In the world of Joyce, however,

---

7 "Elijah" has been discussed by Lane in his translation of The Arabian Nights Entertainments. What Bloom calls "Elijah" is Islamic "Khidr," a wizard noble soul.

there is an indiscriminate flow of both pagan and monotheistic beliefs. He refers not only to Islam, but also to the pagan deities of Arabia, such as the "3 moon goddess"[-es] (Notebook VI.B.31, p.52) of whom Stanley Lane Poole states, "The great objects of worship were the sun, and the stars, and the three moon-goddesses."[8] Polytheism is another prime bond among Eastern cultures and cults prior to Islam, and there are references to it in the Arabian Nights. Even the form of worship of the Hindu and Zoroastrian religions in comparison to the monotheism of Judaism, Christianity and Islam constitute an appropriate juxtaposition of contraries in the Wake.

- Previous critical interpretations of the "cubehouse" passage fail to catch its true import. Campbell and Robinson translate the first sentence of the passage as "what brought about that Thursday morning tragedy? Our house still rocks to the rumour of it; there is a shabby chorus of those who would blame him; the evidence is difficult to evaluate — Therefore, stay us (O Sustainer) in our search for truth."[9] Rose and O'Hanlon hold that, "The flaw was in the bricks" that caused this "municipal sin business"; there gathered "all the hooligans yelling outrageously in celebration."[10] John Gordon has the following interpretation: "No sooner does he stand erect and give us a look at him than a "shebby choruysh" of the ridiculers begins to taunt him. He now sees himself mainly as a different sort of majestic outsider, Mohammed set upon by infidels."[11] Further, Reighard Motz interprets the "cubehouse" as a Euclidean six dimensional-diagram, in which length, breadth and height are the only dimensions knowable to the human senses: "The six-dimensional form of a body is incomprehensible to us...Three-dimensionality is a function of our senses. Time is the boundary of our senses. Six dimensional space is reality. The world as it is."[12] He defines the "arafatas" as "Our Father," from whom urgent hope is invoked out of fear. Motz also suggests that the phrase "The whitestone

---

8   Stanley Lane Poole, translator and editor of The Speeches and Table Talk of Prophet Mohammad, (London: Macmillan, 1882), 22.

9   Campbell and Robinson, A Skeleton Key to Finnegans Wake, 39.

10 Rose and O'Hanlon, Understanding Finnegans Wake, 07.

11 John Gordon, Finnegans Wake: A Plot Summary, 111.

12 Reighard Motz, Time as Joyce Tells It, (Mifflinburg, Pa: Mulford Colebrook Publishing, 1977), 43.

ever hurtleturtled out of heaven" relates to Revelations,II,17:

He that hath an ear let him hear what the Spirit saith unto the churches: To him that overcometh will I give to eat of the hidden manna, and will give him a whitestone, and in the stone a new name written, which no man knoweth saving he that receiveth it.

The mourners do indeed gather around HCE's coffin as a token of respect for him, though at the same time bearing him ill-will. He fell from the skyscraper of his in-built over-vaulting ambition. However, the "municipal sin business," which occurs in the Phoenix Park, has not yet been referred to in the Wake. "The flaw was in the brick" is certainly relevant, as Rose and O'Hanlon explain, but this is not the only possible interpretation. Similarly, the "cubehouse" is indeed six-dimensional, but Motz's interpretation of "the whitestone" is questionable. McHugh's Annotations define the above sentence clearly:

- "cubehouse": Literal translation of Kaba, the centre of Islam;
- "arafatas" : pilgrims must visit the arafatas for prayer;
- "shebby" : likeness;
- "choruysh" : ruling tribe at Mecca at the time of Mohammed
- "blackstone" : Blackstone of Kaba at Mecca (came down white but was blackened by sin). In addition, it should be added that "muzzlenmissilehims," which is an "Arabesque" coinage that clearly seems to allude to Muslims ("Muzzl ... ims"), but also introduces "Muzzle," Missile," and "hims" (which could be a homonym for "hymns").

The truth about the "cubehouse" requires further elaboration. In the Notebook (VI.C. 6-16), Joyce draws a complete sketch of the Hajj ceremony: "hajj, Kaaba, masa, sacred comsi, safa, Merwa, Zanar(sansar), 7 circuits, brush pressed against hair, prayer, kneading place Majan, Kiswa, veil, bab-el-arun, illah, shear the hair, H(iram, dress) labbeyka, circling to Jamrat" (p.339). Unquestionably, the first sentence of the "cubehouse" passage carries a Moslem message. In the context of Islam, the Kaba is the umbilical cord that binds the tree of prophecy from Adam to Mohammed.

i) The Kaba and the Prophet Ibrahim:

The truth of the "cubehouse" according to Islam begins essentially with the prophet Ibrahim. The Quran says that "Ibrahim with Ismail raised the foundations of the House" (2:119). Expelled from his ancestral home in Chaldea, Ibrahim set out for Kanaan. Accompanied by Hajra and the infant Ismail, he arrived at Beer Sheba near Mecca. Ibrahim left his wife and son here in order to continue his journey. Their food and provisions were soon exhausted, and the mother set out in search of water in the fearsome heat of the desert. Moslem tradition holds that Hajra ran for water seven times from the hill of Marva to that of Safa and back. When she returned, she found to her surprise that a spring had erupted at the infant Ismail's feet. This spring is known as the well of Zamzam (Joyce's "By the Stream of Zemzem" (FW 105.07)) and its water is considered holy. Hajra"s desperate search for water between Marva and Safa is commemorated during the Hajj by the pilgrims running seven times between these hills.

The sentence from the Wake quoted at the beginning of the present chapter contains almost all the important elements of the traditions attached to the Hajj and to Ibrahim's time in Mecca.

ii) The Black Stone: "that would blackguardise the whitestone ever hurtleturtled out of Heaven" (FW 5.12).

The stone is not the meteorite "hurtleturtled out of heaven" implied by Joyce, nor was it white in the beginning but subsequently blackened by human sin, as some (like Joyce) believe. The Black Stone is placed in the southeastern corner of the Kaba about five feet from the ground. In the words of Partin, it is:

> "... an irregular oval, about seven inches in diameter, with an undulated surface, composed of about a dozen smaller stones of different sizes and shapes, well joined together with a small quantity of cement, and perfectly smoothed."13 [13]

In Moslem tradition, it is venerated as "Yamin Allah" (the right hand of Allah). According to the Quran, Allah has infinite treasures, armies and domains. A subject testifying his or her loyalty must go personally to the symbolic right hand

---

13 Harry B. Partin, The Muslim Pilgrimage: Journey To the Centre, 19.

embedded in the Kaba, so attaining freedom from evil. The Black Stone also marks the point where the sevenfold circumambulating around the Kaba begins and ends. A.J. Arberry suggests that going round and round the point of confluence between centre and circumference strengthens the spiritual state of the worshipper.[14] Further, according to the Hindu Upanishad, "I return myself with the return of God. I return myself along with the turn of the sun" (II, 9). Thus, by turning and turning, the worshippers follow the endless course of the sun, nature and eternity. Von Grunebaum suggests that the sevenfold rounding of the Kaba is, like the movement of the planets round the sun, a sign of sympathy with the universe.[15]

iii) Arafatah "to the thunder of his arafatas": (FW 5.15)

The Plain of Arafatah lies some twelve miles East of Mecca. Traditionally, it was at Arafatah that Adam and Eve met again after a separation of two hundred years. Here, too, Mohammed (pbuh) delivered his famous address which is held to contain the essence of the Islamic faith. The pilgrims at the Hajj move toward Arafatah on the 8th day of Zul-Hajj. As the sun begins to decline toward evening, the preacher delivers his sermon. He completes the sermon at about sunset and then the whole plain is filled with the litany of Quranic verses. Like other holy places, Arafatah was a centre of festivity and trade in pre-Islamic days. According to Patkin, the pre-Islamic Arabs made two pilgrimages annually, one to Arafatah in the autumn and another to Mecca in the spring. Drinking, racing, gambling, wrestling and literary competitions took place on these occasions. In the words of Syed Amir Ali:

> It was an occasion of profiting for everyone. In these vast assemblages, poets pub-lished their new compositions, orators made harangues before the spell-stricken mass to demonstrate their talents, professional wrestlers fascinated the spectators,

---

14 Quoted in A.J. Arberry, "The Way in Islam" in The Aryan Path: (The Indian Institute of World Culture Banglore), Vol.XXXVII, No.8, (August 1961), 350. During the Hajj ceremonies, Aberry believes, the circumambulating around the Kaaba is a reminiscence of the dance of the Sufis. Arberry quotes Rumi as saying:
"Come forth, O day!
The motes are dancing gay;
The spirits in delight
Dance wildly through the night."

15 G.E. Von Grunebaum, Mohammadan Festivals, (New York: H. Schuman, 1947), 30.

the traders brought the merchandise to make good earnings.[16]

In addition to the mention of "arafatas" (FW 5.15), two further Joycean references are worth noting in this connection. First, "Okadah" (Notebook) is a place like Arafatah, where, according to Stanley Lane Poole as noted by McHugh, "They had an annual fair, the Academie francaise of Arabia...This fair of Okadah has a literary congress."[17]

Second, Joyce shows his familiarity with the artistic achievements of pre-Islamic Arabs by citing the adage "brain of Franks, hands of Chinese, tongue of Arabs" (FW 127.29-30). If the Greek marvelled at his sculpture and saw the truth of rational justice enshrined in his architecture, the Arabs gloried in three things: poetic eloquence, archery and horsemanship.[18]

iv) The Koreish: "but we hear also through successive ages that shebby choruysh of unkalified muzzlenimiissilehims that would blackguardise the whitestone" (FW 5.15-17).

The phrase "shebby choruysh" suggests the tribe of the Koreish into which Mohammed (pbuh) was born. It was this tribe who treated him so shabbily after his declaration of the divine message, though they also became established at Mecca and were entrusted with guarding the Kaba (punned as to "blackguardise"), by the Command of God. The prophet's Koreshite pedigree is traceable from his paternal great-grandfather Hashim. Hashim, who was one of the leading merchants, enjoyed the privilege of collecting taxes to be spent on the poor during annual pilgrimages. He would send one caravan to Yemen in the winter and another to Syria in the summer. He died during one such journey at Gaza in about ad 510. His only son Shayaba was in Yathrib. His civil prerogatives were transferred to his younger brother Muttalib, a man of prodigious generosity. Muttalib took Shayaba back to Mecca and, as they entered the city, the people mistook Shayaba for a slave of Muttalib's. He was, thereafter, known as Abdul Muttalib (i.e., the slave of Muttalib). Mohammed the Prophet (pbuh) was the grandson of

---

16 Syed Amir Ali, The Spirit of Islam (London: Cristophers, 22 Berners Street, 1935), 114.

17 Roland McHugh, "Mohammad in Notebook VI.B.31," AWN, Vol.XVI.No.4, 51. The phrase "days of" occurs in the Notebook (VI.B.31.) and alludes to Lane Poole's reference saying "The Arabs of the Days of ignorance."

18 Ibid., 52.

Shayaba. Thus Joyce's "shebby choruysh" can, on one reading, be interpreted as "Shayaba Koreish."

Like Joyce's Dublin, Christian and Jewish Jerusalem, and the Hindu four corners of the subcontinent, the Moslem Kaba is the navel of faith from which the journey of spiritual salvation begins. Kaba is as powerful a symbol for Islam as Dublin is for Joyce. "For myself," Joyce once said, "I always write about Dublin, because if I can get to the heart of Dublin, I can get to the heart of all the cities of the world. In the particular is contained the universal."[19]

Before the arrival of Adam in Kaba (according to Moslem traditions) no human being had set foot on the Earth. Similarly, Dublin had no recorded history before the coming of Sir Tristram or Saint Patrick, as Rose and O'Hanlon state: "Not yet had anything happened. Not yet had Sir Tristram arrived from Brittany on Howth's craggy isthmus to reduce Isolde; not yet had rocks piled by the river O Conee in Georgia exaggerated themselves into a duplicate Dublin."[20]

It is in the streets of Dublin and along its coasts that the journey of Ulysses begins, ends and resumes again. It is in Dublin that ALP's river runs "past Eve and Adam's" (HCE lying sprawled) "from swerve of shore to bend of bay" in between "Howth Castle and Environs."[21] Ostensibly the river Liffey and Howth Castle, are symbols implying the mysterious energy which dynamizes both masculine and feminine forces of the universe. "Anna Livia Plurabella," the voice of river Liffey (amnis Livia) illustrates the Viconian corso and ricorso as she rolls through Dublin in carrying the metropolitan dirt,[22] from the Wicklow Mountains towards the bay and then back again towards the sea, into the arms of her father. On the other hand, HCE, as the icon of resurrection, is the great cackler Humpty Dumpty. As a unified force of land and water they circumscribe Dublin. Dublin's "them four old codgers" (FW 214.33) symbolise the four provinces of Ireland (Ulster, Munster, Leinster and Connaught); "the four apostles, the Four Masters (early sages of Irish

19 Reported by Arthur Power and quoted in William T. Noon's Joyce and Aquinas, (New Haven:Yale University Press, 1957), 60.

20 Rose and O'Hanlon, Understanding Finnegans Wake, 04.

21 Ibid., 04.The mention of Eve before Adam in the first sentence of the Wake indicates the importance of water over land, a theme which may also be traced in Islamic thought. Joyce was familiar with such a theme as is shown in the phrase "mother of the book [under the throne of God" existing in water] Notebook, (VI.B.31), 56.

22 Adaline Glasheen, "The Opening paragraphs," Vol.II, No.2, pp.06-07, AWN, April 1965.

mythology, the four courts of Dublin"[23] in addition to Blake's four zoas, Jung's four types and four trees on the river Liffey bank. As letters they are "the fout dimmansions" (FW 367.29); as points of the compass they are North, South, East and West, and as gospellers they are Matthew, Mark, Luke and John.

Elaborating the kabalistic symbol "that which is above as being that which is below," Clive Hart says that "Shem's and Shaun's cycles begin in the first place in Dublin, where a conflict between the two always takes place, just as Christ and Satan find a common ground on earth, midway between Heaven and Hell."[24] Like Shem and Shaun, in Ulysses, Bloom and Stephen represent the two opposite poles of Dublin's reality as representatives of their civilization; in the words of Marilyn French,

> "On the one hand, it is a very real place, described in such detail that it feels accurate, as indeed the detail is for the most part accurate. The city is unique and particular; we know its shops and houses, its streets and pubs. On the other hand, it is a representation of the idea of city, and by extension of the twentieth century civilization, and by implication and allusion of all cities, all civilizations."[25]

Like Dublin, the Kaba is the navel of the Moslem faith. Harry B. Partin quotes Halabi as saying about the Kaba, "so it is the origin of the earth and its navel."[26] In the words of Dyar Bakri, "the origin of the clay of the prophet (Mohammad) is from the navel of the earth in Mecca, viz. the Kaba."[27] Al-Azraqi, quoted by Partin, says, "Forty years before Allah created the heaven and the earth, the Kaba was a dry spot floating on the water and from it the world has been spread out."[28] Al-Tabari, also quoted by Patkin, says, "The House was created two thousand years before the earth was spread out."[29] The Quran says, "This is the book we have sent down which is blessed and confirms that which is before it, and (it is) that thou mayst warn the mother of the towns and those round it..." (surah 6: 92).

23 Edmund Wilson, "The Dream of H.C. Earwicker" in james joyce: Two Decades of Criticism, ed. Seon Givens, (The Vanguard Press, New York, 1948), 324.

24 Clive Hart, Structure and Motif in Finnegans Wake, 117-8.

25 Marilyn French, The Book as World: James Joyce's Ulysses (Cambridge: Harvard University Press, 1976), 32.

26 Harry B. Partin, The Muslim Pilgrimage: Journey To the Centre, Thesis (PhD), University of Chicago, (September, 1967), 170.

27 Ibid., 170.

28 Ibid., 170.

29 Ibid., 174.

The "mother of the towns" here is the Kaba in Mecca. Furthermore, surah 42: 5 states: "Thus We have suggested to thee an Arabic Quran in order that thou mayst warn the mother of the towns and those around it." The phrase "those around it," according to Al-Tabari, signifies all the rest of the earth. A tradition quoted from Kisai by Wensinck says: "the polestar proves that the Kaba is the highest situated territory, for it lies over against the centre of heaven;"[30] just as the Polestar is the centre and the highest point of heaven, so is the Kaba the highest point on earth and its centre. A tradition from Ibn Hisham says that the waters of the Flood failed to submerge the Kaba. Von Grunebaum states that "the sanctuary of Mecca is established as the religious centre of the universe and the cosmic significance of any ritual act performed there is clearly demonstrated.[31]

According to Al-Azraqi, "Every prophet, after his people had perished (because they did not heed his warning), would establish himself at Mecca. There, he and his followers would perform worship until he died."[32] Al-Azraqi asserts that prophets of Islam like Adam, Abraham, Isaac, Jacob and Joseph are all buried at Mecca, while Hagar, Ismail and seventy other prophets are buried in Hijr (once a part of the Kaba). Masjid-i-Haram, in which the Kaba is situated, is in the centre of Mecca. If Mecca is the navel of the earth, as it is directly opposite the Polestar (the centre of heaven), and Masjid-i-Haram is the centre of Mecca, then the Kaba is the centre of Masjid-i-Haram.

In metaphorical terms (though Islam disallows such a comparison), then, the Kaba and Dublin are microcosmic navels of the macrocosmic universe. As sanctuaries of religion (the Kaba) and art (Joyce's Dublin) they project the ancient tradition; as Joseph Campbell states:

> The king was the centre, as a human representative of the power made celestially manifest either in the sun or in the moon, according to the focus of the local cult; the walled city was organised architecturally in the design of a quartered circle (like the circles designed on the ceramic ware of the period just preceding), centered around the pivotal sanctum of the palace or ziggurat.[33]

---

30 Ibid., 175.

31 Ibid., 174.

32 Ibid., 18 (Partin is quoting from Burkhardt).

33 Joseph Campbell, The Masks of God: Primitive Mythology, 147.

In transgressing the Natural Order, according to Islam, Adam and Eve were following their own notions of self-hood and independence, contrary to the will of Allah. Tasting the forbidden fruit allayed their consciences with deceit and illusion. Their expulsion from Paradise (the garden) was a heavy blow, made worse by the ensuing terrors of exile. Henry Corbin suggests that Allah took pity on them and sent the angel Gabriel forth and that it was in Gabriel's company that the pair journeyed towards the future site of the Kaba. When they reached the place, a tent descended from Paradise and the Kaba was built exactly where the tent fell.[34] According to another tradition, Allah sent Gabriel to the pair to console them, sending also a white cloud that shaded the spot where the Kaba was to be built as a token of future salvation and recurring divine remembrance.[35] Thus, the Kaba becomes a symbol of redemption, repentance and resurrection — a ricorso back to Paradise. In the celestial hierarchy Adam ranked third, after the Prime Intelligence and the Soul of the World. After the Fall, he ranked tenth, only regaining his initial rank after crossing the seven cherubs, the sub-lunar world, and the Heavens of Moon, Mercury, Venus, Sun, Mars and Jupiter, the seven stages of spiritual resurrection.

The "cubehouse" thus contains the Islamic account of mankind's rise and fall, and this is reflected in the structure of the Wake. The passage from Book I cited at the beginning of the present chapter is preceded by the four paragraphs which, Campbell and Robinson state, "compress all periods of history, all phases of individual and racial development into a circular design, of which every part is beginning, middle and end."[36]

The theme of the "Fall" is underpinned in these three initial pages of the Wake in various ways. At one place, the dreamer explicitly refers to it: "Phall if you but will, rise you must" (FW 3.14). This sentence is reinforced by the thunder of the Fall, echoing Vico's doctrine. This unfamiliar conglomeration of one hundred letters is an icon of heterogeneous languages which balks at any singular idea of human origins. In simple terms, Tim Finnegan comes crashing down like a house of cards, as soon as the wall of his inventive ambition fails to survive the test of

---

34 Henry Corbin, The Cyclical Time and Ismaili Gnosis: Islamic Texts and Contexts, translated by R. Manheim and J. Morris, (London: Kegan Paul International and Islamic Publications, 1983), 38.

35 Ibid., 40.

36 Campbell and Robinson, A Skeleton Key to Finnegans Wake, 13.

Nature. What emerges here as an excessive ambition is what raised (or might have raised) questions in the minds of Adam and Eve; in the words of Henry Corbin, "Is he not their equal? Does he not even precede them? Is he not first and alone, originating in himself?"[37] Corbin is here drawing on the theory of the mystic, kabalistic hierarchy of ten Intelligences, with Adam placed third and groping for the cause of his own and the world's creation. In these introductory paragraphs we glimpse the fallen Adam (Tim) sprawled like the "humptyhillhead of humself" (FW 3.20). Tim's death silences the noise and horror of the battlefield. At his fall, the noise of yelling and shouting, the falling boulders, catapults, grenades, spears — all this chaos and terror ends like the distant rumble of the fast vanishing cloud that a moment earlier filled the environment with the din of the croaking frogs: "brekkek kekkek kekkek kekkek! koax Koax Koax!" (FW 4.02).

High in the sky below which the universal hero lies panting in dust and rubble, there is a rainbow of hope. The theme of hope and renewal is also established through the croaking frogs. L.A. Wiggins alludes to the "thrust and withdrawal of coital movement"[38] of the croaking frogs as symbolising cohabitation and desire. The croaking frog initiates the dialectic of rise and fall, which symbolises the rise and fall of human cultures and civilizations. As William Troy writes:

The Fall is rendered from every one of its possible aspects. There is first of all the fall of the earth from the original chaos: the Humpty Dumpty ballad harks back to the most ancient cosmological myths, like that of the Orphic conception of the universe as an egg upon the waters, whose breaking was responsible for the earth and other planets.[39]

Troy goes on to list other aspects of the fall from unconsciousness towards the initial stages of consciousness; the fall of Adam from the innocence of Eden; the fall of Finnegan in the Phoenix Park incident; the fall of heroes and men. According to Troy, the fall of Finnegan, around which the other falls cluster, is the fall of an icon, the archetype representing Jung's "Collective Unconscious," or the "Great Memory," "by means of which the individual is supposed to carry

---

37 Henry Corbin, The Cyclical Time and Ismaili Gnosis: Islamic Texts and Contexts, 40.

38 L.A. Wiggins, AWN, (August 1969, Vol.6. No.4), "The Voice of the Frogs": An Analysis of Brekkek kekkek koax from Finnegans Wake, 61-2.

39 William Troy, "Notes on Finnegans Wake"- James Joyce: Two Decades of Criticism, ed. Seon Givens, 311.

around in him the mythical formations of the whole racial experience."[40] From the Moslem perspective, it should be repeated that the Fall was the sundering of Adam. Adam fell but was reintegrated. The salvation journey began from the Kaba. As primordial Patriarchal figure of mankind, this means the pedigree and the progeny of Prophet Adam. Joyce has highlighted this by referring to Prophet Mohammed's family. This is important to keep in mind that the Prophet belongs to Abrahim's descendents by blood and faith.

Such phrases in Book I as "sin business," "tragoady" followed by the references to the "cubehouse," "a nod to the nabir is better than wink to the wabsanti," "bedoueen the jebel and the jypsian sea," "Cropherb the crunch bracken shall decide," "ansars helpers," "Heed! Head ! It may half been a missfired brick" and "a collupsus of his back promises" indicate an eclectic sensibility trying to bring different religions into a synthesis, failing which the dreamer is apologetic: "Then we'll know if the feast is a fly day" (FW 5.24), evidently referring to Good Friday but implying a residual doubt about a generally accepted truth. This uncertainty is either because of his dreamy state of consciousness or because his kaleidoscopic mind is penetrating to the truth that has divided Moslems, Jews and Christians. Joyce's insight becomes clearer if we keep in mind that it was the Kaba as symbol which separated the Judaeo-Christians from Islam.

ᐧᐧᐧ

---

40 Ibid., 312.

9.

The Quran in Finnegans Wake
~ in two sections ~

Section I

Although the message of Islam and the Quran's revelations about the earlier prophets connected Moslems with Jews and Christians as belonging to the same group of revealed religions, they were bred and nourished in different times, languages and cultures. Joyce's interest in Islam took account of this. He knew the underlying knot of unity, the navel cord that bound the three religions spiritually each to each, although their outward norms and values were different. What those customs were, how they operated, and what similarity the doctrine of Islam had to other religions seems to have been artistically articulated in Finnegans Wake.

The Quran is similar in approach and theme to the scriptures of the other revealed religions, but its similarity of purpose is almost negated by deep-rooted cultural and political differences. As an artist Joyce had very little interest in discovering the reasons for these differences. The English translations of the titles of the surahs that one comes across quite often in the Wake indicate the influence of Hughes's Dictionary of Islam. The theme of human fall and rise, applicable both on individual and social levels, recurs in almost every surah of the Quran. Joyce in the Wake is telling a similar universal story of human behaviour by applying the theory of Vico. The cyclic aspect of history knits Islam and Joyce's system together, though Joyce is mainly interested in the fourfold phases of the flow of history according to Vico (it must be stated that the Moslem historian Ibn Khuldun had similarly divided history into four periods much earlier than the spectacular work of Vico).[1] On the theme of the fall of nations, Atherton cites six allusions to a

---

1   Ibn Khaldun (Abd ar-Rehman ibn Muhammad, Tunisia 1333-1406) is remembered as the "Father of Historiography" in the Moslem world. He amplifies the desert-dwellers "Saracens" to be the monument of vigour, stamina, stridence, ambition and adventure. The people who live in the cities, according to him are passive, obsessed by evil in its multifarious expressions and hence being sedate, liable to be subjugated by the "Saracens" in every fourth generation of the decaying dynasty. The conquering nomads who emerge from the desert and after a brief struggle, time after time, become the rulers and hence establish themselves in the settled agricultural lands. In the first generation, they infuse new enthusiasm in the lives of their subjects by a sound system of administration and spiritual enlightenment. Unfortunately, this vigour and vigilance declines

single surah, that is surah "Rum" ("Greeks" in Hughes's English version) "the hopes...of his ville's indigenous romekeepers, homesweepers, domecreepers, thurum and thurum in fancymud murumd and all the uproor from all the aufroofs, a roof for may and a reef for hugh butt under his bridge suits tony wan warning Phill filt tippling full. His howd feeled heavy, his hoddit did shake" (FW 6.04-09).

The meanings signified in literal sense may first be taken into account. The phrase "the hopes...of his ville's indigenous romekeepers," suggests the Sick and Indigent Romekeepers Society meant to take care of (as McHugh quotes Horace's Odes III.29.12) "The smoke & and the grandeur & and the noise of Rome" homesweepers, dome creepers." "Thurum and thurum in fancymud murmur" is from Latin dudrum et durum non faciunt murum or sturn measures do not build a protecting wall. "Aufroofs" is commotion, revolt or "and all the uproor from all the aufroofs." "A roof for may and a reef for hugh butt" is Ring-a-ring o'roses: "One for me, & one for you, & one for little Moses." "Under his bridge suits tony wan warning Phill filt tippling full" is about the ballad of Tim Finnegan cited in "Chapter 4: Sindbad and the Sailor and Two Other Tall Tales" ("The Tale of the Hunchback").

From the perspective of Islam, "Rome keepers", "hugh" and "his howd feeled heavy, his hoddit did shake" are meaningful. The author of The Dictionary of Islam is mentioned as "hugh." The "Rome keepers" are the rulers of Rome of surah "Rum" (in Hughes's Dictionary). "Rum" is the word which the Quran uses for the West or Occidentalism. The "homesweepers" are the slaves of this empire among whom Islam was to grow and flourish. Rome is also important because, in his system, Vico alludes to Romulus and Remus as its legendary founders and thus the initiators of human history. According to Vico, the murder of Remus by Romulus unleashed a constant struggle for power in the Roman empire. Remus's blood-sacrifice was thus like the ritual sacrifice in laying the foundation of the

---

in the next generation though the power remains unchallenged until the fourth as stated in The Concise Encyclopaedia of Islam, eds. Nicholas Drake and Elizabeth Davis, (London: 1989, Cyril Glasse), 177: "The princes of the first generation know what is required of them to become rulers; those of the second generation participated in the conquest, so that they have first hand knowledge of the requirements of kingship; the princes of the third generation, however, know of this only by hearsay; and those of the fourth believe that power and respect are no more than their due by birth right. Thus the fourth generation lives in a distorted, and illusory, memory of the past, and it is only a matter of time before it forfeits the right to rule" readily to be consumed by the fresh wave of the "Saracen" warriors. Constant renewal and successive generation and degeneration of dynasties, according to Ibn Khaldun, is a law of history.

Roman civilization (The New Science, 550). The Latin "durum et durum non faciunt murum" from which the verb "thurum" is taken, means "stern measures do not build a protecting wall." This proverb has two meanings: first, in the light of the surah "Rum," it signifies the harsh and painful treatment of Islam by the infidels in Mecca. One of their weapons was propaganda. As this surah is about the defeat of the Romans and Greeks at the hands of the Persians, the Meccan infidels found it an opportunity to slander ("Slanderers Slenderer" Notebook VI.B.27-28: p.206) the Prophet because the Romans were Christians of Constantinople and hence, like Islam, monotheists. In retaliation, the Prophet "his howd feeled heavy, his hoddit did shake" (FW 6.04- 09) (the mental condition of the Prophet during and in the aftermath of revelations) warned them against their self-complaisance as Islam was soon to replace them all. The infidel rhetoric against Islam was doomed to failure. The Persian ruler Khosru Parviz, who defeated the Romans in 615 ac, is referred to in the Notebook (VI. 6-8-10-15-16) as "Chosroes, Kaisar or Kisra." "Hurrah, there is but young gleve for the owl globe wheels in view which is tautaulogically the same thing" (FW 6.29-30), according to McHugh suggests that "There is but one God (Islam)." It is interesting to note that the exclamation "Hurrah" will emerge as "array" in Book IV. "Array" (FW 593.02) is also used for eliciting sudden attention. What strikes the reader in such diversified uses of these exclamations is that though on this page it invokes the God of Islam "Hurrah, there is but young gleve for the owl globe;" in Book IV, on the contrary, it would proclaim another "sandhyas" or reawakening of Hinduism. Joyce's system is a global wheel which "is tautaulogically the same thing" (FW 6.30). Furthermore, "Hurrah, there is but young gleve for the owl globe" (FW 6.29-30) asserts the monotheist claim that there's but one God for the whole of the globe. Finnegan, in this statement does not compromise the possibilities of "wheels in view which is tautaulogically the same thing" (FW 6.29-30). "Wheels" may be interpreted as the cyclical nature of human history according to Vico and the Indic Canon or other systems. Furthermore, all this is "tautologically the same thing" could be an approach due to drunkenness of Finnegan or an utterance in a state of dream or Joyce's own notion.

Surrounding these Islamic statements is a reference to Horace: Odes III.29.12: "Futum et opes strepitumque Romae" (the smoke and the grandeur and the noise of Rome) or "Sick andindigent Romekeepers Society". McHugh quotes the ballad

of Finnegan in which the protagonist's head is described as having felt heavy and shaken after his fall from the ladder. These references reflect Joyce's capacity to diversify the dreamlike vagueness of a meaning which is discernible only after considerable labour. The Quran in surah Rum reveals the real causes of the fall of the Persian and Roman empires. Eroded internally by corruption, these autocratic empires met their fate at the hands of the rising Islamic peoples in the sixth century AD. There is another mention of surah Rum, "Gricks may rise and Troysirs fall" (FW 11.35-36), with the same underlying meaning as above; or as Mutt replies "Rooks roarum rex roome!" (FW 17.09-10) to Jute's "Load Allmarshy!" (FW 17.08). Sometimes only the name of a surah embodies the Quranic meaning as "What if she love Sieger less though she leave Ruhm moan?" (FW 281.22-23). In this sentence, the only reference to surah "Rum" is the noun "Ruhm;" otherwise, it is a well known line from Shakespeare's Julius Caesar III.2.22: "Not that I loved Caesar less but that I loved Rome more." Similarly, in the last Book ALP says in her monologue "She's as merry as the gricks still" (FW 620.30). Surah "Rum" is here alluded to as "gricks," since this surah is named "The Greeks" both in the Dictionary of Islam and in Sale's translation of the Quran. Almost all the Quranic surahs are alluded to in Finnegans Wake in this manner.

The giants Gog and Magog are another theme connecting Finnegans Wake to Islam here: "Agog and magog and the round of them agrog" (FW 6.19). The Quran mentions them as "Yajuj and Majuj"(s.18, v.94-96). "Begog but he was, the G.O.G!" (FW 25.23): "the G.O.G" is "game old Gunne", Michael Gunn, manager of Gaiety Theatre. Most of the Arabian Nights Pantomimes are also associated with this Theatre and its manager in the Wake. In one of the references, though only remotely identifiable with Gog and Magog, there is a statement about walls suggestive of the theme of the Fall: "Now by memory inspired, turn wheel again to the whole of the wall. Where Gyant Blyant fronts Peannlueamoore There was once upon a wall and a hooghoog wall a was and such a wallhole did exist" (FW 69.05-08). Tindall identifies the passage as about a "Magazine wall where Gyant Blyant (Danish, Pencil) confronts Peannlueamoore (Pea, Ann, Penn)."[2] The hole in the wall is "applegate" (FW 69.21) (the fall from Eden motif) and is "triplepatlockt" (FW 69.25) to cordon off Earwicker after his malicious misconduct in the Phoenix Park. It should be kept in mind that in these sentences, Finnegan is being satirised

---

2   W.Y. Tindall, A Reader's Guide to Finnegans Wake, 78.

as a source of constant mental agony for his rivals. "Magogagog" (FW 71.26) are the biblical giants while "thugogmagog" (FW 222.14) and "Gadolmagtog" (FW 246.05-06) mean the great giants in Hebrew. Adaline Glasheen glosses them as the representatives of the nations that have been deceived by Satan. She also hints at the legend of Alexander the Great who had them sealed off behind a great wall in the Caucasus. In support of Glasheen, it must be added that Alexander the Great is the Quran's "Dhu'lkarnein" (surah Kahf (The Cave), s.18 as Hugh puts it in his Dictionary of Islam known to have been read by Joyce). In the Wake, his name appears as "twoheaded dulcarnons" (FW 276.01), though the Wake epithet is also applicable to the proverb "on the horns of a dilemma" or to Euclid. According to the Quran, Gog and Magog had been a curse to the people of Persia. Alexander heeded their complaint and saved them by erecting a strong rampart to protect them from the possible irruption of these giants. The catalogue of "abusive names" compiled by the malignant Cad for Earwicker contains "Magogagog" (FW 71.26) (the very sound resounds like an echo in a cave).

Gog and Magog always embody the motif of the giants in the Wake. On page 6, HCE himself appears as a sleeping giant as "he calmly extensolies" (FW 6.35). His deathbed is a reminiscence of the Apocalypse (of the Bible) and that of the Vichian system: "Eerawhere in this whorl would ye hear such a din again?" (FW 6.24-25). In another reference, (FW 25.23) inserted in the Prankquean's riddle, the sleeping giant is "duddandgunne." He rises suddenly from his deathbed, surrounded by the mourners, and, as soon as the latter console him with words and whisky, he vanishes. In The Mime of Mick, Nick and the Maggies, Gog and Magog appear in two different places. Both these giants and the Prankquean reappear in this chapter. The Prankquean can be seen in the guise of Isabel and the giants appear as beasts "Sobeast!" like Rhinohorn and Hopopodorme. Whisky, tea, pea or pen accompany the giants as inevitable aspects of their protean nature.

The Gog and Magog of Finnegans Wake suggest some clear similarities with the Quranic motif. As surah Kahf or "Cave" relates, Dhu'lkarnein was travelling to the East when the night fell. He stayed with a people who were desperately in need of his help. By the morning the riddle had been solved and peace restored. In the Wake, we read of such a restoration of peace after the "whole thugogmagog" had been "wound up." The passage has the glorious style of Quranic sublimity

"to be wound up for an afterenactment by a Magnificent Transformation Scene showing the Radium Wedding of Neid and Moorning and the Dawn of Peace, Pure, Perfect and Perpetual, Waking the Weary of the World" (FW 222.16.20). The diabolical Chuff was initially an angel — "Chuffy was a nangel then" (FW 222.22). Like the devil, Glugger was "lost-to-lurning" "But the duvlin sulph was in Glugger" (FW 222.25).

Giants according to the Quran, are the progeny of Satan. If "Glugger" is Satan and if he spews or spits his venom "sbuffing and sputing, tussing like anisine, whipping his eyesoult and gnatsching his teats" (FW 222.26-27), then his behaviour is similar to that of the Quranic Gog and Magog (known also in Islam as Dajjal) - "Djowl, uphere!" (FW 222.31). The giant Dajjal would appear before the Day of Judgement, a little earlier than the resurrection of Christ. The Quran in surah (Kahf) (The Cave) verifies this aspect of the events. Phrases like "on the plain of Khorason as though goest from the mount of Bekel" (347.03-04) again imply the regions of northern Persia towards which Dhu'lkarnein was heading one fine day "a white horsday" (FW 347.01) for "skirmishes" against the giants "when we sight the beasts" (FW 347.06) whom he subjugated finally after building the "Crimealian wall."[3]

Most of the Quranic surahs occur in clusters on specific pages of Finnegans Wake. The following passage follows the first exchange of impressions between Mutt and Jute:

(Stoop) if you are abcedminded, to this claybook, what curios of signs (please stoop), in this allaphbed! Can you rede (since We and Thou had it out already) its world? It is the same told of all. Many. Miscegenations on miscegenations. Tieckle. They lived und laughed ant loved end left. Forsin. Thy thingdome is given to the Meades and Porsons... Ramasbatham. (FW 18.17-22:29)

For the purposes of comparison with the Quran, let us quote the first ever revelation to the Prophet. The angel comes to the Prophet and awakens him from

3   The 11th Encyclopaedia Britannica defines this wall as: "Alexander's Wall" — "Derbent or Darband, a town of Persia, Caucasia in the province of Daghestan, on the Western shore of the Caspian...It occupies a narrow strip beside the sea, from which it climbs up the steep heights inland...And to the south lies the seaward extremity of the Caucasian wall (50 miles long), otherwise known as Alexander's Wall, blocking up the narrow pass of the Iron Gate."

his state of introspection in the cave at night:

"Proclaim! (or Read!)
In the name
Of thy Lord and Cherisher,
Who created—
Created man, out of
A (mere) clot
Of congealed blood:
Proclaim! And thy Lord
Is Most Bountiful—
He Who taught
(The use of) the Pen—
Taught man that
Which he knew not."

(Abdullah Yusuf Ali, trans. The Holy Quran: s.96, v.1-5).

The pronouns "We" and "Thou" are used in the Quran (Notebook V1.B,31). "We" is for God, "Thou" for Mohammad and "Ye" is used to address his people. "Stoop" (FW 18.18) as a verb also means to bend or to descend steeply and swiftly. "Stoop" as such is connected with the noun Muslim which means one who has resigned out of self-surrender. "Allaphbed" is the bed of Allah or His Chair which is situated above the hierarchy of ten Celestial Intellects in the heavens. In surah 2, verse 19, the Quran says: "O men of Mecca! serve your Lord who hath created you, and those who have been before you: peradventure ye will fear him; who hath spread the earth as a bed for you, and the heaven as a covering" (trans. Sale p.3). God had also blessed Adam and Eve by procreating them with His Celestial clay (i.e., "claybook") and by teaching them His glorious signs. "Miscegenations" as generations after generations and "It is the same told of all" should be viewed in relation to the tree of Prophets eliciting the reaffirmation of the Divine message, prophet after prophet. Joyce also refers to Hinduism and Buddhism on this page. God Rama- an avatar of Vishnu is stated as "Ramasbatham" (FW 18.28) while the allusion from Buddhism is already discussed in this study in "chapter 3: St. Kevin and the Yoga Way" Part II, Joyce's Use of the Indic Canon."

The Prophet, being unlettered, is asked "Can you rede?" The prophet had told the angel that he did not know how to read or write. The phrase "allaphbed" is a pun on "adcedminded" and also an illustration of the Arabic language which begins with "alaph" for A and "bay" for B. The letter "alaph" is straight, and erect. The letter "bay" is horizontal and hence like a bed. The combination of the horizontal and vertical suggests the meditating Prophet in the cave being told by the Angel to recite in the name of God. The noun "ant" is surah "Naml" or surah Ant according to Hughes "Dictionary of Islam" and "Thy thing dome" is surah "Mulk" or surah Kingdom as Hughes puts it.

The Prophet Mohammed was unlettered, for which he was known as "Ummi". Joyce refers to it in two of the notebooks: Notebook B.41-44 (p.08) and Notebook VI.6-16 as "Mohamad Ana oummi illettre note the sign of HCE" (p.26). In order to preserve the revelations made to him, the Prophet would very often obtain the help of Ansars — the learned community of Mecca and Medina to which Joyce in the first Islamic reference in the Wake refers as "ansars helpers" (FW 5.25). Even Shaun approves of such a method of dictation which is strongly suggested in the above passage. Shaun planned to make use of such a composition through dictation "I'd pinsel it with immenuensoes as easy as I'd perorate a chickerow of beans... the authordux Book of Lief" (FW 425.18-20). Joyce too adopted an amanuensis when his eyesight became weak.

Dictation, however, comes after the experience of the revelation in the cave of Hira where the Prophet was asked to "Heed! Heed!" (FW 5.26). Surah Al-Kahf has also been termed as "Cave." Here Finnegan is making a direct reference to Hughes's translation of Surah Al-Kahf as ("Cave!") (FW 16.03) though in Latin, Cave means "Beware!". In these pages, the names of surahs like Al-Qalam ("Pen") and Al-Tur ("Mountains") are also stated incidentally: "as yet no lumpend papeer in the waste and mightmountain Penn" (FW 19.31-32). "For that (the rapt one warns)" (FW 20.10) is a phrase from the surah Muzzamil according to Hughes's dictionary ("Wrapped Up"): "(may his forehead be darkened with mud who woud sunder!)" is attributed by McHugh to the condition of the Prophet at the time of anger. In the sentence "So you need hardly spell me how every word will be bound over to carry three score and ten toptypsical readings throughout the book of Doublends Jined" (FW 20.13-16), the phrase "three score and ten" is identified

with the condition of Islam before the Last Judgement. Given to vagaries and vicissitudes, the Moslems would by then be divided into seventy-two sects, as counted by Hughes's Dictionary. In the Notebook (VI.C 6-16) Joyce is even more explicit in noting "Koran hey word-70 meanings" (p.26), though this also implies the enormous potential of Quranic interpretations. It is most likely that Joyce is referring here to Sale's explanation of the internal dissension within Islam and other revealed religions:

> For the Mohammedans seem ambitious that their religion should exceed others even in this respect; saying, that the Magians are divided into seventy sects, the Jews into seventy-one sects, the Christians into seventy-two, and the Moslems into seventy-three, as Mohammed had foretold.[4]

In How Joyce Wrote Finnegans Wake (Edited Luca Crispi and Sam Slote [The University of Wisconsin Press, 2007], p.52, "The Beginnings. Chapter I.1, Geert Lernout while discussing Joyce's Notebook [BL 47482a f.78v; JJA44:87]), says that Joyce took these notes from Mardus's translation of the "essential surahs" of the Koran. Lernout mentions Joyce saying that like the Prophet, HCE is "illiterate" formally. About the Queen of Saba, Lernout says that she is "queen of Sheeben" and that the Moslem Holy book was written on "palm leaves, pebbles,shoulder bones, skins." Furthermore, Lernout (p.58), says that the triangular design of the ALP letters drawn by Joyce matches a similar note of triangle in Mardus's work. Furthermore, Lernout cites the phrases such as "a closed book," "delth, page/delta, do" from Mardus's work.[5] On the same page, HCE draws attention to the history of the art of writing. He introduces the mute giants of Vico's first age who communicated by groaning ("groaned for the micies") and who felt the first stirrings on the long journey of consciousness, asking questions like "with for what" as "signs on it!." Gradually the first human ancestors were able to read and decipher the signs of nature surrounding them. Their descendants in this way became familiar with the world mind: "But the world, mind, is, was and will be writing its own wrunes for

---

4   George Sale (Trans.) The Koran, (London: Fredrick Warne and Co., 1891), 122, First published in 1734.

5   How Joyce Wrote Finnegans Wake (Edited Luca Crispi and Sam Slote [The University of Wisconsin Press, 2007], p.52, "The Beginnings. Chapter I.1, Geert Lernout while discussing Joyce's Notebook [BL 47482a f.78v; JJA44:87]),

ever" (FW 19.35-36). Accounting for the diversity of the matters that man has preserved through writing, HCE elicits the scientific simile for the prophetic revelation as "our infrarational senses" (FW 20.01). Before coming to the method of preserving written material, HCE intersperses Arabic customs like hospitality: McHugh explains "the last Michael" (FW 20.01) as meaning that "The last milch-camel must be killed rather than the duties of the host be neglected." How the Prophet Mohammed felt in moments of passion is described as "the heartvein throbbing between his eyebrowns" (FW 20.02), interpreted by McHugh as "Mohammed's eyebrows were divided by a vein which throbbed visibly in moments of passion." His marriage to his cousin and his food of dates and water are referred to next. The Day of Judgement appears as "But the horn, the drinking, the day of dread are not now" (FW 20.04- 05). The Quran was preserved initially on papyrus and palm leaves, "for that (the rapt one warns) is what papyr is meed of, made of, hides and hints and misses in prints" (FW 20.10- 11). "Mahomahouma" (FW 20.17) is the surah "Mohammad." Among his people, the Prophet Mohammed was popular for his honesty, referred to in the Wake as "sedeq" (FW 25.21).

In the Wake, things swirl indefinitely and infinitely due to Joyce's method of word manufacturing and it should therefore be presumed that he scattered references to one culture or religion by immersing them in another. The terms "claybook" and "an allaphbed" may be interpreted in the light of Anna Livia's hen-like burrowing into the dung heap to rescue the sacred Word, "litters from aloft" (FW 17.28).

According to C.G. Sandulescu, the dialogue between Mutt and Jute is meant to be read silently: "A reading aloud of this passage even for oneself, i.e. with nobody else in the room, would disambiguate it beyond the permitted average FW limits, in that would be thinning the webbing of the texture to one layer of patterning only."[6] Mohammed, in talking to the Angel, was talking to himself in an unfathomable prophetic profundity. Not only Mutt and Jute but also prophets like Moses, Isaiah, Jeremiah, Ezekiel and even Jesus showed various symptoms "which" in the words of Jean-Michel Rabate "move from mutism to stammer, from the low tongue of Moses to the unclean lips of Isaiah...because of the uncertainty

---

6   C. George Sandulescu, The Language of the Devil, (Colin Smythe, Gerrards Cross, 1987), 257.

of the status in the beginning."[7] The books of the Islamic traditions reveal the Prophet's state of mental anxiety during the Revelations. Bukhari, to whom Joyce refers in Ulysses[8] (a famous collector of the traditions of the Prophet) says that at the moments of revelations, the Prophet would hear the sound of bells. At times, numbness would overtake him and he would start perspiring out of fear. His face would turn red and even the camel on which he rode, would sweat profusely.[9]

In brief, Joyce has successfully woven the message of the Quran into the first chapter of Finnegans Wake. Though each prophetic experience is unique, yet on the universal human level the profounder experiences are almost alike. The chapter suggests some clear similarities between the prophetic experience in the cave and the occurrence of dialogue in the caves of Finnegan's unconscious. We may note that Joyce's references to Islam are as irreverent as are his references to other religious traditions. His tone, though, remains that of an indifferent observer in a "joco-serious" way. The page following the most comprehensive passage on Islam, the dreamer"s mind piques out these images of erotic nature "...his hodden did shake. (There was a wall of course in erection) Dimb! He stottered from the latter. Damb! he was dud. Dumb! Mastabatroom, mastabadtomm, when a mon merries his lute is all long. For which the world to see" (FW 6.09-12).

10.

The Quran in Finnegans Wake

Section II

Joyce seems to have taken the phrase "al-cohoran" (FW.20.8-9) from George Sale's translation of the Quran titled "Al-Koran." In the Notebook (B.VI.41-44) the Quran is named as "(M) Koran" [p.318], and the "Muslim quran" [p.403]. As the recitation of Allah's signs, the Quran is coherent. The Quran as the Word of

---

7   Jean-Michel Rabate, Joyce Upon the Void, (Macmillan, 1991), 149. Acknowledging his "insight" to Herbert Marks' "The Twelve Prophets" in The Literary Guide to the Bible, ed. R. Alter and Frank Kermode (Cambridge, Mass: Harvard University Press, 1987), 207-33, Rabate says that stuttering of the prophets is a sublime discourse.

8   James Joyce, Ulysses, (New York: Random House, 1961), 80.

9   Dr M. Hamidullah, Introduction to Islam, (fourth edition, Lahore, 1974), 24.

God is the road that links man with God. According to the Moslem mystics, as Dr M. Hamidullah explains, mankind is like a travelling caravan. The Quran provides the true guidelines. When the Prophet Mohammed (pbuh) stressed the need to recite the Quran at least once a week, his saying was understood by the Moslems as follows: The Quran consists of 114 chapters or surahs and each of these consists of several verses or "ayats." When the Prophet enjoined the Moslems to recite the Quran at least once a week he was actually saying that the Quran consists of seven parts (Arabic, Manazils). In Arabic "manzil" means a station during the journey, surah is the enclosed room in that station, and the root of "ayat" (that is "awa") is to go to bed. All three, bed, room and station, are essential for rest in the journey toward Allah.[10] In the Notebook (VI.B.27-28), Joyce mentions the number of the Quranic "ayats" as 6666 [p.223]. The divine dispatches echoed in the following sentence use the word "aya" for verse as, "Ayi, ayi, ayi": "Dispitch desployed on the regions rare of me Belchum. Salamangra! Ayi, ayi, ayi!" (FW 9.12-13) though the Quranic revelations have nothing to do with "the regions rare of" human mind or say, the unconscious. In addition to "Al Cohoran," this paragraph of Joyce contains references to the printing press, the Gutenberg Bible, and telegraphs — a transhistorical tour of "type," with a strong religious focus. Some of Joyce's best puns here ("omniboss" -- .i.e., God). In this way Joyce synthesises by linking Christianity and Islam — the (printed) Bible and the Quran).

In the Wake, the Quran as James Atherton suggests, is better understood as a kind of "telephone directory, or at least phone numbers given in the Wake only acquire significance if they are taken as being references to a chapter and verse of the Quran."[11] In the sentence "reach for the hello gripes and ring up Kimmage Outer 17.67... and he thought the rowmish devowtion known as the howly rowsary might reeform ihm" (FW 72.20-25), the phrase "Kimmage Outer 17.67" should be interpreted as a Quranic reference in which protection is sought against Satan: "Verily my servants, thou hast no authority over them: thy Lord is guardian enough over them" (17:67). The telephone number "17.67" refers to the surah and verse 17:67. The cadence of the Quranic clause "thy Lord is guardian enough over them" is reflected in the Wake's "howly rowsary might reform him." HCE is checkmated by the devil and hence the telephone has been cut off. In another

10 Dr M. Hamidullah, Introduction to Islam, 24.

11 James S. Atherton, The Books at the Wake, 209.

instance, the metaphor of the phone number is stated as "that royal pair in their palace of quicken boughs hight The Goat and Compasses phone number 17:69, if you want to know his seaarm strongsround her, her velivole eyne shipwrecked" (FW 275.14- 19). Joyce seems to have emulated the following verses, though not exactly in accordance with his phone number: "And when a mishap befalleth you at sea, they whom you invoke beside God are not to be found." "Behold! We told thee / That thy Lord doth encompass / Mankind round about" (s.17, v.60, 67). The Quranic phrases like "befalleth at sea" and "thy Lord doth encompass" echo in the Wake's ""sea-arm," "shipwrecked" and in "The Goat and Compass." Or as we read "With Olaf as centrum and Olaf's lambtail for his spokesman circumspect a cyclone" (FW 294.08-10). "Olaf" is the Quranic "Alif" or Allah like the Greek alpha. Allah encompasses the universe as its "centrum" in the cyclic, diurnal course of the sun:

"Stay us wherefore in our search for tighteousness, O Sustainer, what time we rise and when we take up to toothmick and before we lump down upown our leatherbed and in the night and at the fading of the stars!" (FW 5.18-21).

Pertaining to the "toothmick" Imam Muslim quotes several traditions, two of which are as follows (Bukhari, English Translation, Vol.8, Hadith 68):

- a) Abu Huraira reported: The Apostle (may peace be upon him) said, Were it not that I might over-burden the believers — I would have ordered them to use a tooth-stick at every time of prayer.
- b) Ibn Abbas reported that he spent a night at the house of the Apostle of Allah. The Apostle of Allah got up for prayers in the latter part of the night. He went out and looked towards the sky and then recited this verse (190th) of "Al-i-Imran":

"Verily in the creation of the heavens and the earth and the alternation of the day and the night - save us from the torment of Hell." He then returned to his house, used the tooth-stick, performed the ablution and then got up and went out and looked towards the sky and recited the verse again, then returned, used the tooth-stick, performed ablution and again offered the prayer.[12] The rhythmic flow

---

12 Michael Seidel, Epic Geography of James Joyce's Ulysses, 24.

of the quotation from the Wake with its playful swing from day to night is reminiscent of the Quranic style of versification. For comparisons, observe the cyclic turning and turning round of the same theme swinging like the endless journey of day and night on the cosmic map as well as on the Divine scroll revealed through the Prophet Mohammed.

"Verily in the alternation of night and of day and in all that God hath created in the Heaven and in the earth are signs for those who fear Him" (s.10, v.6). "Seest thou not that God causeth the night to come in upon the day and the day to come in upon the night and that He hath subjected the sun and the moon to laws by which each speedeth along to an appointed goal" (s.31, v.28). "It is of Him that the night returneth on the day and that the day returneth on the night" (s.28, v.82). "And it is He who hath ordained the night and the day to succeed one another for those who desire to think on God or desire to be thankful" (s.63, v.255).

These verses should be compared with Butt's story which accounts for this amazing journey of "the Arumbian Knives Riders":

> How Alibey Ibrahim wisheths Bella Suora to a holy cryptmahs while the Arumbian Knives Riders axecutes devilances round the jehumispheure. Learn the Nunsturk. How old Yales boys is making rebolutions for the cunning New Yirls, never elding, still begidding, never to mate to lend, never to ate selleries and never to add soulleries and never to ant sulleries and never to aid silleries with sucharow with sotchyouroff as Burkeley's Show's a ructiongetherall. (FW 346.04-11)

"Alibey" is a Turkish noble. "Ibrahim' is Sura 14 of the Quran. "Bella Suora" is a beautiful nun. "Holy cryptomahs" is happy Christmas. "Axecutes devilances round the jehumispheure" is to execute thw devil dances round the hemisphere. "Jehu" is a furious driver. "Jehumisphere" is also Johannisfeuer in German. "Learn the Nunsturk" is nuns talk. "How old Yales boys" is Yale University. "Is making rebolutions for the cunning New Yirls," is making revolutions for the coming new year. "Never elding, still begidding," is from Dryden's Alexander's Feast "never ending, still beginning." "Never to mate to lend" is a proverb "it's never too late to mend." "Never to ate selleries" is never to eat celery. "Ant sculleries" is Aunt Sally (throwing game). "Burkeley's Show's a ructiongetherall" is Buckley shot the Russian General. The repeated use of "never" for emphasis is alike in religious

texts including the Quran.

The sun is a furious driver like the Hindu deity Jehu which continues its journey "never elding." This ceaseless journey of the sun is "Nunsturk" because its Prime Mover is God who as the Quran says "He begetteth not, neither is He begotten" (s.112, v.3) "never to mate to lend" or "They say, God hath begotten children" (s.2, v.116). Joyce refers to Allah's state of being ever awake in the Scribbledehobble, "Name! Name!...He who sleepeth not (Allah)..." (p.110). The Quranic verse "And Allah does not guide aright the unjust people" (s.2, v.258) is comparable to "and never to aid silleries." The phrase "the Arumbian Knives Riders" suggests the night time tours of Harun al-Rashid. Even more suggestive is the image of the "Riders" who, according to the Moslem mystic Ibn Arabi, are the motivating forces for the sun's rise and fall, the world of night and the world of day.[13] The Prophet Mohammed, in his journey towards the heavens was, according to the Quranic surah "Night of Destiny," ascending with the help of "rabb" — a potential force which is exploited in accordance and in proportion to one's "nefas" (FW 31.36) - a God-given capacity. Every time that the image of the "telephone directory" (FW 118) is used for the Prophet, what is conveyed is the manifestation of divine blessing in this ceaseless journey. According to the Moslem mystics, each stage of the ascension from one heaven to another is like passing through "qiyamah" or resurrection. The "Riders" thus is an Islamic equivalent of the Hindu "sandhyas" of Book IV.

The Wake's coincidence of contraries is the unity of God in Islam. Joyce refers to Al-Farabi, one of the strongest supporters of this concept in Islam—"all for a bit" (FW 19.02). In Islam, the East, associated with the sunrise, substantiates the visible aspect of the Absolute. The West, associated with the sunset, adds to the invisible element of God. These two aspects of the hermeneutics, visible and invisible, are the two great names of God—the outward (al-zahir) and the inward (al-batin). The former constitutes the concrete, material objects and the latter stands for the non-material, spiritual epiphany. The Quranic "what lies between the East and the West" would naturally symbolise those forms that are neither purely material nor purely spiritual, the world of archetypes. Such an interpretation rejects the

---

13 Sir Allama Mohammad Iqbal, Six Lectures on The Reconstruction of Religious Thought in Islam. (Lahore: The Kapur art Printing Works, 1930), 16-18.

element of idolatry or attribution of Divine powers to the objects of nature.

The Quranic motif of unity of Godhood is further traceable in the surah (Fatihah) (FW 52.13). The surah (Fatihah) is the essence of Islamic faith. It establishes the truth of the sublime status of God and man's dependence upon His mercy, who is the all-powerful determining force in the universe or "...the pancosmic urge the allimmanence of that which Itself is Itself alone" (FW 394.32-3). The "all immanence" is an absolute permeation of the inherently permanent Oneness into the things that are in a state of flux. "Itself is itself alone" lays further emphasis on the truth of interfusion between "Itself" as demonstrating, emanating pronoun and as an abstract noun—manifesting the participation of everything individual in the unified, cosmic force.

There are numerous additional references which spell out or imply the Quranic coherence of theme: for example, "a part of the whole as a port for a whale" (FW 135.29-30). (Whale) is one of the surahs of the Quran ("Qaraish" according to Hughes). Another example is "They've come to chant en chor" (FW 234.36). The phrase "en chor" echoes "al-cohoran" as the Quran. In the text it precedes the Moslem congregational prayer in which the Quran is recited:

> They say their salat, the madiens' prayer to the messiager of His Nabis, prostitating their selfs eachwise and combinedly. Fateha, fold the hands. Be it honoured, bow the head. May thine evings e'en be blossful! Even of bliss! As we so hope for ablution. For the sake of the farbung and of the scent and of the holiodrops. Amems.

A pause. Their orison arises misquewhite as Osman glory, ebbing wasteward, leaves to the soul of light its fading silence (allah lah lahlah lah!), a turquewashed sky. Then: (FW 234.36, 235.01-08).

"Madien's prayer" is a song The Maiden's Prayer. "Messiager" could mean Messiah in Arabic for Jesus Christ. In the Moslem traditions, Christ is well-known for his miraculous performances and Messiah is an apt expression for that. "Messiager" may also be considered as the messenger which in the Islamic Canon and tradition is the Prophet, himself. "His Nabis" is Allah's messenger or prophet. "Nabi" is a noun used both in Hebrew and Arabic for a prophet. "His Nabis" may also be his nibs. "Prostitaing" is prostituting but in Islamic Canon, it means the touching of the forehead on the mat during prayer, the final stage of complete

surrender before Allah. "Their selfs each wise" is the prayer said individually. "And combinedly" is praying together. "Fold the hands...bow the head" are the postures during the prayer. "Ablution" is an obligatory washing of particular limbs and parts of the body with water, before praying. The emphasis on "bliss" is an essence of the purpose of praying for oneself and the rest of humanity. To invoke blessing is to request Allah for peace and prosperity achievable when everybody is in peace on this earth. "For the sake of the farbung and of the scent and of the holiodrops. Amems" is "In the name of the Father & and of the Son & of the Holy Ghost, amen." "Farbung" is a dye and "holiodrops" is heliotrope. "Misquewhite" is mist white. "Misquehite as Osman glory," is White as Osman Towels. "Ebbing wasteward" may imply the spread of Islam to the West across Turkey. Through the image of prayer, the entire message of the Quranic argument is explained in the above passage.

In Arabic, this phrase is "La ilaha ill-Allah" (there is no god but Allah). "Ilah" in Arabic means "one who is worshipped." Anything or any being possessing power too great to be comprehended by man is also called "ilah." Everything depends upon "ilah" whereas "ilah" was not dependent upon anything. According to the illustrious Moslem scholar Maulana Maudoodi, "the word ilah also carries a sense of mystery and concealment, that is, ilah would be a being unseen and imperceptible. The words Khuda in Persian, deva in Hindi and God in English, bear more or less the same significance."[14]

"La ilaha illalah" (Non deus nisi deus) as the fundamental and first article of faith in Islam begins with "la illah." that is an absolute negation because "The supreme Godhood is unknowable, inaccessible, ineffable, unpredictable,"[15] that to which the boldest thought cannot attain. The Absolute is inconceivable because He is beyond any relative qualifications, absolutely transcendent, essentially in isolation and hence a Mystery of the Mystery "ankar al nakirat," "the most indeterminate of all indeterminate." Becoming one with God (unio mystica) as mystics vow and claim is like challenging the Absolute Unity because the intervention of "I" (ana) causes the split between the signifier and the signified, subject and object.

14 Michael Seidel, Epic Geography of James Joyce's Ulysses, 16.

15 Encyclopaedia of Seerah, The Editorial Board: Afzalur Rehman, sponsored and published by Seerah Foundation, London, 1989 "True Significance of Islam" Abu'l –A'la Maududi, 407-445), (426).

Are we then, like King Lear, "unaccommodated man" surrounded by the freezing horror of the void? Certainly not, for this proposition "la ilah" of universal negation has been erased by the life-flowing river run "illa," nisi, "except" an equivocal affirmation of "Allah"! Between the two (la illah and Allah) passes the fine line that the true Gnostic must follow without faltering. Allah is like the flash of lightning in the chaos, as Corbin says: "Despite the reticence of the Arabic grammar on this point, it derives the word "ilah" from the root "wlh" connoting to be sad, to be overwhelmed with sadness, to sigh forward, to flee fearfully towards."[16] Corbin elucidates further by stating that "alhaniya" as an ideogram from the root "ilh" suggests Godhood and "alhaynia" as abstract noun means to "desire, to sigh, to feel compassion." The term that Corbin coins for Allah is the "pathetic God, the created being," the most-near and sacrosanct Archangel, the protokistos or Archangel Logos. As the first cause, Allah is "our nimal matte" (animal matter, alma mater/fostering mother; FW 294.05) in the Night Lesson.

Simple affirmation of the authority of God as the absolute power over all creation offers mankind a way out of this void and horror. Joyce's method of describing this void is twofold since he was interested in boring into reality from both ends. His scientific approach deals with it from the psychological, materialistic angle. From a religious point of view, he had studied the concept of creation "ex nihilo" in St Aquinas, among others.

In the passage quoted from the Wake, "Salat" is the prayer said five times a day from dusk to dawn. This message is repeatedly honoured in all the surahs including those mentioned in the text. The noun "Messengers" "messiager" in the Quran stands for surah (Ambyia), "His Nabis" (Prophets). A little later on the same page there is another mention of the surah (Ambyia) as "nab" and "Nebo hood" (FW 235.16). We also find the name of surah (Sajda) stated as "prostituting" (prostating). Like the natural cycle of day and night, the Quranic message has its own coherence "resnored alcoh alcoho alcoherently" (FW 40.05) and regularity "so entirely spoorlessly (the mother of the book...)" (FW 50.11-12). The Quranic surahs could also be cited in the following passages and clauses: "the constant of fluxion, Mahamewetma, pride of the province and when that tidled boare

---

16 Henry Corbin, Cyclic Time and Ismaili Gnosis: Islamic Texts and Contexts, 84.

rutches up from the Afrantic, allaph quaran's his bett and bier!" (FW 297.26-29); "For the people of the shed are the sure ads of all quorum" (FW 312.34-35); "The punch of quaram on the mug of truth" (FW 368.25-26); "Yus, sord, fathe" (FW 379.21); "With his unique hornbook and his prince of the apauper's pride, blundering all over the two worlds! If he waits till I buy him a mosselman's present!" (FW 422.14-17); "The giant sun is in his emanence but which is chief of those white dwarfees of which he ever is surabanded?" (FW 494.27-28); "Hear we here her first poseproem of suora unto suora?" (FW 528.18). Finally, we come back to the same message of harmony: "Echolo choree choroh choree chorico! How me O my youhou my I youtou to I O?" (FW 585.03-05). In these quotations "Mahamewetma" is the name of the surah (Mohammad) who, as the pride of Arabia was blessed with the Quran. "The constant of fluxion" is the ephemeral nature of the reality of the universe described by Hinduism as "maya" echoed in the compound word "Mahamewetma." "Maha" is great made up of the pronouns "me", "we" or the human beings. "Etma" may be glossed as "atma", the ultimate self, in fact the Cosmic Self of Brahma. The phrase "the constant of fluxion, Mahamewetma" could also be interpreted as the constancy of the Selfless Self of Brahma in this world of temporality. "Pride of the province" when viewed in the light of the note "4" at the bottom is "And all meinkind" or the whole of humanity. "Tidled boare" is tidal bore and "rutches" is German rutschen, meaning to slide. "Afrantic" is Atlantic. "Allaph quran" is Al Quran. "Bett and bier!" is bed and beer. "Alaph" and "Bett" could be viewed as Alif and Bay the first two letters of Arabic. Similarly, "with his unique hornook" (FW 422.14-17) may be interpreted as the Quran - a book of guidance. "Apauper's pride" in the context of the Quran is the Prophet of Islam in whom Allah reposes perfection for humanity. "Blundering all over the two worlds!" is the message of the Prophet as in the Quran that the hereafter is as important as here and now. In fact, the hereafter is everlasting and hence more important. "Mosselman's present!" is the Quran as a guide to humanity. Moreover, "emanence"(FW 494.27-28) is Latin emanens, meaning spreading. "White dwarfees" is the stars. "Surabanded" is also used for being surrounded besides a pun on the word "sura." More so, "echolo" (FW 585.03-05) is Italian eccolo meaning here he is. The letters HCE, ECH echo in this line illustrated in the indiscriminate use of the pronouns "How me O my youhou my I youtou to I O?"

The phrase "people of the shed are the sure ads of all quorum" suggests the

concept of the Quranic word "surah" which is also conveyed in almost all the subsequent quotations. "Al" in Arabic is used for the article "the". "For the people of the shed" may be the twelve occupations enlisted by McHugh. The word "surah," according to Hughes's Dictionary of Islam, means a row of bricks. George Sale goes even further and says that the word "surah" is exactly like the "Torah" of the Jews which has "fifty-three sections of the Pentateuch."[17] The Quran binds its different surahs in a "surabanded" structure. The most sublime stage of such a bond implies the immersion of any distinction between mortal categories into "Pukka Yarup!" (FW 10.18).[this word is also mentioned in the Notebook (VI.19- 65 p. 240) as "Pukka"]. "Pukka" is that which cannot be effaced. It is like an indelible ink or ink mark. A "Pukka Yarup" is perfection in the cultural context. It is like the mystic state of becoming one with the entire universe by annihilating ego — a stage of "O my youhou my I youtou to I O?" or "Damadam to infinities!" (FW 19.27). "Damadam" combines two words "dam" which in Urdu means breath and "adam" is creation ex nihilo though it also connotes Adam. Heaving of breath from the state of void in the universe is Allah's blessing for humanity. The Quran, in brief, is such a litany or "reading" of the entire creation as Allah's breath—a "Pukka" or perfection par excellence. "Yarup" in Urdu also echoes "Ya" for the sign of prayer, invocation from "rup" as "rub" or God. Humorously, "Yarup" in Urdu can also be applied to one who keeps on changing his appearance through costumes, gestures or roles—a prototype of pantomime. "Rup" suggests Divine manifestations.

The allusions from the Quran, besides the themes discussed above, are worth observing throughout the Wake. Book after book, these appear like a palpable, tangible thread of gold in the chiaroscuro mosaic of the Wake.

Book I (Chapter 1-8: FW 03-216)

Most of the Quranic surahs whose titles could be read in English are referred to in the Wake. Their titles create interest in the "Countlessness of live stories" (FW 17.26-27) of the Wake. Sometimes a verse or two can be identified as an allusion. At other times, the themes seem to have been reflected in the Wake. Still, the

---

17 Henry Corbin, Creative Imagination in the Sufism of Ibn Arabi (Bollingen Series, XCI), translated by Ralph Manheim, (Princeton: Princeton University Press, 1969: Routledge and Kegan Paul, 1970), 112.

dominant motif of the Quran remains intact: God, His messengers and His moral code. Just as there is a unity of message in the Quran, so there is in the Wake a unity of design based upon the cyclic concept of reality and the coincidence of contraries. Islam figures as a part, however minor, in this multi-cultural framework. Joyce was not interested in any religion at the expense of others which had made their own individual contribution to the growth of human cultures. It is, however, interesting to observe that in Finnegans Wake, Islam is generally concentrated in the first three Books. The unity of Godhead, however, remains the anchor, the gravitational pull which draws every "sign" to its centre.

The sporadic names of surahs and their occasional themes can be observed from the last pages of the first chapter onward. "Tisraely the truth! No isn't it, roman pathoricks?" (FW 27.01-02) contains a number of suggestions. "Tisraely," according to McHugh is the name of the English prime minister Disraeli. Atherton glosses it as an allusion to the surah (Banu Israel) which discusses the story of Moses and Pharaoh in Egypt, a claim further consolidated by the numerous allusions to the Egyptian Book of the Dead on the previous page.[18] "Tisraely the truth" is a pun on "It is really." Similarly, we read "Hold him here, Ezekiel Irons, and may God strengthen you! It's our warm spirits, boys, he's spooring" (FW 27.23-24). "Ezekiel Irons" according to McHugh refers to a "parish clerk and fisherman" in Le Fanu's "The House by the Churchyard." Atherton, however, cites it as the name of the surah "Iron" which points out the value of spiritual strength.[19] The noun "Ezekiel" and the verb "spooring" also mean the enrichment of the soul with spiritual energy. In the surah "Iron," there is also a reference to Maryam and to Christ as the sign of this spiritual glory which coincides appropriately with the passage on Mary on the same page: "They called her Holly Merry her lips were so ruddy berry" (FW 27.15-16). The resurrection of Christ is related to the story of the giants Gog and Magog (a constantly repeated theme). We began our analysis of this page with the assurance of "Tisraely the truth!" and we come to the conclusion with "laus sake" (FW 27.08) [i.e, for Allah's sake]. In fact everything is for Allah's sake in Islam. On the same page we read "yet entirely when the ritehand seizes what the lovearm knows" (FW 27.04) which, according to McHugh, is taken from Matthew 6:3: "Let not thy left hand know what thy right hand doeth." This quotation from Matthew also forms

---

18 George Sale, The Koran Commentary Called the Al-Koran of Mohammed, I-XXII.

19 James S. Atherton, The Books at the Wake, (See chapter The Quran).

one of the most popular sayings of the Prophet Mohammad (pbuh). Almost every book on his sayings quotes it as the most salient feature of Moslem generosity. It means that we should never attach any strings when helping the needy. Two more surahs are named in these last pages of the chapter: Surah "News" "To see is it smarts, full lengths or swaggers. News, news, all the news" (FW 28.20-21).

The introductory pages of Chapter 2 name the following surahs: surah "Mountain" — "Bear in mind, son of Hokmah, if so be you have metheg in your midness, this man is mountain and unto changeth doth one ascend" (FW 32.04-06); surah "Council" — "the vigilance committee and years afterwards, cries one even greater, Ibid, a commender of the frightful," (FW 34.04-06); surah ("Slander") — "Slander, let it lie its flattest," (FW 34.12); surah ("Time") — "at the time" (FW 35.17); and surah "Thunder" — "the ten ton tonuant thunderous tenor" (FW 35.29) whose caller the angel Israfel is stated as "Israfil summoner" (Notebook, VI.B.31: p.56). "Mountain" in the above mentioned surah is the symbol of sublime or prophetic Revelation. Moses saw the Divine miracle of the burning bush on the mountain of Sinai (s.95 v. 2). The mount of Olives is the place where Christ warned his people about the Day of Judgement. Finally, the Prophet Mohammed (pbuh) received his Divine message on the mount of Hira "on Mt Hira" p.53 (Notebook VI.B.31). "Hokmah" is a Hebrew word meaning "2nd Sephira, divine wisdom." From the verb "Hokam" is derived the noun "Hakim," one of the names of Allah in Islam. Allah, furthermore, is also the "jamal" or beauty and glory of the universe which the Prophet Muhammad witnessed at the time of ascension, here emphasized in the syllable "ark sky." "Ark" is the thin veil which separated the Prophet and Allah as they sat facing each other in the seventh heaven or the most beautiful part of the sky "Gamellaxarksky." Elsewhere Prophet Mohammed appear as — "So saida to Moyhammlet and marhaba to your Mount!" (FW 418.17). The Quran calls the mountains as "Tent-pegs" (p.55) (Notebook.VI.B.31). Mountains were thought to have been useful in keeping the earth steady, as pegs do for a tent. "Saida" is Arabic for "good evening." "Marhaba" is "Good morning." "Saida" is also "said I." It echoes the name of the Prophet's adopted son "Zaid" as well.[20] The adjective "Marhaba" is applied to the Prophet as the one who abolished the dreadful time of the Arab "ignorance." He is the hope of a new beginning after bidding "Saida" or "Good evening" to the previous

---

20 Ibid.

ages. It was with good tidings of "Marhaba" that the people of Medina (Joyce's "youthrib city" FW 318.25) welcomed the Prophet. Every morning, the children and the elderly would leave Medina till evening to look for the signs of the migrating (Hijrah) Prophet from the hills far off. At his appearance one morning on the outskirts of the city, his devotees leaped toward him chanting "Marhaba!" "O Mohammed!" "Marhaba!." Joyce has once again woven the motif of the rising and the setting sun in his use of Islam.

Surah "Prophet" in the same chapter is named in the following passage:

> Hay, hay, hay! Hoq, Hoq, Hoq! Faun and Flora on the lea love that little old joq. To anyone who knew and loved the christlikeness of the big cleanminded giant H.C. Earwicker throughout his excellency long vicefreegal existence the mere suggestion of him as a lustsleuth nosing for trouble in a boobytrap rings particularly preposterous. Truth, beard on prophet,..." (FW 33.27-33).

"Hay, hay, hay! Hoq, Hoq, Hoq! Faun and Flora on the lea love that little old joq" is the Little Brown Jug song "Ho, ho, ho. He, he, he." "Hoq" and "hay" in Hebrew mean statue of law ("hoq") and alive ("hay"). HCE's immaculate, taintless character is being compared with Christ. He is as good and excellent as Christ. He is free of any charge leveled preposterously against him, such as the Phoenix Park incident. HCE is the paragon "vicefreegal" or vice regal. In Islamic canon, man in his perfect virtuous state is the vice regal of God "truth, beard on prophet." "Hay" is the Arabic for calling attention of someone. The letter "y" is usually emphasized, as in "Hayyiah." In the above instance, the triple use of "Hay" followed by "Hoq" echoes "Hayyiah" as the caller of the prayers round the day. The proclamation of "Hoq" is another constant theme of the Quran. "Hoq" is the truth of acting according to human "Fitrah" or innocence, as the phrase "the christlikeness of the big clean minded" Earwicker testifies. This purity was destroyed by the "boobytrap" of original sin as was revealed to the Prophet. Man was thus deprived of his purity and innocence of paradise, though he was nevertheless made vice-regent on the earth.

The evil of original sin is mainly caused by the refusal to act in accordance with "Hoq" which is further defined as the norms of "Fitrah" created by God. "Hoq" as

norm means submission to the Divine logos which brings harmony. Opposition to it means discord and chaos. "Hoq" also means "Din." "Dana" as verb derived from "din" means indebtedness to a "dain," the creditor. Indebtedness to the creditor implies "yielding" and "obeying" — being under obligation. Yielding to obligation is possible only in a society which has an established code of law as "madum" or "Madain" with a ruler or governor or a "dayyan." Thus the picture that emerges from the root word "din" is of a society whose purpose is "to civilise, to refine, to humanise" argues Syed Mohammed al-Naquib.[21] Indebted is the one who through Christian humiliation (like Bloom), abasement (like Finnegan before the Jury in Book III), service and dedication to the judge, ruler and governor of his city, atones, for "Verily man is in loss" (surah Al-Asr). Man, on reflection, finds that he is already in loss as Syed al-Naquib states: "for he possesses really nothing himself, seeing that everything about him and in him and from him is what the Creator owns who owns everything."[22] Since indebtedness means the obligation of returning the debt, therefore, such a return demands giving oneself in service. Returning the debt is also returning to man's inherent nature, which is a blessing like that of the recurring rain, as the Quran says: "By the heaven that hath rain." Allah's blessings are also recognised in the Notebook (VI.B.31): "then which of the bounties of your Lord will ye twain deny" (s.27, v.31) from the "Lord of 2 Easts" (p.56). Being "Hoq," Allah is ever awake, as the Quran says: "Nor slumber seizeth him" (s.26, v.3-21), reflected in the Wake as "And he make answer: Add some. Nor wink nor wunk" (FW 74.07-08). There are some more Quranic names of the surahs in these pages of the Wake. The phrase "vigilance committee" (FW 34.04) is suggestive of the surah (Council or Shura). "Ibid., a commender of the frightful" is the title of the prophet as being a servant "vicefreegal" of Allah as "Ibid" suggests "Abid," a word for slave in Arabic. This Divine slavery, however, is bountiful. It is for this service to the cause of Allah that the prophet was made the commander of the faithful ("commender of the frightful").

Furthermore, "Assembly men murmured" (FW 97.28). "Assembly" is the name of one of the Islamic surahs. In Moslem traditions, Allah is so close to us

---

21 Ibid.

22 The Challenge of Islam, ed. Altaf Gauhar, Islamic Council of Europe, London, 1978, "Islam: The Concept of Religion and the Foundation of Ethics and Morality" by Syed Mohammed al-Naquib al-Attas, 35.

that He is known to live nearer than man's jugular vein: "innerhalf the zuggurat" (FW 100.19). Or perhaps the Creator lives in the void from where He breathes His spirit as "an Olaf the Hide" from "a rude breathing on the void of to be... the cluekey to a worldroom beyond the roomwhorld" operating by means of the "(gravitational pull perceived by certain fixed residents and the capture of uncertain comets chancedrifting... Hush ye fronds of Ulma!" (FW 100.26-36). "Ulma" are the Moslem theologians and interpreters of the Quran. These "Ulma" are known by enlightened public opinion to keep their interpretation of reality within the established tradition. "Olaf" is Alif, one of the names of Allah. The passage "(gravitational pull perceived by certain fixed residents and the capture of uncertain comets chancedrifting..." (FW 100.26) as McHugh identifies, pertains to Einstein . "Hush ye fronds of Ulma!" (FW 100.36) is also about the elm tree. "Fronds" is frons in Latin meaning the leaf or thallus of seaweed. "Ulma" (Latin ulmus) is elm in Latin. Moreover, Einstein was born in Ulm. HCE could have any of these in mind along side Islam.

The role of the "Spider" at the time of Hijrah is alluded to in chapter 5. When the Prophet hid himself in the cave, a spider came and built such a strong web as to leave no clue to the frantically searching "infidels" (Notebook: VI.B.15-19). The surah "Spider" which tells this story is alluded to as "their Scotch spider and Elberfeld's Calculating Horses... (Hear! Calls! Everywhair!)... with us in this Aludin's Cove" (FW 108.15-22-26). The following passage throws further light on the Prophet's fugitive condition in the cave: "carrion on the mat of straw; the false hood of a spindler web chokes the cavemouth of his unsightliness but the nestlings that liven his leafscreen sing him" (FW 131.17-19). The phrase "carrion on the mat of straw" suggests the call for prayer or revelation which would sometimes come to the Prophet while sleeping on the mat "lump down upown ourleatherbed" (FW 5.20). Mostly, Joyce inserts the Quran amidst other cultural allusions to Islam. On this page alone, there are references to the Ottomans like "Ostman Effendi, Serge Paddishaw" (FW 131.07). "Paddishaw" is the Sultan, monarch or king. There is another Islamic allusion which is directly relevant to the life of the Prophet: "in the year of mourning" (FW 131.26). This was the year in which the Prophet's uncle Abu Talib (the Prophet's guardian and Hazrat Ali's father) and his beloved wife Khadijah died.

Page 138 also echoes with the names of the Quranic surahs: "if a mandrake shricked to convultures at last surviving his birth the weibduck will wail bitternly over the rotter's resurrection; loses weight in the moon night but girds girder by the sundawn; with one touch of nature set a veiled world agrin" (FW 138.33, 139.01). "Mandrake" shrieks with convulsion when uprooted. The female "weibduck" yells out of pain as the young one is born, enjoying "resurrection" and gains girth rapidly by passing through the cycle of life "loses weight in the moon night but girds girder by the" morning as McHugh refers to Troilus & Cressida III.3.175: "One touch of Nature makes the whole world kin." "Resurrection," "Moon" and "Night" are the names of the Quranic surahs revealing the mysteries of God's sublime status in which there is a rhythmic order in the rising and falling of the sun and moon. This lesson is being taught by the professor on the meaning of "Kismet" (FW 518.10) (fate) — the lot of HCE. His fate is determined by God who reigns "as far as wind dries and rain eats and sun turns and water bounds he is exalted and depressed, assembled and asundered" (FW 136.05-06). This sentence as McHugh cites, is from The Mobinogion Mobinogion: "Thou shalt receive .... Arch baxter: baker the boon...as far as wind dries, as far as rain wets, as far as sun runs, as far as sea stretches."

God is also sovereign over rulers like "hanriech the althe, charge the sackend, writchad the thord" (FW 138.32-33). The chapter also contains general allusions to the Moslem world like "all fitzpatricks in his emirate remember him" (FW 133.26). HCE is being hailed by his humble provincial servants — "boys of wetford hail him babu" (FW 133.28) — as "babu" is a slang in the South Asian languages for a respectable dignitary of the state. "Timour of Tortur" (FW 136.21) — an epithet of HCE — was a Moslem general of the fifteenth century (FW 162.14) whose dominions at one stage were spread across Central Asia from the Mediterranean sea to the Indian sub-continent.

Sometimes the dreamer mixes up the Quran with the general cultural traditions of Islam:

> How is that for low, laities and gentlenuns? Why, dog of the Crostiguns, whole continents rang with this Kairokorran lowness! Sheols of houris in chems upon divans, (revolted stellas vespertine vesamong them) at a bare (O!) mention of the scaly rybald exclaimed: Poisse (FW 177.08- 12).

The phrase "Kairokorran" is a pun on the Quran and its influence on the "whole continents." "Kairokorran" echoes Karakoram, the mountainous region lying to the north of the west end of the Himalayas. "Houris" are the females of the Moslem paradise, compared here with "shoals of herring." Joyce, however, intermingles some other meanings, as "Sheoul" in the Bible is also the grave or hell. The house in which Shem the Penman lives is "Asia in Ireland," "the Haunted Inkbottle" which stinks ("stinksome inkenstink, quite puzzonal") rotten ("wrottel") because he is a "whirling dervish... self exiled in upon his ego... (may the Shaper have a mercery on him!) writing the mystery of himsel in furniture" (FW 182.31; 183.06-07; 184.06-09-10). Shem's stinking appearance requires that he must not budge from the course of mystic seclusion and self-mortification — a profession which in Islam is adopted by the dervishes or mystics. They harmonise bodies and souls by various methods, one among which is a rhythmic dance during which their gowns whirl in a circle suggesting the motion of the entire universe around God.[23]

We may take another such example of assimilating the general Islamic culture as

"...honey and datish fruits and a bannock of barley on Tham the Thatcher's palm. O wanderness be wondernest and now! Listeneath to me, veils of Mina! He would with-say, nepertheloss, that is too me mean. I oldways did me walsh and preechup ere we set to sope and fash. Now eats the vintner over these contents oft ... (FW 318.16-20)

In this passage, the words like "honey", dates as "datish", "barley" are the staple food of the Arabs. Most of the Middle East is well-known for the "palm" tree. Even to the days of Joyce, the houses thatched with palm leaves"Thatcher's palm" was a common feature. "Listeneath to me" is listen to me - a method of speech with which the Prophet preached his message of cleanliness "walsh" and brush the teeth "preechup" before fasting "sope and fash."

The Quran, however, repeatedly insists upon the practical life and social and human harmony for which the Prophet was sent to establish God's rule over the whole of humanity: "(thanks, I think that describes you) Europasianised

---

23 Ibid.

Afferyank!" (FW 191.03-04). The dreamer possibly refers to this stage of the fulfilment of the Prophet's mission:

> ".. pious Aneas, conformant to the fulminant firman which enjoins on the tremylose
> terrian that, when the call comes, he shall produce nichthemerically from his unheav-
> enly body a no uncertain quantity of obscene matter not protected by copriright in
> the United Stars of Ourania or bedeed and bedood and bedang and bedung to him
> (FW 185.27-32).

In this cryptic passage, the Islamic allusion is a mere matter of conjecture. The
Penman Shem is described as "pious Eneas" who at the fulfilment of his "firman"
(an order issued by an Oriental sovereign) is being asked to produce as proof "the
quantity of obscene matter" indicating a parody of the mission's holiness. We may
take another look at this excerpt. "Pious Aneas," is "Pious Aeneas" of The Aeneid.
Being pious, he was obedient in carrying out even the most inconvenient "the
fulminant firman" into the tremulous terrains "the tremylose terrian." He could
produce the pirated editions of Ulysses unprotected by the copyright in America.
He, in this enterprise, was helped by "Ourania" the Heavenly muse of astronomy.
"Ourania" is Greek "Orion" generated from "ouron" or urine. Coupled with "be-
dood" for dead, urine helped making possible the experiments on al-chemy.

2. Book II (Chapter: 1-4, FW 217-399)

Chapter 2 of Book II (FW 260-308) is one of the most complex chapters of
the Wake. It directly asks questions like "As we there are," i.e., here we are but
"where are we there" (FW 260.01). Are we the sum total of existence? One thing is
quite sure — that we are the product of the marriage of eternity with the mortal
— "maker mates with made" (FW 261.08) — on this earth, along this "howe"
hill and stream "en elve, et field" (FW 261.03) and "Cave of kids" (FW 261.15).
The phrase "Cave of kids" is Zeus being suckled by goat in cave. The "Cave" is
also one of the surahs of the Quran. This is relevant here because the dreamer is
dreaming about the real womb of humanity in this chapter. He looks forward to
such a womb as circular like a "wheel" in accordance with Vico's cyclical scheme of
reality. The symbolism of the Cave for Moslems reflects the fact that the Prophet

received his first revelation in the cave of Hira. From Hira to the second experience of the cave in the Saur, there was an absolute change in the Divine injunctions and the prophetic mission. From Saur onward to Medina after the Hijrat, the Prophet was not only a preacher to his own race but also a practical statesman obliged to enforce the Divine injunction through might where necessary. There is a reference to the battles or "Jihad" (Notebook VI.C. 6-10, 15-16) of "Badr" (Notebook I.C.-7, p.373) and Uhud which is punned as "(uhu and uhud!)" (FW 285.12) in glory and praise of Allah — "(madahoy, morahoy...)" (FW 285.14), the Arabic slang for praise and glory.

We also encounter the praise of previous surahs like Thunder — "At furscht kracht of thunder" (FW 262.12) — and Pen "The babbers ply the pen" (FW 285.27). "Furscht" is fear, dread and "kracht" is crashing in German. It was the first crash of thunder that drove men into caves. In this "almightily expanding universe under one" (263.25-6) the previous references to the past imperial powers are repeated: "And Major A.Shaw... And old Whiteman self, the blighty blotchy, beyond the bays, hope of ostrogothic and ottomanic faith converters... Castillian-Emeratic-Hebridian" (FW 263.07-13). "Major A. Shaw" is Asia Major and Minor (East). "Blighty blotchy" is smallpox. "Ostrogothic" symbolises the West while "Ottomanic" is East or Islamic. "Castillian" is one living in a castle (the proverb "The Englishman's house is his castle") ; "Hebridian" is Scottish. Words and phrases like "Nebob" (FW 270.30); "Wherefore Petra sware unto Ulma: By the mortals frost! And Ulma sware unto Petra: On my veiny life!" (FW 264.12-14); "Every letter is a godsend, ardent Ares, brusque" (FW 269.17); and "hath not one,... ya, ya,... end so" (FW 270.29-31) are either Quranic or part of Moslem culture. "Petra" is stone and "Ulma" is elm.. Both are showing their uncompromising identities as the very "veiny" touchstones of reality. "Petra" as stone is the force of silence, unconscious coldness to life's warmth and vegetarian growth on existential level. "Letter" as a sign of divinity notifies the importance of the unknown in our lives. Similarly, "Ares brusque" signifies the theory according to which fate is determined from above or Heaven. "Ares brusque" is also arabesque or Italian "arabesco" having a characteristic of Arabic design of flowing lines in calligraphy in particular. The stemmed leaves emanate from the scroll in a symmetrical rhythm: each line diverging horizontal and vertical from the previous one without breaking the link with the initial stem though enjoying a freedom of its own.

"Petra" may also be read as "Pedra" in Persian for Father. In Sanskrit, it is "Pita." The phrase "ya, ya" is the name of the surah Yasin which begins with emphasis on the syllable "Ya" as "Yaa-sen." "A is for Anna like L is for liv, Aha hahah," (FW 293.18-19) sounds like Allah. "Ante Ann you're apt to ape unty annalive! Dawn gives rise. Lo, lo, lives love! Eve takes fall. La, la, laugh leaves alass!...Allow me anchore!" (FW 293.19-22, 294.05), implies the Quran, and "With Olaf as centrum and Olaf's lambtail for his spokesman circumscript a cyclone... As round as the calf of an egg!," (FW 294.08-11), are clear signs of the dreamer's interest in the Quran and its mystic, kabalistic interpretation. "Olaf" is a straight or vertical letter while "lam" as in "lamb tail" is both vertical and circular.

Book II (FW 309-382)

Chapter 3 begins with a reference to Vico's description of giants:

That the fright of his light in tribalbalbutience hides aback in the doom of the balk of the deaf but that the height of his life from a bride's eye stammpunct is when a man that means a mountain barring his distance wades a lymph that plays the lazy winning she likes (FW 309.02-06).

Observed closely, the passage may be explained as follows: "that the fright of his light in tribalbalbutience" is the fear of lightning that led him or the people like him into the caves where they, out of anxiety and dread, developed a sense of affinity and identity. They began to look after their progeny as a shield against the onslaughts of nature, for self-preservation. From tribal consciousness, they began to develop a language of signs for communication through stammering "butience." "Stammpunct" is German meaning point of view. One of these signs was a "mountain" symbolising the masculine economy. After having waded the distance and the water on the way, he weds a nymph who likes him.

It is the lightning to which Vico refers that causes "fright of his light in tribalbalbutience." Terrified, the giant "hides back," though the experience of explosive noise had shaken him from the "doom of the balk of the dead." In fact, the statement on the giants and the subsequent descriptions of human behaviour in

this chapter are intensely repetitive. The arousal of phallic desire or pride as "a mountain" which motivates HCE to wade through the female lymph reinforces the theme of temptation. "Lympha" is also clear water, which suggests a reassertion of the theme of the fecund ALP and phallic HCE. "Mountain" is the Quranic surah Mountain, and once again there are a number of allusions to Islam. The dreamer refers to the settlement of the earth by the tribes like the "rurik" Vikings in Novgorod and the Milesian who had come to Ireland from Spain to populate "Etheria Deserta" (the old name of Howth, Edri Deserta). In referring to "Etheria Deserta" the dreamer alludes to C.M. Doughty's Travels in Arabia Deserta as McHugh suggests. After this initial allusion there is a reference to the worthy parents of the prophet Mohammed — "and as for Ibdullin what of Himana" (FW 309.13014) — whose son was to be "equipped with supershielded umbrella antennas for distance getting and connected by the magnetic links... with a vital-tone speaker, capable of capturing sky buddies" (FW 309.17-20) connected with the "House of call" (FW 310.22) which "hallucinate ... in the night the mummery of whose deed, a lur of Nur, immerges a mirage in a merror, for it is where by muzzinmessed for one watthour" (FW 310.23-25) and is "as modern as tomorrow afternoon" (FW 309.14-15). "Supershielded umbrella" is the radiotelegraphy pioneered by Bellini and Tosti. The two were able to couple the units in radio amplification "connected by the magnetic links" and enabled the capturing of the sky bodies "sky buddies." From spiritual, esoteric perspective, "super shielded umbrella" are those archetypes "sky buddies" that connect by allowing an interaction between the terrestrial and celestial realms of the universe or eons. Furthermore, "the mummery of whose dead" is The Memory of the Dead. "Mirage in a merror" is mirage in a mirror. "A lur of Nur" is a luring night. "Nur" in Arabic is also night. "Lur" is also a tribe in Western Iran. "Muzzinmessed" besides being a Moazzan (the one who gives the call for prayer in Islam) is also a mizen-mast.

The surah "Nur" to which this refers is an epitome of the soul of the universe:

> God is the light of the heaven and earth; the likeness of His light is a niche wherein is a lamp (the lamp in a glass, the lamp as it were a glittering star) kindled from a blessed tree, an olive that is neither of the East nor of the West whose oil wellnigh would shine, even if no fire touched it; light upon light (s.24, v.35).

Avicenna, in his classic commentary says that the "niche" is the material intellect with a predisposition toward the higher Intelligence. At this stage, the soul as yet is in a state of "potentia" — a potential treasure. By acquiring the reasoning habit, the soul is now capable of reflecting upon the secondary Intelligibles either through reflection (if it is weak) symbolised by the Quranic phrase "the olive tree" or through intuition if strong (a reference to "oil"). A harmonious blend of the primary (reasoning) Intelligence and the secondary is known as "the intellect in habita" ("glass" in the above verse), and at its most sacred it is "whose oil well nigh would shine, even if no fire touched it." As it actualises the potential to the maximum, it acquires the state of "light upon light."[24] That which dynamises the "intellect in habita" into complete actuality is the "fire" of which Mulla Sadra says that its heat, felt in "essence," is hidden from this world, occurring in that state of being which is proper to the soul, and which perceives it through the power of touch. The powers which move the bodily organs don't subsist in them, rather it is the organs which subsist through them. That which inheres in something cannot be separated from that in which it inheres. The soul, therefore, is the form of forms as Sadra complies with Aristotle. By germinating its own substratum and bestowing form upon it, it makes its own progeny as a member of a certain species such as horse or man.[25]

The concept of the soul is further developed in the surah "Iron" referred to as "the man of Iren" (FW 310.20). The rest of the chapter is almost a repetition of the previous surahs of the Quran. "Allamin" (FW 311.02; that is honest and true) is the title by which Mohammed was known in Mecca even before his prophethood. "O, Ana, bright lady" (FW 311.12) echoes the surah ("Rehman") in which the blessing of Allah is invoked as the sender of the sun every morning with a fresh Divine message. The phrase "a maomette to his monetone" (FW 12.20-21) suggests the

---

24 In Letters From the East, (dedicated to Sir Walter Scott, London: Henry Colburn, 1826, 24) John Carne describes his encounter with such mystics for whom he uses the phrase "whirling dervishes." In a certain mosque near to the Bosphorus, Carne observed the cult of these dervishes. They began their prayer by chanting some verses of the Quran following the voice of one of them who was sitting in the gallery. As the voice of the dervish grew louder "the dervishes below began to walk round in a circle, slowly, with their arms folded. At last the music struck up a lively strain; and one of them, advancing into the middle of the circle, began to spin like a top. They all threw off the outer garment, and in their white vest set to spinning, with their arms extended in a line with the top of their heads, and their eyes closed."

25 A Muid Khan, "Some aspects of the Arabic writings of the philosopher Ibn Sina" Islamic Culture. (Vol.25: 42, 1951), 40.

surah ("Mohammed"). "Monotone" is preaching of the Oneness of Allah. The noun "evidence" (FW 314.04) is the surah "Evidence" almost repeated in every chapter of Finnegans Wake just as "thunder" (FW 314.29) is surah "Thunder." "Ho ho ho hoch! La la la lach!" (FW 314.18) is clearly the repetition of "Huq" (truth) of Allah, inserted once again as "Allahbhallah" (FW 317.12). The word "talka" (FW 315.29) refers to surah "Talaq" (Divorce) in the Quran. The phrase "muzzling Moselems" (FW 319.11) is obviously Islamic just "as Omar sometimes notes" (FW 319.33) denotes Omar Khayyam. "That's fag for fig" (FW 322.27) is the name of the surah "Fig" (Al-Tin) while "belly jonah hunting the polly joans" (FW 323.06) is clearly an allusion to the story of the prophet Yunis [the Biblical Jonah] in the belly of the fish. "A lala!...Ala lala" (FW 335.16-17) as Allah is mentioned for the fourth time as "Allahblah!" (FW 340.13), and the surah (Ants or Naml) is referred to as "as your ant's folly" (FW 340.04). In the phrase "For zahur and zimmerminnes" (FW 349.04) "Zahur" is the unanimously accepted phrase for the manifestations of Allah's love as heliotrope—"heliotropically" (FW 349.06). "Zimmerminnies" may be read as the recapitulation of the previously used compound word "muzzlen-imissilehims" (FW 5.15). "Zimmerminnies" may also be interpreted as referring Zimmer (Heinrich Zimmer) whose work on Indian art and mythology was known very well to Joyce. The phrase "grand ohold spider!" (FW 352.24) suggests the surah "Spider" and "Dom Allaf O' Khorwan" (FW 352.34) names the Quran and Omar Khayyam: "maomant" (FW 353.06) is the Prophet Mohammed of Allah (Who is) "the name of the Most Marsiful" (FW 353.02). Mohammed is a servant of "lord of the seven days, overlord of sats and suns" (FW 355.25) "Olefoh" (FW 353.14) or "Hullulullu" (FW 353.28). Most of these Quranic references have already been encountered in the earlier Books of the Wake.

Book III (Chapter 1-4: FW 400-590)

The same pattern is discernible in Book III. What gives them an effect of novelty in every chapter is the difference of context. Each time, the Quranic reference occurs in a new phase of the experiencing mind of HCE. Sometimes a single word from the Quran is almost completely shrouded in other languages: "Hek domov muy, there thou beest on the hummock, ghee up, ye dog, for your daggily broth, etc., Happy Maria and Glorious Patrick" (FW 411.18-20). This is not the general

practice in the Wake as the Islamic allusions can mostly be read in clusters lasting for a page or two. "Hek" is definitely the "Huk," that is truthful, but the next clause in this sentence is from the Czech national anthem "Kde domov muj" (Where is My Home). The rest of the sentence is from the Lord's Prayer: "Give us this day our daily bread." This sentence is preceded by words like the Latin "mat" for mother (though "mata" also means mother in Sanskrit); "bonze" is the term applied by the Europeans to the Buddhist clergy of Japan. Shaun, after replacing his father, is announcing his package of reforms to the people and advising them on the prudence of obeying Divine injunctions. "Boundlessly blissfilled in an allallahbath of houris" (FW 417.27-28), may imply the bliss of houris of paradise, according to Ondt. Obviously, the tone is humorous and punning "allallahbath." "The thing pleased him andt, and andt" (FW 418.09). "In the name of the former and of the latter and of their holocaust. Allmen" (FW 491.08-10). The man of "weltall fellow, raumybult and abelboobied" (FW 416.03) cosmopolitan vision, the well-built and solemn-looking Ondt is having a blissful time as happy and contented as a Moslem among the houris of paradise. The number "and a hundred and eleven other things" (FW 425.30) in the rhetorical flourish of Shaun, suggests the end-lessness of reality, a renewal after completion. The phrase "and as innocent and undesignful as the freshfallen calef" (FW 426.12-13) comes after his sabre-rattling is over and his defeat or loss of power confirmed. While answering the twelfth question, Shaun is reminded of the "annyma" (FW 426.03) (anima) and the jury of the twelve. He becomes conscious of his own plagiarism and that of Shem's writing from his own excretion as an artist. Out of shame and embarrassment, he finds himself almost in tears like an innocent caliph being deprived of his throne. A reference is also made to "ormuzd" (Ohrmazd) — a Persian deity of light who is opposed to Ahriman the divinity of darkness as Shaun is opposed to Shem. In the next chapter, Shaun as transformed into Jaun is delivering a sermon to the twenty-nine girls of St Bride's night school "my sweet assistance" (FW 433.08). "Assistance" is another surah of the Quran. "Lust, thou shalt not commix idolatry" (FW 433.23) has two meanings. First, Jaun is telling them to desist from adultery by warning them to consider it as lust, though to "lust" is also to listen. Second, like the Quranic injunctions which are repeated often, Jaun is warning them not to indulge in "idolatry." When Jaun says "First thou shalt not smile. Twice though shalt not love" (FW 433.22-23) his message is as applicable to the Moslem

injunctions as to his own (which is Christian here). Jaun instructs the girls to keep out of temptation as the "muezzin of the turkest night" (FW 442.32-33) calls loudly upon the help of God and thus keeps Moslems alert against Satan. The compound word "gooandfrighthisdualman!" (FW 442.27) may be read as "go and fight this dualman," the Arabic "zulmat" meaning cruelties and all the attendant evils of ignorance. "Fright" is not only fight as "Jihad" but also the Quranic fear and insecurity against which Islam acts as a shield. "Twick twick, twinkle twings my twilight as Sarterday afternoon" (FW 460.28-29) refers to the surah ("Al-Asr") or "Twilight," while "Arrah of the passkeys" (FW 460.02) suggests the name of surah (Array or Saff) in which Moslems are asked to form a straight line while standing for prayer or war. In surah "Twilight" the fleeting, unstable nature of time is invoked as a warning not to indulge excessively in worldly affairs at the cost of eternal life.

The references to the Quran in the next chapter are scanty and few, but they contain an evident note of the morning and hope in them: "the giant sun is in his emanence but which is chief of those white dwarfees of which he ever is sura-banded?" (FW 494.25). The phrase "surabanded" is the surahs or chapters that Quran is based upon. The emergence of the "giant sun" is like the Divine "Zahoor," the visible epiphany before whose piercing light, everything on the earth seems dwarfed. The "giant sun" could also be Finnegan the dreamer himself for whom these religious books are but parts of the stupendous whole which he himself is. There is another feature of the names of the Quranic surahs in the third Book. Most of the references seem clearly to be coming from the stuttering, stammering tongue of the dreamer — something unforeseen in the previous two Books. In the reference to "the coughs and the itches and the minnies and the ratties" (FW 488.34-35), the "coughs" according to Atherton are surahs "50, 18 and 46: Qaf, Kahf and Ahkaf." The "itches" are the surahs 15 and 70: "Hijr and Miraj." The "min-nies" are surahs 40 and 23: "Mumin and Muminum." The "ratties" are 13 and 49: Rad and Hujurat. In this sentence the names of the surahs are compressed on the tongue — as if the stuttering one is forcing them out but cannot utter them. This is modified into a proper stammer in phrases like "Who you know the musselman, his muscle-mum and mistlemam? Maomi. Mamie, My Mo Mum" (FW 491.28-29). The noun "musselman" is quite clear, and "musclemum and mistlemam" are tolerable distortions of the original. What confuses here is "Maomi. Mamie"

because these words could be read as Ummi or the people of the faith (Islam), or Maomi the island, or as the voice of a cat. "My Mo Mum!" could be interpreted as my Mohammed (the Prophet) or my momin (my fellow Moslem). There is another name of God according to Quran which precedes this passage, "turturs or Arababad" (FW 491.14); here "Arababad" is the Quranic "rubb" or God. The phrase "Arababad" is a pun on the noun "Arab." In addition, "Arababad" echoes the Hindu "Ram Ram." Similarly "Mahmato! Moutmaro!" (FW 499.07) could also suggest the name of the Prophet of Islam, as is evident in almost every reference in Finnegans Wake. "Mahmato!" again echoes the Hindu Mahatama (elderly or fatherly). "Moutmaro!" sounds like the Arabic "moutamir" with a meaning similar to Mahatama. ("Moutmaro!" could also be interpreted as to kill to death in Urdu or Punjabi). There are two references to the surah Al-Naas (or "Men"): "saying good mrowkas to weevilybolly and dragging his feet in the usual course and was ever so terribly naas" (FW 516.10-11) and "on how much family silver you want for a naas-and-pair. Hah!" (FW 522.18-19). The term "Naas" in the Quran is used for the people. It is possible that the dreamer was inserting the name of this surah in the third Book, which is said to be symbolic of the Age of the masses. The phrase "good mrowkas to weevilybolly" is good morning to everybody;" "weevilybolly" is also part of cotton, and "Naas" is a town in County Kildare. "Naas" is also being nice. Yet, "Al-nas" is a surah of Quran. "Lalia Lelia Lilia Lulia" (FW 525.14) could be interpreted as a name implying Allah, just as "Mockmacmahonitch" (FW 529.16) suggests the name of the Prophet Mohammed and "muezzatinties" (FW 552.24) the caller of prayer or "amuezzin," added in the Notebook (VI.C. 1-7) as "allaho-Akbar" meaning God is Omnipotent. It is interesting to note that the Quranic surah (Al-Naas (or "Men") is the last surah. After the mention of this surah, Joyce's Quranic vocabulary also effectively comes to an end.

In sum, what we learn is that when the letters are rejoined by breaking down the grammar of a particular language and by adding up to it letters with different sounds from other cultures and languages, they produce several referents by diversifying meaning. The reason could be the thought's discontentment with word's inability to capture fully by peering in and through the shadowy cevices of a writer's mind. One could expect such cryptic, random portmanteau lexicographic words from HCE's sleepy state of dreaming mind.

Book IV (recorso: FW 593-601)

In Book IV, though, we find a phrase on the prophet Joseph: "before the fourth of the twelfth" (FW 607.06). The verse of the Quran says: "Behold, Joseph said / To his father / I did see eleven stars / And the sun and the moon / I saw them prostrate themselves / To me" (s.12, v.4). None of the previous three verses in this surah refers to Joseph. The story of Joseph begins literally with the fourth verse of the 12th surah—sufficient evidence of the authenticity of the Quranic reference though the said prophet is referred to elsewhere too.

Similarly, Prophet Jesus Christ in Quran is mentioned as Hazrat "Isa" and "Isa bin Maryam". In Finneagns Wake, there are two references to Christ according to Quranic nomenclature, viz: "Poor Isa sits a glooming so gleaming in the gloaming; the tincelles a touch tarnished wind no lovelinoise awound her swan's. Hey, lass! Woefear gleam she so glooming, this pooripathete I...." (FW 226.04). In another context, Christ is stated as "Madame Isa Veuve" (FW 556.09). In the Notebook VI.B.41-44, P.42 Joyce clearly uses the phrase as it appears in Quran "Issa bin Maryam." The Quran remembers the Virgin Mary and her son Christ as "Issa bin Maryam."

If we count the number of allusions to Mary Maryam in Finnegans Wake as calculated by Adaline Glasheen, we find that she appears on twenty-eight different occasions. Atherton adds another five references raising the total to thirty-three. It is worth mentioning that the number of times Mary Maryam has been quoted in the Quran amounts to thirty-four.[26] Furthermore, neither in the Quran nor in the Wake, do we find any other woman referred to so often. The number of times different women appear in the Quran is as follows:[27]

- The idolatrous women s2 v221;
- the unclean women s24 v26;
- the believing women s24 v26;
- the honorable s24 v23;

---

26 The Wisdom of the Throne: An Introduction to the Philosophy of Mulla Sadra, translated by James Winston Morris, (Princeton: Princeton University Press, 1981), 87.

27 Rev. Nilo Geagea. Mary of the Koran: a meeting point between Christianity and Islam; translated and edited by Rev. Lawrence T. Fares, (New York: Philosophical Library, 1984), 116.

- the praying women s33 v35;

- the women of the paradise s36 v56;

- the prophet's wives s33 v28;

- the prophet's daughters s33 v59 ;

- Adam's wife s2 v35;

- Ibrahim's wife s51 v29;

- Lot's wife s11 v81;

- Pharaoh's wife s28 v9;

- Imran's wife s3 v35;

- Zachariah's wife s19 v8;

- Abu Lahab's wife s111 v4;

- Lot's daughter s11 v78;

- Moses' wife s28 v7;

- Moses' sister s28 v11; T

- The queen of Saba s27 v23.

The essential thing to note is that no other lady as above, is quoted by name except Mary in the Quran. Her exclusiveness in the Quran implies, as Nelo Geagea says "It seems as though, in Mary's presence, all other women were something amorphous, evanescent, inconsistent."[28] Mary and Christ were prodigious signs of Allah for the whole of the universe. The Quran uses the term "ayat" for Mary and her son. The term "ayat" in one of its meanings, is "sign."

The Quran is quite explicit in calling Maryam and Christ as the signs of Allah: "Remember in the book the woman who kept her virginity, and in whom We breathed of Our spirit. We made her and her son a sign for the universe" (s21 v91). The term "ayat" occurs 360 times in the Quran, explaining various attributes of divinity. The essence of signs in the Quran collected by Geagea is as follows:

- qualified as "ayat" is the creation of the universe s2, v164;

- sign, the creation of the first man from the dust s30 v20;

- sign the formation of the first woman, with the subsequent differences in sex

---

28 Ibid., 115.

and affection s30 v21.

- Sign, the divinity of men's tongues and colours s30 v22;
- sign, the alternation of the day and night s3 v190;
- sign as sleep and the restorer of human energies s30 v23;
- signs as the winds raising the clouds s30 v46;
- sign as the ship sailing on the water beneficial for humanity s2 v164;
- sign as lightning s30 v24;
- sign as water the blessing of Allah s2 v164;
- sign as the reviver of the dead from the earth s30 v24,
- the green vegetation s22 v63 and symbolises men's final birth s22 v56;
- sign, the she camel drinking her share of water as men do s26 v155.

Particular among these is Allah's protection of His persecuted prophets s13 v38. As s21 v91 points out, Mary and her son are Allah's might and wisdom. The Quran quotes Mary by her name at eleven places while Christ as son appears twenty three times. Christ is always mentioned as "Isa bin Maryam" in the Quran. This shows their intimacy in sharing fears and doubts on the one hand, and hope as Allah's grace on the other. This consciousness of reciprocal interdependence takes its course right from the moment the virgin mother realises herself to be pregnant in those turbulent times of a backward patriarchal system. Christ steps in to fill the void. Even though as yet in the womb, the prophet proclaims her innocence and her being immaculate. The mother needs her son as much as the son needs the mother so that the divine Word is made flesh. Comparing the lot of an ordinary mother-son relationship with this unique Divine phenomena Geagea says that "in those human people, however, when to the link of flesh and blood a supernatural factor is added, this affective cohesion attains a sky high level."[29] Jesus also serves for her as her own self as well as the dark shadow that plagues her with brilliant light. In one of the verses, the Quran calls Mary Maryyum as "ala nisa el alamin" (s3 v42): "Mary Allah has chosen you. He had made you pure, and He has exalted you above all the women of the universe."

---

29 Ibid., 152.

Summation

To sum up, Allah remains a central reference-point in the mazes of Finnegans Wake. Allah is the Divine epithet around which the Quran in Finnegans Wake revolves. The message and the repetitive and hortatory style of the Quran is woven into the arabesque texture of the Wake's universal themes. In these last allusions from the Quran, one important epithet is "Bissmillah," the Wake's "Bushmillah!" (FW 521.15), inserted also in the Notebook (VI.B.31) as "bismillah-bismi-illahi-r-rahmani-r-rahim" (p.56). In another Notebook entry (VI.C.6-16), Joyce has given its English translation by adding the usual Quranic praise of God: "arab, In the name of the most merciful god, the Lord be praised, the gracious God, pray to the prophet and Lord M-+ his people, received your writings, God help them to Islam, you hate God from the beginning, never know religion after death, then we are sure that God sent the Maker" (p.225). Every surah except one begins with this phrase and hence it is regarded as the recapitulation of the whole of the Quran.

The nineteen letters of its Arabic script "Bism Allah al-Rehman al- Rahim" have the following mystic correspondences with the manifested world, as identified by Henry Corbin following Hyder Amuli.[30]

- 1) B (the ba) corresponds to the first Intelligence (the world of the Jabrut).
- 2) S (the sin) corresponds to the Soul of the universe (the world of the Malakut).
- 3) M (the mim) corresponds to the Throne (Arsh): the ninth sphere.
- 4) A (the alif) corresponds to the Firmament (Kursi): the eighth Sphere.
- 5) L (the first lam) corresponds to the seventh Sphere: the Heaven of Saturn.
- 6) L (the second lam) corresponds to the sixth Sphere: the Heaven of the Jupiter.
- 7) H (the ha) corresponds to the fifth Sphere: the Heaven of Mars.
- 8) A (the alif) corresponds to the fourth Sphere: the Heaven of the Sun.
- 9) L (the lam) corresponds to the third Sphere: the Heaven of Venus.
- 10) R (the ra) corresponds to the second Sphere: the Heaven of Mercury.
- 11) H (the ha) corresponds to the first Sphere: the Heaven of the Moon.

---

30 Henry Corbin, Temple and Contemplation, translated by Philip Sherrard with the assistance of Liadain Sherrard, (London and New York in association with Islamic Publications, London, 1986), 122.

- 12) M (the mim) corresponds to the Sphere of Fire: the first element.

- 13) N (the nun) corresponds to the Sphere of Air: the second element.

- 14) A (the alif) corresponds to the Sphere of Water: the third element.

- 15) L (the lam) corresponds to the Earth: the fourth element.

- 16) R (the ra) corresponds to the animal: the first of the three natural kingdoms.

- 17 H (the ha) corresponds to the vegetable: the second of the three natural kingdoms.

- 18) I (the ya) corresponds to the mineral: the third of the three natural kingdoms.

- 19) M (the mim) corresponds to Man, who recapitulates the whole.

If God is macrocosm, then man is microcosm. The zodiac signs, the planetary system and the four elements are in quintessence the cosmic forces also operating in man. Joyce presents his cosmos tinctured with the chaos of human systems in Finnegans Wake.

∾

PART IV

Persian Thought.

II.

The Wake as "persianly literatured" (FW 183.10)

Joyce's use of Persian vocabulary is less rich than that of the languages and thought of Hinduism and Islam. Nevertheless, he has been successful in synthesising the grass-root Persian words with that of other languages of the East. He has taken account of the ancient Zoroastrians and assimilated them into his system of putting together the heterogeneous beliefs of the world, ancient and modern, Eastern and Western, pointing out the universality of the homogenate spirit of mankind.

Joyce's interest in Persian language and culture is quite evident when we study Finnegans Wake, being "persianly literatured"(FW 183.10). McHugh ascribes this phrase to Montesquieu "Persian Letters." The entire passage here seems to be touched by Persian culture (a factor which McHugh overlooks in favour of other possibilities). According to the dreamer, the floor and walls of Shem's lair "were persianly literatured with burst loveletters, telltale stories, stickyback snaps, doubtful eggshells, bouchers, flints, borers, puffers, amygdaloid almonds, rindless raisins, alphybettyformed verbage, vivlical viasses, ompiter dictas, visus umbique, ahems and ahahs,... fallen lucifers, vestas which had served" (FW 183.10-16). McHugh glosses "persianly" as referring to the Italian for "shutter": "telltale," according to him, alludes to the proverb "every picture tells a story." By "ahems and ahahs" he understands "rhyme, reason" and alphabet." However, "Ahems" and "ahahs" echo Ohrmazd and Ahriman, the two sons of the god Zervan. Since Joyce's vocabulary demands multiple interpretations, it should be added that the "Ahems" are also the descendants of those Shans ("Shans" in the Siamese-Chinese family is pronounced as "Thiam") who, led by Chukapha, established themselves in upper Assam in ad 1228. According to some, the last syllable of Assam is simply "Sham" or "Shan". In that case "Ahems" would be an Assamese corruption of

"Assam."[1]

The phrase "persianly literatured with burst loveletters, telltale stories, stickyback snaps,... amygdaloid almonds" (FW 183.10-11-12) also suggests the literature of Persia whose famous mystic poets such as Saadi, Hafiz, Ferdusi, Rumi, and above all Omar Khayyam have contributed so richly to Moslem culture. According to Benstock "neither Glasheen nor Atherton finds a hint of...these poets" though Hafiz "may be intended in "Hafid" (FW 595.03) or "Hajizfijjiz" (FW 347.19)[2]. The phrase "sadisfaction" (FW 445.08) according to Benstock refers to Saadi. Rumi is clearly mentioned in the Notebook (VI.C.12 to 18) as "roumi" echoing in the Wake as "rumilie" (FW 445.34). Saadi's famous Book of morals, Gulistan (Rosegarden) is named as "rosegarden" (FW 597.15) though in the Notebooks (B.41-44) and (VI.C. 6-16) it is glossed under its original name as "gullestan" (97 and 46 respectively). In the Notebook (VI, C.1-7), the noun "ghul" (441) meaning "rose" is used. There is another paragraph in Finnegans Wake (Book I, Chapter 1) which contains allusions to the Persian poet Nizami: "A bulbenboss surmounted upon an alderman. Ay, ay! Duum. (Nizam.) An auburn mayde, o'brine, o'bride, to be desarted. Adear, adear! Quodlibus. (Marchessvan.) A penn no weightier nor a polpost" (FW 13.24-27). "A bulbenboss" according to McHugh is Ben Bulben, the mountain in county Sligo. McHugh has not explained the whole sentence "A bulbenboss surmounted upon an alderman," which in the Persian context is quite clearly an allusion in which a "bulbul" bird is shown to be sitting on the shoulders or head of its owner. Even Khayyam calls himself old Khayyam and his poetry often sings of bulbuls. Joyce further consolidates the theme by referring to Nizami, the poet of Persia. Nizami (Abu Yusuf Mohammed Ilyas ibn Yusuf Nizam ad-din 1141-1202) is famous for the rendition of the tragic romance of "Laylah and Majnun." His tragic vision of life seems to have been interconnected with the plight of Ireland in this context. "Nizam" could also be identified with Nizam al-Mulk (d.1092), a vizier of the Saljuk dynasty famous for patronizing the arts and sciences, as is shown by his constant encouragement of Omar Khayyam's interest in astronomy. "Quodlibus" could be translated as quatrain (four lined stanza), and

---

1 Grierson, Linguistic Survey of India, Mon-Khmer and Siamese-Chinese Families including Khassi and Tai, Vol.II

2 Bernard Benstock, "Persian Elements in Finnegans Wake" Philological Quarterly, Vol.VLIV, (Jan. 1, 1965), 100-109.

"Marchessvan" is the beginning of the sowing season.

The phrase "with burst loveletters and telltale stories" is "persianly litera-tured" for various reasons. In the first place, one of the allusions which Benstock finds in ALP's "mamafesta" is to the ancient Persian religious book Avesta. History knows the compilers of Avesta as the priestly class of Persia's most ancient pagan tribes, though the oldest part of Avesta was written, as the Zoroastrians believe, by Zoroaster himself. As Zaehner explains, Avesta consisted basically of twenty-one books. Its summary appeared in the ninth century AD and is known as the Pahlavi book of the Denkart.[3] The period of its compilation is between the seventh and third centuries BC. The preparation of this text, like that of the Bhagavadgita in India, has to do with faith as conjectured by human intuition and experiences drawn from the writer's immediate surroundings and the realm of transcendence. The Bhagavadgita and Avesta, were the works of the aristocratic priestly classes, the Persian Magi and the Hindu Brahmins. The Indo-Persian mutual exchange of literary values is also worth noticing in the preparation of the Persian "belles letters" to which Joyce makes a punning reference. Written in Pahlavi (middle Persian), these literary, artistic and philosophical texts were transcribed from Sanskrit during the reign of "Anusharwan" (ad 531-78) as Philip K. Hitti argues.[4] In borrowing these ideas from India, the Persians were also to borrow the game of chess echoed in the noun "Marchessvan" (FW 13.27). It is worth noting that the Arabian Nights could not have remained immune from Indian influences. Later on, however, during the age of the Abbasides, Moslem commentators believe that Islam was influenced by the old culture of Persia. As Hitti suggests, the Egyptians, the Syrians, and the Berbers of North Africa all lost their ancient cultures after

---

3   Robert Charles Zaehner, The Dawn and Twilight of Zoroastrianism (Worcester and London: The Trinty Press, 1961), 25. Like the language of Rig-Veda, the different versions of Avesta grafted upon the original script (revealed to Zoroaster) were meant mainly to be chanted as a concatenation of a litany. The text was so complicated that except for its compilers the Magi, none could decipher its meanings. Avesta was to pass through many modifications — each time its suitability reaffirmed the authority of the acting political clique. Regarding Zervan, it should be added that despite his Omnipotence in giving birth to the basic dialectic of the universe, he is not Omniscient. Still, he is the bridge to eternity in whom all opposition is absorbed as in Coincidentia Oppositorum of Bruno. Zervan shares the element of doubt with the Hindu Prajpati. Like Zervan, Prajpati kept on offering sacrificial animals to the deities for a son. His ordeal reached its crisis when he began to doubt the efficacy of his supplication and the irony is that as his bewilderment intensified with a growing sense of horror so did the conception of the son occur at the same time.

4   Philip K. Hitti, History of the Arabs, 6th ed. (London: Macmillan & Company, 1956), 308.

Islam replaced them. That this did not happen in Persia was a severe blow to the Arabism of Islam. It opened new paths in accommodating Greek, Zoroastrian and Hindu learning. When Joyce refers to Finnegans Wake being "persianly literatured" (FW 183.10), the allusion reflects the overwhelming impact of the Persian culture on South Asia. In addition, since "the word Persia we owe to the Greeks"[5] as Zaehner suggests, "persianly literatured" could also be interpreted as the Persian culture in the eyes of the Greeks. "Persia," known to Herodotus as "Persis," was situated in the south-west of Iran.

Avesta is mentioned in the above passage as "vestas which had served" (FW 183.16) in laying the base of the Persia as a distinct cultural and racial identity. The word "vesta" also appears in the first chapter of Book I, when ALP's mercenary habits are mentioned. She would do all she could to "piff the business on" (FW 12.11) even if the Universal Flood had swamped the earth: "Though the length of the land lies under liquidation (floote!) and there's nare a hairbrow nor an eye-bush on this glaubrous phace of Herrschuft Whatarwelter she'll loan a vesta" (FW 12.07- 09). "Length of the land lies" is lie of the land. "Under liquidation" is liqui-dation of debt. "(Floote!)" in German is flut for the Norse Universal Flood. After the passing away of the flood, Ymir's body became the world, his hair "hairbrow" the trees and his eyebrows "an eyebush" the grass and flowers. "Glaubrous phace" is the face of the world. "Herrschuft" is mastery and "vesta" is Avesta or the sacred writings of Zoroaster. That this alludes to Avesta is borne out in a number of ways. First, the passage is preceded by another Persian allusion, "mithre ahead" (FW 04.30) referring to "Mithra," the Indo-Iranian sun god Mitra. Her mother was the goddess Ma who had overwhelmed the world with the primordial flood in which only one man with his cattle was able to escape in an ark. This Flood corresponds with those of the Old Testament and the Hindu Manu.

Secondly, the Persian kings who had been at the forefront as national heroes are quite clearly cited in Joyce's work. In Finnegans Wake, we read "And Egyptus, the incenstrobed, as Cyrus heard of him? And Major A. Shaw after he got the minor smellpex" (263.06-08). These four are translated by Campbell and Robinson as the "Four Old Men: Ignatius Loyola, Egyptus, Major A. Shaw, and old Whitman."[6]

5   R.C. Zaehner, The Dawn and Twilight of Zoroastrianism, 20.
6   Campbell and Robinson, A Skeleton Key to Finnegans Wake, 141.

Campbell and Robinson have not directly mentioned the name of Cyrus, the king who consolidated Persia into a viable state by military conquests of neighbouring civilizations such as Babylon and Chaldea. It is just possible that by the phrase "Four Old Men," Joyce might have meant the formation of an alliance between the Greeks, Egyptians and the Persian Cyrus against the kingdom of the Medes (Asia Minor). From this reference, we can infer the power and influence of Cyrus. In the context of Finnegans Wake and Joyce's strategy, it is quite obvious that he is alluding to the cultural and political whole whose component parts are the East and the West — all woven in the dream, as the West in those days consisted of countries like Greece and Egypt, whereas the East was composed of Persia and India. In another passage in which the battle between Butt (BUD) and Taff (TAF) occurs, the names of three Persian kings are added.

> We want Bud. We want Bud Budderly. We want Bud Budderly boddily. There he is in his Borrisalooner. The man that shunned the rucks on Gereland. The man thut won the bettle of the bawll. Order, order, order, order! And tough. We call on Tancred Artaxerxes Flavin to compeer with Barnabas Ulick Dunne (FW 337.32-36).

"We want Bud" is we went wrong. "Budderly" is utterly or badly. "We want Bud Budderly bodily." Here the emphasis is on human body. "There he is in his Borrisalooner" means the Borsalino hat that he is wearing. "The man that shunned the rucks on Gereland" is the man who shot the Russian General. "The man that won the bettle of the bawll" is the belle of the ball. "Tancred" is the king of Sicily whom the Romans defeated. "Compeer" is to compare, appear or compete in French while "with Barnabas Ulick Dunne" is "Ulick Dean" (W.B.Yeats), see George Moore's Evelyn Innes.

In this passage, "Artaxerxes" is the dynasty of three Persian kings.

The Persian kings "Darius" (FW 307.L) and "exerxeses" (FW 286.08) are to be found in Chapter 10. In the hierarchy of Celestial Intellects, a Cabalistic system which Joyce alludes to at page 307 of Finnegans Wake, "Darius" is the ninth intellect as "If You Do It Do It Now" (FW 307.27). The central myth of pagan Persian religion consists of three main icons. Of these three, Zervan is hardly traceable in Finnegans Wake though his name echoes at several places like "on his Mujiksy's

Zaravence" (FW 340.34). What transpires between Ahriman and Ohrmazd, as shown below, is automatically received by their father Zervan through the facility of TV — "verbivocovisual" (FW 341.18). On page 243 of the Wake, Shem has replaced his father Earwicker. There is a cessation of hostility between the Cad and Earwicker. It is in this spirit that Shem reports while commenting on his authority in the house "zoravarn Ihorde and givnergenral"(FW 243.10). According to Glasheen, Ahriman and Ohrmazd are forms of Shem and Shaun. Zervan can also be identified in one of the Notebooks in which his name appears as "Zarvas" among various Hindu deities: "Indian agni, Vishnu, celestial spouse, Siva Kali Ohmuzd (persian), Salam, (adversary) Zarvas, corrupted due to union of angel Mammon" (VI.C.6,8,9,10,16,15.pp.210).

The central characteristic of the Zervan myth is that Zervan, a universal deity, begged the higher realms to be allowed offspring. In the words of Zaehner, Zervan wished "that perchance he might have a son who should be called Ohrmazd and who would create heaven and earth and all that in them is."[7] Zervan kept on offering sacrifices for a thousand years, after which the element of doubt obsessed him as he believed that his wish had remained unheard. Zervan conceived two sons: Ohrmazd by virtue of the sacrifice and Ahriman by virtue of doubt. He then decided that the first to be born should be king. Ohrmazd was the first to know of his father's wish, but he made the mistake of telling his brother Ahriman, who, on hearing it, tore open the womb and issued forth.

As Zaehner explains, Ahriman and Ohrmazd could not reach an agreement as to who was to rule the universe first. The power, however, would fall into the hands of the good after a long struggle. Ahriman, the earthly ruler, became haughty and ruthless. The ancient Persians, however, believed that his rule would cease one day, after which Ohrmazd or virtue, mercy and balance, was to be the lot of humanity. The ultimate establishment of the rule of Ohrmazd is a great source of hope for mankind. Man, through the intercession of Zervan sitting on the firmament, can by means of will and longing, receive heavenly blessings. But it would take him nine thousand years echoed in the figures of "hasard" (FW 107.21,357.04) which in Persian means one thousand and "nun...sad" (FW

7   R.C. Zaehner, The Dawn and Twilight of Zoroastrianism, 207. (Zaehner here quotes from his book A Zoroastrian Dilemma).

366.36) nine hundred. Both Persian Zoroastrians and the Hindu system of time believe in perpetual creation and constant renewal. The Persian doctrine, however, is like the revealed religions and at variance with Hinduism in anticipating the end of time through the triumph of virtue over the evil of Ahriman.

The names of Ahriman and Ohrmazd can be read in the Notebook (VI.C. 1 to 7): "fire and blow, her place in the dark, Ahriman, satan, Mephisto, that which does not love light, Orimuzd, Ahura Masda, gullphish" (355) and in the Notebook (VI.C.8 to 16): "aryan Aharma" (85), "Parsi (Zoroaster)" (235). Ahriman and Ohrmazd appear in the following pages of Finnegans Wake. "Olivers lambs we do call them, skatterlings of a stone, and they shall be gathered unto him, their herd and paladin, as nubilettes to cumule, in that day hwen, same the lightning lancer of Azava Arthurhonoured (some Finn, some Finn avant!), he skall wake from earthsleep, haught crested elmer," (FW 73.33-35, 74.01-02). "Olivers lambs" is the Irish name of Cromwell's soldiers. They are a treasure ("skatterlings") to be reborn from stone tombs to the Knight-like hero ("paladin") like the accumulation of vapours into "cumuli" or clouds. This pattern would be repeated in the revival and rebirth of the legendary hero King Arthur who is sleeping beneath the earth. Benstock and Glasheen believe that "Azava Arthurhonoured" contains the names of Ahriman and Ohrmazd.[8] If we add the letter "n" to "Azava," the new result would be Azavan — nearer to Zervan. We can then interpret the clause "he skall wake from earthsleep, haught crested elmer" as alluding to the rebirth of Zervan for the completion of the divine plan.

A cleanly line, by the gods! A king off duty and a jaw for ever! And what a cheery ripe outlook, good help me Deus v Deus! If I were to speak my ohole mouthful to arinam about it you should call me the ormuzd aliment in your midst of faime. Eat ye up, heat ye up! sings the somun in the salm...Ja! Ja! Ja!" (FW 162.33-36, 163.01-07). Here "A cleanly line" is the family line. "Ormuzd aliment" is the elemental division between Ahriman and Ohrmazd, the principles of good and evil being described as rivals in the battlefield and also the pub, "champ de bouteilles" (FW 162.10).

After killing their father Finn MacCool, these "twinfreer types" appear on the

---

8   Bernard Benstock, "Persian Elements in Finnegans Wake", 101.

stage. Burrus suffers from the "lac of wisdom" and the other laughs at him for this. Burrus is like Keats's "king off duty and a jaw for ever." As rivals they are evil "arinam" and good "ormuzd" — the two Zoroastrian gods of "the Coucousien oafsprung" (FW 162.14).

The sentence "handsome angeline chiuff...oaths and screams and bawely groans with a belchybubhub and a hellabellow bedemmed and bediab-bled the arimaining lucisphere" (FW 239.29- 34) contains the name of Ahriman as "arimaining" — an angel of evil like Satan. In Chapter 1 of Book II (FW 219-259, The Children's Hour), the children stage a drama in which the basic conflict between the good and evil angels is shown. The twenty-nine girls dance around Chuff, the symbolic embodiment of truth and beauty. Glugg on the other hand is shown as the angel of hell, "belchybubhub" (Beelzebub), who is thrown into the "Erebus" a place of darkness between Earth and Hades. The clause "but I will be ormuzd moved to take potlood and introvent it Paatryk just like a work of merit" contains Ohrmazd as "ormuzd" (FW 425.27). Shaun is telling the pub attendants about the truth of the letter written by Shem — an outright copy with nothing new or original about it. As an angel of abstract beauty, he is like Ohrmazd. His abode is in the clouds and their lightness like his father Zervan. His brother, who writes with the ink prepared from his own excretion, is the angel of darkness or Ahriman: "I will commission to the flames any incendiarist whosoever or ahriman howsoclever who would endeavour to set every annyma...moother of mine on fire" (FW 426.02-04). Igniting "annyma" is like incinerating ones own mother. The phrase "moother of mine on fire" is extremely meaningful. The image of the "mother" is contrasted with that of the "fire." Fire and water are the two contrary entities coexisting as Ahriman and Ohrmazd in Zervan. If fire symbolises the male as Zaehner and others believe, then both in Hinduism and Zoroastrianism water stands for the female. Their coexistence in Zervan establishes his bisexuality.

The Wake's Persian touch also includes the name and palpable themes of Omar Khayyam's poetry. Richard Ellmann, in the biography of Joyce, says that the last song Joyce listened to before death, (on Christmas Day 1940, at the Giedion home in Zurich) was "O moon of my delight" from a record of John McCormack's.[9] The text of these songs was prepared by Liza Lehmann in 1911 under the title "In a

---

9   Richard Ellmann, James Joyce, 753.

Persian Garden." The author had compiled her lyrics from the quatrains translated by Edward Fitzgerald. Sung by soprano and bass voices, these "Rubaiyat" were set for solos and duets, and were heard in concerts in Dublin and at Covent Garden in London. Joyce had known about them through his aunt Josephine Murray (Letters, vol.II, p.198).

Both the translator and transcriber of these quatrains, Edward Fitzgerald, and the original composer, Omar Khayyam, are mentioned in Finnegans Wake. Fitzgerald appears in "a bag of the blues for Funny Fitz" (FW 211.14). Omar's name may be mentioned on the first page of the Wake as "d'amores" (FW 3.04) and "Armorica" (FW 3.05) though in an unintelligible, dispersed way. Still, Joyce's tiny bits may be seen to fit together since, if the name Omar Khayyam derives from the Arabic for worship, then the same word is inserted on the last page of the Wake as "washup" (FW 628.11). Similarly, one of the verses of Omar Khayyam reads "I came like Water, and like Wind I go." [10]

We begin the Wake with "river run" and end it in the drowning waters of the Liffey. The motif of the wind is also relevant as Joyce told Louis Gillet, as reported by Ellmann,[11] that the book's final "the" is like "un souffle." Lehman's "Persian Garden" is encapsulated in the sequence "perssian...oreillental longuardness... (garden)...a wake" (FW 357.09-18-34-35). John McCormack appears as "John... mock...cor" (FW 61.04), and his song "O moon of my delight" becomes "ah Mah" (FW 365.35) in Persian.

The phrase "K.M. O'Mara" (FW 122.19) (Omar Khayyam) is preceded by a direct reference to his quatrains: "from the fane's pinnacle tossed down by porter to within an aim's ace of their quatrain of rubyjets among Those Who arse without the Temple" (FW 122.09-12). "Fane's pinnacle" is the glorious peak from which everybody is eventually "tossed down" to the grave where all people are levelled as they are without the "temple." This should be compared with the quatrain "Think, in this battered Caravanserai / Whose Portals are alternate Night and Day, / How Sultan after Sultan with his Pomp / Abode his destin'd Hour, and went his way" (quatrain 18). "Caravanserai" appears in Finnegans Wake: "caravan series to the

10 Edward Fitzgerald, Omar Khayyam, Rubaiyat of Omar Khayyam, (translated by Edward Fitzgerald, with introduction and notes, by R.A. Nicholson (New ed. London, 1922), quatrain 28.

11 Richard Ellmann, James Joyce, 712.

finish of helve's fractures" with the footnote "Try Asia for the assphalt body with the concreke soul and the forequarters of the moon behinding out of his phase" (FW 285.21-22). The phrase "forequarters of the moon" as McHugh suggests is from Yeats's A Vision. Human destiny in this world is like the constant changes of the moon. Before the evolution of a "concrete man" (Yeats), the traveller of this immense night (like the night book of Finnegan's mind) must pass through and also take his rest in this world. Or "Wone tabard, wine tap and warm tavern" (FW 265.23). "As Omar sometime notes, such a satuation, debauchly to be watched for, would empty dempty him down to the ground" (FW 319.33). Here caravan-serai has been substituted for by "Wone tabard". Finnegan's wish is opposite to Hamlet's desire for death ("devoutly to be wished") as that "other country" to be entered through the portals of discovery. Khayyam's "Portals" of "alternate Night and Day" may be compared with Joyce's "Sein annews" (FW 277.18).

Finnegan applies the microcosmic image of travelling humanity to the entire universe: "nor since Roe's Distillery burn'd have quaff'd Night's firefill'd Cup But jig jog jug as Day the Dicebox Throws, whang, loyal six I lead, out wi'yer heart's bluid, blast ye, and there she's for you, sir, whang her, the fine ooman, rouge to her lobster locks, the rossy, whang, God and O'Mara has it with his ruddy old Villain Rufus, wait, whang, God and you're" (FW 122.12-17). An important feature common to the Wake and the Quatrains is the repetition of ideas and words. "God and O'Mara" is repeated as "God and you're."

Here the name of Khayyam is stated as "O'Mara;" earlier on the same page it is given as "K.M. O'Mara." "Jug" is punned as "jig jog jug." The quaffing of the "Night's firefilled Cup" is the "Morning in the Bowl of Night," and "But jigjojjug as Day the Dicebox throws" embodies the message of morning which "Has flung the Stone that puts the Stars to Flight" (quatrain 1).

Finnegan is advocating the cause of "Eat, drink and be merry": "Smoke and coke choke! lauffed till the tear trickled drown a thigh the loafers all but a sheep's whosepants that swished to the lord he hadn't and the starer his story was talled to who felt that, the fierifornax being thrust on him motophosically" (FW 319.31-34). Metaphysically speaking, the debauched drunkard was "fieri" made from "fornax" (furnace): "With Earth's first Clay They did the Last Man knead" (quatrain 53). Figuratively speaking, Joyce is alluding to the sensuous aspect of the dreamer

(noted by Fitzgerald in the quatrains as well). The dreamer's falling on the ground after heavy drinking and urinating like the trickle of tears is quite natural. What is interesting is the metaphysical implications of such a situation. In brief, wine which causes dizziness by confounding the dreamer's senses stands for soul or spirit in the quatrains of Khayyam. "with hand to hand as Homard kayenne was always jiggilyjugging about in his wendowed courage when our woos with the wenches went wined for a song" (FW 351.09-11). "Homard" is Omar, but it also finds its reflex in the word "Khomar" (in Persian) which is an acute state of being drowsy or being mystically drunk in the love of God. "Jiggilyjugging" recalls the "jug of wine." "Woos" suggests the vows of love between the lover and the beloved. Omar Khayyam drenched with wine is singing such a song about the tavern of love: "And thus within the tavern's secret booth The wisehight ones who sip the tested sooth Bestir them as the Just has bid to jab The punch of quaram on the mug of truth" (FW 368.24-26). "On the mug of truth" is the wine of love and truth revealed as "quaram" or Quran from the "Just" one ("Just" is God who does justice according to His logos of "Hoq") in this mortal tavern of the universe. This paragraph of only three lines mimics the rhyme and meter of the Rubaiyat.

The symbols of the tavern, caravanserai, and wine are crucial in understanding the metaphysical import of Khayyam's mysticism. As Fitzgerald observes, the tavern or Caravanserai is the pilgrimage of the soul in passing through five stages of "Repentance, Renunciation, Poverty, Patience and Acquiescence to the Will of God" (29). The temple is the physical body in which the soul is housed. The temple will pass away but not the soul. Wine is the Divine Spirit. The cup is the "receptacle" or archetype of the spiritual powers. Bread is the heavenly food and the "bulbul" bird is the symbol of the soul "singing in the darkness or hidden depths of man's own being." At the heart of Omar Khayyam's mysticism is the role of the state of wakefulness. Drunk to the core, the poet pleads the reader and the world to awake. "Wake! For the Sun, who scattered into flight / The Stars before him the Field of Night, / Drives Night along with them from Heav'n, and strikes / The Sultan's Turret with a Shaft of Light" (quatrain 1). The Sultan's temple as explained by Fitzgerald is temporal and evanescent, it will collapse only to be replaced by a new one. Does not the same logic apply to the "Bygmester" or builder of Finnegans Wake as he too is lying in a state of Wakefulness? Here the very word with which the Rubaiyat begins forms half of the title of Joyce's book: "Wake!"

Finnegan's passions are the unfulfilled dreams of humanity — a breeding ground of anxieties and fears. These are reflected in his book of the night. His wishfulness is like Omar Khayyam's resort to pleasure and wine. This shimmering of light and darkness, hope and anxiety, day and night is a constant theme of Khayyam and Finnegans Wake.

Supplement

Supplement I

The Vocabulary of Islam

"Annah the Allmaziful". (ALP)

As soon as HCE vanishes from the scene into the waters of Bartholomon's Deep, the stage of the dreamer's mind is suddenly enlivened by the women who start their story in the remarkable style of the women of the Arabian Nights. "Do tell us all about. As we want to hear allabout. So tellus tellas allabouter." (FW 101. 02-03) In the first place, the female narrator of the tales seems to be an "allabout-er" — someone who knows about everything. Secondly, her omniscient nature is supported by the fact that she is introduced on page 101 of the Wake - a number which in Islamic mysticism signifies completion and resurrection. Thirdly, she can prophesy, for, it is she who is urged by the other women to tell what happened to Buckley and who struck him first? Who had spread calamity in Lucalizod? She, as the faithful wife, would first of all collect the data of the whole event in her bag of battle souvenirs introduced on pages 10-11 of the Wake.

We can examine her character in the light of her tremendous experience shown by revealing her 'history-bag'. Her Eastern character is touched upon by her introduction as one who dwells with her man in an haremserai "... spent his strength amok [in] haremscarems." The voice with which she speaks with her female friend is thus coming from such a "haremscarems". Prior to the chapter

in which she introduces her letter, she appears to us as a benevolent force, a symbol of mercy which she demonstrates by curing Naaman of leprosy in Jordan (FW.103.07) "Nomad may roam with Nabuch but let naaman laugh at Jordan!" (II King 5:14). She is both the stone over which her female friends lay their sheets, and the trees which preserve their hearts, though she is the river as well: "For we have taken our sheet upon her stones where we have hanged our hearts in her trees ; and we list, as she bibs us, by the waters of babalong" (FW 10-11). She encompasses everything creative.

ALP's creative instinct can also be judged from her "mamafesta" consisting of several themes at once. Firstly "mamafesta" is her letter to her husband, a great manifesto to the "Mosthighest" or HCE. In the East, she is identified with Kali of Hinduism however her untitled manifesto is applicable to any or all of the religious systems of the world as is her own nature which connotes "laps" or lapsus. It is by falling asleep that HCE reflects the contradictory nature of reality or history through the lapsus of "But there's many a split pretext bowl and jowl" (she uses "bowl" for breakfast for her man in this chapter of her manifesto). If HCE is "the god of all machineries" (FW.253.27) then she is the medium of such a system of procreation "Father Times and Mother Spaces" (FW 602.02) and hence she is the source of perpetuation and recuperation of the creative process. Her "mamafesta" is then also the nourishing food of the mother.

From the Moslem perspective, it is the hymn with which she begins her manifesto that invites attention. "In the name of Annah the Allmaziful, the Everliving, the Bringer of Plurabilities, haloed be her eve, her singtime sung, her rill be run, unhemmed as it is uneven!" (FW.104.01-03). In the dreamlike lapsus and in the light of his habit of stammering there is every possibility that the dreamer might pronounce Allah as "Annah". All the surahs of the Koran begin with similar praise of Allah "In the name of Allah, the Merciful, the Compassionate".

Secondly, ALP is writing a letter and in the Moslem tradition, the letters are always written in the name of Allah. Moreover, it also is a matter of general Moslem practice that a letter begins with a hymn in praise of Allah. Finally, even the words which express man's gratefulness to Allah are written in Arabic irrespective of the writer's original language. Allah is definitely everliving and is thus addressed. Allah is "Allmaziful" that is "al-Rehaman" or merciful, though "Allmaziful" also implies

full of mazes. The syllable "All" is Arabic "El" the eternal logos that never change. As usual, Joyce is combining the Moslem prayer with that of the Christian "Lord's Prayer" "Hallowed be Thy name, Thy kingdom come, Thy will be done, on Earth as it is in Heaven." ALP's "Anna" echoes Allah's dominance as "anndominant" and "preadaminant" an inverted form of "Adam and Eve." Certainly "Annah" subsumes both the "anndominant" or AD and "preadaminant" or BC for His omniscient and omnipotent nature. How far her letter corresponds with Moslem faith, may be judged by observing the views held by Joyce and by Islam in the interpretation of their respective metaphysical ideals. Such an essential point is also addressed briefly in this section.

Allah's mercy is like the release of pent up breath which bursts out sending limitless relief to the sinews of human body. It is ever willing to explode from the compressed existence of the Absolute. That is why Allah's mercy is known as the "breath of the merciful". The state before this explosion is the state of "korb" or extreme tension which must discharge its accumulated energies for the sake of re-lief for which Joyce collects the true Arabic word from the Koran "Kun" (Notebook VI.B, pp.15-117) "Fiat Kun Fa Yakun") or English "Be!" Breathing out all tensions also alludes to the intense creative potential of Allah which bears out the value of the dialectical conflict as an inherent virtue of reality. Such a breathing out is known as "jawhar" in Islam or the Prime Matter in Aristotelian terms. We may now briefly consider such a divine breath that formats the Prime Matter as the essence of the pluralities of phenomenal reality.

Essentially, the pluralities of the phenomenal world owe themselves to the role of the feminine element in the created world.

The prophet of Allah is to have said "Of all the things of your world, three things have been made particularly dear to me, women, perfume and the ritual prayer, this last being the "cooling of my eyes" (that is, the source of highest joy)". By using the number "three" according to Ibn Arabi, the prophet of Allah is un-derpinning the value of "thalath" through which Creation (in its ontological and epistemological dimension) is defined.

Creation is actualized only when the active polarity coincides harmoniously with the passive, which according to Ibn Arabi, Al-Farabi, Avicenna and "Pirs of Moslems Schools of thought" (Notebook B.41-44), is another triplicity:

1. its thingness or quiddity,
2. its hearing, and
3. its obeying the Command of the Creator for the sake of its creation.

Triplicity thus is as important to Ibn Arabi as it is in Christianity. Triplicity or "thalath" is a feminine form. In the above quoted saying of the Prophet, the use of "thalath" according to Ibn Arabi, is meaningful. It implies that the creation is actually a process of the feminine principle "tanith" as Ibn Arabi explains: "The man finds himself situated between an essence (i.e., the Divine Essence) which is his (ontological) source and a woman (i.e., his own mother) who is his (physical) source. Thus he is placed between two feminine nouns, that is to say, between the femininity of essence and the real (i.e., physical) femininity."[1] The Divine Essence known as "dhat" is a feminine noun. Then the Divine Attributes or archetypes known as "sifat" (with "sifah" as singular) is also a feminine noun.

The Omniscient power of "Be!" the Arabic "qudrah" is also feminine. In the words of Al-Qashani "The ultimate ground (or origin) of everything is called Mother (umm), because the mother is the (stem) from which all branches emerge. Do you not see that God describes the matter when He says: "And He created from it (i.e., the first soul, meaning Adam) its mate, and out of the two He spread innumerable men and women" (IV, I). As we know, the wife (of Adam) was feminine. Moreover, the first unique "soul" from which she was created was itself feminine. In just the same way the Origin of all origins above which there is nothing, is designated by a "haqiqa" (feminine noun) or "Reality". Likewise the words designating the Divine Essence, "ayn" and "dhat" are feminine .[2]

Woman is the cardinal agency through which God blesses the spiritual in the sensible. She is the symbol of beauty and the eternal feminine. "Woman is the beam of the divine Light / She is not the being whom sensual desires take as its object / She is Creator, it should be said./ "She is not a Creature" said Jalaluddin Rumi.[3] Besides the creative agency of women the task of creation and fertilization

---

1   What the Seeker Needs: essays on spiritual practice, Oneness, majesty and beauty: with Ibn al-Arabi's glossary of 199 Sufi technical terms/ Muhyiddin Ibn al-arabi, translated by Shaikh Tosun Bayrak Al-Jerrah and Rabia Terri Harris Al-Jerrahi, (New York: Threshold Books, 1992). See also Treatise on Unity [S.I]: Beshara, [19....] Imprint.

2   See: Mysteries of Purity trans. Eric Winkel (Notre Dame, Indiana: Cross Cultural Publication, 1995).

3   See: Ismail Hakki Burseri's translation Kernel of the Kernel of Ibn al-Arabi: Sherborne, nr.

is carried out through water - an element considered passive in comparison to fire or air. The Koran says "Do not the believers see / That the heavens and the earth / Were joined together (as one Unit of Creation), before / We clove them sunder? / We made from water / Every thing living. Will they / Not then believe?" Water covers about 72 percent of our earth and science has proved that the protoplasm which is the source of the procreation of life, is a liquid which remains in a state of instability or flux. Science has further confirmed a similarity between some human organs and those of fish. "And Allah has created / Every animal from water:/ Of them there are some / That creep on their bellies;/ Some that walk on two legs/ And some that walk on four./ Allah creates what He wills;/ For verily Allah has power/ Over all things"

(s.24:v.45). Such a tremendous variety includes the creeping worms, reptiles, snakes, spiders, the swimming fishes and sea-animals. The two-legged animals consist of birds and mankind. Mammals comprise the four legged animals and the rest of the animal kingdom. "It is He Who has / Let free the two bodies / Of flowing water / One palpable and sweet / And the other salt and bitter"/ (s.25: v.53). Of the two types of water, the oceans are saltish. The other is the sweet water fed by rain such as rivers, lakes or underground springs. The Koranic symbols suggest that despite the gravitational pull of the sweet waters to the mighty oceans, the latter still retain their identity in the ocean till some bigger current of water within the sea, swamps them completely by submerging their identity as the signs of Allah. Since on another level, the message of the Koran is purely symbolic, one could interpret the river-ocean analogy as man-God relativity according to mysticism. But the message of the Koran is scientific as well. "And He it is Who sends / The Winds as heralds / Of glad tidings, going before / His mercy, and We send down / Pure water from the sky. That with it, We may give / Life to a dead land, / And slake the thirst / Of what We have created / Cattle and men in great numbers./ And We have distributed / The (water) amongst them, in order" (s.25. v.48-9). The winds bring rain as an activity of the heated water surface or the hot atmosphere. A cycle of water activity is worth observing here. It rises in the form of vapours from the sea and undergoes transformation as soon as it condenses in the air or before it falls down as rain drops, forming rivers which surrender themselves eventually

Cheltanham, Gloucestershire, England, On behalf of the Beshara Trust by Beshara Publications, [1982].

to the sea again. "And He it is Who makes / The Night as a Robe / For you and sleep as Repose, / And makes the Day / (As it were) a Resurrection" (s.25: v.47). Another symbol of the cyclic manifestation of Allah is light, for, light and day here imply heat and activity whereas night is meant for rest and repose - a kind of death before resurrection the next day. The Koran hence delivers its message through the cyclic flow of nature whether in the shape of the planetary system or the "protean" manifestations of the physical, plant and biological life with water at the heart of the whole mystery.

Eve

Three revelationary religions — Judaism, Christianity and Islam - attach a supreme value to Eve and Adam as primordial parents. In the works of Joyce, Eve remains one of the dimensions of femininity to show his vision which is neither religious nor secular, but assimilative of the two.

Eve as we know, sprang from beneath Adam's left rib. "Listeneth! "Tis a tree story. How olave, that firile, was aplantad in her liveside" (FW.564.21). "Olave" is olive tree and "firile" is fir-tree. The olive tree is mentioned in the surah XXIII as "And we also raise for you a tree springing from Mount Sinai". Adam was made of clay which was sticky[4] or "viscous". "Viscous" is that which may be anything not solid and is something that adheres to something else.[5] The soil which composed the clay meant for the creation of Adam, consisted of red, white and black colours. Besides being viscous and coloured, the soil became stinging slime, at a later stage. For forty nights it was allowed to bake before being kneaded into "salsalah", that is, a soil which produces sounds like a potter. During these forty nights, Satan would enter Adam's mouth and leave from his posterior, and he

---

4   Abdullah Yususf Ali, The Holy Koran surah 17, verse. 11.
5   The History of Tabari: General Introduction from the Creation to the Flood, translated and annotated by Franz Rosenthal (New York: State University of New York Press, 1989) p. 249, Vol.I (See also Genesis [2:7] and the Koran s.15,v 26, 28, 33).

would enter his posterior and leave from his mouth.[6] Satan's involvement with Adam is evident even at this stage. As the divine spirit blew into Adam's head, the latter sneezed. As it reached his belly he desired for food and Lo! Adam "jumped up". "When the spirit reached his navel, he looked at his body and was pleased to see it". He attempted to stand on his own but could not. It is to this "jumping up" and the effort he made to stand on his own that the Koran refers to when "Man was created of haste".[7] Adam thus came into being. Allah made him learn the names of all creation as he was to be His vice-regent on earth. The angels, according to Divine decree, were asked to prostrate before Adam which they did, there and then, as a mark of homage to his superiority; but alas, said Satan (out of haughtiness) "I shall not prostrate myself, as I am older and better than he, as well as physically stronger. You created me from fire, and You created him from clay", meaning thereby that fire is stronger than clay. As we have seen, Satan was already maneuvering his roguish role even when the clay destined to create Adam was but at the stage of being baked.

Finding Adam a stinking clay, Satan said "You are not something for making sound. For what then, were you created? If I am given authority over you, I will ruin you and if you are given authority over me, I will disobey you".[8] What was the status of Satan before Allah showered His grace in creating Adam? According to Tabari, there was a time when God had blessed Satan with a beautiful form, endowed him with authority to rule over the "lower heaven and the earth" Satan was the ruler of the "jinns" and God had expected from Satan the dispensation of justice. Instead, Satan became haughty and once his grip over his subjects began to loosen, a reign of "terror, hostility and hatred" set forth in his dominion. God as a consequence, issued His decree and Satan was deprived of his status, and ordered back to heaven while God's fire consumed the riotous "jinns". What is clear is that Satan had lost touch with his true function and responsibilities as an honest arbitrator; while in the case of Adam, we can notice a similar sense of self-complacency. If the former was behaving in a vain glorious, egocentric manner, then the latter was at least showing signs of a rudimentary inclination in the same direction. Even this subtle inclination symbolizes a self-conscious

---

6   The History of Tabari, Vol.I, p. 264.

7   The Holy Koran, s.21, v.37.

8   The History of Tabari, Vol.I, p. 264.

narcissism.

Discussing HCE as primordial Adam, Donn L. Henseler says "If Cad is the potential sin projected by the mind of HCE, then he is synonymous with that which the female effected the male's fall - activated the consciousness of time and simultaneously, consciousness of self as separate and of female as other than self. The confrontation of Cad concerns time and HCE's freedom of will to act or not to act. He chose to answer the Cads question, thus affirming the Cad as real and separate. Or he can ignore him and in doing so deny him actuality".[9] His situation is analogous to the Paradise Lost "Evil into the mind of God or Man/ May come and go so unapproved/ No spot or blame behind; which gives me hope /That which thou dost abhor to dream/ Waking though never will consent to do" (Book 5, lines 117-22). "What corrupts is not the thought of evil but the mind's permission of it" as the twelfth century Abelard says. According to Henseler, HCE's sinful nature is reflected the way he has a "real and separate" identity of Cad in his mind. Cad then symbolises the helpless incitement of satanic influence which is aggressive, rebellious rather than sauve, handsome like that of Orion. Like Lucifer, Cad is the one "who, the odds are, is still berting dagabut in the same straw bamer, carryin his overgoat under his schulder, sheepside out"...(FW35.12-4). HCE with his staff resembles the physique of Cad whereas Cad is the darker shadow of HCE like Milton's Lucifer.

God warned Adam and Eve that they may "Eat freely of its plants where you wish, but do not go near this tree, or you will be wrong doers" (s.2-v. 35). We get the same message from the Old Testament as: ". . But of the fruit of the tree which is in the midst of the garden...Ye shall not eat of it, neither shall ye touch it, lest ye die." (III,3) This is traceable in the Wake as: "In the middle of the garth, then? That they mushn't touch it. The devoted couple was or were only two disappointed solicitresses on the job of the unfortunate class on Saturn's mountain fort?" (FW.90.15). Again, the Wake warns us all whether Jews, Christians or Moslems by referring to the story of Adam and Eve: "Hail, Heva, we hear! This is the glider that gladdened the girl that list to the wind that lifted the leaves that folded the fruit that hung on the tree that grew in the garden Gough gave. Wide hiss, we're wizening!" (FW.271.27).

---

9   Donn L. Henseler, James Joyce Quarterly, Fall 1968.

Satan's initial attempts to lead them astray were, by the keepers of Paradise, nipped in the bud. Like the Prankquean, he had pleaded before a snake who had permitted him to enter his body and thus Satan was enabled to sneak into Paradise with two fangs in the mouth of the snake. Caduccus of Hermes from whom Joyce drew his Cad, bears twin snakes round his head, symbolic of sin and knowledge. As snake, Satan in the Old Testament is cursed by God: "Upon thy belly shalt thou go, and dust shalt thou eat all the days of thy Life." (III,14) This is stated in the Wake as: ". . would go anyold where in the weeping world on his mottled belly." (FW.75.20).

Joyce, in the Wake, refers to the copulation as noted by Roland McHugh: "S is both a policeman and the serpent spying upon Adam and Eve, (F.W.583. 14-25) watching a silhouette on the window blind showing him engaged in the act of copulation with.."[10] In Moslem traditions, A.R. Muhajir elaborates the trial of Adam and Eve. He says that the Koranic terms "Jannat" (the garden of paradise) and "sharajah" (the forbidden tree) are two different things. The garden of paradise is a state of bliss, ease and comfort where, as Allama Mohammad Iqbal says "Wherein no weariness shall reach the righteous, nor forth from it shall they be cast, wherein the righteous will pass to one another the cup which shall engender no light discourse, no motive to sin".[11] It is a state of existence in which man is

---

10 Roland McHugh, The Sigla of Finnegans Wake, (Edward Arnold Pub. Ltd, London, 1976), p. 126. "… S" says McHugh "is both a policeman and the serpent spying upon Adam and Eve" (Notebook VI.B. 21...47 "Spying cop S"). Established exegesis portrays S at FW.583.14-15 watching a silhoutte on Earwicker's windowblind showing him engaged in the act of copulation with ALP. At 586.28-36, S is "pollsigh patrolman Seekersenn", who overhears noises "telling him all, all about ham and livery." If Ham is Shem -Cain, this accords with his opposition to S. But S in III.4 is principally the observer of Earwicker and ALP just as in II.4 Mamalujo is (incorporating Earwicker) the observer of Shem and Isolde. A hierarchy of generations is thereby implicit: the oldest members are S and K, then Earwicker and ALP, and finally Shem and Isolde." The signs used by McHgh in this book are for the following characters:

    Earwicker, HCE.
    Anna Livia
    Shem – Cain
    Shaun
    Snake
    S. Patrick
    Tristan
    Isolde
    Mamalujo

11 Sir Mohammad Iqbal (1877-1938) Reconstruction of Religious Thought in Islam, (Lahore: Sh. Mohammad Ashraf, 1968), p. 81.

unrelated to his environment and bereft of the "sting of want". Muhajir thinks "sharajah"to be the progeny of Adam, the result of the union of opposite sexes from which mankind inherits sustenance.

Commenting on Cad, Donn L. Henseler says that Cad is the sign of potential sin – an inevitable necessity for the multiplication of human generations. HCE would have remained an enclosed potentiality like the Koranic state of Adam and Eve. "It is entirely possible," quotes Henseler, ". . that HCE could have ignored Cad's first inquiry as: 'Guinness thaw tool in jew me dinner ouzel fin?'." (FW 35.15-6). Cad is asking - on the authority of his presence in every cycle of history as a tempting evil which puts the wheels of history into motion by its mysterious grease - "Whether, as before, the intellectual curiosity will kindle a Lucifer-like rebellion, the revolt encouraged by the dim memory of the 'old man' rising in the 'new man' of the present cycle".[12] According to Muhajir, Satan whispered the idea of the private parts to the couple. The word "whisper" suggests that the sexual urge is first born within and reaches its consummation by the stimulation it receives from the external environment. Satan maneuvered this whisper in bringing about their sexual union. As the Koran says "When they both tasted of the tree, their private parts became manifest to each other and they both began to cover themselves with the leaves of the garden." (s.7, v22). The Wake puts this incitement as "..light leglifters cense him souriantes from afore while boor browbenders curse him grommelants to his hindmost; between youlasses and yeladst glimse of Even; the Lug his peak has, the Luk his pile; drinks tharr and wodhar for his asama and eats the unparishable sow to styve off reglar rack." (FW 130.01-03). Milton presents the same as: "They hand in hand with wandering steps and slow / Through Eden took their solitary way." (P L 12.648-9).

Disobedience brought the volte face, the sudden transmutation from bliss to sinfulness, from the state of primitive lack of consciousness to that of an awareness of their identities as individuals breathing in an environment which was totally different, alien as if Plato's thrice removed from reality. The tree of whose fruit was forbidden - as Muhajir says: ". . is used for a sexual act because just as a seed when planted in the soil gradually assumes its stature as a full grown tree and produces

---

12 Donn L. Hennseler, James Joyce Quarterly, Fall 1968.

in its turn millions of seeds to propagate the species."[13] According to Muhajir, we can say that the nourishment of further species emulated the pattern of the trees, as the Koran says: "And Allah has made you to grow out of the earth in the manner of a plant." The frivolous people in the pub are busy enjoying a lively gossip: "Here all the leaves alift aloft, full of liefing, fell alaughing." (FW 361. 18). Their hilarious chitchat, mirth and peaceful past times are suddenly checkmated and everybody is stunned as soon as Constable Sackerson appears in the pub in search of Ear wicker. "And they leaved the most leavely of leaftimes and the most folliagenous till there came the marrer of mirth and the jangtherapper of all jocolarinas and they were as were they never ere." (FW 361.26-29). The pleasure-seekers had to leave their "folliagenous" as soon as their "mirth" was marred and suddenly "they were as were they never ere".

This elaborate pun on leaves is stated in the Koran as: "They began to cover themselves with the leaves of the garden." "Leaves" symbolise love as the dreamer utters about Issy: ". . child of tree, like some losthappy leaf." (FW 556. 19). Or as he says elsewhere: "Everyday, precious, while m'm'ry's leaves are falling deeply on my Jungfraud's Messonge book I will dream telepath posts dulcets on this isinglass stream (but don't tell him or I'll be the mort of him!) under the libans and the sickamours, the cyprissis and babilonias, where the frondoak rushes to the ask and the yewleaves too kisskiss themselves and 'twill carry on my hearz' waves..." (460.19-27).

Anna Livia is fluid like water just as the image of sticky viscous implies fertilization in the process of procreation. The leaves of the trees in this passage stand for the intellectual achievement of the creative artist. The leaves in the Koranic passage symbolise the state of astonishment after the first step, for which Eve is culpable, into the process of procreation – an act of transgression like Promethus or Daedalus. Issy is that sizzling wind which waves the leaves along the babbling Liffey and is like the progeny of Adam and Eve. The bleeding trees do not cleave, they stick for procreation as Tabari says: ". . . where upon God said; Now it is my obligation to make her bleed once every month as she made this tree bleed."[14] "In Tilly," says Eckley, ". . the crimson lotus blooms near water and drops blood from

---

13 Muhajir, Lessons From the Stories of the Koran, p. 67 (Lahore, 1965).
14 The History of al-Tabari: Vol.I, p. 280.

its flowers."[15] As we know, when Dryope tears a branch for her small son, she is punished for an act committed in innocence and becomes a lotus tree and speaks only when her face remains uncovered by the bark. As the Wake puts it : ". . the face in the treebark feigns afear." (FW 279.01) "The bleeding of a tree" according to Eckley, ". . in the Wake, though still that common and natural exuding of resin or 'gum', sticks rather than cleaves and implies procreation." "By gum, but you have resin! Of these tallworts are yielded out juices for jointoils and pappasses for paynims." (FW 564.19-20). The leaves are related to a Lotus tree as the Koran admonishes Adam and Eve: "Cursed is the earth from which you were created, with a curse which will change its fruits to thorns. Neither in paradise nor on earth was there a tree more excellent than the acacia and the lote tree."[16] Abdullah Y. Ali explains the "lote" tree as to have belonged ". . to the family Rahmn aceae, Zizyphus Spine Christi, of which it is supposed Christ's crown of thorns was made - and allied to the Zizyphum Jujba, or the ber tree of India. In the wild it is shrubby, thorny and useless. In cultivation it bears good fruit, provides some shade and can be thornless, thus becoming a symbol of heavenly bliss."[17]

The tree represents endless growth. In this respect, the tree as a symbol of new and inexhaustible life is planted by the river of time. Opposite to the tree is the stone as Shaun stands for petrification- a deadening of conscience, barrenness of soil and terrific astonishment that causes mental stultification. As Grace Eckley comments, one victimized by such a deadly sate of mind would be the one who is transformed into a "stone" or "statue" arrested by bewilderment. In her monologue, as Anna Livia tries to seek peace between her two ever warring sons, her gaze falls on the two ever talking washerwomen while she ponders over their habit of talking too much: "Maybe it's those two old crony aunts held them out to the water front. Queer Mrs Quickenough and odd Miss Doddpebble. And when them two has had a good few there isn't much more dirty clothes to publish." (FW 620.18-21). "Miss Doddpebble" is the stone and the listener. Eckley says that the petrifying state as in the case of Lot's wife, means: ". . the arrest of the soul on its

---

15 Michael H. Begnal and Grace Eckley, Narrator and Character in Finnegans Wake, (Brucknell University Press, London: Associated University Press, 1975), p. 171-80.

16 The Holy Koran, note: Talh and Sidra are two different kinds of trees mentioned in the Koran s56,v28. Even before Islam, these trees were accorded respect for their nourishing of the body with food.

17 ...Ibid.

journey to bliss."[18]

Commenting on Lot's wife, Adaline Glasheen says that: "Lot's wife was turned into salt as she looked back while escaping the cities before destruction."[19] Joyce refers to this: "When the h, who the hu, how the hue, where the huer? Orbiter onswers, lots lives lost. Fionia is fed up with Fidge Fudgesons. Sealand snorres." (FW 257.35). Or as the Wake states: "..may have our irremovable doubts as to the whole sense of lot..." (FW 117.35). Furthermore: "... How to understand the Deaf, Should ladies learn Music or Mathematics." (Lot is quoted in Italics on the left hand side of the page along with other historic personalities, poets, philosophers and prophets) (FW 307.21-22) Or: "..and well shoving off a boastonmess like lots wives does over her handpicked hunsbend, as she would be calling, well, for further oil mircles." (FW 364.35-365.01) or "Lots feed from my tidetable. Oil's wells in our lands." (FW 579.24). The Koran has this to say on the wife of Lot: "The (Messenger) said; O! Lut thee! Now travel/With thy family yet/ A part of night remains / and let not any of you / Look back; but thy wife /(will remain behind): To her will happen / What happens to the people / Morning in their appointed time /Is not the morning right / When our decree issued / We turned the (the cities) / Upside down, and rained down /On them brimstones / Hard as baked clay / Spread, layer on layer..." (s.11, v.81-2) Instead of the pillar of salt into which she was turned, they were buried under rubble. Like her people, she too becomes a brimstone. Like the disobedient wife of Lot, Satan also was turned into a stone, finally. Discussing Satan, Tabari says that like the rest of the creation, Satan was created beautiful, and was appointed viceregent over the lower heaven and the earth. Soon his mind began to inflate with haughtiness. This self-conceitedness tempted him rather furtively to assert himself as the lord of earth. This was "shirk" (polytheism) a vain attempt to rival God. He was a mischief monger and was attempting to jeopardize the natural course of the universe. God, hence, transformed him to a stone.

Tree and stone are two contrary entities subsuming the entire scheme of life and creation. Their symbolic value has a universal import with a cross-cultural

18 Grace Eckley, The Children's Lore in Finnegans Wake, (Syracuse, N.Y.: Syracuse University Press, 1985).

19 Adaline Glashine, Third Consensus of Finnegans Wake, (Berkeley: University of California Press, 1977), p.76

appeal. As symbol of the universal female, Eve is a tree. Satan on the other hand, is the stone. Eve is not mere "body" whose "head"- as Nawal El Saadawi says - is man.[20] According to Saadawi, Eve has proven herself to be more intelligent and creative. By taking the step she risks rather heroically and thus has opened up manifold avenues of life for mankind. The forbidden tree, according to Saadawi stands for the discovery of knowledge: "Be that as it may, but for that light phantastic of his gnose's glow as it slid lucifericiously." (FW 182.04-05). The epithet "gnosis" implies the tree of knowledge. The quick-witted Eve could discern the Divine purpose in imposing such a prohibition: ". . prohibitive pomefructs." (FW 19.13) As Saadawi comments: ". . the fear that once their hands had stretched out to the branches, and once their teeth had bitten into the juicy fragment of flesh, their minds would be able to discern between good and evil. From that moment they would rise to the level of their Creator. Man who was created in the image of God would himself become God." She compares Eve with Isis and says that it was Isis who resurrected what Touphoun had destroyed. Touphoun's malice caused the mutilation of the body of Osiris. A fish from the waters of Nile devoured his sexual organs. Isis, by virtue of her power, restored Osiris to life by reassembling his torn body. The fall was a happy fault: "felicitous culpability" (FW 263.29) determined by: "gracious providence" (FW 69.28) ". . he sat on anxious seat... during that three and a hellof hours' agony of silence, ex profundis malorum, and bred with unfeigned charity that his wordwounder . . might, mercy to providential benevolence's who hates prudencies' astuteness, unfold into the first of a distinguished dynasty of his posteriors." (FW 75.16-24). As the Koran says: "They said; Our Lord! We have wronged ourselves. If Thou forgive us not and bestow not Thy mercy on us, we shall certainly be of those who cause loss to themselves." To this pleading, Allah replies: "Then Adam received words from his Lord and so He turned to him mercifully. Surely He is often returning to mercy, the Merciful."

The Wake's phrase: ". . unfold into the first of a distinguished dynasty of his posteriors," should be observed in the light of these Koranic verses: "We said; Get forth some of you being the enemies of the others and there is for you in the earth an abode and provision for a time." We read the same warning in Old Testament as God punishes the serpent: "And I will put enmity between thee and the woman;

---

20 Nawal El-Saadawi, The Hidden Face of Eve: Women in the Arab World (trans. from the Arabic and edited by Sherif Hetata: London: Zed Press, 1980), p 103.

. . she shall bruise thy head and thou shalt bruise her heel." (III,15) The Koran also insists that: "And for trial will We test you with evil and with good." (21.36).

Establishment of the dynasty on earth reflected the "felicitous culpability" of conflict and cooperation, cycle after cycle. We may say that Eve is the "Ways of God on earth." The Creator substantiates His creation though holds back His will. The freedom of the agent sows the seeds of estrangement. The paradox of freedom is the fear of alienation. Estrangement or alienation then brings about awareness, the casus belli of knowledge of the relationship between mortal and immortal.

It is not through fusion or immersion but rather by means of a relative sympathy of dependence along with independence that the self in man develops and maintains its existence as selfhood. As Jung says regarding the unconscious: "So people generally believe that whosoever descends into the unconscious lends himself in the oppressive confinement of an egocentric, subjective state of mind and exposes himself in this blind alley to the attack of all the ferocious beasts the cavern of the psychic underworld is supposed to harbour."[21] By doing what was forbidden, Eve was putting the cart before the horse. Their sexual interaction exposed them to the devil, the blind dark alley; ". . with apparently no inside and no outside, no above and no below, no here and no there, no mine and no thine, no good and no bad."[22] Exposed thus to the invasion of darkness, there comes a stage when our normal consciousness is suspended. Together with ego and its offshoots, like perception and intellection, spooked into the crucible, lose their identities and we find ourselves in the state of primordial chaos. As Kristeva says: ". . the cells fuse, split, proliferate . . in a body, there is grafted unmasterable, another."[23] Who is this the Other, even the mother is unaware. Why Eve did transgress is impossible to tell. What this economy points to is the human effort in arriving at certain conclusions. Helen Cixous, for example, thinks that masculine economy is centralized, short, reapportioning, cutting, an alternation of attraction and repulsion. While the feminine economy is "continuous, overabundant and overflowing."[24] A handful of dust taken from earth was moistened, baked, and

---

21 Carl G. Jung, Integration of Personality (trans. Stanley M. Dell, London, 1940), p. 69.

22 .....Ibid, p.70.

23 J. Gallop Polylogue, p. 409. See Gallop as quoting Kristeva.

24 Helen Cixous, Writing The Feminine (1968), p. 98.

then with divine spirit breathing into it, became alive. Adam in paradise was in a state of innocence, fused with his environment.

The split occurred at Eve's desire and hence came the proliferation of the creation of life. Adam is masculine, "centralized", "short", "cutting" etc. Eve is "continuous", "overabundant." "With your milk mother, I have drank[25] la glace." Gallop explains la glace as both "ice" and "mirror". Gallop says that mother's fluidity is organically vital for the continuity of life. "Ice" is that which "fixes", "paralyses". Ice therefore is the Adamic, masculine principle. "Mirror" as Gallop interprets is representation. "The representation freezes the nameless flow. Only this liquid which leaves one and arrives in the other, and which has no name." Mirror then is the Eve principle. Life demands active participation of the rigid masculine to keep its identity intact on the one hand and its further proliferation on the other. It is like the liquefaction of the tip of an iceberg after the bottom receives the apparently insignificant yet far reaching affects of warm waves from the exhausting, redundant, loose particles of great explosions occurring in the heart of the earth. "Never one without the other," as Gallop emphasises, and like Eliot's: "No, I do not hope to turn again", or Molly's natural economy of saying: "Yes." Despite contradictions in her character, or as the Koranic verse repeating often; 'Rubbul Mashriquin wal Rubbul Maghribain' ("The Lord of the East and of the West"), establish the fact of the duality of existence.

That which specifies the mother as goddess is the third element: ". . in a body, there is grafted unmasterable, an other." (Polylogue, p. 409) This "an other" which woman thinks of her own, is not so. In the words of Gallop: "The mother calls herself as totality, as self, into question because within her is something she does not encompass, that goes beyond her, is other. This experience, Kristeva thinks might prepare her for a general permanent calling into question."[26]

Woman can enjoy the "sublime repressed" if she identifies herself as mother - the creator of fact and its looming fantasy. Eve by suffering the "pleasure of sin" not only enjoyed the "sublime repressed", but also incarnated the "symbol of goddess." Similarly in Finnegans Wake, ALP in her incarnation as Prakquean, for example, serves the role of "a parody's bird, a peri potmother." (FW 11.9) ALP

---

25 ....Ibid, 121.

26 J. Gallop, Pheminism and Psychology, p. 123.

here is that sixteenth Irish witch - Grace O'Mally - whose powers sway the entire species of her nature. So is the owner of the castle, as, swollen with pride as the imposing castle, overlays the entire landscape. Both are sharply contrasted, the former gifted with the supernatural and the latter as the archetypal aristocrat of the Renaissance. Naturally, the Earl's wife is but a pigmy-sized household pet only. The appearance of the Prankquean is astounding. She bursts in with such dramatic surprise. More so, her humble urge for hospitality. The way she asks for the solution of the riddles is even more stunning. Her flouting of the aristocratic decorum was provocative: "Why do I am alook alike a poss of porter pease." (FW 21.18). In retaliation, the Earl bangs the door shut and throws the shit at her. She in reply kidnaps the two Jiminies, converting the one that is Tristopher into "Luderman" and enlightens, moralises Hilary (a name that sounds like hilarious) by making him learn the joys of the "sublime repressed" (pleasure of the tragic suffering). The situation presents an interesting paradox. She is the goddess of fertility ploughing to cultivate, to harness the aristocratic structure of society with enlightenment while the Earl symbolises barrenness. The stiffened Jarl in his seven fold costume challenges the warrior witch to fight. The "skirtmish" thunders are heard. The duel of the dual ends as the vainglorious pride of the Earl is precipitated. As he now reconciles with his wife for the peace and prosperity of the castle, the Prankquean proves herself to be the real benefactress of the whole family. The way Prankquean conflates the juxtaposed Earl and his submissive wife and the way she teaches the noble arts of suffering, symbolises ALP as the mother goddess endowed with manifold beneficial possibilities.

ALP as Eve has another dimension. Eve had riddled Adam. Similarly the Prankquean questions thrice: "Why do I am alook alike a poss of porter pease" (FW 21.18, 22.05,2.29). J.M Morse suggests that this quotation is from the "piers ploeman" which reads as "make pease portru to pynne the gates." Like Adam, Porter is an aspect of HCE. Porter is Adam standing at the gates of paradise after the fall. "Poss" is boss, as Adam is for Eve. The question then is: "Why I am a piece of Adam, an image of God!" And the answer is: ". . because I am Eve." Why was she deprived of hospitality? The book of Genesis provides the answer: "Therefore the Lord God sent him forth from the Garden of Eden to till the ground from whence he was taken. So He drove out the man; and He placed at the east of the garden Cherubs, and a flaming sword which turned every way to keep the way of the

tree of life." At each of her appearances, a reference is made to the sword: ". . and lit up again and redcocks flew flackering from the hillcombs lit oiut and the valley lay twinkling." (FW.22.04; 22.27) In the Babylonian mythology as adopted by the revelationary religions, the Lord of the heavens drives forth riding on the Cherubins in the flashing of lightening. The thunder is as much a divine miracle as it is related to Thor and to the cyclic appearance of construction and destruction of life and society according to Vico. The two Jiminies according to Morse, are Cain and Abel.[27]

Ibliss, equivalent of Satan
(Notebook VIC 6-16)

Iblis embodies the Islamic concept of evil. Everything evil is Iblis or Satan. It is Iblis who keeps the sense of conflict as inevitable and endless. Since God is even nearer and is Omniscient as well as Omnipotent, therefore what Satan or man proposes, God disposes. For humankind, nearness to God is possible through contrition, suffering and self-realisation. Satan tempts like the temptress ALP but when she appears in the form of the blessed Mary as God's grace, the victim - HCE - is finally exonerated from the taint of sin. Such a dialectical role of ALP - of both a seductress as well as a source of salvation may also be applied to the character of Iblis.

"You have led me astray," complained Iblis to God. Peter J. Awn comments on this complaint by differentiating between God's "Amr" and God's "Irada". Quoting Ibn Ghanim, Awn says that if "Amr" as God's command is a circle then "Irada" as God's will is the circle's circumference. The unavoidable crisis in human life occurs when "Amr" says "Do" and "Irada" responds in negation, "No, do not!" Command is the knot that tightens by binding while Will is the relaxing of this tightness to voluntary possibilities. Awn literally uses "Scylla" for "Irada" and "Charybdis" for "Amr" (the two antithetical facets of phenomenology - the rocks and the whirl-pools around which the Greek, European and Moslem philosophies revolve).

---

27 JJQ Fall 1968, p. 66.

Quoting another Moslem theologian, Al Makki, Awn says that God did will that His Command be actualized, because the basic principle to be observed at all times is that nothing comes into existence without God's will. If God had willed the actualisation and coming into existence of Iblis and his bowing, then the latter would have bowed before God. In other words, what does not exist, was never willed. In this case, therefore, there were two separate things willed by God: the order to bow and Iblis's refusal. "The actual coming into existence of a thing is a clear proof of God's having willed it so." God then determines everything. By creating Iblis, God actually willed him to be that way. This also is a modicum of redemption in the case of Iblis, for God, as has been demonstrated in this study, is all-merciful ("allmaziful").

The Queen of Sheba.

King Solomon and his Queen, Sheba, are referred to in the religious texts of Judaism, Christianity and Islam as E.L. Ranelagh mentions.[28] Ranelagh also cites Mahabharata as another book which describes King Solomon. As we know Joyce's method of locating the nexus of such a common theme and then to spin it around, rehashing its content suitable to his own needs of a wayward dreamer's series of endless reverie in the Wake, he must have availed this theme from Burton's 'the Arabian Nights', Yeats', and the traditions available both in Europe and in Asia.

The story of Solomon and Sheba is a variegated collection of myth and religion. Warning the Pharisees, Christ had said: "The queen of the south shall rise up in judgement of this generation and shall condemn it: for she came from the uttermost parts of the earth to hear the wisdom of Solomon; and, behold, one greater than Solomon is here." (Mathew.12.42). This illustrates as Ranelagh says, Solomon as a prototype Messiah and Sheba as representing the Gentiles

---

28 E.L Ranelagh, The Past We Share: The Near Eastern Ancestry of Western Folk Literature, (London; Melbourne and New York: Quartet Books 1979), See chapter IV, pp.85-90

who were to be converted into Christianity. The Jews became familiar with this story through two sources: The Old Testament and the sixth century A.D. Second Targum, Targum Sheni. Some of the incidents of this story which are common between Jewish folklore and the Koranic version such as "the trick of a pool of glass" as elaborated below, are also found in Mahabharata.[29] Ranelagh also mentions Sheba to be a figure of the cult of the Adoration of Magi. Finally, the tales in Arab literature are full of stories about Solomon. He is a prodigious king of wealth, with thrones made of gold and wielding supernatural powers over the creatures of this earth.

In Finnegans Wake, we read about Sheba: "I considered the lilies on the yeldt and unto Balkis did I disclothe mine glory." (FW.543.13-4) Sheba was like a "lily" on a tall, slender stem. "Lillith" synchronises the theme of promiscuity and perversion attached with the two temptresses of the Phoenix Park. Tracing the roots of "Lillith" in Jewish folklore, E.L. Ranelagh says that she was a cleft-footed demon queen of enormous sensuous appeal.[30] Sheba was a queen but Solomon was a prophet as well as a king, mightier than anything she could ever imagine. HCE is illuminating his achievements. He is the builder of the house of Adam, "Jacobs biscuits and Esans pottage..doubling megalapolitan." (FW 543) "Amtsadam." (FW.532.6) (magistrate Adam and creator), clean living man enjoying affairs with his wife "half wife" "his verawife...niceless to say with helioprope aye lips." (FW. 532.33) Solomon also appears as:

> "...and has been repreaching himself like a fishmummer these siktyten years ever since, his shebi by his shide, adi and aid, growing hoarish under his turban and changing cane sugar into sethulose starch (Tuttut's cess to him!) as also that, batin the bulkihood he bloats about when innebbiated, our old offender was humile, commune and ensectuous from his nature, which you may gauge after the bynames was put under him, in lashons of languages, (honnein suit and praisers be!) and, totalisating him, even hamissim of himashim that he, sober serious, he is ee and no counter he who will be ultimendly respunchable for the hubbub caused in Edenborough" (FW.29.26-35).

The protagonist appears here as a fabulous magus who can assume any shape aided by his Sheba ranging from the animalistic "growing hoarish" to alchemical compounds. A Solomon of bulk for his Balkis in various languages ("lashons") means "language" (in Arabic) including the Koranic surahs like "hamissim and

---

29 .....ibid

30 ......ibid

himashim" (Sura Yasin) In asserting the mortal, religious theme of "the hubbub caused in Edenborough", "Finnno more" is giving way to "Finnagain" (FW. 5.10) That is: "Humme the cheaner, Esc" an older offender . . humile, commune and en-sectuous." (HCE) Joseph Campbell comments that: "By the hocky salmon, there is already a big lad on the premises, with his "Shopillict." Tindall explains: "Shopillict" within brackets as "a shebeen in Chapelized" by ship like a Danish invader.[31] The Egyptian references "Healipolis" (FW24.18): "Totumclmum" or Tut-ankh-amen (FW26.18): the Arabic "hubbub" (love) and the religious "Edenborough" throw an accumulative light on the introvert seeping into the extrovert as John Gordon explains: ". . the outlander dreamer having subsided back into the inlander dream-er", paving the way for continuous creation in the cosmos, "chaoosmos" with a pattern of order imposing itself through the Vichian system.[32]

The queen of Sheba also appears as the "queen of pranks" with Sheba and queen as punned: "A reine of the shee, a shebeen quean a queen of pranks." (FW.68.21-22) A few sentences earlier she has been referred to as: "Houri of the coast of emerald, arrah of the lacessive poghue, Aslim-all- Muslim, the resigned to her surrender...true dotter of a dearmud" . . ."Phenicia or little Asia." (68.11-14... ...29)

Prophet Solomon is mentioned as "A kingly man, of royal mien, regally robed, exalted be his glory!" "Houri" is a nymph of Islamic paradise; "lakeside" is I provoke; "poghue" is Boucicault's "Arrah-na-Pogue". "Aslim-all-Muslim" is a Moslem who resigns himself to God - translated in the fashion of Kipling in the next phrase; ". . he resigned to her surrender." (Kipling usually describes the key words of his Indian vocabulary both in the local Indian language, preceded or succeeded by their translation into English. The chapter III from which the above sentences have been taken according to Tindall, is "full of repetitions and confu-sions, displacements and changes." Unlike the previous chapters disclosing their flagrant hostility against each other, both Hosty and HCE have been interfused into a single identity in this chapter.[33] Even the two girls are seen as admiring this composite figure which interacts the two mortal adversaries such as Napoleon

---

31 Tindall, A Reader's Guide to Finnegans Wake, p.50

32 John Gordon, A Plot Summary, P.120

33 Tindall, A Reader''s Guide to Finnegans Wake, p.67

and Wellington as "elbaroom" and Wellington as "woolsellywelly" (FW 52.23-31). Then, suddenly, the old pattern repeats by relating to the Fall "sukand see whybe!" (FW 52.35) as well as "cherchez la femme" (FW 6.28).

Sheba in this section carries the onus of the Fall levied upon womanhood. The whores like Lupta Loreta and Luperca Latouche are "stripped teasily for binocular man" (FW.68.01-02): Delilah, Gramia, Sheba, Noah's wife are "Angealousmei" (68.18), temptresses like ALP "arrah of the lacessive poghue" (FW.68.12). The third reference to Sheba occurs on page 198 "When they saw him shoot swift up her sheba sheath, like any gay lord salomon, her bulls they were ruhring, surfed with spree." (198.03-04) The tone of the sentence is harsh. Solomon has been compared with invaders like the Goths, the Huns (Huns invaded India) and the Danes. Sheba realises her vulnerable situation and presents some precious gifts to Solomon. Cognisant, she sends "all the neiss (neiece little whores) in the world to him" (FW22.29-30) as "proximate" the term interpreted by Campbell as "negotiator, marriage broker, procurer's procuress".

We read about them further "great gas with fun-in-the-corner, grand slam with fall-of-the-trick, solomn one and shebby, cod and coney, cash and carry, in all we dreamed the part we dreaded, corsair coupled with his dame .." (577.07-10). Solomon is the "corsair" (pirate) while Sheba is "dame" the Damsel. Solomon and Sheba here symbolise "our forced parents". Both would "recoup themselves" for the future course to be pursued. The reference elucidates prayer to God and is preceded by the trial scene over a case of "cheque between Tangoss and Bangos".

References to Solomon in Finnegans Wake.

Adaline Glasheen has pointed out the following references to Solomon:

"Tis as human a little story as paper could well carry, in affect, as singsing so Salaman" (FW.115.35:116.01). Like Finnegan, Solomon is a mythic figure "sports a chainganger's albert solemnly over his hullender's opulence" (126.15-16). "Chain" is a watch: "ganger" is from Ibsen's "Gengangere" (Ghosts) "hollender's" is for a Dutchman and "opulence" is an action of feasting. What the sentence implies is the feasting of the royal Solomon prepared by the supernatural creatures as the entire creation is at his beck and call. His royal souvenir as an opulent ruler, his supernatural gifts are further recognised as "is escapemaster-in-chief from all sorts of houdingplaces" (FW.127.10-11) and "is too funny for a fish and has too much outside for an insect" (FW.127.02-03). The clause "and wannot psing his psalmen" (again alludes to Solomon's song FW

167.16). "Away with covered words, new Solemonities for old Badsheetbaths!". Here the phrase "covered words" are the doubts, whims and shadows that enwrap the substratum, the true soul. "Badsheetbaths" is Solomon's mother, a reference to the role of Eve in the original sin. The Solomon's oath cannot assuage the original doubt (FW 188.25). "Salmonson set his seel on a hexengown." (FW297.04) implies the way Solomon subjected Sheba and set his seal on her lands and fate. ". . And be that semiliminal salmon solemonly angled, ingate and outgate." (FW.337.10) The emphasis seems to be on the theme of fall and the role of the prophets including Solomon in purgating the original sin. The cyclic appearances and returns of the prophets in their divine missions. "And you'll sing thumb a bit and then wise your selmon on it," (FW 625.16) suggests the proverbial wisdom endowed to Solomon and his song.

As in the Wake, we find the theme of Bilkis and the Prophet Solomon in the Koran as: "We gave (in the past) knowledge to David and Solomon." (27.15) The Koran recognises his sagaciousness and acumen in observing and deciphering the mysteries of Nature: "And Solomon was David's heir /He said O ye people! / We have been taught the speech / Of Birds, and on us / Has been bestowed (a little)/ Of all things: this is /Indeed Grace manifest. (from Allah)" (v.16) The ants remarked as they heard Solomon's armies approach fast in the words of the Koran: "O ants enter ye into your habitation, lest Solomon and his armies tread you under foot and perceive it not." (v.18) The prophet heard and said with a smile: "O Lord excite me that I may be thankful for Thy favour wherewith Thou hath favoured me, and my parents, and I may do that which is right and well pleasing unto Thee . ." (v.19) Then he cast a glance at the birds and inquired about the missing "lapwing." "Is she absent? Verily I will chastise her with severe chastisement or I will put her to death, unless she bring me a just excuse." (v.21) The bird appeared before the king in the twinkling of an eye. "I have viewed a country which thou has not viewed." (v.22) Then the lapwing described the queen of Saba, who according to George Sale and the Encyclopedia of Islam was known as Bilkis, the daughter either of Hodhad ibn Sharhabil or Sharabil ibn Malec and belonged to the tribe of Yaran ibn Kahtan.

Abdullah Y. Ali identifies Bilkis to be the biblical Sheba (Kings X-10), the ruler of Saba-a city of Yemen in the Hadramount territory irrigated by the Marub dam. Biblical account is similar to that of the Koran as the latter accounts for the prosperous state of her economy: "There was for Saba / Aforetime, a sign in their / Homeland two gardens / To the left and the right /Eat of the sustenance

(provided) /by your Lord and be grateful / To Him: a territory fair and happy / And a Lord Oft forgiving." (34.15) The Marab dam had tremendously contributed to the prosperity of her rule, "A city termed "Araby the Blest" for its greenery, spices and frankincense" as Abdullah Y. Ali says.

As the noun "abyssania" derives from the tribe "Habasha" which had come originally from Yemen just twenty miles from Babal Mandeb, the Queen had extended her territories covering Abyssania as Abdullah Y. Ali comments:

> "In the 10th or 11th century B.C there were frequent invasions of Abyssania from Arabia, and Solomon's reign of forty years is usually synchronised with BC 992 to 952". Her people worshipped the sun and the moon – an influence to which they were subject because of the Chaldeans to which the Koran refers by alluding to prophet Abrahim "When the night covered over him, he saw a star: He said: "This is my Lord". But when it set, he said: I love not those that said. When he saw the moon rising in splendour, he said: this is my Lord. But when the moon set, he said: Unless my Lord guide me, I shall surely be among those who go astray" (5.76-7). These verses refer to the story of Abrahim. Solomon, according to the Koran had despatched the bird "lapwing" reaffirming the message of prophet Abrahim in revoking the worship of the sun and the moon.

Even the bird, the envoy "lapwing" is symbolic. This lynx-eyed bird could detect water deep in earth. Solomon had sought its services when the prophet wanted water for ablution. One version is that the queen was asleep when the bird appeared to her. According to another, she was busy discussing the state matters with her courtiers when the bird appeared. The queen read the message to the courtiers. The Koran says: "She said, Ye chiefs! Advise me in this/My affair; no affair/Have I decided. Except in your presence."(V.32) The bloated chiefs felt insulted and responded, in the words of the Koran: "We are endowed with strength, and are endowed with great prowess in war, but the command appertaineth to thee, see therefore what thou wilt command." (V.33). As the Koran reveals in emphatic tones: "In the name of the most merciful God, rise not up against me; but come and surrender yourself to me." (V.31) And the Queen warns her courtiers: "She said, 'Kings when they/ Enter a country/ despoil it/ And make the noblest/ Of its people its meanest/Thus do they behave." Knowing too well the might and political supremacy of the King, the queen felt content to mellow the king by escorting a caravan of gifts as a custom as Sale quotes Jallalu-d-din: "Bearing the presents, which they say were five hundred young slaves of each sex, all habited

in the same manner, five hundred bricks of gold, a crown enriched with precious stones, besides a large quantity of musk, amber, and other things of value."[34]

Even though the shrewd Queen knew of the powers of the king, yet she dressed the male slaves as females and vice versa only to see how wise he was. Furthermore, she sent him "in a casket, a pearl not drilled, and an onyx drilled with a crooked hole."

Solomon could distinguish between the male and female slaves by the way they urinated, "and ordered one worm to bore the pearl, and the other to pass the thread through the onyx." Sale also mentions that Solomon had been pre-warned by the bird regarding the strength and needs of the queen's retinue. He "ordered a large square to be enclosed with a wall built of gold and silver bricks, wherein he ranged his forces and attendants to receive them." The queen's furtive attempts proved abortive. The king retaliated by ordering her presence along with her paraphernalia to which she consented. Her splendid throne was carried by the "jinns" to the awe-inspiring palace of Solomon. She was surprised when she witnessed the power of the king over the elemental forces both natural and supernatural. Her acknowledgement of the truth spared her the throne. To exorcise the demons of idol-worship, she was given another shock. As she advanced towards the throne of the king for reception, she had to pass across the pavement which was transparent like glass and was constructed over a water channel full of fish. Sensing the water ahead, she let her bare feet and ankles hover in sight - as any mean and lowly, barefoot slave entering the holy palace.

Kebra Nagest in "The Queen of Sheba" traces the queen's native land in Saba, the South West of Arabia, the sabian worshippers of the sun. Her Arabic name, according to Nagest is Bilkis while the Ethiopians call her Mekeda. According to the manuscript available at Oxford (see Dillman, catologues Bibl. Bodeley, P.26), Makeda was preceded by five kings named as Arawi 400 years, Angabo 200 years, Giedur 100 years, Siebado 50 years and Kawnasy 1 year. Makeda, the model of beauty and brightness, received the most cordial welcome from the king. According to Nagest, they fell in love, were married and she remained with the king for quite sometime. As a token of remembrance, Solomon gifted her with his ring which was eventually worn by her son Menyelek, a mirror image of his father.

---

34 George Sale, The Koran (London: Fredrick Warne, 1891)

The son came to see the father and everybody in the court was surprised to see the likeness of the father in the son and the son in the father. Menyelek's visit to his father was a matter more of interest than affection. The ambitious prince became determined to take away the Tabernacle of Zion from the Temple of Jerusalem. Makeda sent her son to carry out this ambitious enterprise in order to claim his lawful heritage of the throne of Solomon. Further more, he wanted to prove that the lineage of prophet Abraham was from his house in Saba.

On page xxxix of the introduction, Nagest says that the Lord wished an earthly counterpart of the heavenly Zion in the form of a Tabernacle. As the builders employed their tools in breaking the stones, to their surprise, not the stones but the tools would break up. Annoyed by the mystery, the prophet summoned his hunters to fetch him a bird called "Rukh" ("... playing lallaryrook cookerynook,..." FW.184.14). They brought him the bird and put a pot over it. In the meantime, the bird's mother found her young one missing and in agony, she flew round and round the earth till she detected the pot in the holy city of Jerusalem. The mother could not lift the pot and hence soared up towards the heaven where, in the lower zones of the Eastern part of Eden, she found a piece of wood. The piece of wood split the pot in the middle and thus the mother was able to rescue her young one. The miracle fascinated Solomon. They employed the wood as tools and thus were able to break the stones and erect the earthly Temple of the heavenly Zion.

Nagest says that the Queen was a malformed child and as such, one of her feet was that of a goat, because at the time of her conception, the queen mother had cast envious looks at a beautiful goat, "How handsome the goat is! And how handsome its feet are." The princess Sheba had grown up as an abnormal child. The miraculous wood was submerged in the water and she had to dismount from her throne to walk through the water. "She stretches out her hands and drums up the lower part of her cloak...thus Solomon saw her feet without asking... and her feet touch the piece of wood...and as the feet designed after the fashion of a goat's foot touched the wood, the goat's foot by the grace of God became like that of a man's."

Nagest draws a dramatic picture of their marriage: "I came to thee a maiden, a virgin; shall I go back despoiled of my virginity and suffer disgrace in my kingdom?" The king replies: "I will take thee to myself in lawful marriage!" The king

then strikes a deal, "When thou shalt come to me by night as I am lying on my bed, then shalt thou be my wife by the law of the kings." During her time away from the king she was fed mainly with foods full of spices, pepper and pungent herbs. On the third night, she received a meal without water, "Thou wilt find no water except by the couch of the king," which was kept in the king's bed chambers. She went in, assuaged her thirst and as she turned around, the wide-awake king, though pretending to be asleep, reminded her, "Verily thou hast become my wife by the law of the kings."[35]

ᕽ

---

35 Kebra Nagast, The Queen of Sheba and Her Only Son Menyelek, (trans. E.A. Wallis Budge), London 1932, See ch. 31, 35, 52, 69.

Appendix I

The Finnegans Wake
Notebooks at Buffalo

Forward Note:

Detailed discussion of these terms and allusions is based on the references cited as "Notes" at the back of individual themes and motifs. Notes on the Oriental Vocabulary in the Notebooks are taken from various sources. Some of these notes are taken from the Hobson-Jobson dictionary by Col. Henry Yule and A.C. Brunell (edited by William Crooke (London: Routledge and Kegan, 1886)). These notes establish Joyce's study of this dictionary for Finnegans Wake in addition to Ulysses. For others, such as the Persian and words in Arabic, I have made use of the dictionaries of these languages. In places, I had to rely upon my own judgement of the Eastern background. These notes are in accordance with the chronology of the Notebooks and the pages of that particular Notebook or register. Clive Hart's A Concordance to Finnegans Wake (Minneapolis: University of Minnesota Press, 1963) has been the most useful source book for collecting words from the Wake for me. The following abbreviations have been used:

EF: *The English Factories in India* (1618-1669), *A calendar of documents in the India Office, British Museum, and Public Record Office,* ed. Sir William Foster (13 vols., Oxford, 1906-27). New Series: vol. 1, *Western Presidency,* (1670-1677), ed. Sir Charles Fawcett (Oxford, 1936); vol. 11, *The Eastern Coast and Bengal* (1670-1677), ed. Sir Charles Fawcett (Oxford, 1952).

OED: *The Oxford English Dictionary. A new English dictionary on historical principles founded mainly on the materials collected by the Philological Society,* ed. Sir James A.H Murray, Henry Bradley, Sir William A. Craigie, and C.T. Onions (Oxford, 1933).

S.P.E: Society for Pure English.

The Finnegans Wake Notebooks at Buffalo

Notebook: VIB: 27-8

207 'Agni' (noun) in Sanscrit means fire, 'ignis' in Latin and 'after the elements — Agni (fire), Varuna (water) and Surya (the Sun) and the Devas (the gods of Heaven). As a warrior, he uses his famous weapon 'thunderbolt' (Vajra), a bow and a net riding a four-tusked elephant 'airavata' and lives in the clouds (svarga) around Mt. Meru. He hosts the deceased warriors and entertains them through

the dance of the 'apsaras' and games.

VIC 1-7

132. **Dhaki ricksha.** 'Khaki' is dusty or a light drab, the colour of the uniform worn by some of the Punjab regiments at the siege of Delhi. The 'khaki' uniform became popular in the army generally during the campaigns of 1857-58. Later on, it was adopted as a convenient uniform by many other corps. 'Khaki' is a stout cotton cloth.

VIC 6-16

25 **Abhidharma**

Sanscrit, Pali 'abhidharma' is composed of two words: 'abhi' is higher or special. 'Abhi' also means 'about'. 'Dharma' is 'teaching' or 'philosophy'. Abhidharma, therefore, denotes 'higher teachings' or 'about the teaching'. Abhidharma was the interpretations of the sayings of Buddha. These were in the form of manuscripts, which emerged from several monastic orders. Xuanzang, the 7th century Chinese pilgrim had collected seven such texts. Two of the Abidharmas are still available in their original form: the Theravada Abhidharma written in Pali and the Sarvastivadin Abhidharma in Chinese. It is believed that soon after his awakening or enlightenment, Buddha again slipped back into meditation. Abidharma is the fruit of this period of meditation. Buddha taught this text to the heavenly beings on his visit, which happened after the revelation of Abhidharma. This text was entrusted to Sariputra, a monk. He handed it over to the next generation. Abhidharma, therefore, is a pure, undiluted religious text of Buddhist sutras. A touch of Buddhist sanctimoniousness may be glanced by the words of Leopold Bloom as he says to Molly on their visit to the National Museum in Dublin (which also has the statue of a reclining Buddha; that it 'was a bigger religion than the Jews and Our Lords both put together all over Asia' (U.18.1203-4).

VIC 11-14, 17-8

331 **Agam**

Agam is used in many languages, with different meanings. In Gaelic and Irish, agam means 'at me'. In German, it means 'agamic', in Gurbani 'unapproachable', in Hebrew (transliterated) 'pond', in Indonesian 'hefty, manly, sturdy, virile', in Malay 'immeasurable' and finally in Urdu, agam means 'unfathomable.'

VIB 27-8

207 Ahi Indra Agni Vishnu Celestial spouse

'He under whose supreme control are horses, all chariots, and the villages, and cattle; He who gave being to the Sun and Morning, who leads the waters, He, O men, is Indra.' Rigveda, (2.12.7, trans.Griffith). Besides Agni, Indra who enjoys soma is one of the leading deities according to Rigveda. He defeated Vritra and smashed the stone that led to the liberation of the cows and rivers – the productive forces of life. He is engaged in a timeless battle against evil: cares for and looks ignite' in English. Agni is also a Hindu deity – a messenger between gods and is worshipped as fire, lightning and sun. Agni synthesises both destructive and constructive dialectical nature of reality. His black eyes, hair, three legs and seven arms show his complex character. Goats pull his chariot and he rides a ram. He radiates seven rays of light that also represent the planetary system around the sun. Agni's name appears in the first hymn of Rigveda as 'agnim ile purohitam / yajñasya devam rtvijam / hotaram ratnadhatamam."I praise Agni, the priest of the house, the divine ministrant of sacrifice, the invoker, the best bestower of treasure.'

VIC 1-7

401 M. Ahmedinger

Situated in the state of Maharashtra, Ahmednagar was founded by Ahmad Nizam Shah in 1494. The Nizami Shahi dynasty ruled the area until it fell to Shah Jahan, the Moghul emperor in 1636. Auranegzeb, the greatest Moghul emperor spent the latter part of his rule (1681-1707) in this region (known as the Deccan region). He died in Ahmednagar and was buried there. Though restored to the Marathas,

Ahmednagar came under British influence after the capture of the city by General Wellesley. Among its valuable pieces of architecture, is the Ahmednagar fort, built by the Moghuls. The British established a military cantonment in the suburbs of the city.

VIC 6-16

139 Ancient Brahman

Blavatsky refers to Jacolliot as describing the supernatural powers of a Hindu 'sannyasi' - demonstrating that he was both, present and absent at the same time.

The 'spectre' is that of an 'old Brahman'.

'The fakirs, although they can never reach beyond the first degree of initiation, are, notwithstanding, the only agents between the living world and the "silent brothers," or those initiate who never cross the thresholds of their sacred dwellings. The Fukara-Yogis belong to the temples, and who knows but these cenobites of the sanctuary have far more to do with the psychological phenomena which attend the fakirs, and have been so graphically described by Jacolliot, than the Pitris themselves? Who can tell but that the fluidic spectre of the ancient Brahman seen by Jacolliot was the Scin-lecca, the spiritual double, of one of this mysterious sannyasi? Although the story has been translated and commented upon by Professor Perty, of disappearance of the hands, the fakir continuing his evocations (mantras) more earnestly than ever, a cloud like the first, but more opalescent and more opaque, began to hover near the small brasier, which, by request of the Hindu, I had constantly fed with live coals. Little by little, it assumed a form entire human, and I distinguished the spectre -- for I cannot call it otherwise -- of an old Brahman sacrificator, kneeling near the little brasier.

"He bore on his forehead the signs sacred to Vishnu and around his body the triple cord, sign of the initiates of the priestly caste. He joined his hands above his head, as during the sacrifices, and his lips moved as if they were reciting prayers. At a given moment, he took a pinch of perfumed powder, and threw it upon the coals; it must have been a strong compound, for a thick smoke arose on the instant, and filled the two chambers.' Brahman's prayer is described as 'his lips moved as if they were reciting prayer.' (Notebook VIC 6-16 27 'brahmin's lips')

- Blavatsky, Isis Unveiled, Vol.2, PP.104-5 'The Living Spectre of a Brahman'.

Notebook VI B.41-44

Annie Besant (1847-1933), the daughter of William Wood and Emily Morris, had

a hard life as a child because of the death of her father. Helped by her brother, she married the young Rev. Frank Besant at the age of 17. As the wife of a minister, she involved herself in alleviating the problems of her husband's parish. She realised that human problems required a drastic social change. The husband and the wife felt themselves polls apart on the social issues. Soon, she stopped visiting the Church communion and in retaliation, the reverend divorced her. She came to London and began working for a radical paper the 'National Reformer'. Together with Charles Bradlaugh- the editor of the paper, she wrote a book fighting for the cause of the birth control. Both were sentenced to six months prison for 'obscene libel' though the sentence was overturned

Besant continued to write against social injustice, the problems of the poor living in unfavourable conditions due to population flux into the cities after the industrial revolution. She openly criticised religion advocating the cause of free thought and atheism. During the 1880's she joined the Theosophical Society under the influence of Madame Blavatsky. Inspired by this new cult, she went to India for spiritual insight from where she wrote and established contacts with other prominent figures interested in Occult and theosophy.

VI.C.11-18

37.

Aryan. In Sanskrit, the adjective 'Aryan' means 'noble'. All those peoples whose languages stem from the roots of Sanskrit, are known as Aryans. The Aryans are an ancient race whose traditions cover many a legend. One of the earliest Aryan kings was Darius in Persia, on whose tomb the name Aryan is inscribed.

VI.C.6-16

169 **Asiatic cholera** A water-borne disease, cholera or Asiatic cholera is caused by the bacterium 'vibrato cholera'. Garcia de Orta is the first Portugese physician who describes about it in his book Coloquios dos Simples e Drogas da India (1563). According to him, contaminated water and improperly cooked fish are the direct factors that cause cholera. The bacterium-contaminated faeces transmit this

disease through ingestion. Among the causes of contamination may be the diluted sewage water released into waterways, food washed with it or the shellfish inhabiting such water.

VIB 23-4

289 **Atma** or self means the boundaries of consciousness imposed by time and place. Self or 'Atma' is relative and aware of the subject and object, a duality due to ego. Self-realization comes only when this shell of duality is broken, and a new awareness permits an initiate to see the illusion which is this world, its pains and suffering (dukha) conditioned by the sinful nature, some of these sins are as a consequence of our predecessors in the form of prejudices which could be racial, religious, or tinctured by caste and colour.(See The Teachings of Sri Ramana Maharashi, edited by David Gorman).

VIC 1-7

394.

Ayah. Ayah is the maid servant of her children. It is a popular Indian vernacular word also used in Portuguese as 'aia' for a nurse or governess.

VIC 6-16

266 Bagheli

 Bagheli dialect is spoken in the Baghelkhand, central India. Bagheli Rajputs are the descendants of the Sloanki Clan, which ruled Patan in Gujarat.

VI C 1-7

Bunday matiave (songs in audience). This phrase sounds like 'Bande Mataram' meaning 'I revere the Mother land'. This was the song chanted in public rallies by the Hindus during the Freedom Movement in India. These kinds of songs aggravated the already hostile relations between the Hindus and the Moslems.

Meant to arouse Hindu nationalism to fever pitch, the first song of this nature could also be read in Bankim Chandra Chatterjee's novel Ananda Math (published in Calcutta, 1882). The hero of the novel, Bhavananda, is obsessed with the idea of an active revolt aimed at elimination of the Moslem rule of Bengal sometime in the beginning of the eighteenth century. While canvassing for support, he meets one Mahendra to whom he hums the song of 'Bande Mataram': 'Can the Hindus preserve their Hinduism unless these drunken 'nereys' [a term of contempt for Moslems] are driven away'. The spirit of these songs was reflected in the national Indian anthem of the Congress Party of India. (See Satyapal; Prabodh Chandra, Sixty Years of Congress (Lahore: Lion Press, 1946), p.98.

VIC 269

269.

Bapka gora, bapki ghori: both of these phrases mean the wheeled vehicle pulled by the slaves of India. The phrase 'goreevallahs' (p.395) means the same as 'bapka gora'. 'Gora' is horse. 'goreevallas' is the horsekeeper.

Notebook, (VI.B.21).

69 Bhagavat Upanishatem!

Originally, a part of the Mahabharata (Book 6), Bhagavat Gita is based on the dialogue between Lord Krishna and Arjuna at a very quiet moment — the stasis followed by the titanic warfare between good and evil. Arjuna, the hero hesitates to fight against the forces of evil. Lord Krishna convinces him to stand up and face the evil even if it he were to take up arms against his own kith and kin. Arjuna is told that good will prevail. Krishna, then, surprises Arjuna when the former reveals his identity that he was Lord Krishna. Bhagavat Gita is about the problem of living clean in an imperfect world. The nature of this world becomes clear when we read the next part of the sacred text, which is about cannibals, vampires and oceans of blood and so on.

Upanishad is a detailed catalogue of Hindu faith, discussing themes such as 'karma' (action), 'punarjanma' (reincarnation), 'moksha' (nirvana), the 'atman' (soul),

and the 'Brahman' (Absolute), and above all self-realization, yoga and meditation. 'Upanishad' as a noun implies 'sitting down near' the guru (a spiritual teacher) gifted with the knowledge of the fundamental truths of the universe. The message in Upanishad relates to a time when teaching was imparted in the pin-drop silence of the forests 'ashrams' or hermitage. Upanishad also symbolizes the annihilation of ignorance by 'Brahma-knowledge'.

VIC 6-16

266 **Bihari**

Bihari is an Indo-Aryan language spoken in Bihar as well as in the neighbouring provinces of India.

Following is the list of different forms of Bihari spoken in the province.

Angika (30,000,000 speakers). Written in Anga, Kaithi and Devanagari scripts.

Bhojpuri (26,254,000 speakers). Written in the Kaithi and Devanagari scripts.

Kudmali (37,000 speakers)

Magahi (11,362,000 speakers). Written in the Kaithi and Devanagari scripts.

Maithili (7,500,000 speakers). Written in the Maithili and Devanagari scripts.

Panchpargania (274,000 speakers)

Sadri (1,965,000 speakers)

Sarnami Hindustani (150,000 speakers) Form of Bihari with Awadhi influence spoken by Surinamers of Indian descent.

Surajpuri (273,000 speakers)

Vajjika (500,000 speakers)

VIB 9-12

333 bombay drink

The town Bombay was named after the Mumba-Devi. Situated on the southern edge of India, the foreigners (Europeans) used Bombay as the launching pad for their commercial pursuits. Originally Mumbai, the English transposed the name of the town giving it a new name, Bombay.

VIC 6-16

440.

Bombay duck. 'Bombay duck' is a small fish that exists in the coastal waters of India. In Bengal, the fish is known as 'nehare'. It is famous for its delicacy and freshness. It was imported into England after being dried.

VIC6-16

27 brahmin's lip

Piety means the purity of head and heart. A conscientious Brahman knows that piety lies in the purity of head and heart. In order to keep his heart clean and conscience clear, he must take care of a clean body. He must take a daily bath and shave himself properly. Only then, could he perform the 'puja' properly and preach truth to his disciples.

VIB 22

208.

burra sahib. Hindi 'bara' great; the great sahib (or master). It occurs constantly say in a family to distinguish the father or the elder brother, a civil servant especially during the British rule.

VIC 1-7

278 Canning, (Lord) was the Governor General 'Gabbarnaur-Jaggarnath' (FW.342.13-14) of India from 1856 - 1862 and the first Viceroy of India from 1 November 1858. Born on 14 December 1812 Charles John Canning was the third son of the famous statesman, George Canning and was educated at Putney, Eton and Christ Church, Oxford. The most significant event during his administration was the outbreak of the 'sepoy it and this great event was followed by the Parliamentary Act of 1858. By the Proclamation of the Queen, the East India Company's rule ended and the Crown of England took over the government of India. Lord Canning did not spare the partisans in the uprising. Nevertheless,

his avoidance of an indiscriminate vengeance earned him the title of 'Clemency Canning'. He restored law and order in an effective way and introduced a new system of administration. He reorganised the British Indian army and restored financial stability by introducing income tax, uniform tariff and convertible paper currency. He introduced the Bengal Rent Act 1859 to improve the circumstances of the peasants of Bengal. It helped curb the high-handedness of the Europeans. He also reformed Judiciary. Lord Canning's introduction of the Indian Council Act 1861 was a major step in introducing democratic reforms to India. By this Act, the respected members of public could nominate themselves to the Viceroy's Legislative Council. Over-worked and ailing, Lord Canning left India on March 18, 1862 earning the rank of an earl.

'Cash', a small coin in Tamil (1621 EF, 1711 OED) appears in Finnegans Wake viz: FW.24.01, 24.01, 65.15, 133.13, 134.19, 150.24, 161.06, 161.07, 201.14, 404.30, 451.05, 492.20,538.16, 574.30, 577.09.

VI C 1-7

266.

Cawnpore. A city in India (Cawnpore or Cawnpur) situated on the river Ganges at a distance of about 245 miles south east of Delhi. It was garrisoned by British troops in 1778. The Indian freedom fighter Nana Sahib is recorded to have carried out a systematic killing of the soldiers of this garrison on 15 July 1857 during the 'Sepoy Mutiny'.

VIB 27-8

207 Celestial Spouse.

We may find two references to this phrase, first in The Divine Comedy (Canto the Thirteenth) where Beatrice's descent enables her to address Dante:

'THUS stood these Lights that guide the wand'ring Soul ;
For, as the Stars, that circle round the Pole,
Conduct the Keel, remote from East and West;
So these supply the never setting Beam:

Sin only can obscure the golden gleam
That points the Passage to eternal Rest.

II.

And now the Bands, that march'd in order bright
'Twixt the triumphal Wheels and seven-fold Light,
Fac'd to the winged Car in full parade;
While kindling rapture beam'd from ev'ry eye,
Fix'd on the Pledge of everlasting Joy,
While thus a silver voice the Song essay'd:

III.

"Descend from LEBANON, celestial Spouse!
Thy Consort waits thee, to receive thy Vows!"---
Three heav'nly Echoes to the Song reply'd;
Thrice the loud Chorus fill'd the Concave round ;
Thrice EDEN's Vales return'd the joyous sound,
To Æther wafted on th' aerial Tide.

The second reference may be cited from Tantra(a religious text). According to Tantra, 'Celestial Spouse' is the Spouse of Indra (See stanza 8).

p. 168 p. 169

I SEEK refuge with Tripurasundari, (1)
Who wanders in the Kadamba forest; (2)
The spouse of the Three-eyed One, (3)
Bank of cloud (in the sky of the heart) of numbers of sages, (4)
p. 170
Whose hips defeat the mountain by their greatness. (1)
Who is served by celestial women,
Whose eyes are like the newly blown lotus,
And who is dark as the colour of a freshly formed rain-cloud. (2)
2
I seek refuge with Tripurasundari,
The Spouse of the Three-eyed One,
Who dwells in the Kadamba forest,
And who is ever wandering;
The Large-eyed One who holds a golden vina, (3)
Wearing a necklace of priceless gems,

Whose face is glowing with wine, (4)
And who of Her mercy grants prosperity to Her devotees.

3

Ever are we protected by Her whose abode is the Kadamba forest,
The weight of whose breasts are garlanded with glittering gems,
Whose breasts are rising, (5)

(p. 171)

And excel the mountain in greatness;
Whose cheeks are flushed with wine, (1)
Ever singing sweet songs; the playful one, dark as a cloud, (2)
Ever compassionate to all.

4

I seek refuge with Tripurasundari,
The Spouse of the Three-eyed One,
Who stays in the Kadamba forest,
Who is seated in the golden circle and dwells in the six lotuses, (3)
Ever revealing like lightning the great power (of devotees), (4)
Whose beauty is like that of the Jaba flower, (5)
And whose brow is adorned with the full moon.

5

I take refuge with Her, the sweet speaker,
Daughter of the sage Matanga, (6)

(p. 172)

Whose breast is adorned with the vina. (1)
And whose head is beauteous with locks of curling hair;
Who dwells in the lotus; (2)
The destroyer of the wicked,
Whose eyes are reddened with wine; (3)
The charmer of the enemy of the God of Love. (4)

6

I take refuge with Tripurasundari,
The Spouse of the Three-eyed One,
Who should be meditated upon as in the first flush of Her nubile youth, (5)
Her blue garment stained with drops of blood. (6)
Holding the wine-cup, (7)
Her eyes rolling with wine; (8)

p. 173

With heavy, high, and close-set breasts, (1)

Dark of colour, and with dishevelled hair. (2)

9

At time of recitation I remember the Mother,
Lustrous as the scarlet hibiscus, (3)
Her body pasted with saffron and sandal,
Her hair kissed by musk; (4)
The Mother with smiling eyes, (5)
With red garland, ornaments, and raiment,
Who holds the arrow, bow, noose, and goad; (6)
The charmer of countless men. (7)

(p. 174)

8

I worship the World-Mother
Who is served by celestial women,
The Spouse of Indra,
 Skilful in plaiting hair;(1)
The devoted Spouse of Brahma,
 Anointed with sandal paste;
 The Spouse of Vi??u,
Adorned with pleasing ornaments.

VIC 11-14, 17-8

333 Chanda In Hinduism, Chanda is a monster that Chamunda Devi killed.

In Pali texts, Chanda is a sincere wish free of 'lobh' or greed.

'Chandavato kim nama kammam na sijjhati?' 'Who has a serious wish to do, everything is possible.'In Urdu, Chanda means 'moon.' It is an honorific title used for the most respected person in the family. Usually, a mother on citing the moon, uses it for her brother before her children.

VIC 11-14, 17-8

Chenab River

The noun Chenab is composed of 'chen' moon and 'ab' for river. The name could be due to the place of its origin, i.e. Chandra whose water after mixing with that of

Bhaga at Tandi in the upper Himalayas in the Lahaul District of Himachal Pradesh (where the river is known as 'Chandrabhaga'), flows through Jammu and Kashmir and then Punjab before dropping into the Indus at Mithankot. Like river Ravi, it was known to the people of the Vedic period as Ashkini and as Ascesines to the Greeks. Alexander established a town 'Alexandria' at Mithankot-the place where these rivers merge. Like the Rhine and Danube, Chenab River appears quite often in native literature.

VIB 13-20

105 coco echoh choroh choree chorico!

The noun 'choree' or 'chowree' is a town hall building 30 feet square, with square gabble-ends, and a roof of tile supported on square wooden posts. Here, the public-related matters were settled in the presence of the Government officials during and before the Raj.

VIC 6-16

96 chutney curry

In Indian cuisine, a 'chutney' (British spelling), 'chatni' (Urdu or Hindi transliteration) is a strong relish produced from a mixture of sweet and spicy condiments. As a genre, chutney is like Latino salsa or European relish of freshly chopped vegetables / fruit with added seasonings. In the Indian context, chutney also means the crushing together of ingredients and is eaten afresh contrary to the preserved tin-chutney, popular in North America or Europe. Chutneys usually have fresh green chilli peppers. Others may have one major ingredient of a wide variety of fruits and vegetables. Some of these require cooking, others a blender. Sugar, salt, garlic, tamarind, onion and ginger are used to add flavour alongside spices like fenugreek, coriander, cumin and hing (asafoetida).

Some of the popular types of chutney are listed below:

Coconut chutney

Onion chutney

Tomato chutney

Cilantro (coriander leaves) and/or mint chutney (both are often called Hari chutney, where 'Hari' is Hindi for 'Green')

Tamarind chutney (Imli chutney)

Mango chutney (made from unripe, green mangos)

Lime chutney (made from whole, unripe limes)

Garlic chutney made from fresh garlic, coconut and groundnut

Green tomato chutney. Common English recipe to use up unripe tomatoes

Apples, peaches or tomatoes are also used in temperate countries.

VIC 395.

Cummerband yellow, blue, green. 'Cummerbund' is a girdle in Hindi and 'kamar-band', in Persian. 'Cummerbund' is worn by domestic servants as an item of ornament as Yule and Brunell quote from Pioneer Mail, June 17th: '1880....The Punjab seems to have found out Manchester. A meeting of native merchants at Umritsur...describes the effects of a shower of rain on the English-made turbans and 'Kummerbunds' as if their heads and loins were enveloped by layers of starch'.

VIC 6-16

96 Curry: Indian curry is a distinctly spicy dish and is full of variety. It usually consists of meat, fish, fruit or vegetables cooked with a quantity of bruised spices and turmeric that adds flavour.

VIC 11-14, 17-8

344- 346 deva diva Deva-duta. These words carry different meanings in different religions. According to Buddha, deva-duta is the karmic fate, which each individual is indebted to, in his earthly cycle of life. Secondly, deva-duta is those Buddhist messengers who bring the news of old age, sickness or dukha. In Hinduism, Deva is a divine being. Dive-Deus is from the root 'div' meaning 'to shine'. As a celestial being, Deva inhabits all the three modes of existence - good, bad or indifference: ranging from sub-human level to super-human beings. According to

Zoroastrianism, deva symbolises devil or evil spirit.

VI.C.1-7

71. dhoti-clad babu ji.

Nehru (Pandit Jawaharlal 1889-1964) in his Autobiography (London: John Lane, 1942: p.469) while marking the obvious cultural differences between the Hindus and Moslems says that the Moslems wear a particular type of pyjama which is neither too long nor too short. They have a particular way of shaving or clipping the moustache, allowing the beard to grow, and always keep a lota [deep water bowl] with a special kind of spout, just as the Hindus wear a dhoti, possess a topknot, and keep a lota of a different kind. In the Notebook, (VI.C. 12-18) p.59, the phrase reappears as 'pyjamas trousers'. To explain it further, the Hindi 'pae-ja-ma' is literally the leg-clothing. A pair of loose trousers, tied round the waste. It is worn by various persons—women of various classes, by Sikh men, and by mostly Mohammedans of both sexes. It was adopted from the Mohammedans by Europeans as an article of dishabille and of night attire, and is synonymous with long-drawers or Moghul breeches. The next word 'dhoti' in Hindi means a loin-cloth worn by all the respectable Hindu castes of Upper India, wrapped around the body, the end then being passed between the legs and tucked in at the waist, so that a festoon of calico hangs down to either knee.

VIC 1-7

85. Dravidian.

As Yule and Brunell identify, the term Dravida was used to denote the Conjeveram Kingdom (4th-11th century AD). The term 'Dravidian', according to Encyclopaedia Britannica (15th ed. p.697-699) was first coined by Robert A. Caldwell in his Comparative Grammar of the Dravidian or South Indian Family of Languages (1856). The Sanskrit word 'dravida' is also used in Pali meaning 'tamil'. The Tamils of India and Sri Lanka are the largest group of Dravidian speakers. The Dravidian languages consisting mainly of Telugu, Tamil, Kannada, and Malayalam are spoken in the southern, eastern, and central India; Sri Lanka; the Indian settlers

in Southeastern Asia; southern and eastern Africa and Sindh (Kalat, Khairpur, Hyderabad) in Pakistan.

Tracing its origins, the Encyclopaedia Britannica (15th edition) posits that it must have been the Aryan language which, while coming from Central Asia, expanded into northwest, east and south of India. Shrouded as its origins are in mystery, the Dravidian language has defied any solid connection with other languages like those of Mitanni, Basque, Sumerian, or Korean. Yet its linguistic relations with the Uralic (Hungarian, Finnish) and Altaic (Turkish, Mongol) are supposed to be more probable. The Dravidians might have been the stock which had evolved after the 'dolichocephalic (longheaded from front to back) Mediterraneans mixed with branchycephalic (short-headed from front to back) Armenoids' (p.698, E.B.). During their migration from this region, they must have mixed up with the 'Ural-Altaic speakers' in the third or fourth millennium before moving further from northwest to southeast India in between 2000 and 1500 BC.

VIB 13-20

67 Drogheda's

The word 'darogha' was used, among others, during the Moghul period for a government official. During the Raj, 'darogha' was a local chief of police. The word is also traceable in a Mongol inscription of 1314, found in the Chinese Province of Shense, mentioned by Pauthier in his book Marco Polo, p.773. The Mongol Governor of Moscow, during the Tartar (FW.346.01'tartery': FW. 339.18 'tatattar') rule over Russia, was honoured with the title 'Doraga' (See Hammer, Golden Horde, p. 394). The servants responsible for the care and management of the Imperial stables during Moghuls were also known as droghedars.

VIC 11-14, 17-8

269 **Fakir foretells Hb   Fakir**

To dream of an Indian fakir, according Dream Dictionary, foretells several possi-bilities. The dreamer is easy to seduce and tempt if he lurks into unreal fantasies. Such a meeting with a fakir may be a foreboding for an unusual change in life.

The change may be an unhappy one.'fakir foretells' (Notebook VI.12-18), p.269, c.1609, (Mohammedan or Hindu) religious mendicant, devotee.

VIC 6-16

266 Godhia prabut

Prabhu is one of Hindu deities. Joyce's phrase 'godhia prabut' may signify this. In From the Caves and Jungles of Hindustan (1890), Blavatsky talks about her Indian experience and describes her host, Sham Rao Bahunathji, who comes from the Patarah Prubhu caste. 'Prabhu' says Blavatsky, means 'lord and this caste descends from the Kshatriyas. The first of them was Ashvapati (700 B.C.), a lineal descendant of Rama and Prithu, who, as is stated in the local chronology, governed India in the Dvapara and Treta Yugas, which is a good while ago!' (Chapter VI 'Brahmanic Hospitalities', p.7-8). 'Prabhus' live in Bombay occupying clerical jobs. As Blavatsky states, one of the Prabhu kings, Ashvapati, annoyed a Bhrigu- a seer, whose curse, in return, drove the people of his caste out of power to work as 'Patans', from their previously privileged status of pious 'Patars'. In this state of 'the fallen one', they have to earn their livelihood by working as clerks - 'to earn by their pens' as Blavatsky puts.

VI.B. 23-24

287. 'Gurumukhi'

is the alphabet used for writing the Punjabi language. Guru is the one who is a teacher of sacred thought and mukha is his mouth. Gurumukhi is an improved and legible form of Landa, invented some three hundred years ago for writing the Sikh scriptures. Gurumukhi is thought to be the sacred language of the Sikhs. The phrase 'Gurumaki' echoes 'gau-mukh', the chasm in the Himalaya mountains through which the Ganges flows (conceived to be shaped like a cow's mouth).

VI.C. 9 -12

27 Hlaing

U Chit Hlaing (B.1879-d.1952)is a famous politician in Burmese history. He was known as the King of Burma without a crown. He was imprisoned when the British Crown Prince of Wales (who later became King Edward VIII) visited Burma in 1921. In 1937, Hlaing attended the ceremony of King Edward's Coronation. He studied law in England and had founded Y.M.B.A. (Young Men's Buddhist Association) on his return to Burma.

VIC 11-14, 17-8

334 Haldi

Also pronounced as 'hull-thee' is turmeric and is used for yellow colour in food in South Asia. It has antiseptic qualities and its commonly available fine powder is used for curing wounds.

VIC 11-14, 17-8

132 'Huray Krishna, huray Ram'

is a bhagan (hymn) to gods such as'Jai Jai Ram Krishna Hari ! Jai Jai Ram Krishna Hari ! Jai Jai Ram Krishna Hari ! Jai Jai Ram Krishna Hari!'

Hari

The adjective 'har' means something great and intense.

The term 'puja' means the worship of deities, which has three different forms: temple worship, domestic worship and communal worship. In the Temple worship, the priests serve the deities. In the domestic worship, the prayers are said in a corner of the house kept clean for the ritual. In the communal worship, prayers take the form of singing of hymns such as Hare Ram Hare Krishna. Recitation from religious text is also part of the prayer.

'Hari' is also one of the names of Vishnu. Vishnu as 'hari' according to Vishnu sahasranama, is one who annihilates the 'samsara' cycles of incarnations due to ignorance (See Commentary by Adi Sankara). In Sanscrit, 'hari' means yellow or fawn-coloured/khaki (which is also the colour of the Sun and 'Soma'). 'Hari' is 'zari'

according to Avesta identified with 'Zara' for Zarathustra. 'Hari' means 'daylight' in Indonesian, 'day' in Malay and 'king' in Tagalog. Such a wide spread use of the word 'hari', indicates the influence of Sanscrit.

One of the names of God, according to Sikhism, is 'Hari'. The most prestigious Sikh Temple - the Golden Temple is also called 'Harimander' or 'Temple of God.'

VI B 22

225. **Ram hury.**

Ram is one of the incarnations of Siva. Out of ten such incarnations, which include such as fish, tortoise, bear, man-lion, and dwarf, Rama symbolises the use of the axe in exterminating his enemies in battle. Rama or Ramacandra is also one of the heroes of the epic, Ramyana.

VIB 13-20

107. **Hashsay:**

'Hash' is motion; departure; mud, clay; hish, the part of the plough to which the oxen are fastened; hush is like calling for attention.

VI.B.23-24

288   **Hathi**

Elephant brayboshy: language in Bengal. (Bosh is 'dhut' - a sound expressing: repulsion, aversion, slight mistrust etc; sh, pish, psh, bosh.)

VIC 11-14, 17-8

334 **Hemavati**

is one of the rivers in the Western Ghats of India besides the Bedthi River, the Varada River and the Nethravathi River.

VIC 1-7

217 Hindu Fakir

Madame Blavatsky refers to the phrase 'Hindu fakir' in the following letter.

[Banner of Light, Boston, Vol. XLI, April 21, 1877, p. 8]

To the Editor of 'The Sun':

Sir, -- However ignorant I may be of the laws of the solar system, I am, at all events, so firm a believer in heliocentric journalism that I subscribe for The Sun. I have, therefore, seen your remarks in to-day's Sun upon my "iconoclasm."

No doubt, it is a great honor for an unpretentious foreigner to be thus crucified between the two greatest celebrities of your chivalrous country -- the truly good Deacon Richard Smith, of the blue gauze trousers, and the nightingale of the willow and the cypress, G. Washington Childs, A.M. But I am not a Hindu fakir, and therefore cannot say that I enjoy crucifixion, especially when unmerited. I would not even fancy being swung round the "tall tower" with the steel hooks of your satire metaphorically thrust through my back. I have not invited the reporters to a show. I have not sought notoriety. I have only taken up a quiet corner in your free country, and, as a woman who has travelled much, shall try to tell a Western public what strange things I have seen among Eastern peoples. If I could have enjoyed this privilege at home, I should not be here....'

Religiously, the 'fakir' is one who has attained such a level of spiritual strength through ascetic vigil that he could lay down on a bed of nails without demur. One could see him sticking pins and needles into himself. He is also the fire-eater. In the Indian fairs, he may be seen pulling his head back, thrust the burning torch between the lips and blow the flame which flares like a blast furnace as his eyes redden and cheeks glow. With dexterous self-control, as the crowd gets excited, he closes his lips and the fire disappears.

VI.B.9-12

45. Hoogly.

Hoogly is a town situated on the western delta branch of the Ganges. Its left bank is occupied by metropolitan Calcutta. Hoogly is important because it was the first town which was built by the Europeans (Portugese) in the early sixteenth century. In 1640, the English established their factory in Hoogly though the enterprise, owing to a dispute with the local Nawab, had to be abandoned in 1688. It was at Chuttanutty (Calcutta) that the English, through a peace treaty, regained the lost trade privileges and thus were able to resume their further penetration of Bengal as Yule and Brunell state. Yule and Brunell quote from Elliot: 'c.1632. Under the

rule of the Bengalis a party of Frank merchants...came trading to Satganw (see Porto Pequeno); one 'kos' above that place, they occupied some ground on the bank of the estuary...In course of time, through the ignorance and negligence of the rulers of Bengal, these Europeans increased in number, and erected substantial buildings, which they fortified...In due course a considerable place grew up, which was known by the name of the Port of Hugli...These proceedings had come to the notice of the Emperor (Shah Jahan), and he resolved to put an end to them'. Abdul Hamid Lahori in Sir H.M. Elliot's (K.C.B.) The History of India as told by Its own Historians, (London: Trubner and Co., 1867).

VIC 6-16

251 Huderabad Nizam,

Deccan Maharao Hyderabad and Berar was an autonomous princely state of south-central India. Located in the south-central India, the princely state of Hyderabad was ruled by an autonomous, hereditary Moslem family from 1724 to 1948. Founded by the Qutb Shahi dynasty of Golconda, the city of Hyderabad was built on the architectural pattern of Isphahan and was popularly known as 'Isfahan-e-Neu'. The architects based the design of the city on the model of Paradise as described in Quran.

The state fell into the Moghul hands, remained under them until the defeat of the governor by Asif Jah- another Moghul official who declared himself 'Nizam-al-Mulk' in 1724. Prince Asif Jah and his successors ruled the state like royals and enjoyed the title of 'His Exalted Highness.' In the 1930's, Nawab of Hyderabad was the richest man on earth, his state the wealthiest in India. Nawab used the Jacob Diamond as a paperweight. Like the Nizams of Hyderabad, the Deccan region was also ruled by a similar dynasty.

The successors of both the kingdoms still exist, enjoying a privileged status within the existing political system of India. We may consider the history of the title 'Maharao' from the life of the battle-hardened fourteen-year-old Rao Madho Singh, the son of Rao Matan- ruler of Bundi in Deccan. Shah Jehan, the Moghul emperor was much impressed by Madho Singh's qualities as a warrior. The Kingdom of Kora was entrusted to him in 1579. After his death, Mukund Singh,

his eldest son, was made the new ruler. When Emperor Aurangzeb rose against his own father, the whole of the Rajputana stood firm with Shah Jehan. Once in office, the new emperor, Aurangzeb Alamgir thought it better to avoid confrontation and struck a deal with Mukund's son, Jagat, who was put on the throne respecting Moghual interests. At his death in 1670, the kingdom was without an heir. Kishore Singh by this time had recovered from wounds due to a previous battle against emperor Aurengzeb. The former made alliance with Aurengzeb and on his death in which he had received fifty wounds in a battle in Arcot, his son Ram Singh came to power. After Ram Singh, the next ruler was Bhim Singh. Bhim Singh struck a deal with the Sayyid brothers against the Moghuls expanding his kingdom into three directions- to Bhilwara in the west, Gagron in the south and Baran in the east. Bhim Singh was the first Rajput leader to enjoy the title of the 'punj hazari' (leader of five thousand men). He was also the first king of the dynasty who was titled as 'Maharao' the Great King.

Following the tradition, Maharao had an intimate contact with his subjects. The day of his accession to the throne was celebrated with all the pomp and glory of a royal: princes led the procession in addition, courtiers, commanders and priests, mahouts and musicians, dance girls and foot soldiers. Maharao Bhim Singh was also very religious. He would keep the family god with him. After his death, the deity was lost. On its recovery, the deceased Maharao's son, Durjan Sal, travelled for fifty miles to get it back, with all the state honours, from a party of the Nizam of Hyderabad.

VI B 22

278. **In gangetu Doab.**

'Doab' in Persian means two waters i.e., 'Mesopotamia' a piece of land carved up between the two confluent rivers. Applied to the topography of Upper India (as Joyce is implying), the term identifies the piece of land lying between Ganges and Jumna. These 'Doabs' are proverbial in Punjab where the land tracts are chiselled by various rivers merging together at a certain point of confluence into a single and bigger river before starting another course of carving up the next land mass with another river in the central and southern parts of Pakistan. The famous

'Doabs' of Punjab are Richna Doab, between Ravi and Chenab, and Jech Doab, between Jhelum and Chenab.

VIC6-16

58) Indian Poison

The phrase 'Indian Poison' may be interpreted as the claustrophobia of religious and caste-related differences.

VIC 6-16

267 Indian Sanscritto!

Rig Veda is the first recorded script of Sanscrit - a language that grew out of oral transmission over time. The word 'sanscrit' means purified, and refined. Sanscrit's consecrated status owes to the religious 'gurus' who were also teachers. The transmission was special and the exercises were imparted in a rigorous manner just like St. Ignatius Loyola's Spiritual Exercises. The grammar was closely analysed based on the rules laid down by grammarians like Panini. The work on grammar began around 5th century B.C. Sanscrit took nearly a thousand years to refine itself and become a model dialect. Heinrich Roth, Johann Ernst Hanxleden and Sir William Jones are some of the European scholars of Sanscrit.

VIC 11-14, 17-8

194 Indus

The Indus (Sanscrit: Sindhu; Urdu Sindh; Tibetan: Sengge Chu ('Lion River'); Persian: Hindu; Greek: Sinthos; Pashto language: Abaseen). ('The Father of Rivers'); Mehran (an older name)) is the longest and most important river in Pakistan. Originating in the Tibetan plateau near Lake Mansarovar, the river runs a course through Kashmir and Northern Areas in Pakistan. Flowing in the south along the entire length of Pakistan, it merges into the Arabian Sea near Karachi. The total length of the river is 3200 km (1988 miles). The river has a total drainage

area exceeding 450,000 square miles. Indus is the key provider of water to the agriculture of Pakistan. The confluence of river Indus and the rest such as Ravi, Sutlej, Jhelum, Beas and the extinct Sarasvati River - forms a delta known as the 'Sapta Sindhu' (seven rivers) in Sindh with 20 major tributaries.

VIC 11-14, 17-8

214 **Prathan Lord** Ishwar (is god).

The following sample explains the usual nature of a hymn in Hinduism.

'My Lord, O God
My lord, O God why in Thy world
Is there hate and killing?
Whilst Thou are so large hearted
Why is the human heart so petty?
Why are there borders at every step?
If the whole earth belongs to Thee
If the earth moves around the sun
Why is there such darkness?

Why is the garment of this world
Stained by the blood of man? Screams echo all around
Who will listen to words of love?
Dreams shatter every moment
Who will gather the splinters?
Why are there locks on every heart?
Why is there rust on every lock?

My lord, O God why in Thy world
Is there hate and killing?
Whilst Thou are so large-hearted
Why is the human heart so petty?
The Urdu Version is here

Ishwar Allah Ishwar allah tere jahaan men
Nafrat kyun hai jang hai kyun
Tera dil to itna bada hai
Insaan ka dil tang hai kyun

Qadam qadam par sarhad kyun hai
Saari zameen jo teri hai
Suraj ke phere karti hai
Phir kyun itni andheri hai
Is duniya ke daaman par
Insaan ke lahu ka rang hai kyun

Gunj rahi hain kitni chikhen
Pyaar ki baaten kaun sune
Tut rahe hain kitne sapne
Inke tukre kaun chune
Dil ke darwaazon par taale
Taalon par ye zang hai kyun

Ishwar allah tere jahaan men
Nafrat kyun hai jang hai kyun
Tera dil to itna bada hai
Insaan ka dil tang hai kyun

Lyrics (English & Urdu) : Javed Akhtar

Composed by A R Rahman

VIC 1-7.

250. **Java.**

Lassen (referred to in the Notebook, (VI.B.9-12) as 'Lassan' p.87) identifies the ancient name of Java (Hobson- Jobson, p.346).

VIC 6-16

266 **Jainism or Jain Dharma**

A religion and philosophy, which has influenced Indian religions, ethical and political spheres of life for the last three thousand years. Human soul can realise its true nature by way of ascetic self-control and non-violence. Rather than idol worship or the 'Sthanakvasis', Jainism emphasises on 'Gunas' or virtues and qualities. All

humans are equal and spiritual elevation is due to the cultivation of these qualities. Accountability of deeds is individual as souls are independent and eternal. Umasvati, a monk, wrote the most popular scripture on Jainism Tattvartha Sutra or Book of Reality about 1800 years ago.

VIC 1-7

153. Lama Masjit.

'lama' in Arabic is jama and collective or congregational in English. Masjit is Masjid or mosque. The phrase 'lama Masjit' suggests the Jama Masjid, the largest mosque which was completed in 1658 in Delhi by Shah Jehan, the Moghul king of India. The precincts of the mosque are over 92 meter square and the minarets are 34 meter high.

VIC 11-14, 17-8

Jhelum River

Arising from northeastern Jammu and Kashmir and feeding on glaciers, Jhelum River presents a picturesque view from Srinager city. The Neelum River flows into it near Muzaffarabad like the Kunar in Kaghan Valley. Jhelum river courses into Punjab at Jhelum district, flows on through the Chaj and Sindh Sagar Doabs before merging into Chenab at Trimmu in Jhung district and then into Sutlaj. Alexander the Great met stiff resistance by the natives at the Battle of the Hydaspes on this river. It is the largest river of Punjab.

'Jodhpur' (FW.329.02), a town in south India.

VIB 27-8

208 **Siva m Kali Olmuzd Satan Zarvas Mammon**

Kali is feminine to the Sanscrit 'kala', which means 'time' as well as 'black'. Kali is a goddess who may be translated as 'she who is time': 'she who devours time': 'she who is the mother of time': 'she who is black' and 'she who is black time'. In

contrast to her consort Shiva, who symbolises 'white', Kali is 'smasana' or black like cremation ashes. As Shakti, Kali is also prana or energy, which enters the body giving it life. Kali is mentioned in Rigveda as Agni's (the god of fire) black tongue.

VIC 11-14, 17-8

320 **Kama**

Kama may refer to several things Kama, a Hindu god, the God of Love, son of Lakshmi. The term "Kama" also refers to one of the four goals of life according to Hindu traditions (Purusharthas) - these include Dharma, artha, kama, and moksha. It is also the name of a river - the Kama River, a tributary of the Volga River, in Russia. Kama is a sickle-like Japanese weapon used for cutting weeds. Furthermore, Kama is an iron pot used for heating water in Japan, for tea ceremonies. Kamasutram or Kama Sutra ('Aphorisms of Love') is an ancient book on sexual behaviour written by Vatsyayana between the Ist and 6th centuries A D. Kama means desire and sutra is a thread. Kama Sutra is a text whose fabric is woven with a series of aphorisms.

VIC6-16

413 **kasba in collar**

Kasba is small like a town in English. Kasba is a frequently used word for a village, which has grown in size depending on the arrival of people from the outside. 'Kasba colour' is also a phrase used for fashion designs. The emphasis is on the native, indigenous form of traditional designs in clothes. It could consist of the homespun fabrics ('kurtas' or flowing shirts) woven with colourful tribal, caste or religious motifs. It usually has an earthy tincture. Alternatively, the design may also be bright like wild rose, scarlet, and tulip and flamingo.

VIC6-16

8 **Krishna**.

An avatar of Vishnu, Krishna is brave and heroic like Hercules. Krishna and Vishnu complement each other in their divine attributes. In The Bhagavad Gita, Krishna helps Arjuna by driving his chariot. Krishna's sense of humour as a child is well known despite being a God. Krishna is 'Sat Cit Ananda' - one who blesses and is knowledgeable. Radha and Krishna are the fountainhead of spiritual energy of the universe.

VIC 1-7

153 **Kutb Marar, Minar.**

The foundation of the famous Kutb Minar was laid by Qutubud-din Aibek at the time when in 1193, Delhi was made the seat of Mohammedan power in India. During his time, five storeys (29.05 meters) of the Minar were constructed. Iltumish (next ruler) added another five and Feroz Tughlok Shah III raised it to its presently existing height of 71.24 meters with 379 steps.

VI.C. 1-7

286 **'Mahtma's** (utters) to A.P. Simrett' (Sinnett)

'Mahatmas' are the holy people who have achieved 'nirvana' or liberation from the chains of karma or incarnations which shackles humanity, through constant vigil and disciplined spiritual exercises. They are not super humans but have risen to this level through worship, meditation and ascetic self-control. They do not even urge anything like reverence, worship or allegiance. Being the masters of wisdom and compassion, they approach humanity with profound sympathy and affection. In them alone their adepts have found a blend, a reconciliation of the carnal, animal soul with the selfless Self of the universe.

As to Mahatma's letters to A.P. Sinnett, we may gloss the spiritual relationship, which developed among the theosophists like Madame Blavtasky and her guardian, Master Morya. There were other adepts and masters in the field like Master Koot Hoomi, Col. Olcott and A.P. Sinnett. These theosophists, at one stage, decided

to settle in the Himalayas (Simla) for which there was continuous correspondence between all these spiritual gurus such as A.P. Sinnett, Mr. A.O. Hume, Damodar, Blavatsky and others.

VIC 6-16

266 Mahrathi

Marathi is the language of Maharashtra. It is the southern-most language belonging to the Indo-Aryan family of languages. Like Saurseni and Magadhi, Marathi has deep roots in Sanscrit.

VIC 11-14, 17-8

260 Mamluk

A Mamluk was a slave soldier who, on embracing Islam, served the Muslim caliphs during the Middle Ages. Unlike the Janissaries, the Mamluks as in Egypt, became so powerful that they themselves became rulers, overtime. The Abbasides were the first to hire their services by recruiting them from mainly areas of Caucasus (Georgians, Circassians and Turkic) and in areas north of the Black Sea. Like the Janissaries, Mamluks were loyal to the caliphs only and had no link with tribal leaders, their families or nobles of the established power structure. Because they were strangers and came from poor backgrounds, they could never dare challenge the rulers through rebellion or conspiracy.

As soldiers, Mamluks were to follow the dictates of 'furusiyya', a code of conduct that included values like courage and generosity but also doctrine of cavalry tactics, horsemanship, archery and treatment of wounds. They lived within their garrisons. Their entertainments included sports like archery competitions and presentations of mounted combat skills at least twice a week. The intensive and rigorous training of each new recruit helped ensure a great deal of continuity in mamluk practices. With the passage of time, the local governors or emirs - allowing thereby, their gradual assimilation into the establishment, were also recruiting Mamluks. They grew in power, held top positions in the army and civil administration and could transfer their ranks to their sons. The Mamluk dynasty

of India (1206-1290) is one such example of the rise of a faithful commander to the position of a ruler.

VIC 6-16

266 **Mantra**

'Man' means mind; 'tra' means control; a mantra is a means for the control of the mind: to keep the mind from rambling in endless thoughts, in this world of illusions.

VIC 1-7

27. **Mantram.**

Mantram is that part of the four of each Veda which comprises the hymns (as distinguished from the Brahmanas, or logical portions). Mantram is a formula sacred to any particular deity. It is an incantation, a charm, spell and philtre etc.

VI C 1-7

153 **Moti Masjid.**

Moti Masjid (Pearl Mosque) was also built during the reign of Shah Jehan at Agra in 1648. It was completed in 1653.

VIB 9-12

82. **Nullah.**

Nullah is 'nala' in Hindi meaning a watercourse. Yule and Brunell quote from the Life of Napier, Vol.II, p.310 '1843. Our march tardy because of the 'nullahs'. Watercourses is the right name, but we get here a slip-slop way of writing quite contemptible.' Lieutenant General Sir W. Napier, K.C.B. The Life and Opinions of General Sir Charles James Napier (4 vols). (London: John Murray, Albemarle Street, 1857).

VIC 11-18

33: Hindu fell in war, O M

Established in 1902 by King Edward VII (based on the Prussian Poure le Merit), O M or the Order of Merit reward recognised the distinguished services of the British and Commonwealth citizens in the armed forces, science, art and literature. The military award had a pair of crossed swords behind the medallion. The reward is still in practice and is of very high honour. Florentine Nightingale was the first woman to achieve the Order of Merit in 1907. The civilian O M looks like a red cross with a golden crown and red and blue ribbon.

Hindu symbolism

VIC 6-16

227 **OM or 'AUM'** is the omphalos enjoying both, the prefix and suffix of Hindu mantras. OM is the sound sense symbolization of divine breath and its protean manifestation as existence of all that exists. The symbol for such a phenomenon reality is 'swastika' or the movement of matter in all the four directions in a harmonious way like a wheel. In the centre of the hub resides Brahma in peace and harmony, according to Vedas.

VIC 6-16

266 **Oude**

Oude or Awadhi is another Indian language - a derivative form of Hindi dialect and is spoken in Awadh (Oudi), Bihar, Madhy Pradesh, Delhi and Nepal. Raamcharitmaanas of Tulsidaas is written in Awadhi language.

VI.B.29.

Pagoda Shweet Dagôn

11th EB, 'Rangoon' 891c: The great golden pile of the Shwe Dagôn pagoda dominates the city, the centre of Burmese religious life.

Shwedagon Pagoda

The famous Shwedagon Pagoda was visited by Ralph Fitch — the first Englishman, in the fifteenth century. Fitch had sailed from the Thames in 'the talle shippe' Tyger mentioned by the 'witches' in Macbeth. The ship was indeed wrecked in and around Aleppo though Fitch managed to escape drowning. Ralph Fitch wrote of the mighty Pagoda, as The Light of Dhamma (Vol.1, No.1, Union of Burma Buddha Sasana Council, Rangoon, 1852) quotes 'It is the fairest place, as I suppose, that doe bee in the worlds!' It remains the oldest and the mightiest shrines of Buddhism. Across the globe, the pilgrims throng enchanting Anicca, Dukkha, Anata ('All is Impermanance, a source of discontent, without any unchanging soul or ego').

According to the archives, Topussa and Bhallika, the two Burmese merchants had the blessing of meeting Buddha soon after his long-sought Enlightenment. Buddha further blessed them with the gift of eight of his hairs. The merchants, on return, saw the Burmese King, who, much impressed by this as an auspicious occasion, enshrined the present in the Golden Pagoda or Shwedagon. The Pagoda is 326 feet high and is situated on a hill overlooking Rangoon. It is surrounded by shelters embellished with some of the finest woodcraft and mosaic work. The shelters have five to nine storied roofs culminating in a spire. One could see innumerable figures of Buddha of brass or alabaster. The Pagoda is one of the supreme art treasures due to grace, dignity and splendour.

VIC 1-7

42. Paly.

Paly is the discourse of Sakya Muni, the Southern Buddhists of Bihar. Paly, one of the ancient languages of India, was vernacular during the Aryans. As Pali in Sanskrit means 'a row or series', the Buddhists used it 'for the series of their Sacred Texts', state Yule and Brunell. Being the text of the Buddhist sacred texts, Pali is respected as a sacred language. Its influence in Asia is as pervasive as the profound impact of the Indian religions.

VIC 1-7

Panditani.

Panditani is the wife of the one who is learned in language, science, laws, and religion (Hindu) of India.

VIC 1-7

170 **Passive resistance**

Passive resistance is a protest by non-active means as practiced by Buddha. It denies an active or open protest of any kind such as economic or political non-co-operation, civil disobedience, lobbying, tax refusal, sanctions, picketing, leafleting, vigils or general strikes. Passive resistance is the lesson we learn from Jesus Christ when he advised to turn the cheek so that the aggressor may slap the other side as well. Passive resistance, according to Buddhism is renunciation of everything that may tempt us; even one's own self for the sake of 'sukha.'

VIC 11-14, 17-8

163 **The plain tail of the ills,**

Plain Tales from the hills / Rudyard Kipling

As we know Rudyard Kipling's relation with India, the Plain Tales from the Hills is an accurate portrait of the life-style of the Sahibs in which the author grew up. The Sahibs represented the ruling elite of India and as such, they had their own way of living as if in a cantonment, away from the mainstream milieu, in their own circle. They had clubs, playgrounds and went out for hunting as a group. They cherished the idea of a benevolent ruler who was in India for the good of the country. They were taught to bear responsibilities with fortitude and tolerance. Yet, they were very aware of their own national identity and hence were great promoters of the idea of national jingoism 'by jingo' (38, Notebook, VI.C.6-16) because of the growing influence of other European Powers in and outside Europe. Kipling describes their social and personal lives in this book.

VIC 6-16

139 **Prakriti**

Composed of 'pra' for 'beginning' or 'origin' and 'kruthi' meaning 'to form' or 'to perform', Prakriti means 'natural or original form, deviation form which brings 'dukha' or dis-ease'. 'Prakriti consists of five animate and inanimate elements. Besides the four basic elements such as 'vaayu' or air, 'agni' or 'teja' or fire, 'jala' or water, 'prithivi' or earth there is the all-pervading substratum of 'space'.

VIB 9-12

64. **Puckwan.**

Puckwan is from Pakka in Hindi, meaning also ripe and cooked. 'Puckaun' (FW.210.35) is the cooking of various foods in the Indian languages, especially Hindi, Urdu and Punjabi.

VIC 11-14, 17-8

346: **Pukka fires**

'Pukka' means authentic, top notch. 'Fire' beside other meanings also stands for a hot and spicy dish. 'Pukka fire' may be interpreted as hot curry with ingredients such as water, scotch bonnet peppers, cane vinegar, modified food starch, salt, approved spices etc, etc. Fire is also the digestive fire with qualities such as hot, light, dry, sharp, penetrating, pungent, luminous, and transforming. The digestive fire sharpens absorption, assimilation, metabolism, digestion, perception, taste, touch, hearing, vitality, clarity, alertness, regular appetite, and combustion according to Indian cuisine.

Madame Blavtasky accounts for 'pukka fire' while on her Indian visit as:

> 'In Champara there is no lack of bamboo and grass. The school hut they had put up at Bithivara was made of these materials. Someone, possibly some of the neighbouring planters' men set fire to it one night. It was not thought advisable to build another hut of bamboo and grass. The school was in charge of Sgt. Soman and Kasturbai. Sgt. Soman decided to build a 'pukka' house, and thank to his infectious labour, many co-operated with him...'

- Blavatsky Baboon, (p.225)

VIC 6-16

139 Purushan

Purushu in Sanskrit means a heavenly man. After identifying 'purushan' a 'heavenly man' Blavatsky explains further by saying that Purshan is the Primordial Entity of Space - equivalent or interchangeable with Brahma or Adam Kadmon. He is the 'evolver' - a dynamic force that animates by inspiriting 'Prakriti'. Purushan and Prakriti are the two eternal forms of the Same Brahma.

(See Blavatsky, Secret Doctrine, I, p. 281).

Purushan is also an auspicious deity of blessing. Hindus believe that while laying the foundations of a building, it should be considered that 'purushan' remains well awake. Following are the situations, which temper with the auspicious blessings of the deity:

> 'Thundering in the skies
> Sight of a firebrand
> Quarrel with the enemies
> Grieving of the priest fixed
> Breaking or/and scattering of a coconut by accident
> Occurrence of Menstrual period of the wife
> Hearing the sound of someone is crying
> Hearing the sound of the drum beat
> Toppling the holy water pot kept for worship
> Hearing the sound of someone sneezing
> Scattering of articles meant for worship
> Sighting of the guests for the function
> Sight of a weapon
> Sight of a widow
> Sight of a snake charmer
> Scattering of sparks of fire from the holy-fire-pit
> Scattering of sparks of fire from the cancer
> Scattering of cotton from an exploding silk cotton pod.'

386. Rajah.

A Sanskrit word meaning a king, though with the passage of time, its use has

degenerated and thus even the petty chiefs and landlords hold it as a title. Both the Moslem rulers and the British conferred the title of Rajah upon the Hindu nobility, a counterpart to the Islamic Nawab. In the vernacular dialects of South India, it is pronounced as 'Rai', 'Rao' and 'Raya'. Yule and Brunell think that the word Rajah might be a derivation from Pliny's 'Rachias'.

Tippoo with gross impropriety addresses Louis XVI. as 'the Rajah of the French'- Select Letters of Tippoo Sultan to various Public Functionaries...arranged and translated by W. Kirkpatrick, London, 1811, p.369.

VIC 6-16

266 **Rajasthan**

The largest province of India in terms of area bordering Sindh in the west, Gujarat in the southwest, Madhya Pradesh in the southeast, Uttar Pradesh and Haryana in the northeast and Punjab in the north.

Cairo, Constantinople, Delhi, Kabul, Mecca, Peking, Rangoon, Tehran, Tokyo.

VIB 29-41

Rangoon

Located where the Yangon and Bago rivers meet, about nineteen miles from the Gulf of Martab, Rangoon (Burmese 'Yangon') was the capital and the largest city of Burma during the Raj. Rangoon enjoyed the privilege of being the city with one of the largest number of public buildings throughout Asia - such as the High Court, City Hall, Bogyoke Market and the General Hospital, along with the Military Cantonment constructed by the Raj. Added to the Raj in 1852 along with the rest of lower Burma, the city was reconstructed by military engineers like Fraser and Montgomerie, the Public Works Commission and the Bengal Corps of Engineers. Judson College was built to cater to the needs of modern education, Judson College was built. Respecting the needs of the natives, a Theological

College for Karens was also established. To teach English, Anglo-Burmese, and Christian Karen children, boarding schools also came into being. Rangoon made a phenomenal progress as a port for the export of rice and timber, raw cotton, precious stones, cheroots and ivory. In the early twentieth century, Rangoon was as developed in public services and infrastructure as London. It was a melting pot of cultures, and a business hub of Asia due to its location, a meeting place of South Asia and South East Asia during Raj.

VIC 11-14, 17-8

320 **Ravi**

The River Ravi rises from the Himalayas in the Chamba district of Himachal Pradesh, takes a north-westerly course initially and then turns south-west, passing through the Dhaola Dhar range and entering the Punjab near Madhopur. From Madhopur, its course lies along the Indo-Pakistan border before entering the Chenab River. "The Ravi" is also called the "river of Lahore" ("O how the waters come down at Lahore", U 755.15) as it passes through this metropolis of the Punjab with such deep calm and majesty like the River Thames. According to the Rig Veda, the famous battle of the ten kings happened on the Iravati (Ravi) in the Punjab (See Macdonell and Keith, Vedic Index, 1912).

VI.B.27-28

208. **Rudra.**

In The Gods of India, Alain Danielou, probing the origins of the god Rudra says that he symbolised for India what Dionysus meant to the Greeks and Osiris to the Egyptians1. Danielou divides the tradition of Hindu philosophy into the pre-Vedic, Vedic and finally that of the Upanishads. If Siva as (tamas, darkness) had been the known god of the pre-Vedic period, then Rudra incarnates Siva during the age of Vedas, the time of the penetration of the Aryans into India and the period of the Upanishads2. Rudra of the Vedas, symbolises terror and destruction, an instigator of storms and howling winds. He is also the god of fire. Since the spirit of holiness and piety springs from the dark womb of (tamas), Rudra in this paradoxical

feature of Hinduism (akin to the coincidence of contraries say of Bruno), is also a benevolent deity of the Rig Vedas3. According to Danielou, the Rig Vedas speak of Rudra as 'the lord of songs, the lord of sacrifices, the healer, brilliant as the sun, the best and most bountiful of gods who grants prosperity and welfare to horses and sheep, to men, women, and cows; he is the lord of nourishment who drives away sin; he is the wielder of the thunderbolt and the bearer of bow and arrows'.

VIB 13-20

Rupees

Originally, Sher Shah Suri used a Sanscrit word 'rupyakam' (which means silver coin) as a standard currency during his reign (1540-45). It weighed 178 grains of silver at the time. Rupee as a currency has been in use since then, even during the Raj. In the late nineteenth century, one rupee was worth nearly one shilling and four pence. It was divided into 16 annas, 64 paise or 192 pies. India, Pakistan, Sri Lanka, Nepal, Mauritius, Seychelles, Indonesia and Maldives use rupee as currency.

VI B 13-20

332. **Sakti.**

Sakti is the active power of a deity personified as the male' deity's female counterpart. At the clasping of Sakti, Siva the lord-of-sleep, is shaken up and hence the ignition of creative process. The lord-of-sleep is dynamised by the all pervading power of Sakti which includes lust, enjoyment and liberation from the bonds of Nature. Siva hence is a static principle whereas it is Sakti from whose fecund womb all things are generated. The noun Sakti also means a spear or sword.

VIC 6-16

266 **Sher Tiger**

'Sher tiger' or Shere Khan is one of the famous characters who appear twice in

Rudyard Kipling's Jungle Book stories. It is believed that Kipling had met an Afghan prince, Sher Khan Nasher while in Afghanistan. However, the king of the Jungle in fiction has a habit of his own: aggression and arrogance. An Afghan prince of the days of Kipling could not behave like this due to political uncertainties in the country. He had to be sensitive to the political set up which demanded vigilance and shrewdness. In South Asia, Sher usually symbolises bravery and dauntless-ness. In Kipling's story 'Mowgli's Brother' Sher Khan cannot bear with humans, chases them out of the Jungle but for one little baby. The baby is followed by Sher Khan but is protected by the wolves, Raksha and the Father Wolf. They name him Mowgli. Sher Khan vows to snatch the baby back but fails due to Bagheera and Baloo. Sher Khan manoeuvres the rest of the wolves to revolt and expels Akela, the chief. The attempt fails. During this period, Mowgli has grown up into a strong, athletic youth. Sher Khan learns about his activities and calls a meeting threatening to deny the wolves using his territory for hunting. Mowghli was there. Unable to bear with this threatening attitude, Mowgli takes him by surprise by attacking him first. Sher Khan and his cronies flee while Mowgli swears to return to the human village with Sher Khan's skin, one day.

'Sher' has several other connotations such as 'sher' or 'she'r - a common word for poem in Arabic and Persian. A sher is also a form of dance in Eastern European folk music, notably Russian and Klezmer music. Sher or Shir is also a Persian word meaning Lion or Tiger. Sher Shah Suri was the king of Suri dynasty in India. Sher-e-Punjab (the lion of Punjab), is the title by which Maharaja Ranjit Singh is known to his votaries. The Shirokhorshid (Lion and sun) was the Flag of Iran.

'Sher' is also a surname.

VIB 27-8

208 Shiva

The Supreme God according to Vedas. Shiva means God who purifies because He cannot be affected by'Prakrti' or matter/nature and its three forms which are satva, rajas and tamas. As part of Trinity, if Brahma is the creator, Vishnu the preserver, then Shiva is the destroyer. Shiva is the Lord of ascetics. He is represented by three

horizontal stripes and is thought to have immersed Himself in profound state of meditation on Mount Kailash. (Courtesy Yahoo)

VIC 6-16

Sindhi

A recognised language of South Asia, spoken mainly in Sindh. Besides its predominant Indo-Aryan roots, it does have Dravadian touch. Sindhi is written is modified form of Arabic. Its dialect gives a feel of Saraikee, put together, the shades of influences then go as far as Baluchistan, North Western Frontier Province, Gujrat and Rajasthan.

VIC 6-16

139 Singh

Derived from Sanskrit 'simh', meaning 'lion', Singh is commonly used among different castes of India such as Rajputs, Dogras, Gurkas, Gujjars, Juts and Marathas. The Hindu Rajputs- well known for their pugnacious, martial race originally used it. With the arrival and flourishment of Khalsa brotherhood of Sikhs during Guru Gobind Singh, the title became an icon symbol of this religion. However, the title did bring about a radical change in the caste system of India especially the Sikhs. All Sikhs being 'Singhs' made them equal to each other; and women, their counterparts, now entitled as 'Kaurs', also became equal. Gur Gobind Singh sanctified these title= 'Singh' and 'Kaur' in April (during Vesakhi - Sikh festival), 1699.

VIC 11-14, 17-8

331 Takhta

Takhta in Indonesian language 'takhta' means accepting the Will of God (Bhana Mannana) as in the sentence "Indonesian-Bahasa Sehari-hari Maka kedua puluh empat pemimpin dan keempat makhluk yang di sekeliling takhta itu tersungkur dan menyembah Allah yang duduk di atas takhta. Mereka berkata, Amin! Pujilah

Allah!" We should also view "takhta" in the light of the Sikh religion, established by Guru Nanak in India towards the last decade of the fifteenth century. Every true Sikh respects the advice of his Guru. "Gurubani" means a king who must dispense justice in the mlost democratic way and is thereby known as "panchayati raj". - "Takht bahai takhta ki layik" i.e. a ruler or king should be allowed to rule only if he deserves it and if he can guarantee the safety and prosperity of his people. To bear "Takhta" or "takht" means a just ruler.

VI C 1-7

248. **Tansin.**

Mian Tansen, the glorious singer of the Moghul king Akbar's court who died on 6 May 1589.

VI.B.27-28

206 the Indian scene, Devil Slanderers, Slenderer

VIC6-16

37 " ...tries to convert to karma"

Conversion to karma means acceptance of the truth of reincarnation according to Hinduism. Karma is a doctrine according to which the actions in one human life cycle bear on the next: good yielding good, and bad, bad. With the help of "ahimsa" (respect for all living things, and non-violence), one can achieve good karma for a better life in the future by keeping on the path which leads to a final mergening with Brahma. Karma is also a recognition of one's identity on earth i.e., one's caste and status. Hinduism has it that deviation from one's karma leads to suffering. Dedication to duty is an avenue to peace and nirvana.

VIC 1-7

283 **Twilight of gods**

In theosophy, "twilight" means "sandhya", the interval when light and darkness co-mingle and as a moment of pause or waiting before the beginning of a new day or cycle. The phrase "Twilight of [the] gods" may refer to the fourfold body of Brahma, which suggest the beginning of the cycle of creation of the universe: night, day, and evening and morning twilights. According to Hindu mythology, the "pitris" (the higher forms of the gods) were born in the womb of night, whereas the four lower classes were created from the evening twilight; gods were born from the body of Brahma during the day and men during the night.

VIC 6-16

266 "Anna [s] only "

Except for the symbol of the new sovereign, the King's Portrait and a corn sheaf, the rest of the present Indian monetary system, such as the currency and the coinage, was still in use during the Raj. 192 paisa constituted one rupya.

1 Rupya = 16 Annas

1 Anna = 4 Paisa

1 Paisa = 3 Pai

VIC 6-16

267 **Urbu Zban** (lay of camp)

Urdu is indeed a language (Persian "zban", "zaban") which means language of the camp, originating as a new lingau franca. Urdu is the touchstone of India's absorptive capacity: the foreign (the Other) feeding on the indigenous. It grew out of a long, persistent, interaction between the natives and the foreigners during a period of about six centuries, 1200-1800 A.D., from the Delhi Sultanate to the time of theMoghuls. As part of the Indo-Aryan family of languages, Urdu is an interesting lingua franca metamorphosis of the still existing languages (such as Persian, Turkish, Arabic, Hindi, and Hindi) plusSanskrit. Joyce's "Urbu" is indeed is a camp lingo; the Sultans of Delhi and the Moghuls recruited soldiers speaking different languages and without any one lingua franca. In the course of living

and fighting together, they generated words which claimed the loyalty of these soldiers, a synthesis of heterogeneous slang and vocabulary drawn from various sources. Today one may drop in at any hotel, visit any part of South Asia and communicate in Urdu. The dominant people in the remote parts will hesitate, signalling disapproval or indifference towards English but not towards Urdu. The affinity between Hindi and Urdu is very close, yet the two differ in their scripts, the former being written in Devangari and the latter in Arabic and Persian. The stock influence of foreign languages, such as Arabic, Persian and others, on Hindi is also a treasure. At times, spoken Hindi sounds as half-Urdu and half-Punjabi.

VIB 27-8

207 Vishnu

Honoured as Shri,Vishnu is another god. Just as is Shiva for Shavites, so is Vishnu for Vaishnavas. In the Hindu trinity (Trimurti) of gods, he is one of the aspects of godhood beside Brahma and Shiva. Vaishnavas believe that Vishnu is the Ultimate Reality rather than an incarnation. Vishnu is from the root "vis", which means "to enter and pervade". Add the suffix "nu" and we get "the All-pervading One." According to the commentators, Vishnu enters everywhere at all times because He is free from the chains of Maya. According to the Rigveda, Vishnu's "three strides" enlarge his reach by incorporating both time and place in the eternal: the first two strides encompass earth and sky; the third carries him to the celestial abode of the gods. The word for "stride" in Sanskrit is "kram" or "chakram", modified further as "chakra", which means "wheel". In other words, Vishnu's reach is like a wheel., in this universe, the cycles of "karma" and incarnations, and beyond. One may wonder at the study made by Clive Hart on the concept of such cycles, which weave the Wakes fabric. Vishnu is Bhagavat or Bhagavan, meaning "possessing bhaga (Divine Glory)".

VIC 1-7

325 Warren Hastings

Warren Hastings (1732-1818) was employed by the East India Company as a

clerk. He was promoted to the rank of manager to work in a commercial post in Bengal. At the annexation of Calcutta (1776) by Nawab Siraj-ud-Daula, he was taken prisoner but was soon released. When the British re-took Calcutta, he was appointed to the British Council (1761). He resigned in1764 and returned to England. He went back to India in 1769, served as a member of the Madras Council and became Governor of Bengal. He is remembered for a series of reforms for the people of Bengal aimed at improving the judicial and financial systems of the province. The reforms were intended to win hearts and minds among the native populationand prepare the ground for direct British rule in the area. He became the Governor General of India in 1774.

VI.C.1-7

281 "..a white man"

The phrase "a white man" may allude to Kipling's poem 'The White Man's Burden', which promotes colonialism and imperialism. As such, the phrase suggests the way the USA justified itself in the colonization of the Philippine Islands. Despite the cost that imperialism entails, the poem extols the nobility of mission (on the part of the imperial power) for the good of the natives. "A white man", as supposed by gratious and more civilized claims to know well what is in the best interest of the coloured.

'Adi' (FW.29.26) is Turkish for 'his name' 'The African touch' alludes to ancient and modern African cultural achievements. It may include the African art and folklore handicrafts, music and dance, but may just as well be an advertisement promoting tourism: the excitement, magic, and beauty of the countryside and the wild life by staying close to nature rather than in the luxury hotels

VIC 1-7

351 Dita.

A Punjabi word used for one who offers help without strings. It is also used as a name as in Allah Dita or Dita Ram. Dita is also a salad, hence "Scotta Dita" for "tricolour salad" in Michael Romano's Lamb Chops as well as in Ming Tsai's Asian

Marinated Pork Loin with Five-Spice Tea Rub...Dita Salad "Bosh" (FW 125.22), "Boshiman" (FW 594.23), "Culubosh" (FW 51.36), "Truthbosh" (FW 348.32) suggest the Turkish word "bosh", meaning frivolous, worthless chatter. "Bosh", though, also denotes "language" in South Asia. The word nearest to "bosh" in Urdu is "fohush" meaning immoral and indecent manners and the use of offensive language.

V1C 1-7

327 Gazzela

Found in the savannas of Africa and the Asian forests, the gazelle is an antelope famous for its speed and its racing stamina. Feeding on tender plants and leaves, gazelles live in herds. When chased by predators (lions and cheetahs), gazelles react instinctively: a few wobbly paces in the bushes, followed by a sudden jump in the air before racing off. Molly talks of 'gazelle' as "I never loved a dear gazelle ... but it was sure..." (U 476:24), as does Bloom, to indicate his woe and sorrow: "Gazelles are leaping, feeding on the mountains. Near are lakes. Round their shores file shadows black of cedar groves. Aroma arises, a strong hair growth of resin. It burns, the orient, a sky of sapphire, cleft by bronze flight of eagles. Under it lies the womanicity, nude, white, still, cool luxury. A fountain murmurs among damask roses, mammoth roses murmur of scarlet winegrapes. A wine of shame, lust, blood exudes, strangely murmuring."

VI.C.1-7

301 Rickshaw pullers

The term 'rickshaw' is drawn from Japanese "jinrikisha" ("jin" means human, "riki" force, strength, and "sha" vehicle), translating literally as "human-powered vehicle". Claude Gillot's painting Les deux carrosses (1707) shows two cartoons of cart-like rickshaws. Known as 'vinaigrettes' (for their resemblance to the wheel barrows of vinegar makers), they were a cheap mode of transportation in the streets of Paris during the seventeenth and eighteenth centuries. In Japan, they appeared during the Meiji period (1868-1912), gaining popularity as a swifter

means of transportation than palanquins. Rickshaws appeared in India, first in Simla, and later in Calcutta around 1880. In China, they were used first as a means of transporting goods. By the last decade of the nineteenth century rickshaws were being used in all the major cities of Asia as a cheap and readily available means of livelihood for the peasantry.

VIB 13-20

255 Alfala

Alfala is the cloth worn as protection against the wound due to circumcision.

VIB 21

96 Sindabad Aman-Ullah Shah

Amanullah Shah (June 1, 1892 –April 25, 1960) was the ruler of Afghanistan who led his nation to independence from the Raj. After the death of his father, Habibullah Shah, the then a governor of Kabul Amanullah, came to power. He reformed the state treasury as well the army and established peace in the country. The Third Afghan War, which marks his reign, ended in an armistice signed with the Raj after a brief stalemate as the British, in 1919, were in sever difficulties from the just-ended First World War. He seized the opportunity of establishing endur-ing relations with the newly formed Soviet Union to which development the Raj responded with envy, but at the same time a more accommodating approach than previously. Getting the Afghan nation back on its feet, he introduced positive reforms based on the Iranian model developed by Reza, Shah of Iran. In respect of education, the wearing of the veil (hijab) and human rights, the new constitution proved to be more democratic and liberal. The King was catching the "wind of change" coming from Moscow and Iran.

VI B 13-20

18 Amir O bama

(Amir al bahr)

Richard Burtons gives the tonnage of ships using the Suez Canal, Baghla weighing over fifty tons and Samuk about fifteen to fifty. 'Amir al-Bahr' is the captain who carries pilgrims via Suez to Jeddah, for the pilgrimage to Mecca and Medina. Burton sailed on one of these himself (see ref. 28-9: Burton, The Pilgrimage).

VI.B. 13-20

18 emir O ma ma! is 'Ameer' or 'Omara'.

'Ameer' in Arabic (root 'amr') means Commander or Chief. The phrase 'emir O ma ma!' refers to 'Amiru'l Muminium' meaning 'the Amir of the Faithful' or the Caliph, the vice-regent of God on earth. In the age of the Patriarchal Caliphate, the Caliphs (Hazrat Abu Bakr, Hazrat Umar, Hazrat Usman and Hazrat Ali) were honoured with this title.

VIC. 1-7

180 Asia Major

Asia Major is the major part of the Asian region, both land and sea, while the area of the northeast of Turkey (Anatolia) and its neighbourhood is known as Asia Minor. Asia Major may also be defined as the region of greater mountain ranges (Himalayas, Karakorum, Pamir in the North, and South China Sea, the Pacific Ocean, the Indian Ocean, and Persian Gulf in the South.

There is also a journal named 'Asia Major'. It was founded by Bruno Schindler (1882-1964), a scholar and publisher, in Germany in 1923. 'Asia Major' was published in German, English and French. It covered cultural, economic and political affairs affecting the region as well as the interests of the European Powers. The journal was shut down after the rise of National Socialism in Germany. Dr Schindler left Germany for Great Britain. The journal was revived in 1949 under

the aegis of Cambridge, Oxford and London Universities.

'Atabey' (FW.541.17) 'bey' denotes Sir, Mr or father in Turkish

VIC 6-16

86) **Azrael:**

'Azrael' in Arabic is 'Izrail' or (more commonly 'Israel' in English for the angel of death in Islam. In the Quran, Azrael is mentioned as 'Malaikat Maut'. Azrael was also known as an 'azra', a descendant of the high priests of Aaron.

'Babau' (FW.466.01) has 'baba' for 'father', just as 'ana' or 'anne' is mother

'Batin' (FW.29-30) is Turkish and Urdu for 'abdomen'.

VIB 27-8

211 **'beyt-ul-mal.**

The Department of Treasury in Islam. Osaman'

Beyt-ul-mal, as Joyce observes, is the Islamic treasury meant to serve the needy, the orphans and the poor. As the Quran states:

"Alms are for the poor and the needy, and those employed to administer the (funds); for those whose hearts have been (recently) reconciled (to Truth); for those in bondage and in debt; in the cause of Allah; and for the wayfarer: (there is it) ordained by Allah, and Allah is full of knowledge and wisdom" (Al-Tauba, v. 60).

Again, the Quran says:

"The Believers, men and women, are protectors one of another: they enjoin what is just, and forbid what is evil: they observe regular prayers, practice regular charity, and obey Allah and His Messenger. On them will Allah pour His mercy: for Allah is Exalted in power, Wise" (Al-Tauba, v.71).

The earliest institution from which this help was made available was 'Masjid Nabavi' in Medina (434, 'medina' Notebook VIC 1-7). The Moslems, who had fled Makkah for the sake of their lives, were in desperate need of food, clothing and shelter. The generous Moslems of Medina came to their help by collecting whatever they could and putting it in this mosque, where people in need were given assistance. During the forty years of the Patriarchal Caliphate ('Osaman',

or Sayyadana Uthman, Sayyadana Ali [cousin and son-in-law of the Prophet], Sayyadana Umar and Sayyadana Abu Bakr), the treasury served its true phil- anthropic purpose. The practice has become a cherished norm of the Islamic societies.

Beyt-al-Mal denotes of the revenue collected from 'Zakath' (a compulsory tax levied upon the property and income of every Moslem), charities and other state taxes.

'Bosh' (FW.125.22), 'Boshiman' (FW.594.23), 'Culubosh' (FW.51.36), Truthbosh' (FW.348.32) suggest the Turkish word 'bosh', meaning frivolous, worthless chat- ter. 'Bosh', though, also denotes "language" in South Asia. The word nearest to "bosh" in Urdu is "fohush", meaning immoral and indecent manners and the use of offensive language.

VIC 1-7

77. "...buries own daughters: "

The Quran tells how the pre-Islamic Arabs would, out of a false sense of pride and prestige, and also the fear of poverty or loss of livelihood, take their infant daugh- ters into the desert and bury them alive. Islam condemned this cruel custom and extirpated it.

'Caftan' (FW 343.10), 'Caftan's (FW 187.08): this denotes an ankle-length costume

VIC 6-16

152 Cacheimire

Cashmere is a soft fabric made of the downy wool which grows next to the skin beneath the outer hair of a Cashmere goat. The goats producing this hair occur in Mongolia, Iran, Afghanistan and Australia.

VIB 29-41

Cairo

Cairo, is 'Al-Qahirah' in Arabic, translates as 'The Victorious'. It is said that, at the time of its foundation, the planet Mars appeared in the sky. According to ancient mythology, Mars was thought to bring destruction 'Al Najm Al-Qahir'. The city was named after this planet in the belief that the force of the planet would destroy whoever tried to capture the city. Cairo, the Jewel of the Middle East, glorified by thousands of minarets, as is Rangoon by pagodas, is situated on the banks of the Nile and extends into the delta. Cairo is a great blend of time and civilizations: its Eastern zone bears the stamp of contributions made by Judaism, Christianity and Islam, while on the Western side lie the remains of ancient civilization (the city of Memphis and the Great Pyramids) Cairo lies at the crossroads of three continents: Asia, Africa and Europe. It has retained its independence, despite a brief period of foreign occupation.

Caliph Mamoon (see Abbasides) is remembered as "...remembore long ago in the olden times momonian" (FW 397.17). According to Burton's tale 'The Caliph Al.Maamun and the Pyramids of Egypt' (The Arabian Nights, Vol.V, pp.105-6), he sought to get to the ancient treasures by burrowing deep into the Pyramids. Burton analogizes 'pyramids as haram for "well-esteemed" in Arabic, to which the Wake refers as "haram's way round ... bestpreserved whole wife" (FW 532.32). According to Encyclopedia Britannica (11th edition, which Joyce consulted), the Pyramids are named separately, and one among them is termed as 'The Glorious' by Burton, who took the name from the Encyclopedia (see vol.22, p.684). As Scheherazade puts it, the curious caliph enters the Great Pyramid, or 'the Glorious' to dig out the 'mysteries preserved until the day of resurrection' because "there is none of the face of the earth aught like them for ... mysteries; ... for they are built of the rocks" or the Wake's "mysterbolder" (FW 309.13). Joyce transposes these images variously as "glorisol which plays touraloup with us in this Aludin's Cove of" (FW 108.22) and "... the glory of a wake ...allatheses" (FW 309. 6-8). The Caliph could only dig in a small tunnel given the formidable nature of these ancient mysteries. Scheherazade puts it as "he expended his mint of money, but succeeded in opening only a small tunnel in one of them", transcribed by Joyce as "we all would fain make glories. It was minely well mint" (FW 313.27).

VI.C.1-7

189 Cape of good hope

Kaap die Goeie Hoop (Afrikaans), Kaap de Goede Hoop (Dutch) and Cape of Good Hope (English) lies on the Atlantic coast of South Africa. A rocky headland, the Cape of Good Hope was the first European colony, established in 1628, both in the Cape Peninsula and in Africa as a whole. In 1488 the Portuguese explorer Bartholomeu Dias became the first European to reach the Cape. It was John II of Portugal who gave it the name of 'Cape of Good Hope' - Cabo da Boa Esperanca in Portuguese. Not far from the Cape, the Dutch East India Company in 1652 laid the foundations of Cape Town, whence the Europeans expanded into the interior by penetrating North and North East in the next two centuries. The European wars of the seventeenth century contributed to the development of the Cape and surrounding areas. Bands of refugees, fleeing from religious persecution in France and elsewhere, were readily available to the Dutch East India Company as skilled workers. The British had a vital interest in the Cape in that control of it could shorten distances to the East, which was so important for commercial and, ultimately, political reasons. The British occupied the Cape first in 1795 and then again in 1806; British control lasted until 1910, when the Cape it was incorporated into the independent Union of South Africa.

VI.B.29.

35 chihari chatah

Formerly, the greatest ornament of the city of Kabul was the arcaded and roofed bazaar called the Chihâr Châtâ, construction of which is ascribed to Ali Mardan Khan, a noble of the 17th century, who left behind him many monuments testifying to his munificent public spirit both in Kabul and in Hindustan.

VIB 29-41

Constantinople

Located between the Golden Horn and the Sea of Marmara, geographically a

meeting point of Europe and Asia, Constantinople was honoured as the 'Queen of Cities' because it was the wealthiest city in Europe during the Middle Ages. It served as a capital city during both the Roman and the Ottoman empires. Mustafa Kamal Ataturk renamed the city 'Istanbul'. Constantinople was supposedly founded by the legendary Byzas in 667 B.C. during the earliest era of expansionism launched by the Greeks. In 330 A.D., the emperor Constantine put an end to its Greek identity by renaming it in his own name. Constantine well knew its importance - a land and water link between the two continents, along with a vibrant harbour in the Golden Horn. In 1453, the city fell to the Ottomans. The Moslems did not interfere with the freedom of the Orthodox Patriarchy as the latter remained neutral to Vatican influence from Rome. Fatih Sultan the Second however, converted the Christian Hagia Sophia into a mosque. Suleiman the Magnificent built a monumental mosque along the sea adding glory to the city.

There are several references to this city in the Wake:

'Constituently' (FW.155.09), 'Cunstuntonopolies' (FW.357.30), 'constantineal' (FW.442.06).

VIC 1-7

365 Crusades

The Crusades comprise a series of military campaigns sanctioned by the Catholic Church and the Pope that occurred between the 11th and 15th centuries. The ultimate aims the Crusaders were to liberate Jerusalem from the Moslems and to checkmate Islamic (Seljuq) expansion into Anatolia in the interests of the security of the Byzantine Empire. In the Fourth Crusade the Crusaders succeeded in re-claiming Constantinople.

Besides religious and political aims, these were also Crusades launched for economic reasons, such as the Albigensian, the Aragonese and the Northern Crusades.

VIC 1-7

Eastern sensuality

Another phrase which clearly indicates the mind-set of the Orientalists as they viewed what they considered to be excessive and deleterious interest and activity in relation to human body (especially the female), as if physical, especially sexual, pleasure or satisfaction were solely preserves, the Western Orientalists had the notion, of the "East".

VIC 1-7

240 extreme Orientales

The "Far East" refers to the Eastern part of Asia (including South-East Asia) and the Eastern part of Russia.

VIC 1-7

435 Moorish gate

The phrase 'Moorish gate' refers to the Moorish times in Spain. The towns, as everywhere, whether East or West, were well-protected during the Middle Ages. The towns were surrounded by walls. The inhabitants couldn't leave or enter the town after certain hours in the evening, the town gates were protected by sentries (to which Bloom refers in 'Lotus Eaters'). The gates symbolized the authority of the Emir or Caliph. They were built with abundant use of iron, stone and cement. They looked imposing. In Ulysses, Molly Bloom refers to 'Moorish wall': "he was the first man kissed me under the Moorish wall .... It never entered my head what kissing meant till he put his mouth in my tongue" (U 18.768). She refers to the 'Alamada gardens': ".... and O that awful deep down torrent O and the sea crimson sometimes like fire and the glorious sunsets and figtrees in the Alamada gardens .... Yes when I put the rose in my hair like the Andulusian girls used....". She also talks about the 'handsome moors' as ".... handsome moors all in white and turbans like kings asking you to sit down in their little bit of a shop and Ronda with the old windows of the posadas glancing eyes a lattice hid for her lover to kiss the

iron...." (U 782:38-41). Ira b. Nadel traces Molly's background and says that she belongs to the Laredo family which had migrated to Morocco after the expulsion from Spain in 1492.. In the celebrated Buffalo Notebooks, Joyce notes "(the chief) nien to casile morocco, granada, medina, sidonia" VIC 1-7). She remembers this as "almost the bay of Tangier white and the Atlas mountains with snow on it" (U 18.856).

VIC 1-7

434. Gebel al Tarith.

'Gebel' is Arabic for 'mountain' and 'al Tarith' echoes the name of the Moslem general Tariq (bin Ziad). Musa ibn Nasayr, the Arab conqueror of Morocco, had established Tariq as governor of Tangier before leaving for Syria. The Visigoth rulers of Spain had thrown their country into the chaos of civil war. Witiza, one of the sons of the recently assassinated king, asked Tariq to intervene and place him on the throne. In May 711, Tariq bin Ziad landed on Gibraltar with an army of 7000 soldiers. From that time onward, the rock in the Muslim world has been known as Gebel al-Tariq. Molly knows Gibraltar, having been born of Major Tweedy, (who was serving the Pax Britannica in the race for power in the Mediterranean) "... Gibraltar, situated at the crossroads where the 'Greeks and the Jews and the Arabs and the devil knows who else' come together as cultures of different origins. Her romance-like trance is notable: 'Gibraltar my goodness the heat there the levanter came on black as night and the glare of the rock standing up in it like a giant ... they think is so great with the red sentries here and there the poplars and they all white hot and the mosquito nets and the smell of the rain water ...."

'Ghazi' (FW 56.11) and 'Ghazi Power' were titles given to Kemal Ataturk for the bravery and the warrior qualities with which he defended the Turkish cause during and after the First World War.

Golden Horn

Name given to the land where the united Alibey and Kagethane rivers enter the Bosporus on the north side of Istanbul, about one mile from latitude 41 degrees

North. The Golden Horn has been in use as a port for centuries since ancient times.

VIC 1-7

434 Granada

Granada or the 'Illiberi Liberini' of Pliny, is situated at the north-eastern foot of the Sierra Nevada mountains where the Darro and Genil rivers meet. Granada is an ancient city: the Ibero-Celtic inhabitants had contacts with Phoenicians, Carthaginians and Greeks. The Greeks established a colony here in the 5th century B. C. The Visigoths prospered in this city and maintained a strong military presence. The Moorish force led by Tariq bin Ziyad took the city in 713. The famous 'Al-hambra' citadel and palace is a great tourist attraction. The city bears a remarkable legacy of contributions made by Jews, Christians and Moslems.

VI.C.1-7

302 Grand Turk

Taken up by Bermudan salt-makers about three hundred years ago, this Caribbean island is an ideal place for holidays. It has been the capital of the Turks and Caicos Islands, a British possession since 1766.

"Grand Turk" can also be applied to a well-established Turkish citizen — the effendi, as Molly Bloom remembers: "like those Turks with the fez used to sell" (U 18.405).

VIB 27-8

226 Hadis

Translated as 'al-hadith', these are the collections of the sayings of the Prophet of Islam. "Ahdaith" (plural) is a treasure of the entire life span of the Prophet: words, deeds and sayings (sunnah). The Quran has this to say on the importance of 'hadith':

"Those who follow the messenger, the unlettered Prophet, whom they find mentioned in

their own (Scriptures), in the Law and the Gospel; for he commands them what is just and forbids them what is evil; he allows them as lawful what is good (and pure) and prohibits them from what is bad (and impure); he releases them from their heavy burdens and from the yokes that are upon them. Therefore, those who believe in him, honour him, help him, and follow the light that is sent down with him, - it is they who will prosper," (Sura 7:157)

- (Yusuf Ali translation).

Some of the 'hadith' may be noted here:

"The first thing created by God was the intellect."
"The ink of the scholar is more precious than the blood of the martyr."
"One learned man is harder on the devil than a thousand worshippers."
"Riches are not from an abundance of worldly goods, but from a contented mind."

VIC 11-14; 17-18

260 The Helmand

River Helmend known as Darya-ye Helmand in Persian and the Erymandrus in Latin, is the longest river of Afghanistan. It begins in the Hindu Kush mountains, flows to the west of Kabul and thence south-westwards through the desert, the Seistan marshes and Lake Hamun-i-Helmand to the Afghan-Iranian border. The river is of vital importance to the farming communities of Afghanistan. In ancient times, the caravans travelled along this river, crossing Kandahar to southern Persia and the Persian Gulf.

'Hittit' (FW.346.35). The Hittites flourished in Turkey around 1500 B.C.

VIC 6-16

Inshallah

"Insha'Allah" is an Arabic term used in the Quran, Surah Al-Kahf (18):24:-

"And never say of anything, 'I shall do such and such thing tomorrow, except (with the saying) 'If Allah wills!' And remember your lord when you forget..."

The Moslems always use this term when referring to a thing they intend to do in the immediate or distant future. The Spanish word "ojala" and the Portuguese

word "oxala" (I hope, I will) are derived from this Arabic word meaning "God willing."

VIC 11-14; 17-18

260 Imam Janissary

The Janissaries (or janizaries; in Turkish: Yeniçeri (yeni çeri, meaning "new soldier"); in Greek: Getsa; in Bulgarian: enichari or yanichari; in Bosnian: Janjicari) were the infantry units that formed the Ottoman sultan's household troops and bodyguard. The force originated in the 14th century; Sultan Mahmud II abolished it in 1826. Sultan Murat I, who laid the foundations of the Ottoman Empire, needed devoted soldiers, whom he recruited from the Dhimmi (non-Moslems), i.e. Christian youths, exempting from religious taxes. These were the Janissaries, who became the first Ottoman standing-army around 1365. They were exempted from state tax (jazia) and constituted a shrewd replacement for the tribal warriors, most of who did not wish to be infantryman, considering it beneath them. By the middle of the nineteenth century, their numbers swelled as more and more youth were recruited from such diverse ethnic groups as Greeks, Albanians, Serbs, Bosnians and Ukrainians. They were trained under strict discipline, with hard labour. They lived in what were effectively monastic conditions and were expected to remain celibate. They were expressly forbidden to wear beards (restricted to Muslims), but moustache were permitted. The Janissaries kept to these rules, at least until the 18th century, when they also began to engage in other crafts and trades, breaking another of the original rules. For all practical purposes, the Janissaries belonged to the Sultan, carrying the title "kapikulu" ("door slave") to indicate their collective bond with the Sultan. Janissaries were taught to consider the corps as their home and family, and the Sultan as their father.

The Janissaries enjoyed a privileged status in Turkish society in return for their loyalty and fighting spirit in war. By the mid-18th century, they were also recruited to serve as law-enforcers, and were also permitted to become administrators and scholars. In return for their services, they were given pensions on retirement. The institution of the Janissaries began to lose its vitality as soon as its members began to move into other professions.

VIB 13-20

312. **Humidon.**

In Arabic "humidon" denotes "feminine". Furthermore, it carries the implication of "worn out", "obsolete", "withered", "barren", "extinct". The "Humidon" are also one of the tribes in the Najd region of Saudi Arabia.

VIC 6-16

153 **Jehad**

"Jehad" means sacrifice in the name of Allah; it covers nearly everything a Moslem is and has: property, family, and (above all) his own self. The most valued Jehad is the sacrifice of one's own self by working for the welfare of society and one's family. Jehad can also denote "Jehad-bil-Saaf" (armed struggle), "Jehad-e-Akbar" (keeping oneself from indecent, shameful behavior), "Jehad-bil-alum" (keeping people on the path of righteousness) and "Jehad-bil-Maal" (self-sacrifice in the form of donation and charities).

VIB 29-41

Kabul

Situated in a valley flanked by high mountains and through which flows the Kabul River, Kabul, the capital city connects with Central Asia via the Hindu Kush Mountains. Its multicultural and multi-ethnic population is composed of Pashtuns, Tajiks, Hazaras and others. An ancient city, Kabul has been a host to almost every invader of Afghanistan from abroad. Kabul recovered quickly from Mongol aggression, especially during the time of Tamerlane, and became a trading hub of the region. Kabul was the capital (1504) when Zaheer-ud-din Babur planned to expand into India from this region. Nadir Shah of Persia captured Kabul in 1738. In 1826, when Dost Mohammad came to power the British asked for a deal which, on refusal, resulted in his removal and his placement with another King in 1836. The natives rebelled at this, leading to the expulsion and virtual extermination of the British, both civilian and army, from Kabul. The British retaliated by attacking

Bela Hissar from Jalalabad, retook Kabul and re-instated the deposed king, Dost Mohammad in 1878-9. Afghanistan and the Raj were locked in a game of endless charges and counter-charges, skirmishes and forays, arising probably from, above all, the increasing Russian presence in Central Asia.

VIC.09 -33

57 Orthospanna

Kabul is believed to be the Ortospanum or Ortospanna of the geographies of Alexander's march, a name conjectured to be a corruption of Urddhasthâna, "high place." 11th EB. "Kabul"

VIC 1-7

141 Kohibaba, Pamir-roof of the world, karakorum

"Kohibaba" or Kuh-e-Baba, is the southwestern branch of the Hindu Kush highlands and lies due West of Kabul. Kuh-e-Baba is the source of many of the rivers of Afghanistan. Helmund, the longest river, originates from here, as also do the Kabul River and the river Hari Rud and Oxus. The highest peak of Kuh-e-Baba, Shah Fuladi, is 5143 meters high.

VIC 11-14; 17-18

320 Kubango

An alternative name is O·ka·van·go; an alternative spelling is Cu·ban·go. It is the name of a river of Botswana and Angola, flowing about 1,609 km from central Angola to the Okavango Basin (or Delta), a marshy region in the north of Botswana.

'Kuschkars' (FW 365.17, 'Kuss' (FW 383.18), 'kus' means 'bird' in Turkish.

'Lydias' (FW 294.20) is an ancient kingdom of Asia Minor. 'Lydias' appears in a sentence preceded by another reference to a 'Turk' - 'flavourite turvku', (FW 294.19)

VIC 6-16

211 The Mahdi, faki/learned man

The Mahdi in Muslim exegesis is the one destined to create an ideally perfect society on earth before the Day of Resurrection. The Quran says that the Mahdi meaning the guided one, shall redeem humanity from suffering and injustices (See surahs Anbiyaa: 105, Araaf: 128, Noor: 55). We also learn about the Mahdi through the "sayings" of the Prophet, such as "Even if the entire duration of the world's existence has already been exhausted and only one day is left before the Day of Judgment, God (Allah) will extend that day to such a length of time as will accommodate the kingdom of a person out of my Ahl al-Bayt who will be called by my name. He will then fill the Earth with peace and justice whereas it was filled with injustice and tyranny previously then" (Sahih Tirmidhi, V.2, p.86, V.9, p.74-75). According to Islamic eschatology, the Prophet Jesus Christ will accompany Imam Mahdi, in the war against Dajjal (the false Messiah).

VIC 1-7

203 Mauretania

Named after the Mauri tribe, which later appears in history as the Moors, Mauretania was an ancient kingdom of North Africa ruled by Berbers; in extent it encompassed North Morocco and West and Central and Algeria of today, so bordering the Mediterranean. Mauretania was subjugated by the Romans, who, after the death of Juba II, placed his Roman-educated son Ptolemy on the throne. On his death, the kingdom was made into a Roman province divided into two parts: Mauretania Tingitana (modern Tangier) and Mauretania Caesarensis, to-day's western and central Algeria. The people of Mauretania believed that their kings were gods.

VIB 13-20

56. M hubs. Habb (v.n.)

in Arabic means awakening, rising from sleep; blowing with violence or being

windy; being active, brisk, nimble and swift (like a camel). Haba is dust, especially the finer particles which fly about and are only conspicuous in the sun's rays.

VI.B 5

303 **Mufti:**

A mufti is an Islamic scholar who interprets Sharia (Islamic canonical law) and has the power to ordain its implementation by fatwa. Below is an example of the way a Mufti requires Muslims to observe the sanctity of the month of Ramadan (378 'ramdan' :Notebook VIB 17-20), ninth month of the Muslim year by reading from surah Al-Baqara v. 2:185 "Ramadan is the (month) in which was sent down the Quran, as a guide to mankind, also clear (Signs) for guidance and judgment (between right and wrong). So every one of you who is present (at his home) during that month should spend it in fasting, but if anyone is ill, or on a journey, the prescribed period (should be made up) by days later. Allah intends every facility for you; He does not want to put you to difficulties. (He wants you) to complete the prescribed period, and to glorify Him in that He has guided you; and perchance ye shall be grateful."

VIC 1-7

342. **Mullah** ("mulla" in Hindi):

the word is derived from Arabic "maula" or "wila" meaning "propinquity". This is the legal bond which still connects a former owner with his manumitted slave; in virtue of this bond the patron and the client are both called "maula". In India, "mullah" is a learned man, a teacher, a doctor of law. He is also one who reads the Quran in a house for 40 days after a bereavement. When oaths were administered on the Quran, the person who held the book was called the "Mulla Qurani".

VIB 13-20

418. Night of nights.

In Islam, the 'night of nights' is the best of all the nights of the year. According to sura 'Al-Qadr' (s.97) of the Quran, this night is 'the Night of Power'. It can be any of the nights of the last week of the month of fasting but generally the 27th of the month of fasting is reckoned to be the 'night of nights'. The Quran was completed on this night of the year.

VI.C.1-7

185 Nimrod (king)

Nimrod, son of Cush, grandson of Ham and great grandson of Noah was Monarch of Mesopotamia. He appears in the religious books of all the three revealed religions: the Bible, in the Table of Nations (Genesis 10); the First Book of Chronicles; and the Book of Micah. He is mainly remembered for the Tower of Babel, built during his reign. The Quran in chapter 2, Surat Al-Baqarah (The Cow), verse 258 refers to Nimrod as follows:

Translation:

'Have you not considered him who disputed with Abraham about his Lord, because God had given him the kingdom? When Abraham said, 'My Lord is He who gives life and causes to die", he said, 'I too have power to give life and cause death.' Abraham said: 'Surely God causes the sun to rise from the East. You make it rise from the West." Thus was the unbeliever confounded. God does not guide the unjust aright" (2:258).

Nimrod was the king, and the Prophet Abraham a subject. However, Nimrod claimed that he was an incarnation of the sun god, and as such, a divine king. The Prophet, though a mere messenger appointed by Allah, preached that there was no one on this earth or in the universe who could dare to associate himself with God because He is One and Alone, above and beyond any need of partnership with humans. Nimrod felt threatened as his ears were 'poisoned' by the mischief-mongers. The Prophet was thrown into the fire but, to the astonishment of all and taken as evidence of God's miraculous mercy, the Prophet survived unscathed.

VIC 1-7

141 Noah's ark

According to the Bible, 'Noah's Ark' was a vessel on which Prophet Noah, his relatives and some valuable animals were able to escape from the Great Flood. (See Genesis, chapters 6-9). The Ark came to rest in north-east Turkey, on the mountains of Ararat. Blavatsky writes extensively on the "Deluge" (Noah's Flood) by reference to different religions and to mythology. Quran also reveals a great deal about the Prophet Noah and his travails due to the social evil he was sent to warn against.

'Odalisque' (FW 226.32), 'Odalisks' (FW.335.33): from Turkish 'odalik' for a dancing-girl in the royal palace.

VIC 11-14; 17-18

37 'Orang (of Asia)

Mongol Orang' is a phrase that alludes to the Mongol national identity in history, comprising the regions of former Mongolia which are now parts of China and Central Asia, etc. In 1911, Mongolia declared itself independent when Dr Sun Yat-Sen overthrew the Qing Dynasty. Four years later, the Chinese government invaded, and Mongolia became an autonomous region under the protectorate of the central government. In 1921 Mongolia became an administrative district. The Mongolians then retaliate, their army occupying the capital city Urga on 3 February 1921. The flag of national identity the soldiers carried was the same flag that the Mongols had had in the Middle Ages, a yellow square with orange borders.

The flag is ripe with mystical import: the soyombo is the national emblem associated with the saffron-yellow colour of Lamaism. The three tongues of fire represent the past, present and future. Beneath the fire are symbols of the sun and moon; do these represent the pre-Buddhist belief pattern of the Mongols? The ancient Mongols indicated their hatred, or threat of death to the enemy, with an arrow pointing downward, represented in the new map by two triangles pointing

in the same direction. There are also two horizontal rectangles, which symbolise justice between rulers and ruled. Inside the horizontal rectangles lie the Chinese characters for 'yin' and 'yang', respectively the female (submissive) and the male (dominant) opposite forces of darkness and light. In addition there are two fish set in the 'yin-yang' dichotomy to represent the secret of wisdom. At the top of the design is the fortress, which signifies the bond of unity among the people of Mongolia.

VIC 11-18

38 Osmanli

Osmanli is the founder of the Ottoman caliphate Osmanli caliphate

In James Joyce, Richard Ellmann cites these words from a poem written on 'Thanksgiving Day', 1937:

> *'At last I reached a banquet-hall - and what a sight to see!*
> *I felt myself transported back among the Osmanli*
> *I poured myself a bubbly flask and raised the golden horn*
> *With three cheers for old Turkey and the roost where*
> *I was born'*

(Ellmann, James Joyce, p.719)

'Ottomanic faith-conveters' (FW 263.10-11) are the Moslem preachers engaged in proselytising the natives. 'Parasangs' (FW.586.27): 'para' means 'money' in Turkish.

VIC 1-7

141 ...**Pamir** -roof of the world silkworm karakorum

"Silkworm" here strongly suggests the 'Silk Road' or "Silk Route", denoting several interconnected networks of travelling routes between South Asia and X'ian in China, distance of about 5,000 miles. The German geographer, Ferdinand von Richthofen, coined the term in 1877. In German, the "silk road" is translated as "Seidenstrafe"

The "Silk Road" was a vital link in the exchange of ideas, people and goods among such diverse civilizations as China, ancient Egypt, Mesopotamia, Persia, India and Roman Empire. Two routes are distinguishable: i) the northern route links the Bulgar-Kypchak zone to Eastern Europe, the Crimean peninsula, the Black Sea, the Sea of Marmora, the Balkans and Venice; ii) the southern route connects Turkestan-Khorasan, Mesopotamia and Anatolia to the Mediterranean Sea, the Levant, Egypt and North Africa. There is also a "Sea Silk Road", which extends from Southern China across the Philippines, Brunei, the Maldives (141 'Bad-il-maudat' (Notebook VIC. `1-7)), Siam (Thailand), Malacca (Malaka), Ceylon (Srilanka), India, Persia (Iran), Egypt, Italy and Portugal.

VIC 1-7

141 **Pamir** meaning in Persian "the Roof of the World"

Extends over the region from Tajikistan to Kyrgyzstan republics. Consisting of a dizzying panorama of overpowering peaks and cliffs, staggering ice rivers, oceans of white and blue mountains, craggy gorges and formidable glaciers, the Pamir mountain system comprises the longest range of mountains in the Asian continent and the highest peaks after Mount Everest in the Himalayas. It includes the Hindu Kush in the North-West, the Tian Shan in the North-East and the Karakorum and the Himalayas in the South-East. Situated on the southern edge of Central Asia, the Pamir is a source of interaction between East with West. The nomads of this vast region (comprising Uzbekistan, Kyrgyzstan, Tadzhikistan, Kazakhstan and Turkmenistan) paved the way for the "Silk Road" and provide a "road-map" to the devastating campaigns of Genghis Khan.

The Central-Asian region of the Pamir has produced cities such as Samarqand, the city of blue domes and Bokhara, where Marco Polo stayed. Another notable area is the fertile Ferghana Valley, whence came the Moghuls to India in the fifteenth century AD and whose inhabitants played so important a role in the flow of trade on the "Silk Road" by checking the growing demands of the third- century B.C. Chinese emperor who sought to gain for his and China's own advantage the lucrative business of providing food, shelter and fodder for the trade caravans passing through.

Marco Polo, helped by the local shepherds, was the first noteworthy European to cross, and give descriptions of the Pamir. The first Russian expedition to the Pamir set out in 1866.

VIB 22

Panjabee

Punjabi from Sanskrit 'pan ca' (five) and Persian 'aab' (water) is a language spoken in the region through which flow five famous rivers of North-Western India. Punjabi is written in two scripts: Punjabis of Muslim background use Shahmokhi ("from the mouth of the Kings") script, derived from Persian script, while the Sikhs of East Punjab i.e. East of the river Ravi, use the Gurmukhi ("from the mouth of the Gurus") script. Some Punjabi-speaking Hindus living in the states of Haryana and Himachal Pradesh use the Devanagari script.

VI.C.1-7

301 Rickshaw pullers

The term 'rickshaw' is drawn from Japanese 'jinrikisha' ("jin" means human, "riki" force or strength and "sha" vehicle, translating literally as "human-power vehicle". Claude Gillot's painting 'Les deux carrosses' (1707) shows two cartoons of cart-like "rickshaws". Known as 'vinaigrettes' (for their resemblance to the wheel-barrows of vinegar makers), they were a cheap mode of transportation in the streets of Paris during the seventeenth and eighteenth centuries. In Japan, they appeared during the Meiji period (1868-1912), gaining popularity as a swifter means of transportation than palanquins. Rickshaws appeared in India, first in Simla and later in Calcutta, around 1880. In China, they were used first as a means of transporting goods. By the last decade of the nineteenth century rickshaws were being used in all the major cities of Asia as a cheap and readily available means of livelihood for the peasantry.

NOTE VOC

VIC 1-7

250 **River of Jordan**

The River Jordan is known in Hebrew as the Yarden, and in Arabic as the Urdun. It arises from the place where the Hasbani River (Lebanon) and the Banias (Syria) meet. It passes through Israel, Palestine and Jordan, and ends in the Dead Sea. In addition, it passes through the swampy area along the eastern shore of the Sea of Galilee and receives inflow from the River Yarmuk. The place that separates the Sea of Galilee from the River Jordan is the spot where, according to Christianity, Jesus Christ was baptized.

VIC 11-14; 17-18

336 **Rumi**

Mawlana Jalal ad-Din Muhammad Rumi (Turkish: Mevlânâ Celâleddin Mehmed Rumi (1207 — 1273 CE)), known simply as Rumi, was born in Balkh then in Khorasan and now in N.E. Afghanistan. Maulana Rumi is to Islam what Dante Alighieri is to Christianity, especially in regard to mysticism. They were contemporaries and evidently had literary and mystical common interests. Rumi emerges as the icon guiding Allama Mohammad Iqbal in his theosophical masterpiece, Javed Nama. Widely known across Asia, Rumi's religious ethics were mystical in spirit and based on human tolerance and sympathy. His "Mevlevi Order", still popular among Islamic mystics, is an innovative approach to reaching transcendence. The worship is based on Sema, and the worshippers appear in a group robed in "togas". To the rhythmical beats of music the dervishes ("Dervilish" FW 513.16) dance, whirling ("whirling dervishes" FW 184.06) round and round and chanting Divine hymns in deep-throated voices, symbolizing the heart's quest for spiritual exaltation through music. Just as the revolutions of the planets and the universe supposedly produce "heavenly" music, so the limbs of the human body are imagined as dancing round the heart in spiritual exultation. Maulana Rumi died in Konya, Turkey.

VIB 13-20

339 Sabir Mohamistan

A sabir is one who observes patience in all circumstances. The Quran calls such Moslems as "As-Sabirin" in surah Al-Baqara , chapter 2, verse 177:

> "It is not righteous that ye turn your faces towards East or West; but it is right-eousness- to believe in Allah and the Last Day, and the Angels, and the Book, and the Messengers; to spend of your substance, out of love for Him, for your kin, for orphans, for the needy, for the wayfarer, for those who ask, and for the ransom of slaves; to be steadfast in prayer, and practice regular charity; to fulfill the con-tracts which ye have made; and to be firm and patient, in pain (or suffering) and adversity, and throughout all periods of panic. Such are the people of truth, the God-fearing."

VIB 21

70 Saracen

The term 'Saracens' appears in Western chronicles to denote the Saracen Empire or the Arab Caliphate of the Umayyad and Abbasid dynasties. It appears in Greek as Sarakenoi, a borrowing of the Arabic word "sharqiyyin" (easterners). During the Roman Empire, nomadic Arabs from the desert were called "Saracens". The term was widely used during the Crusades for Moslems. The Crusaders also called the Moslems "those empty of Sarah" because they had descended instead from Hagar, the prophet Ismail's mother, according to Biblical Genealogies.

"Silkhouetted" (FW 56.07) is the silk hat which Ataturk wore after banning the use of the fez.

VIC 1-7

255 Slave trader Macpherson

Charles Macpherson published in 1808 Memoirs of the Life and Travels of the Late Charles Macpherson, Esq. in Asia, Africa and America. He describes the con-tents as follows:

"the book is illustrative of Manners, Customs, and Characters; with a Particular Investigation of the Nature, Treatment, and Possible Improvement of the Negro in the British and French West India Islands. Written by Himself Chiefly between the Years 1773 and 1790."

The book presents slavery as he saw it during the Romantic period. William Blake, Samuel Taylor Coleridge, William Wordsworth, Robert Southey and John Thelwell all raised their voices against slavery, so criticizing their own government, which, however, abolished slavery in 1807. In 1833, the British government also declared emancipation of slaves in the British colonies. Slavery and colonialism contributed in their own way to voices of discontent and to the rise of Romanticism.

VIC 11-14; 17-18

260 **Suffee** (Sofo) mosque

Situated in Istanbul, **Hagia Sophia** ([Temple of] Holy Wisdom), a former Eastern Orthodox church, was converted to a mosque in 1453. Hagia Sophia, or Sancta Sophia (Latin) and Ayasofya (Turkish), is one of the first architectural achievements in the world. Hagia Sophia is covered by a central dome (diameter of 31 metres (102 feet) and height 56 metres slightly smaller than that of the Pantheon. The dome seems appears weightless from the unbroken arcade of arched windows under it, which help flood the colourful interior with light. The dome is carried on pendentives, in four concave, triangular, sections of masonry which solve the problem of setting the circular base of a dome on a rectangular base; the weight of the dome passes through the pendentives to four massive corner piers, the dome seeming to float on four great arches. At the western (entrance) and eastern (liturgical) ends, half-domes carried on smaller semi domed exedras extend the arched openings. Thus, a hierarchy of dome-headed elements creates a vast, oblong, interior crowned by the main dome, a sequence without example in antiquity. All interior surfaces are sheathed with polychrome marbles (green and white with purple porphyry and gold mosaics) encrusted upon the brick. On the exterior, simple stuccoed walls reveal the clarity of massed vaults and domes.

The following allusions indicate the richness of Joyce's imagery with regard to the

Eastern Question and the reign of **Sultan Abdul Hamid:-**

(U 322. 30-31); "On which the sun never set" (U 329. 20); "Even the grand Turks sent us his piastres"..."Entente Cordiale" (U 330. 22); "Sold by custom in Morocco like slaves as cattle" (U. 327. 1-2); "nominate our faithful hereditary Grand Vizier" (U 483. 9-10); "We do not want to Fight, But, by Jingo if We do.." (FW 67) ; "Sublime Porte" (i.e. the Ottoman Court at Constantinople (FW 72); "Whiteman's burden Kipling" (FW 112); "Effendi": Turkish title of respect for Officials (FW 113) ; "balance of power" (U 686.25); "Gordon at Khortum" (U 757.21) ; "Hassan Khan" (Persian ambassador who visited England in 1819) (FW 497);

Sultan Abdul Hamid.

Difficulties and embarrassments marred Sultan Abdul Hamid's ('hamid' — FW 357.07) reign. Neither he nor his predecessors had taken effective steps for ruling the huge land mass and its heterogeneous peoples, and Turkey "rubbed shoulders" with Europe geographically ("The Isles in Greece" (from Don Juan) ; "Turkey-in-Europe" (FW 464) ; "Great Trek" (1836-40) ..Turkey divided in Turkey-in-Europe and Turkey-in Asia" (FW 483), "Tukurias-in-Asies" (FW 155.05); "1796 Napoleon seizes Leghorn" (FW 8.30) ; "Wellington, battle of Gawilagarh Aragaum, Salamanca" (FW 1812); "Napoleon III defeats Franz Joseph in the battle of Solferino 1859" ; "Austerlitz, battle won by Napoleon in 1805"; "Prince Bismarck battling against Napoleon III" ; "St. Helena"; "battle of Talavera, 1809, Vimeiro 1808"; "Viscount Wolseley Irish field marshal in Crimea" (FW 49). Napoleon had warned that the geography of a nation determines her foreign policy. The Ottomans did not move to adjust to this dire warning. As a result, we see Turkey giving in to the Powers of Europe in the Greek War of Independence (see Stephen's reading of Shelley's poem "Hellas", or Lord Byron's "The Isles in Greece" from Don Juan). We may consider the overwhelming odds of the "balance of power" (U 686.25), [366 'balance of power' (Notebooks VIC. 11-14, 17-8)] that the Sultanate faced in the nineteenth century.

PLEVNA (U 56.27)

With four references in Ulysses, Plevna currently known as Pleven in North East Bulgaria, as the historic site of another showdown between the Porte and the Tsar, must have interested Joyce through Montague Hozier's History of the Russia-Turkish War (1877-79). Hozier's book, as Gifford and Seidman (Annotated Notes for James Joyce's Ulysses, University of California, 1988) explain, must have

been given to Bloom by Major Tweedy (U 693:31-33; 709:5-7) from "The Garrison Library" at Gibraltar.

The 1877 war between Russia and Turkey was a result of long simmering discontent among the peoples of the Balkans. Tracing the background of the conflict between the apparent rivals such as the Great Britain, Russia, the Porte and France, the historian Fisher says that the disagreements in the Balkans arose from racial differences and consciousness of separate identities. The Austro-Hungarian Dual Monarchy of 1867 was an amazing settlement between the German and the Magyar races. "You look after your barbarians," said Andrassy, the Hungarian, to Beust, the German, "and we will look after ours." The written constitution came near to satisfiying the ruling classes, but omitted the restless Slavs, who, as Fisher says were nonetheless members of a very large and diverse ethnic group spread from the Arctic Ocean to the Eaxine, and from the Baltic to the Bering Straits (1038)

In 1824, according to Fisher, Kollar, a Slovak poet, launched a movement for the awakening of the Slavs in Europe, this at the time when the Greeks were asserting their right to self-determination against the same enemy, Turkey. Bohemia was the first region affected by the revolutionary message. Soon, the Bohemian revolution of 1848 spread throughout the Slav regions of Russia at the time when Alexander II, trying to catch up with Western Europe, was struggling to enforce his reform programme. "The measures were great", says Fisher, but "the men who were called upon to carry them out were not great." The world soon came to know that, despite his sincerity of purpose, the Tsar could not eliminate ethnic prejudice among the Serbs; on the contrary, they were getting closer and closer together across the region. The Bulgarians, an Achilles heel to the Ottomans, were soon to challenge the latter, while Russia busied itself in driving deeper into Central Asia, adding Samarqand to its annexations.

The Serb revolt, which started in Herzegovina and Bosnia in 1875, enveloped also Montenegro, Serbia and Bulgaria. The situation, however, was brought under control by the Turks after heavy losses on the part of the insurgents. The lull, unfortunately, proved temporary, due to the deep differences of race and religion among the peoples of the Balkans. Unable to contain the growing national solidarity among Slavs, Russia declared war on the Porte in April 1877, capturing Kars rapidly but faced stiffened resistance. Turkish resistance in Plevna lasted 143

days, but, as Gifford and Seidman note, it could not stop the Russians, who as a result were soon camping in sight of the Ottoman capital, Constantinople, a city of symbolic division between Asia and Europe in the form of the Bosporus and the Dardanelles (see Richard Ellmann, Ulysses on The Liffey). Constantinople was of strategic importance to England's commercial-cum-imperial interests; as Fisher comments, "that Turkey should become a satellite of Russia seemed to imperil the whole position of Britain in the East, and in England the Brits were going jingo: 'We do not want to fight, but by jingo if we do, we've got the ships, we've got the men, we've got the money too.'"

The Tsar though, sued for peace at Berlin in 1878 after a dire warning from the British. At the Congress of Berlin in June 1878, "the whole question of the Near East was settled upon lives which safeguarded British interests, extended Austrian influence, and administered a check to the Pan-Slavish ambition of the Tsar", writes Fisher (1041).

EGYPT:

"It was Napoleon writes Fisher, "who had recovered Egypt for Europe, [and] it was Mehmet Ali, Napoleon's admirer and pupil, who had made Egypt a modern state; it was Ferdinand de Lesseps, a French engineer of genius, who had succeeded in constructing the Suez Canal in 1859-1869. All three were opposed to England" (1069). Construction of the canal "grand canal" (406 Notebook. VI. C. 1-7) was a project more rewarding in the end to the British than to France, whose colonies were mainly in the West. No sooner were the lavish, royal celebrations of the canal's construction over than the British — out of their interests, from Malta and the Cape of Good Hope (189 Cape of good hope Notebook, VI. C. 1-7) through Suez, the Levant, the Fertile Crescent and the Persian Gulf to the Indian Ocean - won over the sympathy of the Khedive and assisted him in straightening out his debt-ridden treasury.

The British established sound administration, gave military training to local recruits, and were soon to face another contender for power from within Egypt, viz. Mohammad Ahmad, a self-proclaimed Mahdi (The Mahdi Notebook, 211 VIC6-16) or Messiah from Dongola in Sudan. Mohammad Ahmad had succeeded

in wiping out the scattered English garrisons in the scorching wilderness of Sudan as the conflict had expanded. To save the English face, Gordon, a visionary soldier with distinguished service in the Civil War in China, was appointed as Governor General of Khartum in February 1884.

A year later, in January 1885, Gordon was killed by the Dervishes: "whirling dervish, Tumult, son of Thunder, self exiled in upon" (FW184.06). After a decade of war between the fearless Dervishes and the English defenders of the long Egyptian-Sudanese borders in 1896, Kitchener advanced to Dongola, bringing the region "King of upper and lower Egypt" (21, Notebook B. 41-44) under his control after another two years of relentless warfare.

The next conflict occurred in the same region between the British and the French over the Fashoda incident. Engaged in exploring "darkest Africa" for three years, a team of French scientists under Capt. Marchand reached Fashoda, a village on the upper Nile (170 "White nile Blue" Notebook, VIC. 1-7) in late summer 1898 and planted the French flag there. Kitchener demanded the immediate withdrawal of Marchand and his team and removal of the flag. Since the English had suffered so badly in Sudan, the public opinion was drummed up, persuading the Government to despatch a naval fleet in case war broke out against French. The French public also was reluctant to give in once their national flag had been hoisted on soil which, they considered, was not English.

The French fleet also followed suit. Anglo-French rivalry, which in recent centuries is traceable to the Seven Years War in not only America, but also in India and the Middle East, was about to break out again. Mutual balancing of respecting the English and French averted a showdown between the two over Africa and relations further improved after Great Britain, France and Russia signed the Entente Cordiale treaty (U 330. 22). The Russo-Japanese war ("The Russians, they for the Japanese" — U 58.9-10) of 1904-5 raised hopes of improvement in British relations with Russia.

- **H. A.L. Fisher**, *A History of Europe (Boston and New York Press, 1935-6).*

VIC 6-16

21 Sultan of Mat

Sultan of Mat is a title used by the chief of the Sulu tribe, who live in the east coast and in the North of the state of Sabah, Malaysia. His real name was Datu Muhammad Salleh. He was born in Inanam, Sabah and was a relative of the Sultan of Sulu. Known as Mat Salleh, he was at war with the British during and after 1895. He died in battle in January 1900.

'Sulvans of Dulkey' (FW.616.11) ...'I believe in Dublin and the Sultan of Turkey' (FW.266.F.4). 'The Bey for Dybbling' (FW.29.22), 'Alibey' (FW. 346.05), 'Ailbey' (FW.484.23), 'Aubeyron',

VIB 29-41

Tokyo:

One of the most populous and rich metropolis of the world, Tokyo's spectacular rise in importance owed much to Tokugawa Ieyasu (1545-16116) and the Emperor Meiji (1868-1912). Tokugawa Ieyasu established his base in Edo (Yedo) (now Tokyo) after defeating the formidable warlords and unifying the country in 1603. The 263 years of the Shogunate came under the imperial banner in 1869, when the 17-year-old Emperor Meiji took over the Castle of Edo Castle, renamed it as Imperial Palace, and made Tokyo the de facto capital of Japan. Rapid industrial and commercial development by the turn of the century was enhanced by the introduction of a suburban railway-network. A hugely devastating earthquake hit Tokyo in 1923 at magnitude 8.3. Tokyo's greatest boast is the Nijubashi Bridge at the Imperial Palace, open to the public on the eve of the Japanese New Year and the Emperor's birthday only. The Emperor greets the loyal citizens from the royal balcony on this day. The Moghuls also followed a similar tradition of appearing before the public.

Turkey (FW 483-7-8) "He would preach to the two turkies"

"Turkey Coffee" (FW 43.08);

"Turkey's delighter" (FW 248.20) - a mixed sweet of fruits and nuts sprinkled with sugar.

VIC 6-16

152 Turkman

The origins of the Turkmens lie somewhere in the Turkman Sahra, the region east of the Atrek River in the Eastern part of the Elburz mountains south of Turkmenistan. Of light-yellow complexion, they are inhabitants of Central Asia. According to Turkmen pre-Islamic mythology, Aghooz Khan, the headman, is considered as primordial as Adam Kadmon. There exists reference to Noah and his three sons. Tatars and Turks believe themselves to be offshoots of the same family tree. Like the Pushtuns of Afghanistan and Pakistan, the Turkmens moved ceaselessly the Persian-Russian border except during the time of the Soviet Communist revolution. They are Moslems of the Yamoots, Tekkehs, Saloors and Sarighs tribes. Turkmens are passionate lovers of horse-racing and wrestling.

VIC 1-7

325 Whiteboy

An offensive or derogatory slang term used by "coloured" people for "whites" in response to their being called "niggers" as in racially motivated "pop" music.

VIC 1-7

170 White nile

The White Nile and the Blue Nile are the two major tributaries of the Nile. Rising from Lake Victoria, the White Nile flows North across Uganda and Sudan, including the vast swamps of the sudd (area of floating vegetation)before mixing with the Blue Nile at Khartoum. The White Nile arises from the confluence of such earthen rivers and streams, most flowing North out of Uganda. Its discovery and exploration mark the modern civilization and its ability to penetrate the unknown. The Blue Nile originates from Lake Tana (Northern Ethiopia) and flows initially southwards and then northwards through Ethiopia and then through Sudan after meeting the White Nile near Khartoum, whence the river crosses Egypt before discharging into the Mediterranean sea across a vast delta.

Appendix II

Glossary

The list of the Eastern vocabulary in the Wake gives an overwhelming impression. Despite Joyce's complicated use of words and textures of thought taken from different times and religions, this vocabulary stems directly from daily life and from the times and occupations of sleeping and waking, eating and drinking. Despite his strong interest in Eastern mysticism ranging from the Indian systems of Hinduism and Buddhism to Persian Zoroastrians and the Moslem Kaba, Joyce, through this vocabulary, has encapsulated the ethos of a popular culture in Finnegans Wake. Though it eludes detection, behind each of these camouflaged tiny bits there is an elaborate background texture. Here one can observe the way in which Eastern cultures have actually evolved from the roots of their soil.

A

Ack, ack, ack   (FW 65.34). Used by Kipling as "Ack, dum, ak dum, ek dum" for at once or quickly. "Ack, ack, ack" in Finnegans Wake denotes the sharp banging sound produced by the click of a camera.

Ahim   (FW 458) is an Urdu word for something which is of a certain importance as Shem in this instance is emphatic toward his sister in telling her to "please kindly think galways again or again" (FW 458.10-11).

glimpse agam   (FW 346.17). "Agam" is an Arabic word c.1614 used for dyed clothes. The term was borrowed into Indian language as Walt Taylor explains in "Arabic words in English" (S.P.E. Tract No XXXVIII).

amuckst   (FW 499.35) means the furious speed with which the moon appears and disappears among a thin sheet of clouds: "the rugaby moon cumuliously godrolling himself westasleep amuckst the cloud scrums". This term was used on the Coromandel Coast in 1669: "One of them (the slaves) ...wounded many people in a kinde of muck he did runn". The English Factories in India 1668- 1669, ed. William Foster; 1670-1677. p.283. According to Foster, this idiom "running amuck" was first used by Oxford English Dictionary in 1672.

Anna   (The English Factories E.F. 1620, Oxford English Dictionary OED 1727) appears in several combinations in the Wake. The anna is an Indian coin which is equivalent to one- sixteenth of a rupee. In the Wake the term Anna used for ALP appears on these pages: 07.26, 28.31, 104.08, 128. 14, 195.04, 196.03, 196.04, 196.04, 196.05, 198.10, 199.11, 200.16, 200.36, 207.19, 209.35, 215.12, 215.24, 277.12, 293.18, 325.04, 506.34, 562.14; "anna" 182.27.

anander   (FW 581.33) according to McHugh means another, each other. "Ananda" is one of the blessed traits of Brahmin (Max Muller, Theosophy, 1892)..

Ananias   (FW 171.31) is Pineapple

Apsaras   (FW 60.20), a class of female deities and wives of Gandharvas (Max Muller, Theosophy, 1892). McHugh says that apsaras were the maidens who, while Buddha was meditating, dropped on him from the mango tree.

arsoncheep   The phrase "arsoncheep"(FW 357.03) is a compound of the Persian "arzen" translated into English as "cheap".

atta   (FW 79.08), a Punjabi word used for wheaten flour. The verb "atta" is also used for some kind of favour say in terms of money or even God given gift of beauty.

aubergine   "Aubergines" (FW 163.18) is the fruit of the eggplant (French) drawn from Arabic "al- badinjan", Persian "badin-gan" and Sanskrit "vatin-ganah."

azure   "Azure" (Persian) is "Azores" (FW 468.34), "azurespotted" (FW 477.19). The stone was collected by Marco Polo at "lajward" (Turkestan) known as "lajward" in Arabic.

Avider   "whichever you'r avider to like it and lump it, but give it a name" (FW 455.07-08). "avider" has not been identified by McHugh but according to Max Muller it means "avidya" or nescience, spiritual ignorance (Theosophy, 1892).

B

babouche	Babouche is from Arabic "babush", Persian "papush" meaning "foot" and "covering" ("babushkas" FW 268.18); ("baooshkees" FW 417.12).
Babu	(FW 133.28) 1782, a Hindu gentleman, clerk.
Ban	(Persian) is "ban" (FW 020.01); "Ban" (FW 072.03) for prince, lord, chief, governor," related to Sanscrit Pati "guards, protects."
Bandy	(FW 12.18, 187.26) 1761, carriage (Telegu).
Bangle	(FW 207.07) "Bangled" (FW 620.08), ring bracelet or anklet 1787.
"Batt in, Boot!	Sell him a breach contact" (FW 374.19-20) is a "breach of contract" (McHugh) in business, reaffirmed by the word "Sell". The Indian term nearest to "Batt in, Boot!" is Batta (1632 EF, 1680 OED) which means difference in exchange or extra allowance.
Bazaar	(FW 597.14) and "Bazar" (FW 497.25) is an Indian word (c.1599 OED) used for market.
Begum	(FW 526.26) and (FW 590.24) is an Indian word (1626 OED, 1634 OED) used for queen, princess or a well-to-do lady.
Bengalese	(FW 179.14) 1678 OED, native language of Bengal.
bearer	(FW 408.13, 575.17, 590.04): "Bearer" (FW 463.05): "bearers" (FW 43.01). Bearer in the Indian languages is used for the palanquin-carrier; 1760 domestic servant (Bengali).
Buggy	(FW 85.10) is a light one-horse vehicle in the Indian context.
ber	(FW 345.18) (c.1874), a thorny tree of Asia (grown in Europe as well).
Bibby Buckshee	(FW 52.18). This phrase is preceded by "soorkabatcha" which in Urdu and Punjabi means the son of a pig (a term of abuse) as an Indian proverb says: "Tulsi! the man who Ram loves not, nor dwells upon, nor worships him, Is as an ass, or hog, or dog, what profit is his life". "Bibby" was used by Coryat (c.1612-17) as "Bibee Maria" for Mary Virgin. "Bibby" is a female who is clean of mind and heart as well as body. Elsewhere in the Wake "Bibby" can be traced at FW 329.22, 520.26, 529.33. "Buckshee" was the allowance given as baksheesh in addition to the basic salary. "Buskshee" also means a higher rank in the Mughul army dealing with the payment of salaries. Thirdly, "Buckshee" is the proper noun for a lady in the Indian aristocracy.

Bulbul	In another cluster of words, "Bulbul, bulbulone! I will shally. Thou-shalt-willy" (FW 360.23-4), the bulbul is as vital a symbolic bird as the cuckoo for William Wordsworth, the nightingale for Keats and the swan for Yeats. Every poet and storyteller of Central and South Asia uses this symbol to express the true state of his soul. Usually it symbolises love, and since "faraq" or "Alys!" (FW 359.32) (alienation, isolation) is a common theme of Eastern literature, the word "bulbul" is used as the personification of this loss. The "bulbul one" is the distorted name of another Punjabi bird with lesser beauty and virtue than the "bulbul" proper. In the song of the nightingales conducted in the radio "hookup" and sung by singers like Jenny Lind (the Swedish Nightingale), there are other allusions to Eastern fauna and flora. The fruits that are mentioned are basically Eastern. "I soared from the peach and Missmolly showed her pear too" (FW 360.28-9). The two singing nightingales, hiding in the thick grove and the shadows of roses are hypnotised ("hypnot") and mesmerised ("remesmer") (FW 360.24) in the intoxicating pain of the blossom and fragrance. They have lost their own selves and hence are now in the state of "I will shally", "Thou shalt willy" — a melting of identities into a whole of a deeper mystic nature. The phrase "Moths the matter?" has to be seen in a similar context. Moths are the sign of barrenness. They thrive in the winter when the trees are withered and dry. The moth, however, has been replaced by another adversary — a bee. "Whet the bee as to deflowret greendy grassies yellow horse" (FW 360.29-31). The flowers" concern at being deflowered by the voracious bees is also shown in this sentence: "Did you aye, did you eye, did you everysee suchaway, suchawhy, eeriewhigg airywhugger? Even to the extremity of the world?" (FW 360.31-33). Even the word "yellow horse" from the Eastern perspective communicates the paleness, the ruination of the lush, brilliant greenery by the vagaries of weather and bees. These two (the bee and bulbul) are traditional antipathetic images of Eastern poetry. The tone of their mutual eyeing and ayeing, winking and murmuring while communicating about HCE suggests a symbolic gesture of love, doubt and desire in Eastern lyrical poetry. The image of "bulbul" may also be gleaned in this excerpt as "palpably wrong and bulbubly improper, and cuddling her and kissing her, tootyfay charmaunt, in her ensemble of maidenna blue, with an overdress of net, tickled with goldies, Isolamisola, and whisping and lisping her about Trisolanisans, how one was whips for one was two and two was lips for one was three, and" (FW 384. 28-36)
Burr	(FW 34.36) is a banyan tree (Southey).
buzkashi	Buzkashi is "Basqueesh" (FW 287.F.4); "basquibezingues" (FW 350.20); "basquing" (FW 556.33). From Persian. Buz "goat" + kasha "drawing", Buzkashi is an Afghan sport, played like polo with a goat carcass.

C

calabash	Calabash (Persian) is "Calabashes" (FW 336.33); "Calaboose" (FW 952.24); "calaboosh" (FW 240.24) Calabash is a "dried, hollowed gourd used as a drinking cup," from Spanish "calabaza", possibly from Arabic "qar'a yabisa" for "dry gourd," or Persian "kharabuz", used of various large melons.
calico	(FW 240.25) 1616, cotton cloth derived from Calicut, one of the ports of India.
Canaries	(FW 260.F1), c.1875, adjective and substantive used in Dravidian language.
Candy	(FW 92.20; 176.14) is a Marathi and Malayalam term used for weight. Candy (Persian) is "candy kissing" (FW 300.15). Arabic "qandi", Persian "qand" or "cane sugar" is probably from Sanskrit "khanda" or "piece of sugar".
Caravan	(FW 031.21; 333.10;602.28) is Persian "karwan" (group of desert travellers). The word was picked up in the Crusades. Usually the word used is "caravanserai" for "inn" (with a large central court) catering to the travellers.
Cash	a small coin in Tamil (1621 EF, 1711 OED) appears in Finnegans Wake viz: FW 24.01, 24.01, 65.15, 133.13, 134.19, 150.24, 161.06, 161.07, 201.14, 404.30, 451.05, 492.20,538.16, 574.30, 577.09.
Cassock	(FW 311.29) is from Turkish "quzzak" meaning "nomad or adventurer". It is also a coat used for riding. In Persian, it is known as "kazhagand" meaning "padded coat" from "kazh" for "raw silk" and "agana" or "stuffed".
Cha	(FW 54.12), used for tea (c.1616).
Cheayt	The phrase "Taylor's Spring," (FW 365.33-34) is followed by the word tailor in Persian as "cheayt": "Taylor's Spring; a little cheayat chilled (Oh sard! ah Mah!)" (FW 365.34-35).
Chick	(FW 20.25, 446.10) 1698, screen blind made of bamboo.
cinnabar	Persian Cinnabar "cinnabar" (FW 030.24); "cinnamon" (FW 097.17; 184.20; 419.21; 456.20). Cinnabar is a "red or crystalline form of mercuric sulphide," . Originally, "zanjifrah" in Persian, cinnabar is also a red resinous juice of an Eastern tree, whose colour, it is thought, is due to a mixture of dragon's and elephant's blood.
Chop	(FW 190.04, 208.03, 467.14) 1614, seal impression, license, passport, first rank.
Coss	(FW 459.24, 293.01), measure of distance as in miles or kilometres.
Cot	(FW 330.28, 556.14), light bedstead E F. 1614). crores (FW 256.31) c.1609, ten million.

crores	(FW 256.31) c.1609, ten million.
Curry	(c.1598-1681), dish of meat, cooked with bruised spices and turmeric (Tamil): FW 138.12, 295.18, 351.02, 456.20.
Chatty	(FW 76.27, 307.15, 523.27, 528.31), (c.1781), earthenware water pot.
chee-chee	(FW 38.16, 53.16, 53.36, 106.19, 166.31, 221.08), minced English c.1781.
Chuckler	(FW 107.07), c.1759, tanner or cobbler (Tamil).
chir	(FW 209.06), pine tree c.1885.
Chutney	(FW 456.20), strong hot relish, a condiment (c.1845).
Chuttor	(FW 300.19), used in Punjabi for four walls or corners enclosing a square.

D

Dal	(FW 186.10, 281.19) c.1645 (EF), 1698 (OED), pulse.
Dammad	(FW 291.24), son-in-law (Urdu).
Damman	(FW 243.12). Zamman is a metaphysical term used for representing time and place in Persian.
Dandy	(FW 92.20, 172.14, 345.24, 464.24), c.1685, boatman.
Darras	(FW 388.01): lesson (in Arabic and Persian).
darr	(FW 584.07), door in Persian. In Punjabi "darr" is the flight of birds exactly as the English proverb says "birds of a feather flock together".
das	(FW 130.16, 481.33, 482.04), used as a surname by Hindus.
Dasht	(FW 199.36), used in Urdu, Punjabi for jungle, forest.
Dawk	(FW 207.08): Dawk Chowkee (c.1727 OED), post or transport by relays of men.
Dharma	(FW 93.22), doctrinal word for faith in Hinduism.
dhee	(FW 123.02), used for daughter in Punjabi.
divans	(FW 177.10). A "divan" was a court in the palace where the king sat and held meetings with courtiers, generals and ministers.
divane	(FW 536.18), minister of finance department (c.1608, 1690).
Dinar	(FW 170.03), (c.1634). Various oriental coins.
dam	(FW 139.18, 215.16, 277.F6, 339.06, 645.20) is used for money in general terms and is a copper coin in particular. "Damdam" (FW 19.30) is the continuous breathing from birth to death.
Dama	(FW 471.02) is the disease called asthma.
Dom	(FW 22.18, 197.18, 352.33. 568.23, 625.20) c.1828: member of a Dravidian caste.

Door   (FW 043.09;046.09;046.10;064.10;073.28;075.12;078.25) etc, etc, is Sanscrit Dvárah "door, gate" and Persian duvara- "door".

Dumdum   "domatium" FW 567.12; "Dumstddumbdrummers" FW 497.17 Named for Dum-Dum arsenal in Bengal, where the British made them to use against fanatical charges by tribesmen. It was outlawed by international declaration, 1899. The arsenal was situated on a hill or mound, was known as hill battery, cognate with Persian damdama.

durbar   (FW 497.29) c.1609, court kept by a guardian ruler; leve'e held by native prince, British governor or viceroy in India.

E

Emerald   (FW 068.12;263.22;440.33;603.09 and "emeralds" FW 492.11) is "emeraude" in French, "Esmaraldus or smaragdus" in Latin, "smaragdos" or "gren gem" in Greek "baraq and bareqeth" or "shine" in Hebrew. In Arabic, emerald is known as "barq" (FW "burqued" 503.36) "lightning") "Macadam" in Sanscrit, "zumurrud", in Persian, "zümrüd", in Turkish and "izumrud" in Russian.

Erin   The phrase "sons and daughters of Erin" is interpreted by Benstock as denoting the liberation of both the Irish and the Persians at almost the same time. The new nation of Iran was formed in the 1920s, and its old name "Persia" was replaced by Iran in 1934, just three years before the Irish Free State became "Eire". Phrases like "Come Back to Erin": "Come big to Iran" (FW 144.18), "the man of Iren" (FW 310.20), and "Aran chiefs" (FW 475.12) might be concerned with Ireland, but in the latter case the addition of the phrase "parish...mead" in the next paragraph (475.22-23) adds a Persian element. Furthermore, Iran (FW 358.21; 491.36) is Persian "Eran" (sahr) "(land) of the Iranians," from old Persian "arriya" - a self-desigination of the Aryan people. It became the official country name in 1935 under Reza Shah. His wife is a shahbanu (from banu "lady"); his son is a shahzadah (from zadah "son").

Esther   (FW Esther FW 069.14;429.18; "esthers" 03.14;624.25) is from Hebrew for "Ester", Persian "sitareh" (star) related to Avestan star. Esther is also the name of the Persian king, Ahasuerus.

F

Firman   (FW 185.27) c.1614 H J, 1616 OED: edict of a sovereign, grant, license, passport.

Flying the Perseoroyal	Persian language and history are again readable in the paragraph preceding the radio broadcast. "Flying the Perseoroyal" (FW 358.19-20) might indicate the Shah of Persia's flight into exile during the first World War. The passage continues: "Withal aboarder, padar and madar, hal and sal, the sens of Ere with the duchtars of Iran. Amick amack amock in a muck tub" (FW 358.20-22). According to Benstock, the entire family of Noah seems to be on board the ark. Obviously the following are the Persian names used for a family relationship: "baradar" for brother, "padar" for father, "madar" for mother, "doctor" for daughter and "amu" for paternal uncle. "Amu" echoes "mamun" for maternal uncle in Urdu and Punjabi.

G

Gadi,	an Indian word meaning throne, regal position (Marathi, Bengali) which can be detected in the passage "My globe goes gaddy at geography giggle pending which time I was looking for my shoe all through Arabia" (FW 275.F2).
Gazebo	(Persian) "gazebocroticon" (FW 614.28) means a beautiful sight. benared my ghates (FW 551.35) according to McHugh means "Hindus must wash in Ganges at Ghats of Benares". Ghaut c.1639 EF, 1675-80 SM, 1698 OED, mountain pass; flight of steps leading to the river side; burning ghat.
Gazzelle	(FW 595.04). Gazel (c.1800), species of lyric poetry.
Ghee	(FW 411.19) c.1665, butter clarified to resemble oil.
giaour	Giaur in Persian is "giaours" FW 107.22; "Giaourmany" FW 355.22; Giaur is a Turk. term of contempt for non-Muslims. Originally from Persian "gaur", giaur is the variant of gabr "fire-worshipper," originally applied to the adherents of the Zoroastrian religion.
Godown	(FW 456.05, 565.21) c.1583 Fitch; (1588) 1625 OED, warehouse (Malay, Tel, Tam).
Googul	(FW 265. F4) 1813, aromatic gum resin.
Grab	(FW 72.01, 464.31) is a large coasting vessel (Marathi).
Gunne	(FW 25.22, 44.12, 104.08, 271.17). Gunny according to 1619 EF, 1711 OED, is a coarse material used for the making of sacks.
Gup	(FW 529.14) 1617 1A 1VIII 1806 OED, gossip; silly talk (Partridge
Gurrahgrunch	(FW 342.17, 347.17). Gurrah (c.1865) is an earthen jar.

H

Hakemouth	(FW 263.02) echoes Hakemit in the Islamic world which means a judge or physician (c.1585, c.1622 EF, c.1638 OED).

hasard	The word "hasard" (FW 357.04) is both "hasad" — that is envy or jealousy — and "hasard", one thousand in Urdu and Persian.
hindustand	(FW 492.17) c. 1616 OED, language formerly called "Indostan".
hinndoo	(FW 10.06, 10.09, 10.14) c.1662, one who worships Hinduism.
Hing	(FW 206.03), "hing" (FW 391.08) c.1583 Fitch, 1586 OED; in Indian languages "hing" is an essential part of the aromatic flavour of meals and is translated as "asafoetida".
Hobson's	[Jobson] (FW 63.02) Indian words in English.
Hoolies	(FW 138.11) Holi, c. 1622 EF, c.1687 OED, the great festival or carnival of the Hindus.
hooper	(FW 486.30) (c.1707) is a cake made of rice flour.
Hoope's	(FW 449.12) or hoopoe, a bird of fabulous nature.
hoon	(FW 200.11), gold coin.
Howday	(FW 517.31), Howdah (c.1774), seat erected on the back of an elephant.
Hum	(FW 6.33. 114.19, 199.32, 441.19): "hum" (FW 52.23, 339.21, 369.21, 431.07, 447.04, 465.29, 512.22, 514.04, 611.08). "Hum" in Urdu is used for "we", the plural of "I".
Huzoor	(FW 244.19), c.1775, Indian potentate's title of respect.

I

inam	(FW 237.26) c.1619 EF, 1803 OED, gift of rent-free land.

J

Jack tree	(FW 211.15, 307.20, 330.22, 459.27, 460.27, 496.03): "Jack" (FW 168.11, 179.08, 308.24, 320.34, 549.23). Jack tree (c.1613) is also the Malay for the same tree.
Jaggery-yo	(FW 256.19). 1598 OED, coarse, dark brown sugar.
jackal	"Jackal" (FW 212.31) is from Turkish "cakal", Persian "shaghal" and Sanskrit "srgalas" meaning "the howlers" figurative "skulking henchman".
Jambos	(FW 471.23). c.1630 rose apple.
Jaggarnath	(FW 342.13). c.1616, c.1638 OED, Hindu deity to which persons blindly devote themselves or are ruthlessly sacrificed.
Jasmine	(FW 613.34 jasminia) is "yasamin" in Arabic and "yasmin" in Persian for a plant that breathes fragrance.
Jaun	(1851), small palanquin-carriage which though in the Wake is used as the name of a character (FW 429.01, 430.17, 430.33, 431.09, 431.13, 431.20, 431.21, 437.35, 439.27, 441.34, 448.34, 453.14, 454.16, 469.19, 470.24).
Jodhpur	(FW 329.02), a town in south India.

jujube	Jujube or Sisyphus (Persian) is "jujube" (FW 444.22);"juju-jaw" (FW 256.19) "Jujuba" (Latin zyzyphum). It is an Asiatic tree with date-like fruit, first recorded 1835.
julep	"Julep" (FW 464.29);"julepot" (FW 559.15). Julep is a syrupy drink:"gulab" (Persian) from gul "rose" and ab "water"-known as rose water is usually flavoured with mint. It was also used to give medicine to patients.

K

Khan	(FW 32.02, 24.35, 497.34). Persian title of nobility in South Asia specially applied to Pathans.
Khyber	(FW 464.10), one of the narrow hilly passages above Peshawar (the capital city of the North West Frontier Province of Pakistan) through which the invaders like Alexander penetrated the subcontinent from Afghanistan.
Kiosk	(FW 135.28) is "kushk" (Persian), Turkish "kiosque" for "palace, portico."
Kurds	Accounting for the food imagery in this passage, Benstock refers to "curds on the table" (FW 374.05). "Curds" could also imply the Kurds who have their own national and cultural identity. There is another reference to the Kurds: "The kurds of Copt on the berberutters and their bedaweens!" (FW 241.23-24). (In this sentence, the Christian Copts of the Middle East, the Berbers of Africa, the Bedouin and the Kurds are all alluded to).
Kush	"Kush" as Benstock suggests may mean "a Turkish bird". In addition, "kush" from "kuschkars" signifies the mountain ranges of Iran. The verb "khuschk" implies dryness and barrenness. Since these mountains are known to be dry, "bad of wind and a barran of rain" (FW 365.18-19) brings in a coincidence of contraries. "Bad of wind and a barran of rain" in itself is a poetically balanced phrase repeating the initial word in Persian followed by its translation into English. "Bad" is Persian for wind and "barran" is rain. In languages like Urdu and Punjabi the phrase used is "bad-o-baran". In this sentence, the dreamer combines four aspects of elemental reality: the plains of Iran, the mountains, winds and waters.

L

lac	(FW 162.23, 378.04); lakh c.1608-13 Hawkins, 1613 OED. Lac has two meanings: a) as a number it stands for one hundred thousand: b) resinous incrustation produced on certain trees, used as scarlet dye.
lala	is both a flower and the elder in the family (FW 250.21, 250.21, 295.24, 335.16, 335.17, 335.23).

Lemon or "limun"	(Persian) is cognate with Sanskrit "nimbu" the lime is "lemoncholic" (FW 453.07; "lemon holy" (FW 555.23); "lemon sized" (FW 059.08); "lemon orange" (FW 596.01).
Lilac	(FW "lilly" 396.26; 352.22; "Lilly" 373.03) is French shrub with mauve flowers from Spanish "lilac", Arabic "lilak", Persian "lilak" with variant of "nilak" (bluish) from "nil" (indigo) and Sanskrit "nilah" or (dark blue).
lunger	(FW 165.10, 331.06, 349.35): "Lunger" (FW 131.04). Lunger is a meal open to everybody irrespective of religion or class.
Leep	(FW 626.02) c.1895 (Kipling), to wash with cow-dung and water.
Lotta	(FW 062.34, 241.33), a water pot (1809).

M

Madrasattaras	(FW 10.16) 1654 EF, 1833 OED, handkerchief (place-name): 1878 native of Madras.
magi	Magi (Persian) is "Maggi" (FW .211.22); "Maggies" (FW 219.19); "maggies" (FW 039.13;048.11;142.30;560.15;586.14). Latin magi, pl. of magus, from Gk. magos, is a word used for the Persian learned and priestly class as portrayed in Bible (said by ancient historians to have been originally the name of a Median tribe). From old Persian "magus" "magh" meaning "to be able to have power" or magic (Persian) may be cited in the Wake at (FW 013.17;421.22;451.08;470.03;565.29;608.190).
Magnificat	Magnificat in Persian is "magnifica" (FW 100.04); "magnificent" (FW 060.25; 377.20;539.25); "magnificently" (FW 032.20); "magnifying" (FW 183.21).
Maistre	(FW 177.30) in Punjabi is a mason who builds a house with bricks (c.1798).
mantra	(FW 553.32), sacred text or passage used as magic formula.
Mard	There are other allusions to the East in this chapter. The phrase "To tell how your mead of, mard, is made of" (FW 374.01) contains the word "Mard" which is "man" not only in Persian but also Urdu and Punjabi. Mard is basically manliness in the sense of chivalry, magnanimity and tolerance. The word also appears in the *Notebook* (41-44): "Mardi mard mard mard maroha" (p.35). Here "Maroha" is Arabic "Marhaba", eliciting the mystical path of vigil and self-mortification. Benstock points to another "merde-mard" pun: "Fingool MacKishgmard Obesume Burgearse Benefice" (FW 371.22), a sentence gloating with obscenity. Three literary figures are being defamed here: Wilde, Macpherson and Kierkegaard. The language used is Italian dialect (ba fangool), French (merde), German (fick) and English (bugger, arse). The Persian "mard" is used to convey a similarly derogatory meaning. Benstock establishes another link between the Medes and "mead".

Mash	(FW 140.32): "mach" (FW 240.01, 407.09), a pulse c.1880.
Masta	(FW 515.12) "mast" is one who is frenzied.
math	(FW 288.08) is a Hindu convent of celibate mendicants (1834).
Matty	(FW 398.01, 482.27, 614.2) is a slave to his master's orders, c.1810.
Meerschaum	(Persian) is "meerschaum" (FW 050.30; 241.14). It is a tobacco pipe with a bowl made of meerschaum, a type of soft white clay.
Meter	(FW 398.14; 531.19) is French metre from Greek "metron", Sanskrit "mati" - "matra", Persian ma for "measure" or unit of length.
Moghul	(FW 277.03) "moghul" (FW 97.24) c.1583-91 Fitch ("Great Mogor") c. 1616-19, Terry ("Great Mogoll"); autocratic ruler(1678); kind of plum(1718); locomotive (1884); playing cards (1842). M.breeches: and long-drawers or pyjamas.
moochy	(FW 11.06), leather worker (1837).
mora	(FW 28.20): "Mora" (FW 131.23), a foot-stool, stool.
Mucktub	The word "muck tub" (FW 358.22) in one sense refers to Swift's "Tale of a Tub" with Peter, Jack and Martin as "Amick amack and amock" (an Irishman, his son and a sham), with echoes of the nursery rhyme "Rub-a-dub-dub, three men in a tub", as Benstock claims. "Maktub" in Persian, Urdu and Punjabi is a common phrase for a library, a school and a tradition of thought.
Mufti	(FW 462.32) "muftis" (FW 497.30) "muftlife" (FW 261.19). A mufti is a religious scholar of Islam.
Mugger's	(FW 54.20): "mugger" means crocodile, c.1814.
Mull	(FW 193.18), "mull" (FW 286.31, 371.31), is to rub, c.1881.
Mummy	(FW 194.22; 194.33; 194.33; 411.17); "mummyscrips" (FW 156.02), is "mumiva" or asphalt (wax) in Persian.
Musk	(FW 191.24; 280.33; 359.09); "musked" (FW 512.09); "musky" (FW 541.31). Musk is from "mushk" Persian, "muska-s" Sanscrit, and Arabic "al misk" applied to various animals and plants - especially the deer glands.

N

nabobs	(FW 414.05): Title of certain Mohammedan officials, who acted as deputy governors of provinces or districts in the Moghul empire; person of great wealth, especially one who has returned from India with a large fortune acquired there.
narghile	"Narghile" (Persian) is "nargleygargley" (FW 234.3) is from "nargil" for "coco-nut"."Narghile" is oriental water pipe for smoking. The bowl is made of coco-nut.
Navel	(FW 018.29;323.05;447.05;447.06;475.14;480.17) is Persian "naf" Sanskrit "nabhila" or hub and "bembix" or "whirlpool" in Greek.
Nun, lemmas	Similarly, the phrase "Nun, lemmas- quatsch" (FW 296.1-2) is a pun on the original "lebbens- quatsch" (FW 270.L). "Nun" is "bread" not only in Persian but also in Pushto, Punjabi and occasionally Urdu. The English "lemon" according to Benstock comes from the Persian "lemu".

P

pagoda	(FW 228.10, 466.19, 466.21) 1634 OED, idol; person extravagantly rever-enced; gold coin (EF c.1619).
pan	(FW 14.12, 15.34, 50.27, 243.07, 340.31, 363.29, 466.01. 466.02, 619.02). Pan (c.1616), betel leaf; combination of betel leaf, areca nut, lime etc., used for chewing.
Paradise	(FW 020.15;076.34) or "Garden of Eden", is "pairidaeza" for "enclosure, park" according to *Avestan*. In modern Persian and Arabic, paradise is termed as "firdaus" for "garden" - a compound of "pairi" meaning "around" and "diz" which is "to make, form a wall". "Pairi" is cognate with Greek "peri" (around, about) while "digen" in Sanskrit means "firm", "solid" originally "kneaded into a compact mass".
Pariah	(FW 192.32), a person of degraded or despised class; social outcast.
Parsee	(FW 296.F1): "parsee" (FW 495.03), an Indian adherent of Zoroastrianism.
Pice	(FW 256.31, 604.03) c.1615, coin (one-fourth of an anna).
Puckaun	(FW 210.35) is the cooking of various foods in the Indian languages, especially Hindi, Urdu and Punjabi.
Puggaree	(FW 52.24) is a light turban (c.1665).
Punch	(FW 176.06, 255.26, 514.13, 620.23): "punch" (FW 116.23, 368.26, 514.33) is a beverage.

pundit   (FW 505.27). Pundit c.1661 EF, 1698 OED, learned expert or teacher.

Punkah's   (FW 297.18), c.1610 Finch, 1625 OED, fan.

Purdah   "Purdah" itself has twice been mentioned in Finnegans Wake. It occurs in the following sentence: "Number Thirty two West Eleventh streak looks on to that (may all in the tocoming of the sempereternal speel spry with it!) datetree doloriferous which more and over leafeth earlier than every growth and, elfshot, headawag, with frayed nerves wondering till they feeled sore like any woman that has been born at all events to the purdah and for the howmanyeth and howmovingth time" (FW 274.12-20). The second reference is: "KATE (Miss Rachel Lea Varian, she tells forkings for baschfellors, under purdah of card palmer teaput tosspot Madame d'Elta, during the pawses)," (FW 221.12-14). Phrases like "teaput" and "Madame d'Elta" are by all accounts images of eroticism, sex and female fertility. "Purdah" in Urdu is "hijab" in Arabic and curtain in English

R

rack   (FW 130.05), "racky" (FW 114.25), aphetic form of arrack.

rupee   (FW 492.36), 1608-13 Hawkins, 1612 OED, coin.

ruth   (FW 58.31, 255.12, 596.21) :"Ruth" (FW 147.13, 192.28, 257.21), c.1813, vehicle or carriage.

Rutty   (FW 525.04, 537.10). "Ruttee" (c.1625) is a seed of Abrus precatorius used as a goldsmith's weight.

S

Sad pour sad   "Those sad pour sad forengistanters, dastychappy dustyrust!" (FW 357.05- 06) contains "sad pour sad" which is Persian for one hundred percent, "farangi" meaning European and "dasty chappy, dasty rast" which is "on the left, on the right". The allusion invokes "The Charge of the Light Brigade" , Tennyson's poem on the Crimean war. The paragraph is replete with sexual vocabulary: "orefices, Culpo, Ars, classies, assasserted, freequuntly, Kunstful, Cunstuntonoploies, etc)". The nouns "Hamid" and "damid" (FW 357.07) are quite well-known symbols in Moslem culture. "Hamid" is one who praises, a Moslem given to glorifying the name of God and Prophet Mohammed. "Damid" is son-in-law in Urdu and other related languages. "Hamid" and "damid" are mystic terms as well — meant to reflect the longing of the subject for the object out of "A dard of pene" (FW 357.10). The Eastern "dard" is English "pain", though the former is also a poetic term for the alienation of the seeker from the sought. "Dard" is one of the titles of a famous Urdu poet of 18th and 19th century India. In French "dard" implies "dart", and "pene" is Latin for sorrow.

Saffron	(FW 203.24;611.36;"Saffron" 455.07;"saffron breathing" 550.17) is Persian "zaferoon."
Sahib	(FW 492.23),"sahib" (FW 54.13, 121.19, 302.03),"sahibs" (FW 497.31).A great sahib or master in a family or a high official."Burre" (FW 130.12) in Urdu is used for brown colour.The white colonial masters were called "burra sahib" in India.
Saki	(FW 317.02) wine, used also as a simile for the beloved in Urdu poetry.
Sal	(FW 358.20), c.1678 EF, OED, timber tree or Shora robusta.
Salam	(FW 360.27) c.1613, ceremonious obeisance; respectful compliments (used as verb c.1669-79 Bowery, 1698 OED).
Salam	"Salam, salms, salaum!" (FW 360.27) is the traditional Moslem greeting, welcoming the stranger.
Sambat	"Sambat" according to Benstock is from "shambeth" implying Saturday, but "sham" is also evening in Persian, Urdu and Punjabi.[1] This is appropriate to the character of "Shem" who represents the darker facet of reality, its instinctive, blind and diabolical aspect."Sham" in Punjabi signifies the sinking of the sun — darkness and uncertainty; fears, thefts, enmity; the time of the devil and his devious antics. Sham also implies the time of rest after daylong sweat and toil. In other words, Sham is a time of testing the strength of a Moslem's faith."Sambat" also means the bond of marriage in Hindi. One needs to recall the strict adherence of a widow to the rite of *sati* (self-immolation at the death of her husband) as a bond of "sambat". Furthermore, the phrase "Foraignghistan sambat" (FW 493.02) incorporates "farangistan" (the land of the non-Europeans or the place of non-Occidentals).The noun "farahang" in Persian is also the name of an Urdu magazine (published from Karachi) interested in discovering the linguistic, etymological and cultural roots of that language. "Faharangistan" in Persian means an educational academy.

Sard and Mah	"Sard" is cold in Persian and "Mah" is moon or month. Accounting for the traditional celebration of "No Ruz" in Iran, Benstock suggests that in this annual spring festival, seven dishes whose first letter is "s" find their echo in the following seven English words: "sure, straight, slim, sturdy, serene, synthetical, swift" (FW 596.32-33). These seven words occur in Book IV of Finnegans Wake which introduces both the final ricorso and fresh beginning. The spring festival of "No Ruz" is a celebration of the year that has just been completed and a prayer for the year to come. In addition to the above, there are numerous words which belong simultaneously to Persian, Punjabi and Urdu. The difference is that they do not form a cluster placed in one particular chapter, but are scattered throughout Finnegans Wake. For example, the noun "nabob" means a landlord — a title especially used since the Moghul dynasty in India. The official language of the Moghuls was Persian. It remained the same until the English colonisation of the subcontinent. "Nawab" is also used in the languages of India as an equivalent to the English and European "knight". Words like "vizier" and "khan" are also used in Finnegans Wake. Words like "mishe" (FW 3.09) or "bibby buckshee" (FW 52.20-21) are used to seek pardon and forgiveness; "hamman" (FW 205.30) is the bathroom ; "Ahdahm" (FW 205.31) means person; "rang" (FW 360.22) is colour; "dustydust it razed" (FW 314.16) could be interpreted as "dasty rast" (FW 357.6-7) as used for a reliable right hand man; and "Khubadah" (FW 609.32) is both good and bad since "Khub" is good and "bada" is bad. "Khubadah" can also be translated as one who is dreaming. A "mesfull" (FW 415.06) is from "mesquel" an instrument used for measurements. "Meshallehs" (FW 550.12) can be understood as "mashallah" in the sense of the above-mentioned "valleh" (praise be to God); from "meshallehs" can also be derived "masaleh" (interests, materials or spices). The word "masael" meaning metaphysical questions and "mosalleh" signifying well-armed. Many other examples could be given.
buzkashi	Buzkashi is "Basqueesh" (FW 287.F.4); "basquibezingues" (FW 350.20); "basquing" (FW 556.33). From Persian. Buz "goat" + kasha "drawing", Buzkashi is an Afghan sport, played like polo with a goat carcass.
Sari	(FW 333.20), long wrapping garment worn by Hindu women.
Saul	(FW 306.L2) is the sal-tree (India).
seer	(FW 108.04, 174.12, 611.20): "seers" (FW 342.04, 342.04): "seer's" (FW 096.28) is the denomination of weight, measure of capacity.
seersucker	Persian seersucker is "shukar" (FW 357.02), "sirsakar" (Hindi), "shir" (Persian) is "ksiram" (Sanscrit) for "milk" while "shakar" (Pali sakkhara, Sanskrit "sarkara" is "gravel, grit, sugar."
shamiana	(FW 182.01) c.1609, awning or flat tent-roof without sides; flat awning or canopy.

shawls   (FW 007.32;117.01;144.04;213.29 393.16).The Persian word shawl (c.1662) has been adopted into Urdu and other Indian as well as European languages. Shawl is a type of scarf worn in Asia.

shiek   (FW 494.22). Sheikh is a Hindu converted to Islam and is generally noble in rank or learned in Islam.

Shukar   The phrase "shukar in chowdar" (FW 357.02) is in one sense "shukar-i-khuda" (thanks be to God — conveying a sense of humility and resignation)."Chowdar" implies the tent or sheet of cloth used by a woman as "purdah".

shudder   (FW 358.05, 487.04), c.1787, sudder chief, applied to higher governmental officials.

Sola   (FW 102.15):"sola" (FW 189.19, 314.34), tall leguminous plant; pith of this plant employed in making light hats (Bengali).

souckar   (FW 362.15), Hindu broker or money-lender.

Sublime Porte: "Sublime Porte" (the Ottoman Court at Constantinople)" (FW 72).

Sundry   (FW 147.25) c.1831, a tree abundant in the Ganges delta (Bengali).

susa   (FW 345.19). Susa 1801, Gangetic dolphin (Platanista gangetica) (Bengali).

Syce   (FW 94.06) c.1653 is the servant who attends to horses; groom.

T

taffeta   Taffeta (Persian) is."taffeta" (FW 012.23);"Taft" (FW 277.11).Applied to various fabrics or tapestry at different times, "taffeta" is a shiny silk or linen cloth.

Tambourine   (FW 248.09) c.1585, musical instrument.

Taraf   Similarly, "taraf" is a corner, as for example the four corners of the earth (both of these words are in daily use in Urdu and Punjabi).

Tartar   (FW 105.25;136.21;233.34;407.04;491.14) imples "Tartary" or the land of the Tartars.Tatar (Persian) was used first in the 13th c. in reference to the hordes of Ghengis Khan (1202-1227).Tatars were a horde mixed of Tatars, Mongols and Turks. Lord Byron used it as "tartarly" (1821).

Thug   (FW 212.03):"thug" (FW 240.12, 495.03, 618.29) c.1810, a professional robber and murderer, cut-throat, ruffian, rough.

Thugg   (FW 485.11):"Thuggeries" (FW 540.31),"thuggery" (FW 177.35).

Thunder   (FW 093.26; 176.01; 187.15; 221.21; 227.06) etc, etc is Persian
             "tundra" and Sanskrit "tanayitnuh".

Til   (FW 13.22, 104.10, 312.08, 316.36, 320.22, 326.18, 537.10, 546.15,
             577.29, 596.08). Til (c.1840), timber plant (Sesamum Indicum).

toon   (FW 117.32). Toon (c.1810) is a timber tree (Indian mahagony,
             Cedrela toona).

Tulip   (FW 015.01; 570.04) is Turkish "tulbent" for "turban", Persian "dulband"
             (turban), so called from the fancy resemblance of this flower to a turban,
             introduced to Europe from Turkey in the 16th century.

Turk   (FW "Turk" 080.10;366.19; "Turk" 098.10;181.22;520.02 "Turc" in
             French, Byzantine Gk. Tourkos and Persian turk. Said to mean "strength"
             in Turkish, is the name of people who live in the south of the Altai
             Mountains. In Persian, "turk" means a beautiful youth. The Young Turk
             (1908) was a Turkish citizen loyal to Turkish nationalism. The phrases
             "Turkish bath" and "Turkish delight" are used by Joyce in *Ulysses* and the
             Wake.

V

Vallad, vallahe   Similarly, the word "vallad" (FW 493.03) according to Benstock, means
             ballad and "vallahe" (by God)! "Vallahe" is used in Persian, Urdu and
             Punjabi as an exclamation denoting beauty and wonder. "Vallad" in these
             languages implies the patriarchal family tree; valid (father): aulad (children):
             waldiat (fatherhood), etc.

Velayat   The word "velayat" in "villayets prostatution precisingly kuschkars tarafs"
             (FW 365.16-17) means a province in Persian.

Z

Zillahs   (FW 102.03), c.1800, administrative district.

ॐ

Appendix III

Bibliography

James Joyce Primary Texts

A Portrait of the Artist as a Young Man
(New York: Viking, 1964), First Printed, London 1916, The Egoist.

Finnegans Wake
(London: Faber and Faber, 1989), First Printed, Faber and Faber, 1939.

The Letters of James Joyce, Vol. I, ed. Stuart Gilbert
(New York: Viking Press, 1957); reissued with corrections 1966. Vols. II and III, ed. Richard Ellmann (New York: Viking Press, 1966).

Finnegans Wake: Notebooks, prefaced by David Hayman arranged by Danis Rose with assistance of John O'Hanlon
(New York and London: Garland Publishing, 1978).

Scribbledhobble: The Ur-Workbook For Finnegans Wake, edited with notes and introduction by Thomas E. Connolly
Connolly (Evanston, Illinois: Northwestern University Press, 1966).

Ulysses,
(New York: Random House, 1961), First Printed Shakespeare and Company: Sylvia Beach, Paris, 1922.

Secondary Texts:

Anderson, Chester. "Baby Tuckoo: Joyce's "Features of infancy"
Approaches to Joyce's Portrait": Ten Essays, ed. Thomas F. Staley and Bernard Benstock, 135-69.

Attridge, Derek and Ferrer, Daniel eds.
Post-Structuralist Joyce: Essays from the French, (Cambridge: Cambridge University Press, 1984).

Atherton, J.S.
The Books at the Wake: A Study of Literary Allusions in James Joyce's Finnegans Wake, (London: Faber and Faber, 1959).

Aubert, Jacques.
"Riverrun" in Post-Structuralist Joyce: Essays from the French, ed. Derek Altridge and Daniel Ferrer, (pp.69-78).

Beckett, Samuel et al
Our Examination Round His Factification For Incamination of Work in Progress (1929; London: Faber and Faber, 1969).

Begnal, Michael H. and Eckley, Grace.   *Narrator and Character in "Finnegans Wake", (Lewisburg, Pa: Bucknell University Press, 1975).*

Begnal, Michael H. and Senn, Fritz eds.   *A Conceptual Guide to Finnegans Wake, (University Park: Pennsylvania State University Press, 1974).*

Beja, Morris et al., eds   *James Joyce: The Centennial Symposium, (Urbana: University of Illinois Press, 1986).*

Benstock, Bernard.   *James Joyce: The Undiscovered Country, (New York: Barnes and Noble, 1977).*

Benstock, Bernard.   *Joyce-Again's Wake, (Seattle: University of Washington Press, 1965).*

Benstock, Bernard.   *"The Kenner Conundrum." JJQ, 13 (1976): 428-35.*

Benstock, Bernard.   *"L. Bloom as Dreamer in Finnegans Wake". PMLA, 82 (1976): 91-7.*

Benstock, Bernard.   ed. *Critical Essays on James Joyce (Boston: G.K. Hall, 1985).*

Benstock, Bernard.   ed. *The Seventh of Joyce, (Bloomington: Indiana University Press, 1982).*

Benstock, Shari.   *"Nightletters: Woman's Writing in the Wake" in Critical Essays on James Joyce, ed. Bernard Benstock, 221- 33.*

Benstock, Shari.   *"The Genuine Christine: Psychodynamics of Issy" in Women in Joyce, ed. Suzette Henke and Elaine Unkeless, 169-96.*

Bishop, John.   *Joyce's Book of the Dark: "Finnegans Wake". (Madison: University of Wisconsin Press, 1986).*

Boldereff, Frances Motz.   *Reading Finnegans Wake, (Woodward, Pennsylvania: New York Public Library, 1959).*

Bowen, Zack   *Musical Allusions in the Works of James Joyce, (Albany: State University of New York Press, 1974).*

Boyle, Fr. Robert, S.J.   *"Penelope". In James Joyce's "Ulysses": Critical Essays, edited by Clive Hart and David Hayman (Berkeley: University of California Press, 1974), pp.407- 33.*

Brivic, Sheldon.   *Joyce Between Freud and Jung (Port Washington: NY: Kennikat Press, 1980).*

Brivic, Sheldon.   *"Joyce in Progress: A Freudian View." JJQ, 13 (1976): 306-27.*

Brivic, Sheldon.   *Joyce the Creator (Madison: University of Wisconsin Press, 1985).*

Brivic, Sheldon.   *The Mind Factory: Kabbalah in Finnegans Wake". JJQ, 21 (1983): 7-30.*

Brown, Richard.   *James Joyce and Sexuality, (Cambridge: Cambridge University Press, 1985).*

Budgen, Frank.   *James Joyce and the Making of "Ulysses", (Bloomington: Indiana University Press, 1967).*

Burgess, Anthony.   *Joysprick: An Introduction to the Language of James Joyce, (London: Faber and Faber, 1965).*

Campbell, Joseph and Robinson, Henry Morton.   *A Skeleton Key to Finnegans Wake, (London: Faber and Faber, 1947).*

Card, James Van.   *An Anatomy of "Penelope" (Rutherford, NJ: Fairleigh Dickinson University Press, 1984).*

Cheng, Vincent John.   *Shakespeare and Joyce: A Study of Finnegans Wake (University Park: Pennsylvania State University Press, 1984).*

Cheng, Vincent John.   *Joyce, Race, and Empire (Cambridge University Press, 1995).*

Colum, Padraic and Mary.   *Our Friend James Joyce, (London: Gollancz, 1955).*

Derrida, Jacques.   *Dissemination, trans. Barbara Johnson. (Chicago: University of Chicago Press, 1981).Johns Hopkins University Press, 1976).*
"Two Words for Joyce" in Post-Structuralist Joyce: Essays from the French, ed. Derek Altridge and Daniel Ferrer, 145-59.

Devlin, J. Kimberly   *Wandering and Return in Finnegans Wake: An Integrative Approach to Joyce's Fiction, (Princeton, New Jersey: Princeton University Press, 1991).*

Eckley, Grace.   *The Children's Lore in Finnegans Wake, (Syracuse, NY: Syracuse University Press, 1985).*

Ellmann, Richard.   *The Consciousness of Joyce, (Toronto and New York: Oxford University Press, 1977).*
James Joyce, (New York: Oxford University Press, 1962).
Ulysses on the Liffey. (London: Faber and Faber, 1972).

Epstein, Edmund L   *The Ordeal of Stephen Dedalus, (Carbondale: Southern Illinois University Press, 1971).*

French, Marilyn   *The Book as World: James Joyce's "Ulysses", (Cambridge, Mass: Harvard University Press, 1976).*

Freud, Sigmund   *Beyond the Pleasure Principle, trans. and ed. James Strachey, (New York: Bantam Books, 1959).*

	The Interpretation of Dreams, trans. James Strachey, ed. Angela Richards, (Harmondsworth: Penguin, 1976).
	Totem and Taboo. trans. James Strachey, (New York: Norton, 1950.
Frye, Northrop.	*The Great Code, (London: Routledge, 1982).*
Gaiser, Gottlieb., ed.	*Reading Lacan, (Ithaca: Cornell University Press, 1985).*
Gifford, Don	*Joyce Annotated: Notes for "Dubliners" and "A Portrait of the Artist as a Young Man", (Berkeley: University of California Press, 1982).*
Gifford, Don and Seidman, Robert J.	*Notes for Joyce: An Annotation for James Joyce's "Ulysses", (New York: E.P. Dutton, 1974).*
Gilbert, Stuart.	*James Joyce's Ulysses, (New York: Vintage Books, 1955).*
Gillet, Louis.	*Claybook for James Joyce, trans. Georges Markow-Totevy, (London and New York: Abelard-Schuman, 1958.*
Glasheen, Adaline.	*Third Census of Finnegans Wake, (Berkeley: University of California Press, 1977).*
Goldberg, S. L.	*The Classical Temper, (London: Chatto and Windus, 1961).*
Goldman, Arnold.	*The Joyce Paradox: Form and Freedom in his Fiction, (London: Routledge, 1966).*
Gordon, John.	*Finnegans Wake: A Plot Summary, (Dublin: Gill and Macmillan, 1986).*
Gose, Elliott B., Jr.	*The Transformation Process of Joyce's Ulysses, (Toronto: University of Toronto Press, 1980).*
Groden, Michael.	*Ulysses in Progress. (Princeton, NJ: Princeton University Press, 1986).*
Harkness, Marguerite	*The Aesthetics of Dedalus and Bloom, (London and Toronto: Associated University Presses, 1984).*
Hart, Clive.	*A Concordance to Finnegans Wake, (Minneapolis: University of Minnesota Press, 1963).*
	ed. James Joyce's Dubliners: Critical Essays, (New York: Viking, 1969).
	James Joyce's Ulysses, (Sydney: Sydney University Press, 1968).
	Structure and Motif in Finnegans Wake, (London: Faber and Faber, 1962).
Hart, Clive and Hayman, David, eds	*James Joyce's Ulysses: Critical Essays, (Berkeley: University of California Press, 1974).*

Hart and Senn, eds.	*James Joyce's Ulysses: Critical Essays, (Berkeley: University of California Press, 1974).*
Hart and Senn, eds.	*A Wake NewsLitter, Vol I, March 1962 to Vol.XVII, Dec. 1980). (New York: Viking Press, London: Faber and Faber).*
Hayman, David and Anderson, Elliot, eds.	*In the Wake of the Wake, (Madison: University of Wisconsin Press, 1978).*
Henke, Suzette A,	*"Gerty MacDowell: Joyce's Sentimental Heroine" in Women in Joyce, ed. Suzette Henke and Elaine Unkeless, 132-49.*
	"James Joyce and Women: The Matriarchal Muse." In Work in Progress: Joyce Centenary Essays, ed. Richard F. Peterson, Alan M. Cohn, and Edmund L. Epstein, (pp. 117-31).
	Joyce's Moraculous Sindbook: A Study of Ulysses, (Columbus: Ohio State Universiy Press, 1978).
	Politics of Desire, (New York and London: Routledge, 1990). Henke, Suzette, and Unkeless, Elaine, eds.(Urbana: University of Illinois Press, 1982).
Herr, Cheryl.	*Joyce's Anatomy of Culture, (Urbana: University of Illinois Press, 1986).*
Herring, Phillip F.,	*Joyce's Uncertainty Principle, (Princeton, NJ: Princeton University Press, 1987).*
Kenner, Hugh	*"Circe" in James Joyce's Ulysses: Critical Essays, ed. Clive Hart and David Hayman, 341-62).*
	Joyce's Voices, (Berkeley and Los Angeles: University of California Press, 1978).
	The Pound Era (Berkeley and Los Angeles: John Hopkins University Press, 1978).
	"Signs on a White Field" in James Joyce: The Centennial Symposium, ed. Morris Beja et al., 209-19.
Kopper, Edward A.	*"but where he's eaten: Earwicker's Tavern Feast / Book II, chapter iii" in A Conceptual Guide to Finnegans Wake, edited by Michael H. Begnal and Fritz Senn, 116-38.*
Kristeva, Julia.	*The Powers of Horror, trans. S. Roudiez, (New York: Columbia University Press, 1982).*
Litz, A. Walton	*The Art of James Joyce: Method and Design in Ulysses and Finnegans Wake, (Oxford: Oxford University Press, 1964).*
MacCabe, Colin.	*James Joyce and the Revolution of the Word, (London: Macmillan, 1978).*

	ed. James Joyce: New Perspectives, (Bloomington: Indiana University Press, 1982).
Maddox, James H., Jr.	Joyce's Ulysses and the Assault on Character, (New Brunswick: Rutgers University Press, 1978).
Manganiello, Dominic.	Joyce's Politics, (London: Routledge and Kegan Paul, 1980).
McCarthy, Patrick A.	The Riddles of Finnegans Wake, (London and Toronto: Associated University Presses, 1980).
	"The Structures and Meanings of Finnegans Wake", in A Companion to Joyce Studies, ed. Zack Bowen and James F. Carens, 559-632.
McHugh, Roland.	Annotations to Finnegans Wake, (Baltimore and London: John Hopkins University Press, 1980).
	"Mohammed in Finnegans Wake", AWN, Vol. XVI. No. 4 (August 1979).
	The Sigla of Finnegans Wake, (London: Edward Arnold Limited, 1976).
Misra, B.P.	"Sanskrit Translations", AWN, Vol. I, No. 6 (Dec. 1964: Feb. 1965).
Motz, Reighard.	Time as Joyce Tells It, (Mifflinburg, Pa: Mulford Colebrook Publishing, 1977).
Noon, William T.	Joyce and Aquinas, (New Haven: Yale University Press, 1957).
Norris, Margot.	"Anna Livia Plurabelle: The Dream Woman" in, Women in Joyce, ed. Suzette Henke and Elaine Unkleless, 197-213.
	The Decentered Universe of Finnegans Wake, (Baltimore: Johns Hopkins University Press, 1976).
	"The Last Chapter of Finnegans Wake: Stephen Finds His Mother". JJQ, 25 (1987): 11-30.
	"Mixing Memory and Desire: The "Tristan and Iseult" Chapter in Finnegans Wake". In James Joyce: The Centennial Symposium, edited by Morris Beja et al., 132-36.
O'Brien, Darcy.	The Conscience of James Joyce, (Princeton, NJ: Princeton University Press, 1968).
O'Hehir, Brendan and Dillon, John M.	A Classical Lexicon for Finnegans Wake, (Berkeley: University of California Press, 1977).
Parrinder, Patrick.	James Joyce (Cambridge: Cambridge University Press, 1984).

Peake, C.H.
James Joyce: The Citizen and the Artist, (Stanford: Stanford University Press, 1977).

Power, Arthur
Conversations with James Joyce, ed. Clive Hart. (New York: Harper and Row, 1974).

Rabate, Jean-Michel.
Joyce Upon the Void, (Basingstoke: Macmillan, 1991).

Reynolds, Mary
Joyce and Dante: The Shaping Imagination, (Princeton, N J: Princeton University Press, 1981).

Rose, Danis and O'Hanlon, John
Understanding Finnegans Wake: A Guide to the Narrative of James Joyce's Masterpiece, (New York and London: Garland, 1982).

Sandulescu, C. George.
The Language of the Devil: Texture and Archetype in Finnegans Wake, (Gerrards Cross, Buckinghamshire: Colin Smythe, 1987).

Scherman, Katharine
The Flowering of Ireland, (Boston: Little Brown, 1981).

Scholes, Robert and Kain, Richard M., eds.
The Workshop of Daedalus: James Joyce and the Raw Materials for A Portrait of the Artist as a Young Man, (Englewood Cliffs, NJ: Prentice-Hall, 1968).

Scott, Bonnie Kime.
Joyce and Feminism, (Bloomington: Indiana University Press, 1984).

ed. *New Alliances in Joyce Studies, (Newark: University of Delaware Press, 1988).*

Joyce's Dislocutions: Essays on Reading as Translation, ed. John Paul Riquelme. (Baltimore: John Hopkins University Press, 1984).

Seidel Michael.
Epic Geography: James Joyce's Ulysses, (Princeton: Princeton University Press, 1976).

Senn, Fritz
"One White Elephant", AWN, Vol.1, No.4, August 1964, p.02.

Shechner, Mark
Joyce in Nighttown, (Berkeley: University of California Press, 1974).

Sollers, Philippe
"Joyce and Co." In In the Wake of the Wake, ed. David Hayman and Elliott Anderson, 107-21.

Solomon, Margaret.
Eternal Geomater: The Sexual Universe of Finnegans Wake, (Carbondale: Southern Illinois University Press, 1969).

Strong L.A.G.
Sacred River: An Approach to James Joyce, (New York: Haskell House, 1982).

Sultan, Stanley
The Argument of Ulysses, (Columbus: Ohio State University Press, 1958).

Thornton, Weldon. — *Allusions in Ulysses, (Chapel Hill: University of North Carolina Press, 1968).*

Tindall, William York. — *A Reader's Guide to Finnegans Wake, (New York: Thames and Hudson, 1959).*

A Reader's Guide to James Joyce, (New York: Ferrar, Straus Giroux, 1959).

Troy, Mark. — *Mummeries of Resurrection: The Cycle of Osiris in Finnegans Wake, (Uppsala: Acta Universitatis Upsaliensis, 1976).*

Tucker, Lindsey. — *Stephen and Bloom at Life's Feast: Alimentary Symbolism and the Creative Process in James Joyce's Ulysses, (Columbus: Ohio State University Press, 1984).*

Walkiewicz, E.P. — *"Sandhya" AWN, Vol. XVII, Dec. 1980.*

White, David A — *The Grand Continuum: Reflections on Joyce and Metaphysics, (Pittsburgh: University of Pittsburgh Press, 1983).*

Wright, David. — *Characters of Joyce, (NJ: Barnes and Noble, 1983).*

Yared, Aida. — *"In the name of Anah: Islam and Salam in Joyce's Finnegans Wake" (Vol. 35, No 2-3, Winter/ Spring 1998), 401-438.*

Texts from Eastern Cultures and Thought:

Abbott, Nabia — *"A Ninth-Century Fragment of the "Thousand Nights": New Light on the Early History of the Arabian Nights." Journal of Near Eastern Studies Vol.8 (1949): pp.129-164.*

Amir Ali, Syed. — *The Spirit of Islam, (London: Christophers, 1935).*

Bachchan, Harbans Rai. — *W.B. Yeats and Occultism: A Study of His Works in Relation to Indian Lore, the Cabbala, Swedenborg, Boehme, and Theosophy, (London: Books From India, 1976).*

Bhattacharyya, Narendra Nath. — *The Indian Mother Goddess, (Columbia, Missouri: South Asia Books, 1977).*

Blavatsky, H.P. — *The Secret Doctrine, 2 Vols. (London: The Theosophical Publishing Company, Limited, 1888).*

Isis Unveiled, 2 Vols. (New York: J.W. Bouton, 1872).

Bodley, C. Ronald Victor. — *The Messenger: The Life of Mohammed, (London: Robert Hale Limited, 1946).*

Braybrooke, Neville. — *"T.S. Eliot in the South Seas" in T.S. Eliot: The Man and His Work, ed. Allen Tate (New York: Delacorte Press, 1966).*

Burton, Richard F.   *(trans.) The Book of the Thousand Nights and a Night with Introduction, Explanatory Notes on the Manners and Customs of Moslem Men and a Terminal Essay Upon the History of The Nights [together with] Supplemental Nights to the Book of the Thousand Nights and a Night with Notes Anthropological and Explanatory. (London: The Burton Club for private subscribers only. 17 Vols. 1886).*

Campbell, Joseph.   *The Masks of God: Primitive Mythology, (London: Secker and Warburg, 1960).*

Caracciolo, Peter L. ed.   *The Arabian Nights in English Literature, (Basingstoke: Macmillan, 1988).*

Carne, John.   *Letters From the East, (London: Henry Colburn, 1826).*

Corbin, Henry.   *Creative Imagination in the Sufism of Ibn Arabi, (Bollingen Series, XCI), trans. Ralph Manheim, (Princeton: Princeton University Press, 1969, and London: Routledge and Kegan Paul, 1970).*

Corbin, Henry.   *Cyclical Time and Ismaili Gnosis: Islamic Texts and Contexts, trans. R. Manheim and J. Morris, (London: Kegan Paul International and Islamic Publications, 1983)*

     Temple and Contemplation, trans. Philip Sherrard with the assistance of Liadain Sherrard, (London: Islamic Publications, 1986).

Danielou, Alain.   *Hindu Polytheism, (London: Routledge and Kegan Paul, 1964).*

Doughty, Charles Montague.   *Travels in Arabia Deserta: With an introduction by T.E. Lawrence, 2 Vols. (London: Jonathan Cape, 1964).*

Deussen, Paul.   *The Philosophy of the Upanishads, (Edinburgh: T. and T. Clark, 1906).*

Eliade, Mercia.   *The Myth of the Eternal Return, trans. Willard R. Trask, (London: Routledge and Kegan Paul, 1955) —Yoga: Immortality and Freedom, trans. Willard R. Trask, (New York: Pantheon Books, 1958).*

Gauhar, Altaf. ed.   *The Challenge of Islam, (London: Islamic Council of Europe, 1978).*

Hobson J. Peter, Consultant ed. Nicholas Drake and Elizabeth Davis.   *The Concise Encyclopaedia of Islam, (London: Cyril Glasse, 1989).*

Hughes, Thomas Patrick.   *A Dictionary of Islam (London: W.H. Allen, 1885).*

Gerhardt, Mia.   *The Art of Story Telling: A Literary Study of the Thousand and One Nights, (Leiden: E.J. Brill, 1963).*

Gibb, H.A.R.   *"Literature", in The Legacy of Islam, ed. Thomas Arnold and Alfred Guillaume (Oxford: Clarendon Press, 1931).*

Hamidullah, M.   *Introduction To Islam, 4th ed. (Lahore: Ashraf, 1974).*

Hegel, Georg Wilhelm Friedrich.   *The Philosophy of History, trans. J. Sibree. Intro. C.J. Friedrich, (New York: Dover, 1956).*

Khan, A. Muid.   *"Some aspects of the Arabic writings of the philosopher Ibn Sina", Islamic Culture, Vol. 25:42, (Hyderabad-Deccan, 1951).*

Lane, Edward William.   *The Arabian Nights, (New York: Tudor Publishing, 1927).*

Metlitzki, Dorothe.   *The Matter of Araby in Medieval England, (New Haven: Yale University Press, 1977).*

Morris, James Winston.   *The Wisdom of the Throne: An Introduction to the Philosophy of Mulla Sadra, (Princeton: Princeton University Press, 1981).*

Muller, Max, ed.   *Maha Bharata: The Epic of Ancient India, condensed into English verse by Romesh Dutt, C.I.E. (London: Dent, 1899).*

ed. Rig Veda- Sanhita, the Sacred Text of the Brahmans, commentary by Sayanacharya, (London: W.H. Allen, 1849-74).

Nicholson, Reynold A.   *A Literary History of the Arabs, (Cambridge: Cambridge University Press, 1969).*

Olcott, Henry S.   *A Buddhist Catechism, (Colombo, Ceylon, and London: The Theosophical Society, 1882).*

Organ, Wilson Troy.   *The Hindu Quest for the Perfection of Man, (Athens, Ohio: Ohio University Press, 1970).*

Philip K. Hitti,   *History of the Arabs, 6th ed. (London: Macmillan, 1956).*

P.M., Holt.   *The Cambridge History of Islam, ed. P.M. Holt, Lambton, Ann K.S, and Lewis, Bernard. 2 vols (Cambridge: Cambridge University Press, 1970).*

Poole, Stanley Lane. ed. and trans. *The Speeches and Table Talk of Prophet Mohammed, (London: Macmillan, 1882).*

Partin, Harry B.   *The Muslim Pilgrimage: Journey To the Centre, (Chicago: University of Chicago Press, 1967).*

Said, Edward W.   *Orientalism, (New York: Random House, 1978).*

Sale, George.   *The Koran, (London: Fredrick Warne, 1891).*

Santayana, George.   *Winds of Doctrine (New York: Doubleday, 1963).*

Schopenhauer, Arthur.   *The World as Will and Representation, trans. E.F. Payne. 2 Vols (New York: Dover, 1969).*

Published

Whyte Tracks
Møllehavevej 11
3200 Helsinge
Denmark
http://www.whytetracks.eu.com